# Information Issues
# for Older Americans

# Information Issues
# for Older Americans

### Edited by William Aspray

ROWMAN & LITTLEFIELD
*Lanham • Boulder • New York • London*

Published by Rowman & Littlefield
A wholly owned subsidiary of The Rowman & Littlefield Publishing Group, Inc.
4501 Forbes Boulevard, Suite 200, Lanham, Maryland 20706
www.rowman.com

86-90 Paul Street, London EC2A 4NE

Copyright © 2022 by The Rowman & Littlefield Publishing Group, Inc.

British Library Cataloguing in Publication Information Available

**Library of Congress Cataloging-in-Publication Data**

Names: Aspray, William, editor.
Title: Information issues for older Americans / edited by William Aspray.
Description: Lanham : Rowman & Littlefield, [2021] | Includes bibliographical
  references and index.
Identifiers: LCCN 2021035464 (print) | LCCN 2021035465 (ebook) | ISBN
  9781538150191 (cloth) | ISBN 9781538188323 (paper) | ISBN 9781538150207
  (ebook)
Subjects: LCSH: Older people—Services for—United States. | Information behavior—
  United States. | Information literacy—United States.
Classification: LCC HQ1064.U5 I5425 2021  (print) | LCC HQ1064.U5  (ebook) | DDC
  305.260973—dc23/eng/20211108
LC record available at https://lccn.loc.gov/2021035464
LC ebook record available at https://lccn.loc.gov/2021035465

# Contents

Preface    vii
*William Aspray*

**1**  Everyday Information Behavior of Older Americans    1
*William Aspray*

**2.**  Information, Knowledge, and Successful Aging    17
*William Jones*

**3**  One Senior Citizen's Information Ecosystem and Infrastructure    63
*James W. Cortada*

**4**  AARP and Its Competitors as Information Providers    91
*William Aspray*

**5**  Age and Technology in Action    123
*Claudia Grisales Bohorquez, Marilyn Kay, Noah Lenstra,
and Kate Williams*

**6**  Health Insurance Literacy and Older Adults    143
*Emily Vardell*

**7**  Active Aging in the Era of Smart Devices    163
*Pallabi Bhowmick, Clara Caldeira, Kay Connelly, Ben Jelen,
Novia Nurain, and Katie A. Siek*

**8**  Telephone-Based Communities for Information and Social
Connectedness    199
*Robin N. Brewer and Mary Janevic*

**9** Not Your Grandparents' Family Tree: Practices of Privacy in Genetic Genealogical Networks                 221
*Judith Pintar*

**10** The "One Hundred Percent Corner": Situational Awareness and Successful Aging in Community                 247
*David Hopping*

**11** Mapping the Research on Digital Information Issues for Older Adults                 263
*Unmil Karadkar*

Index                 279

About the Editor and Contributors                 000

# Preface

## William Aspray

If you are an American, your chances of living to an old age are relatively high. As of 2020, average life expectancy at birth was approximately seventy-eight for males and eighty-two for females.[1] This was not so true in the past,[2] and it is still not true in many other countries.[3] All major demographic groups in the United States are living into old age, regardless of income, gender or sexual orientation, level of education, region of the country you live in, or whether you reside in a rural or urban area. However, as textbox P.1 shows, there is some variation in life expectancy across these demographic groups.

As one reaches older ages, a number of changes take place. Most people are freed from working, and they become more financially reliant on Social Security, pensions, annuities, or savings. Most people have more time and more schedule flexibility at their discretion. Most people have greater flexibility in the geographic location in which they live, and new kinds of fifty-five-plus communities become available to them, but they may have new limitations in the type of housing they can live in because of health issues. Most people have growing health issues, and their health insurance typically changes from one associated with their employer to one associated with the Medicare system. Often more attention is paid to financial and other legacy issues. These issues and others set older Americans apart from younger ones. There is also great heterogeneity within the class of older Americans. For example, the needs and opportunities of the recently retired, active sixty-five-year-old may be different from those of someone who is eighty-five years old.

All these changes in life as one ages means that one faces new information needs and new uses of information and communication technologies in their everyday activities. This change is the topic of this book. The book is intended to appeal both to the general reader and the academic who is interested in either information issues or aging issues. It contains both overview essays

## TEXTBOX P.1.   LIFE EXPECTANCY (YEARS) BY DEMOGRAPHIC GROUP IN THE UNITED STATES[1]

**Gender** Men 77.9, Women 88.4

**Race** White 78.6, Hispanic 81.9, Black 75.0, Asian 86.3, American Indian/Alaskan Native 77.4

**Geographic Region** California 81.6, Hawaii 82.3, Mississippi 74.9, West Virginia 74.8

**Socioeconomic Status** Top 1%: Men 87.3, Women 88.9; Bottom 1%: Men 72.7, Women 78.8

**Population Density** Large metropolitan areas 78.8, Rural areas 76.8

**Education** White female: <HS 76.9, High school 83.8, Some college 86.1, College or more 88.4

## NOTES

1. One has to be careful in reading this table because the sources of statistics are different for each demographic class considered here. So, the data is useful within a demographic class, but it is not possible to compare the numbers by race with the numbers by educational attainment, for example. We could find no single source that provided all this information. "US Census Bureau Life Table 2020; Race and Health in the United States," Wikipedia, accessed March 30, 202, https://en.wikipedia.org/wiki/Race_and_health_in_the_United_States; Raj Chetty et al., "The Association between Income and Life Expectancy in the United States, 2001–2014," *Journal of the American Medical Association* 315, no. 16 (April 26, 2016): 1750–1766; Ghopal K. Singh and Mohannad Siahpush, "Widening Rural-Urban Disparities in Life Expectancy, U.S., 1969–2009," *American Journal of Preventative Medicine* 46, no. 2 (February 2014): e19–29; Arun S. Hendi, "Trends in Education-Specific Life Expectancy, Data Quality, and Shifting Education Distributions: A Note on Recent Research," *Demography* 54, no. 3 (June 2017): 1203–1213. The data on educational attainment are taken from 2009, for total life expectancy at age twenty-five. For the other demographic groups, it lists life expectancy at birth.

about general information issues that older Americans typically experience and more narrow examples of specific issues or specific types of solutions involving information institutions, such as libraries, and information technologies, such as smart homes and specialized telephone networks.

This book has been written primarily by information studies scholars. (Biographies of the individual authors can be found at the back of the book.) Information studies is a discipline that has emerged over the past quarter century. It is an interdisciplinary field that draws on natural science and engineering (especially computer science), social sciences such as psychology and sociology, humanities disciplines, design, and health disciplines such as medicine and nursing. Most of the authors are or have recently been affiliated with one of the major information schools at leading public universities in the United States: Indiana, Illinois, Michigan, North Carolina, Texas, and Washington. A strength of this approach of having chapters written by many different authors is that it provides us with a chance to demonstrate the many different perspectives that one can gain on issues involving information and older adults.

The first three chapters provide overview information. In chapter 1, William Aspray surveys the many kinds of information that older adults commonly access. The chapter also discusses the sources of information available to older adults and their care providers, in particular the role of the federal, state, and local governments and nonprofits in providing this information. In chapter 2, William Jones addresses how older Americans can compensate for their gradual decline in raw cognitive abilities by better leveraging information and experience. In chapter 3, James Cortada examines in detail the information ecology of a single older American as a way to better understand the multiple information sources that are available and the ways in which an individual can use them to navigate successfully in life.

The next three chapters explore in greater detail specific sources, strategies, and competencies that older adults live with in the complex information world of modern America. In chapter 4, William Aspray explores the nonprofit organizations that have been established in the United States to serve older people. The principal focus of this chapter is on the largest of these organizations, the AARP, and its many resources and services, but there is also discussion of organizations created to compete with AARP for political or religious reasons. In chapter 5, Claudia Grisales Bohorquez, Marilyn Kay, Noah Lenstra, and Kate Williams give an overview of the ways in which older adults can and do interact with technology. Their analysis is based on their experiences in working with older adults in community settings as well as field research, and they not only describe the various ways in which older adults interact with technology as they go about their everyday lives but also recommend some strategies and practices for both individuals and institutions. In chapter 6, Emily Vardell uses the lens of information literacy to explore how older adults deal with the myriad complexities of health insurance as they negotiate through the various parts of the Medicare system and interact with the players involved, including the Medicare administration, insurance companies, insurance brokers, and the AARP.

The next two chapters consider technology and the design of systems to provide a better life for older Americans. In chapter 7, Pallabi Bhowmick, Clara Caldeira, Kay Connelly, Ben Jelen, Novia Nurain, and Katie A. Siek give an overview of how internet-connected technologies (i.e., the Internet of Things) affect older adults' independence, safety, health, social connection, and security in their daily lives. They consider a number of technology examples, focusing on opportunities to better support older adults, and highlight the design issues that arise in making these technologies serve well in their intended roles. In chapter 8, Robin Brewer and Mary Janevic explore the use of a more traditional technology, the telephone, for creating communities with information and social connectedness. They point out that much of the recent research has been on employing text messaging, video conferencing, and social media platforms as technical enhancements for older adults, but these technologies are unevenly available, and their use can be limited by age-related vision or motor impairments, so they return to the well-established technology of the telephone and illustrate how it can be effectively used for these purposes.

The final three chapters focus on more specific topics or more targeted audiences. In chapter 9, Judith Pintar focuses on an information activity—genealogy research—that is popular among older adults. She explores how the practice of genealogy has changed through the use of both electronic communication and genetic markers by companies such as 23andMe and how these changes introduce new privacy concerns. In chapter 10, David Hopping explores the importance of social engagement to successful aging. In particular, he explores the information architecture present in the design of retirement communities to enhance aging in community and in particular the importance of the "one hundred percent corner" pattern, which provides physical awareness and line-of-sight features to enhance residents' situational awareness. In chapter 11, Unmil Karadkar presents a chapter directed primarily at information researchers and aging researchers, which maps out the strengths of the existing research literature and points to future needs and opportunities for research.

This book was written during the COVID-19 pandemic. The elderly population, the subject of this book, have been hard hit by the pandemic both because of their relatively frail health and the close confines of assisted living facilities. But the pandemic has caused many other, unexpected casualties as well. Four authors, all of them relatively young, have had to drop out of this project. One had to be hospitalized with COVID, another lost childcare facilities, a third had to pick up work for a colleague who was out with the disease, and a fourth was injured in a serious car accident while moving out of a city to a place to work remotely during the pandemic. It will be a long time before we understand the many different ways in which this pandemic has affected our lives.

Thanks to our editor Charles Harmon at Rowman & Littlefield and all the staff working with him: Erinn Slanina, Melissa McClellan, and Daniel McNaughton for his work on this index. It was a pleasure working with them, as it has been in the past.

## NOTES

1. "Life Table for the Projected Total Population in the United States: 2020," US Census Bureau, accessed March 30, 2021, https://www.census.gov/content/dam/Census/library/publications/2020/demo/p25-1145-supplemental-tables.pdf. The numbers have dropped slightly because of COVID.

2. For example, in 1900, the average life expectancy for White men was forty-seven, for Black men was thirty-three; for White women was forty-nine, for Black women was thirty-four. Jeffrey Hoyt, "1900–2000: Changes in Life Expectancy in the United States," Seniorliving.org, updated April 27, 2021, https://www.seniorliving.org/history/1900-2000-changes-life-expectancy-united-states/.

3. The world life expectancy overall is 70.8 for males and 75.6 for females—lower than in the United States. However, the United States has only the forty-sixth-highest life expectancy among all countries. On average, a person in Hong Kong, for example, has a life expectancy six to seven years longer than a person in the United States, while a person in the Central African Republic has an average age expectancy that is twenty-four to twenty-five years shorter than a person in the United States. "Life Expectancy of the World Population," Worldometer, accessed March 30, 2021, https://www.worldometers.info/demographics/life-expectancy/.

*Chapter One*

# Everyday Information Behavior of Older Americans

## William Aspray

This book is about the information behaviors of older Americans. It addresses a number of closely related concepts: information needs, information wants, information use, learning, decision-making, information seeking, unintended search, identifying relevance, selecting information, and sharing and collaborating.[1] It is also about technological artifacts and physical and organizational structures that have been designed to provide information, communication, and a sense of connectedness and community for individual older people or groups of them.

It is common in information studies scholarship for people to study the information behaviors of particular populations, such as specific occupations (e.g., scientists, lawyers, farmers), specific social roles (e.g., consumers, hobbyists, citizens), or specific demographic groups (e.g., as defined by age, race and ethnicity, or socioeconomic class). In information studies organized by age, the most frequently studied ages have been children and teenagers (e.g., studying teens' heavy use of social networking technologies). There have been a few studies specifically about the information behavior of older people, many of them focused on seeking health information.[2] There has, however, been no comprehensive, systematic study of the information behavior of older Americans prior to this book. This book includes a variety of approaches to this topic, ranging from traditional library and information approaches, such as information literacy and information ecology, to design and technology approaches, such as those employed by human-computer interaction scholars.

There is a large and growing population of older people in the United States. Fifteen years into our new century, there were some forty-eight million residents in the United States over the age of sixty-five, approximately 15 percent of the population. A mere fifteen years later (by 2030), there is

1

projected to be seventy-five million, with women outnumbering men. Of the forty-eight million seniors in 2015, nearly 83 percent had at least a high school education, which means they knew how to read and use information. Nearly twenty-six million of them had completed an undergraduate degree or more, which means they were practiced in seeking information to facilitate their journey through life. They were a socially stable lot. Fifty-eight percent were married, and contrary to their image as being technologically compromised, a third lived in a home with some sort of computer.[3]

This cohort is living longer too, and they are in better health. In a survey conducted in 2019, 45 percent of noninstitutionalized seniors (sixty-five or older) reported their health as "excellent or very good," although most had one chronic condition, in descending order of frequency: hypertension (75% of those seventy-five years or older), hyperlipidemia (48%), arthritis (54%), heart disease (28%), or diabetes (28%)—all of which could be controlled to some degree through medication. But as any senior will attest, *energy* is a key indicator of quality of life, and they report having a great deal of it in their sixties and seventies, less in their eighties. Energy is important for successful physical functioning, which is required to varying degrees in handling information. Eighty-five percent of people in this group are comfortable with their ability to live independently, with only 10 percent experiencing cognitive difficulties, 7 percent reporting vision problems, and 14 percent reporting hearing issues.[4] So, generally speaking, this is an energetic, alert cohort active in their largely postcareer, postparenting phases of life, pursuing active retirements, and their educational levels demonstrate long familiarity with information and its ephemera, tools, and uses.

There are some problems with studying this population, however. One is definitional. How old does one have to be in order to be an "older American"? There has long been an association between being "older" and age sixty-five. However, the US Social Security Administration has recognized that Americans are living longer, so it has moved its "normal" year for drawing benefits to ages sixty-six or sixty-seven, depending on one's birth year. The organization formerly known as the American Association of Retired Persons, now simply AARP, does not require people to be retired to join, only that they be age fifty or over. The US military offers half benefits after twenty years and full benefits after forty years; so people who joined the military at age eighteen might qualify for military retirement as early as their late thirties. This author once had a landlord who had made a fortune as a junk bond trader and retired at age twenty-eight. On the other hand, one can often find US senators and university professors still at work in their seventies. We won't try to answer this question about how old is old in this book, but we will try to give you a sense in each chapter of the population we are discussing.

Another issue is the diversity in this group of older Americans. The older old—also a definitional problem, but call it eighty-plus—is typically different in terms of health needs, energy, and mobility than people in their sixties. Older adults are also widely varied socially, culturally, and economically. Fewer and fewer people personally remember World War II, some were flower children of the 1960s, and the newer members of this group are more likely to have their first presidential memories be of the Reagan administration. All this is to say it is tricky and not absolute when one talks about the information needs of older adults.

While we focus on older Americans in this book, this population shares some information behavior characteristics with other older people in Canada, Western Europe, Australia, and Japan, for example. But because of cultural differences from one country to another, and because of differences in the ways countries handle retirement income and health care for their older citizens, especially as regards national governmental programs, it is safer to restrict our focus to the United States in the coverage here. Many information issues are the same for older people from one developed country to the next, but others remain significantly different.

It is beyond the scope of this chapter to look in detail at how information issues for older Americans have changed over time, such as the increasing longevity and improvement in health of the older US population, the creation of the Social Security program in 1935, increasing general wealth since 1945, and the creation of the Medicare program in 1966.[5]

## INFORMATION-SEEKING BEHAVIOR OF OLDER AMERICANS

One of the oldest and most traditional topics studied in information behavior studies is information-seeking behavior. This is about the conscious—and sometimes unconscious—search for information to solve a problem or satisfy a curiosity. The remainder of this chapter is about two aspects of the information-seeking behavior of older Americans: the typical questions they seek to answer and the sources they use to answer these questions. There are multiple ways in which an information scholar might go about answering these questions. One might do a survey of the research literature on this topic and pull from that the topics that are being searched. In a sense, this is what Unmil Karadkar does in chapter 11, but his focus is not so much on the questions asked but on the strengths in the existing research and the opportunities for future research. Examining the totality of chapters in this book will give some sense of the information seeking of older Americans, but this book is not comprehensive—no single volume on this topic could be—and thus we are likely to miss some major categories of questions asked by taking this approach.

Another common approach of information scholars is to carry out an empirical study of the everyday information-seeking behavior of older Americans. Following this approach, a researcher might first conduct some focus groups to identify some of the major issues, craft a survey questionnaire to administer to a group of older Americans, and then analyze the results using the qualitative and quantitative methods honed by the social sciences. The difficulty with this approach is that it is time-consuming and expensive, and one has to take care to ensure that the people who completed the questionnaire were representative of this older population in the whole. Another approach commonly used by information scholars is to build models of information-seeking behavior—often framed around theories from psychology or sociology—and use the model as a lens to understand our issues at question. However, because of the diversity in our population of older Americans, as well as the diversity in their information needs, any such model would need to be complex and would require thorough testing in order for us to trust the results.

For the sake of practicality and time constraints, we have blended two methods here. First, we have started with a list (see textbox 1.1) of information issues sought by a subset of our target population—namely, older Americans with disabilities.[6] This list was created by the Library of Congress's National Library Service for the Blind and Print Disabled as a resource for people over age fifty-five with disabilities and their caregivers. Their information was culled from "a spectrum of organizations, online tools, and articles from government, academic, and nonprofit sources. All nonprofit sources are checked against the IRS Exempt Organization and Revoked Organizations, Charity Watch, and ProPublica Nonprofit Explorer."[7]

## TEXTBOX 1.1.   INFORMATION ISSUES FOR OLDER AMERICANS WITH DISABILITIES

Financial Issues
   Financial resources
   Taxes
Federal, State, and County Benefits
Issues about Living
   Utilities

Housing
   Aging in place
   Nursing homes, memory care, and palliative care
   Transportation and driving
Work and Volunteer Opportunities
Health Issues
   Medication costs
   Resources for caregivers
   Physical health
   Alzheimer's and Dementia
   Falling
   General health resources
   Hearing
   Nutrition
   Vision
   Cataracts
   Diabetic Retinopathy
   Glaucoma
   Macular degeneration
   Resources for eye health
   Psychological health
   Depression, anxiety, and suicide
   Drug and alcohol abuse
   Vision rehabilitation
Legal
   Legal (general)
   Guardianship, conservatorship, and power of attorney
   Wills and advanced sirectives
   Abuse and fraud
Other
   Quality of life
   Assistive Technology, accessibility, and adult literacy
Safety and Emergency Preparedness

However, as we indicated earlier, many older Americans have considerable energy and good health, and if they are living with a disability, they are often nevertheless able to lead a rich, active, and fulfilling life. As a result, there are a number of additional issues that are of interest to older Americans. We offer a sample of them in textbox 1.2.[8] This list is based primarily on an open-ended literature review of academic research on older Americans conducted

## TEXTBOX 1.2. ADDITIONAL ISSUES THAT OLDER AMERICANS SEEK INFORMATION ABOUT

- Travel
- Entertainment (concerts, theater, movies, puzzles, reading)
- Active involvement in sports
- Sex
- Family caregiving
- Political involvement
- Intergenerational teaching and relationships
- Deciding when to retire
- Where to live
- Insurance
- Financial planning
- Preserving one's legacy (work, financial, family)
- Remaining engaged (social networking, keeping a sharp brain, clubs and organizations, working after retirement, mastering technology, leisure and recreation)
- Freedom for and necessity of second careers

by two student research assistants, Vaughan Nagy and Hannah Weber, at the University of Colorado, Boulder, during the spring 2020 semester.

Textboxes 1.1 and 1.2 provide a sense of the general topics that older Americans are interested in, if not the specific questions they ask. Many of these topics are similar to those that might be raised by adults in their twenties, thirties, or forties. However, there is perhaps heightened attention given, especially in textbox 1.1, to concerns about health issues and government support programs. We believe this heightened interest is representative of the interests of this older population.

## WHO PROVIDES INFORMATION TO OLDER AMERICANS?

Another common topic in information-seeking academic research is the sources of information consulted by the seeker. There are numerous places where older Americans can obtain information to help them live richer and more effective lives. Table 1.1 provides an overview of the various providers of information for seniors.[9]

**Table 1.1.   Information Providers to American Seniors**

| | |
|---|---|
| **People** | |
| Strong ties | Close friends, family |
| Weak ties | People from work, church, clubs; neighbors |
| Experts and skilled providers | Doctors, financial advisers, accountants, longtime home repair and maintenance people |
| Counselors | Religious, social service |
| **Organizations** | |
| Government | Social Security, Medicare, local zoning boards, police |
| Nonprofits | Professional organizations, cultural organizations, retirement organizations, libraries, museums |
| Media | Television, radio, print (newspapers, books, magazines), online (websites, blogs, social media sites) |

It is beyond the scope of this chapter to cover all the information sources used by seniors. Many of the later chapters discuss friends and family, neighbors and coworkers, the use of technology, built environments, and institutions such as libraries in the information-seeking activities of older Americans. However, we will make some brief overview comments here about older Americans as they interact with technology and cultural institutions. A key observation is that older Americans tap into a diverse collection of information providers as a routine practice.

There is a widespread belief that older Americans are inadequate in their interaction with information technology. However, prior research on the role of computing and smartphones demonstrates that many seniors have been using computers longer than their children or grandchildren have been alive.[10] A seventy-five-year-old in 2020 was fifty-five when flip phones went into wide use in private and work life, thirty-five when IBM introduced its personal computer in 1981, and just graduating from high school in the 1960s when computers first entered business and industry. This generation has been bumping into technology for a long time, and despite some difficulties they did begin to be digitally connected. By 2017—a decade after their invention—smartphones were in the hands of four in ten seniors, and of those in their seventies, even more had one. Of those in their seventies who had a college education, 65 percent owned one. In James Cortada's study of a woman in her midseventies (chapter 3), two-thirds of her cohort had home broadband and 92 percent of those friends with a college education accessed the internet, a rate of usage exceeding that of the population at large. Just over half of her cohort owned a tablet, and a third had an e-reader. Roughly a third of all seniors used social media in 2017, including 42 percent in their seventies and 56 percent of those in their seventies with a college education.[11]

But these older adults still faced difficulties using new technologies. Many experienced frustration when learning to use their smartphones and e-readers. They did not always understand the language of the technology, let alone what user manuals were explaining, despite the fact that they were spending more than half their daily leisure time (four hours a day) with such devices as TVs, computers, tablets, and smartphones. By 2019, some 73 percent of seniors were accessing the internet. However, their issues with technology literacy were not holding them back; survey data indicated they were "eager to learn." Seniors were interested in helping vendors design devices more suitable for this large cohort. Seniors in their sixties and seventies had typically already received some training on these technologies if they had worked outside the home, while older seniors complained they had left the workforce before they could grasp basic concepts of the internet and smartphones.[12] Chapter 5 discusses these issues (and solutions) in some detail.

Also, a brief word about libraries and other cultural institutions. Older adults comprise a large part of the audience at museums, ballet performances, classical music concerts, and nonmusical plays.[13] What do seniors think of public libraries, which for over a century have been regarded as enormously valuable as a source of information frequently used by over 70 percent of the American public? In 2017, Americans over the age of seventy-one reported that they found information there that was trustworthy and reliable (68%), that libraries taught them new things (68%), and that they obtained information helpful with decisions they have to make (48%); boomers (aged fifty-two to seventy at the time of writing) posted even higher approval ratings on these three counts: 74 percent, 72 percent, and 55 percent, respectively.[14] So, while Americans in their seventies had become extensive users of digital sources of information, they had not given up on their lifetime use of public libraries.[15] In chapter 6, Emily Vardell discusses this topic in connection with health insurance literacy.

Having sketched this general overview of seniors and their use of technology and cultural institutions, we now focus our discussion on government agencies and nonprofit organizations by listing those that are particularly important to older Americans. Although these lists are long, they are nevertheless incomplete. Table 1.2 lists organizations that primarily target the needs of older Americans, while table 1.3 lists organizations that have a broader mission but are actively involved with older Americans.

These organizations fall into several categories: some are government agencies focused on the general needs of older Americans (e.g., Administration on Aging). There are also numerous private nonprofits: ones that serve the general needs of older Americas (e.g., AARP), organizations focused on a specific disease that is of particular importance to older Americans (e.g.,

**Table 1.2. Organizations Primarily Focused on the Needs of Older Americans[1]**

American Association of Retired People (today AARP)
Academy of Nutrition and Dietetics
Administration for Community Living
Administration on Aging (AoA)
Agewell Foundation
Aging 2.0
Aging Safely, Inc.
Aging Well Hub
Aging with Dignity
Alliance for Aging Research
Alliance for Retired Americans
Alzheimer's Association
Alzheimer's Disease Education and Referral Center
Alzheimer's Foundation of America
American Academy of Hospice and Palliative Medicine
American Association for Geriatric Psychiatry
American Association of Retirement Communities
American Bar Association Commission on Law and Aging
American Federation for Aging Research (AFAR)
American Foundation for the Blind SeniorSite
American Geriatrics Society
American Health Assistance Foundation
American Health Care Association
American Seniors Association
American Society on Aging (ASA)
Asociacion Nacionale Pro Personas Mayores (ANPPM)
Assisted Living Foundation of America (ALFA)
Association for Gerontology in Higher Education (AGHE)
Association of Mature American Citizens
Buck Institute
Caregiver Action Network
Caring Across Generations
Center for Advocacy for the Rights and Interests of the Elderly (CARIE)
The Center for Social Gerontology (TCSG)
Centers for Medicare and Medicaid Services
The Christian Association of Primetimers
CICOA Aging and In-Home Solutions
Cooperative Development Foundation
Corporation for National and Community Service Senior Corps
Diverse Elders Coalition
Encore
Families USA
Gay and Lesbian Association of Retiring Persons
Generations United
Gerontological Society of America (GSE)
Hartford Institute for Geriatric Nursing

*(continued)*

Table 1.2. *(continued)*

International Network for the Prevention of Elder Abuse
Jewish Association for Services for the Aged
John A. Hartford Foundation
Justice in Aging
Leadership Council of Aging Organizations (LCAO)
Leading Age
Legal Advocates for Seniors and People with Disabilities (LASPD)
Live Extension Advocacy Foundation
Long-Term Care Community Coalition (LTCCC)
Medicare Rights Center (MRC)
National Academy of Social Insurance
National Academy on an Aging Society
National Adult Day Services Association (NADSA)
National Aging in Place Council (NAIPC)
National Aging Pacific Center on Aging (NAPCA)
National Alliance for Caregiving
National Association for Geriatric Education
National Association for Homecare and Hospice
National Association of Area Agencies on Aging (n4a)
National Association of Conservative Seniors
National Association of Nutrition and Aging Services Programs (NANASP)
National Association of State Long-Term Care Ombudsman Programs
National Association of States United for Aging and Disabilities
National Caucus and Center on Black Aging (NCBA)
National Center for Assisted Living
National Center on Elder Abuse (NCEA)
National Citizens' Coalition for Nursing Home Reform
National Clearinghouse on Abuse in Later Life (NCALL)
National Committee to Preserve Social Security and Medicare
National Consumer Voice for Quality Long-Term Care
National Council for Aging Care
National Council on Aging (NCOA)
National Guardianship Association
National Hispanic Council on Aging (NHCOA)
National Indian Council on Aging (NICOA)
National Institute on Aging
National Long-Term Care Ombudsman Resource Center
National Nursing Home Social Work Network
National Resource Center on Nutrition, Physical Activity and Aging
National Resource Center on Supportive Housing and Home Modification
National Senior Citizens Law Center (NSCLC)
National Senior Games Association
Oasis
Paraprofessional Healthcare Institute (PHI)
Pension Rights Center
Pets for the Elderly Foundation
Points of Light

Programs of All-Inclusive Care for the Elderly
Red Hat Society
Retirement Research Foundation
Second Wind Dreams
SeniorCare.com
Senior Corps
Senior Job Bank
Senior Medicare Patrol
SeniorNet
Senior Service America
The Seniors Coalition
The Service Corps of Retired Executives (SCORE)
Services and Advocacy for GLBT Elders (SAGE)
Shepherd's Centers of America
60 Plus Association
Social Security Administration
Socks for Seniors
The Spry Foundation (Setting Priorities for Retirement Years)
Vantage Aging

---

1. The lists presented in tables 1.1 and 1.2 were compiled from the following sources: "Organizations for Older Americans to Know," Diversity Best Practices, April 28, 2011, updated July 29, 2015, https://www.diversitybestpractices.com/news-articles/organizations-older-americans-know; Kristen Hicks, "15 Organizations Working to Advocate for Seniors," SeniorAdvisor.com, June 19, 2017, https://www.senioradvisor.com/blog/2017/06/15-organizations-working-to-advocate-for-seniors/; "National and Internation Private and Public Organizations," West Virginia Bureau of Senior Services, 2020, http://www.wvseniorservices.gov/GettingAnswers/LinkstoHelpfulSites/NationalInternationalPrivatePublicOrgs/tabid/102/Default.aspx; Amy Clark, "7 Top Charities that Benefit Seniors," The Senior List, May 20, 2020, https://www.theseniorlist.com/blog/7-charities-that-benefit-seniors/; "Organizations Supporting Issues and Services Important to Senior Citizens," SeniorJournal.com, December 31, 2016, http://seniorjournal.com/NEWS/Aging/2016/20160204_Organizations-supporting-issues-and-services-important-to-senior-citizens.htm; "Organizations and Research Centers," Old Anima, accessed August 30, 2020, https://www.oldanima.com/organizations.htm; "10 Resources for Living Independently as a Senior," Aging in Place, updated August 2020, https://aginginplace.org/10-resources-for-living-independently-as-a-senior/; "10 Charities for Elderly People," Preferred Care at Home, accessed August 30, 2020, https://preferhome.com/senior-resources/common-senior-concerns/10-charities-for-elderly-people-2/; "What Are the Organizations for Older Adults," modified December 23, 2019, https://elder-law.laws.com/organizations-for-older-adults/organizations-for-older-adults; "Our Members," Eldercare Workforce Alliance, 2020, https://eldercareworkforce.org/our-members/; "List of NGOs Accredited to the OEWG on Ageing," UNDESA, 2011, https://social.un.org/ageing-working-group/accreditedngos.shtml; Hanscom Federal Credit Union, "23 Organizations Dedicated to the Needs of Seniors," Money Wisdom, October 11, 2019, https://go.hfcu.org/blog/23-organizations-dedicated-to-the-needs-of-seniors; Vin [no surname], "Learning the Importance and Benefits of Senior Organizations," Shield My Senior, March 19, 2017, https://www.shieldmysenior.com/senior-citizen-organizations/; Gregg Parker, "6 Organizations Dedicated to Helping the Elderly," Wiki.ezvid.com, October 22, 2019, https://wiki.ezvid.com/m/6-organizations-dedicated-to-helping-the-elderly-lFsZJnsNSOZPq; "Related Professional Organizations," Gerontological Advanced Practice Nurses Association, August 30, 2020, https://www.gapna.org/resources/related-professional-organizations; Joseph Slife, "Search for an Alternative to AARP? Here Are 6 Options," Sound Mind Investing, July 27, 2017, https://soundmindinvesting.com/articles/view/seven-alternatives-for-seniors-fleeing-aarp; Cheryl Cirelli, "5 Senior Citizens Organizations to Check Out Today," LoveToKnow, accessed August 30, 2020, https://seniors.lovetoknow.com/Senior_Citizen_Organizations; "National Senior Services and Resources," Seniors Resource Guide, accessed August 30, 2020, https://seniorsresourceguide.com/directories/National/search.php?region=US01&topic=609; Ana Cocarla, "US Organizations that Serve Seniors," Senior Care Center, 2019, https://srcarecenter.com/article/us-organizations-that-serve-seniors/.

**Table 1.3.   Organizations with a Broader Purpose that Are Actively Involved with Older Americans**[1]

American Academy of Home Care Medicine
American Automobile Association Foundation for Traffic Safety
American Cancer Society
American Lung Association
American Nurses Association
American Public Health Association
American Red Cross
Commonwealth Fund
Community Transportation Association of America
Employee Benefit Research Institute
The Faith and Service Technical Education Network (FASTEN)
Family Caregivers Alliance (FCA)
Healthy People 2020
Henry J. Kaiser Family Foundation
Honor Flight Network
Independent Transportation Network
Institute for Healthcare Improvement
Joint Commission on Accreditation of Healthcare Organizations
Meals on Wheels America
National Academy for State Health Policy
National Alliance to End Homelessness
National Association of Insurance Commissioners
National Association of Social Workers
National Coalition for the Homeless
National Commission for Health Education Credentialing
National Consumer Law Center (NCLC)
National Family Caregivers Association
National Law Center on Homelessness and Poverty (NLCHP)
National Pharmaceutical Council
Office on Women's Health, Health and Human Services
Peace Corps
Pharmaceutical Research and Manufacturers of America
Rebuilding Together
Robert Wood Johnson Foundation
The Roundtable on Religion and Social Welfare Policy
Rural Transit Assistance Program (RTAP)
Urban Institute
U.S. Department of Veteran Affairs
Volunteers of America

1. The sources used to compile this list are the same as those used to prepare table 1.1.

Alzheimer's Association), professional organizations for caregivers (e.g., Paraprofessional Healthcare Institute), organizations focused on a particular demographic community (e.g., National Hispanic Council on Aging), organizations concerned with housing or transportation (e.g., National Aging in Place Council), organizations involved with caregiving facilities (e.g., National Citizens' Coalition for Nursing Home Reform), organizations protecting against abuse and fraud related to older Americans (e.g., National Center on Elder Abuse), and organizations focused on healthy diet and exercise (e.g., Academy of Nutrition and Dietetics).[16] These lists indicate how large and complex the information ecology for older Americans is. Further case studies of individuals' preference of some sources of information over others, or of the order in which sources are used, would be revealing but is beyond our scope here.

In summary, to better understand the relationship of older Americans to their information needs, we accept three realities: (1) they share common behaviors and identities shaped by the social, historical, and economic realities of their lifetimes as well as by the technologies they have used for many years; (2) they seek out information in a multitude of ways and exhibit a great propensity to find it methodically, following well-established habits of information seeking; and (3) American society is honeycombed with organizations that assist older Americans in their information-seeking activities. These three realities are observed, in one way or another, in most of the chapters of this book.

## NOTES

1. For an excellent analysis of these related concepts, see Donald O. Case and Lisa M. Given, *Looking for Information*, 4th ed. (Bingley, UK: Emerald, 2016), chapters 5 and 6. On the theories employed in information behavior studies, see Karen E. Fisher, Sandra Erdelez, and Lynne McKechnie, *Theories of Information Behavior* (Medford, NJ: Information Today, 2009).

2. For a discussion of the literature on information behavior of various populations, see Case and Given, *Looking for Information*, chapter 12. For a discussion of the literature on information behavior of older adults, including citations to the existing literature, see Case and Given, *Looking for Information*, 353–355.

3. All demographic statistics are drawn from the US Census Bureau (www.census .gov).

4. "2019 Profile of Older Americans," Administration for Community Living and Administration on Aging, accessed August 16, 2020, https://acl.gov/sites/default/ files/Aging%20and%20Disability%20in%20America/2019ProfileOlderAmericans 508.pdf.

5. For a study of how to introduce historical change into the study of information behavior over time, see William Aspray and Barbara M. Hayes, eds., *Everyday Information* (Cambridge, MA: MIT Press, 2011) and in particular William Aspray, "One Hundred Years of Car Buying," 9–70.

6. "Resources for Senior Citizens and Their Families," National Library Service for the Blind and Print Disabled, Library of Congress, accessed October 5, 2020, https://www.loc.gov/nls/resources/general-resources-on-disabilities/resources-senior-citizens-families/. The Library of Congress list has been reordered to group like information needs, but the contents have not otherwise been altered. Note that some of the categories seem to be narrower than others; this is more likely to be an indicator of the interest in particular topics than weakness in categorial scheme.

7. "Resources for Senior Citizens and Their Families."

8. Table 1.2 is prepared in part from a literature review of academic research on older Americans conducted by this author's research assistants, Vaughan Nagy and Hannah Weber, at the University of Colorado, Boulder, during the spring 2020 semester.

9. The notion of strong ties and weak ties that is employed in this table is based on a famous paper by the sociologist Mark Granovetter, which has been widely adopted by researchers in information studies: Mark S. Granovetter, "The Strength of Weak Ties," *American Journal of Sociology* 78, no. 6 (May 1973): 1360–1380.

10. A. Berenguer, J. Goncalves, S. Hosio, D. Ferreira, T. Anagnostopoulos, and V. Kostakos, "Are Smartphones Ubiquitous?: An In-Depth Survey of Smartphone Adoption by Seniors," *IEEE Consumer Electronics Magazine* 6, no. 1 (January 2017): 104–110.

11. Monica Anderson and Andrew Perrin, "Tech Adoption Climbs among Older Adults," Pew Research Center, May 17, 2017, https://www.pewresearch.org/internet/2017/05/17/tech-adoption-climbs-among-older-adults/.

12. Robin Seaton Jefferson, "More Seniors Are Embracing Technology. But Can They Use It? UCSD Researchers Suggest Asking Them," *Forbes*, June 28, 2019, https://www.forbes.com/sites/robinseatonjefferson/2019/06/28/more-seniors-are-embracing-technology-but-can-they-use-it-ucsd-researchers-suggest-asking-them/#1e43fe832323.

13. See, for example, American Academy of Arts and Science, "Humanities Indicators: Art Museum Attendance," accessed March 31, 2021, https://www.amacad.org/humanities-indicators/public-life/art-museum-attendance; and "A Decade of Arts Engagement: Findings from the Survey of Public Participation in the Arts 2002–2012," National Endowment for the Arts, Research Report #58, accessed March 31, 2021, https://www.arts.gov/sites/default/files/2012-sppa-jan2015-rev.pdf.

14. A. W. Geiger, "Most Americans—Especially Millennials—Say Libraries Can Help Them Find Reliable, Trustworthy Information," Pew Research Center, August 30, 2017, https://www.pewresearch.org/fact-tank/2017/08/30/most-americans-especially-millennials-say-libraries-can-help-them-find-reliable-trustworthy-information/.

15. Wayne A. Wiegand, *Part of Our Lives: A People's History of the American Public Library* (New York: Oxford University Press, 2015).

16. In these tables, we have included not only organizations that are targeted at older Americans but also professional organizations and trade associations that serve older Americans. We have also listed in these tables government organizations that serve older Americans primarily or frequently in carrying out their missions. We have not discussed for-profit organizations, even though they often provide information to older Americans.

*Chapter Two*

# Information, Knowledge, and Successful Aging[1]

## William Jones[2]

To live is to age. Age is a lifetime giver of experiences, knowledge, and wisdom. But age is a taker too. After bringing us to a peak of raw mental and physical ability sometime in our twenties, age begins to take it all away.

The ultimate, inevitable end to our life story is never in doubt. But a growing body of research, loosely grouped under the rubric "successful aging," provides intriguing, suggestive indicators that we might compensate for and counter declines in raw cognitive ability through methods that better leverage both information "out there" and our accumulated knowledge "in the head." In ideal circumstances, methods combine so that the declines of age are minimal, and we remain active, engaged, and self-reliant until the very end of our biological lives.

Staying sharp. Aging gracefully. Still in the prime. Notions of successful aging have been around for as long as people have been fortunate enough to grow old. Successful aging as a focus of scientific inquiry is more recent. Academic definitions for successful aging, like those we might hold informally, are varied.

This chapter adopts the MacArthur model definition advanced by Rowe and Kahn, wherein successful aging is a convergence of contributing factors: "minimize risk of disease and disability . . . continue engagement with life [and] . . . maintain physical and cognitive function."[3]

Contributing factors of successful aging are not independent of one another, and each factor affects the others (see figure 2.1). As we stay engaged with life, for example, we are more likely to stay informed, connected, and active in ways that minimize our risk of disease and disability and that help us maintain high physical and cognitive function. Likewise, as we avoid disease and disability, so too can we more readily stay engaged and maintain function, both cognitive and physical. Maintenance of physical and cognitive

Figure 2.1.   A depiction of the MacArthur Model of Successful Aging.
William Jones

function, similarly, supports engagement in life and the avoidance of disease and disability.

The list of contributing factors for successful aging can be expanded and its items elaborated. Bowling and Dieppe include the following:[4]

- life satisfaction and well-being (includes happiness and contentment)
- mental and psychological health, cognitive function
- personal growth, learning new things
- physical health and functioning, independent functioning
- psychological characteristics and resources, including perceived autonomy, control, independence, adaptability, coping, self-esteem, positive outlook, goals, sense of self
- social, community, leisure activities, integration and participation, social networks, support, participation, activity

What other factors might we add? Spirituality, mindfulness, a regular practice of meditation, a sense of purpose, and so on.

Regardless of the actual list of contributing factors, a key point of Rowe and Kahn's work is that infirmities, physical and cognitive, which may correlate with advancing age, are not an inevitable, foregone outcome of aging:

> Our purpose was to counteract the longstanding tendency of gerontology to emphasize only the distinction between the pathologic and nonpathologic, that is, between older people with diseases or disabilities and those suffering from neither. The implicit assumption of that earlier gerontology was that, in the absence of disease and disability, other age-related alterations in physical function (such as increases in blood pressure and blood glucose) and cognitive function (such as modest memory impairment) were "normal," determined by intrinsic aging.[5]

Rowe and Kahn argue further that environment, including our various lifestyle choices, makes a substantial contribution to variance in measures of successful aging and that this contribution (as opposed to the contribution of genetics) increases dramatically as we age. With reference to the results of the famous "Swedish twins" study,[6] for example, they note that for some measures of physical health, the percentage of variance accounted for by environment versus heredity increases from a range of 20 percent to 30 percent for people in their fifties and early sixties to 75 percent and more as people age through their sixties and seventies and on into their eighties.

With respect to the list of factors contributing to successful aging, we might wish for most of these to be present, regardless of our age. Indeed, we might better use the term *successful living*. We stick with *successful aging* because *aging* more directly denotes change with time, for better and for worse. Many things improve with age as we live and learn and as we gain in knowledge and wisdom. But aging also brings decline.

By some measures of function, age-related declines begin as early as our early twenties. Aging successfully, then, is not just a concern for older people—in other words, something we begin to plan for along with retirement and health care coverage as we near the age of sixty-five. If we mean to age successfully, it is best to start *now* regardless of where we are in our adult lives.

Successful aging isn't just for us as individuals but also for us as members of families, workgroups, and societies. Collectively, we are growing older. In the United States, "from 2000 to 2010, the population under 18 years of age increased by 2.6%, while the population of those 65 years of age and older increased by 15.1%."[7] Other countries are aging too. For example, more than 20 percent of the population in Germany, Italy, and Japan are age sixty-five or older.[8]

There is a concern often expressed that increasing numbers of older people may stress our systems of Social Security and medical care to the breaking point. But if these people successfully age, we can imagine that many will continue (by choice or sometimes economic necessity) to work or otherwise contribute as productive members of society. We need the expertise and the experience of these people! As a society ages successfully, we might even hope for a "longevity dividend"[9] as, for example, when the experience and wisdom of older people is synergistically melded with the energy and raw processing ability of younger people. We can already think of people who continue to serve successfully, especially in public office, even as they age into their late seventies and beyond. If these people no longer have the vigor of youth, perhaps they more than compensate with their knowledge and wisdom gained through a lifetime of experiences.

Collectively and as individuals, we can take successful aging to be about reducing, even reversing, or at least compensating for, the declines in function that typically accompany aging even as we take full advantage of the improvements in function (and happiness) that aging brings.

## WHAT CAN WE DO RIGHT NOW?

Researchers have been consistent concerning key steps we can take to promote good health and maintain good cognitive and physical function:

- Get regular exercise. It's good for brain as well as body.[10]
- Watch your weight.
- Stay engaged and involved, and maintain good connections to friends and family.
- Get good sleep (although for some this may not be so easily controlled).
- If you drink, do so in moderation.
- And, of course, give up bad habits such as cigarette smoking.

What else? The focus of this chapter moves beyond the certain benefits associated with the steps listed above toward efforts of less proven potential with special focus on cognitive functioning. Much as we may fear and seek to diminish or delay the physical declines that come with aging, research indicates that we especially fear cognitive decline. For example, in a survey of six hundred people aged seventy or older,[11] 60 percent indicated that they would not wish to live any longer under a condition of severe cognitive impairment. Cognitive decline had a greater impact on a participant's valuation of life than did physical impairment or pain.

## A PLAN FOR THIS CHAPTER

In three sections, this chapter raises key questions and offers a few suggestions concerning the cognitive dimensions of successful aging:

1. Are we getting slower or smarter as we age? We consider the notions of fluid versus crystallized intelligence and relate these to underlying notions of information "out there" versus knowledge "in the head" and then further to notions of bottom-up (data-driven) processing versus top-down (expectation-based) processing.

2. What can we do to keep our brains in shape? The efficacy of selected activities and programs of brain training are reviewed. With sufficient training, people, regardless of age, can achieve impressive, even incredible, performance gains on a given skill (e.g., playing a piano or recitation of a span of digits). But, alas, there is typically little if any transfer of this performance to other skills (e.g., playing another musical instrument or recitation of a span of letters) nor to everyday activities. But some recent studies suggest that certain forms of practice and training (e.g., playing certain video or virtual reality games) may lead to the development of skills that are more general and have practical value in our everyday lives.

3. Can our information tools work like "cognitive eyeglasses" to help compensate for some declines in cognitive abilities? We take inspiration for the cognitive from the physical, not only with respect to quotidian disciplines (e.g., walk a mile every day) but also with respect to tools and technologies that might function analogously to the various tools, including prosthetics, that we routinely employ to extend the reach of our physical bodies and to overcome infirmities. For example, can information tools be designed to reduce demands on working memory, which is known to decline gradually in capacity with normal aging? Conversely, might these tools take greater advantage of abilities related to vocabulary and general knowledge, which continue to improve through adulthood?

The following sections provide a highly selective review of a broad swath of relevant research topics. Exploration of any topic is, of necessity, brief. Consider this chapter, then, as a starting point and not as a conclusion. For the layperson, the chapter provides ample references for further reading. For researchers working to extend our knowledge, may this chapter's review serve as an encouragement—an incitement even—toward the work so urgently needed if we are, individually and collectively, to age successfully.

## ARE WE GETTING SLOWER OR SMARTER AS WE GET OLDER?

In an impressive analysis involving data from nearly fifty thousand web participants and including normative data from standardized IQ and memory tests, Hartshorne and Germine found that when in their lives people reach a peak of performance varies greatly for different measures of cognitive ability.[12] For some abilities, people peak and then begin to decline just around the age of twenty. For other abilities, people reach a stable plateau in early adulthood that may persist for several decades. And then for some abilities, people don't reach a peak of performance until sixty or older.

In a selected depiction of measures in figure 2.2,[13] performance on one cognitive measure, a digit symbol coding task,[14] begins to decline before age twenty, while performance on a vocabulary task (given a word, provide its definition) continues to improve through a person's sixties—in other words, throughout the range of ages included in the study.[15]

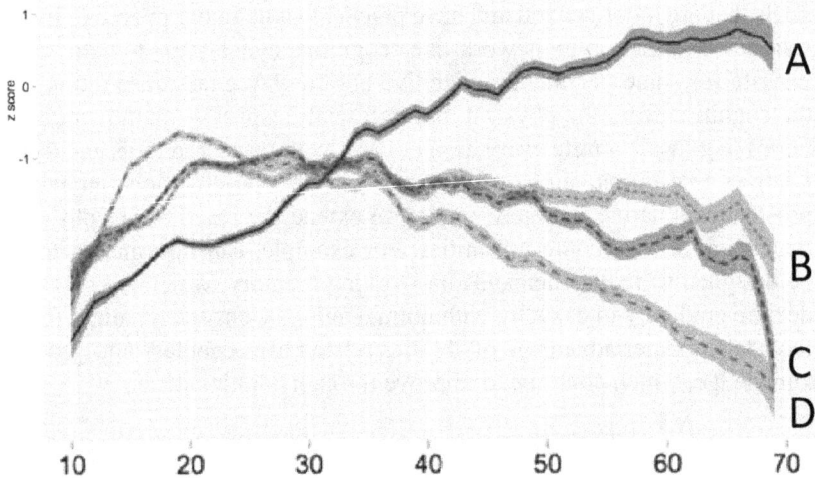

Figure 2.2. **Performance on some cognitive tasks, e.g., the digit symbol coding task (D), begins to decline early in adulthood even as performance on other measures, e.g., the vocabulary (A), continues to increase as people age into their 60s and beyond. (Shaded areas represent standard errors.) Working memory digit span, B, after a modest initial decline in a person's early 20s, remains stable as a person ages into their 60s. (The other measure, C, is for visual working memory.)**
William Jones

Performance on some cognitive tasks (e.g., the digit symbol coding task, labeled as D in figure 2.2) begins to decline early in adulthood even as performance on other measures (e.g., the vocabulary, labeled as A in figure 2.2) continues to increase as people age into their sixties and beyond. (Shaded areas represent standard errors.)

Age-related discrepancies in performance across tests of intelligence and cognitive ability have given rise to a proposed distinction between fluid and crystallized intelligence.[16] Horn notes that fluid intelligence is "relatively independent of education and experience; and it can 'flow' into a wide variety of intellectual activities," whereas crystallized intelligence is "a precipitate out of experience. It results when fluid intelligence is 'mixed' with what can be called the 'intelligence of the culture.' Crystallized intelligence increases with a person's experience, and with the education that provides new methods and perspectives for dealing with that experience."[17]

Crystallized intelligence is represented by measures of cognitive function that continue to increase well into later adulthood. In Hartshorne and Germine's study, these include measures of vocabulary (provide definitions for words), information (answer general knowledge questions), and comprehension (explain, for example, why we have parole). Per the quote by Horn earlier, crystallized intelligence is much more than a simple rote-like accretion of facts. Rather it represents an integration of raw information, acquired through facilities of fluid intelligence, into a more coherent whole—possibly as shaped through prior learning and the experiences of formal education.

Fluid intelligence is represented by measures of cognitive function that declines early in adulthood, including measures of abstract reasoning, the ability to reason in novel situations, working memory, and raw processing speed. Salthouse argues for a unifying explanation in which these early onset declines are explained to reflect an underlying decrease in processing speed.[18] By this explanation, declines in working memory occur, for example, because items in working memory "fall out" with normal decay before an older person can make use of them in the current problem situation.[19]

Are we getting slower or smarter as we get older? Both, it would seem. Even as measures of fluid intelligence began to decline in early adulthood, where declines may follow from an underlying decrease in processing speed, we are getting smarter by other measures as we learn and gain experience with increasing age. Clearly the distinction between fluid and crystallized intelligence is a simplification—but a useful one for this chapter's exploration into cognitive issues of successful aging. The distinction aligns nicely with two other distinctions commonly made:

- Between information ("out there")—or, more precisely, information drawn from sensory data—and knowledge ("in the head").
- Between bottom-up and top-down processing, as used in cognitive psychology to explain human information processing, most especially perception and pattern matching.[20] Bottom-up processing works from sensory data to classification and comprehension, whereas top-down processing is more heavily influenced by expectation and previous experience. (More about both later.)

These distinctions will prove useful as we consider a key question of successful aging: Can continued improvements in crystallized intelligence compensate for a gradual degradation in fluid intelligence? This question relates to a general observation that, drawing on the knowledge we have already acquired, our top-down, expectation-based processing can frequently speed up and streamline the bottom-up processing of incoming information.

In many circumstances, of course, there is redundancy such that we have a choice between the knowledge in our heads (e.g., our memories) and an external lookup of information. If, for example, we mean in an email message to ask how a friend's daughter is doing in her first year of college at Drexel, we might trust our memory for the daughter's name ("Hanna? Or is it spelled Hannah? Or . . . is her name Emma?"), or we could take extra time to look through past emails or perhaps Facebook posts for this information.

The trade-offs between remembrance and lookup will shift as a function of the cost of an error (a friend is likely to be forgiving of an error in our remembrance, a boss perhaps less so) versus the cost, in time and energy, of a lookup. The costs associated with remembrance versus lookup are constantly shifting. The cost of external lookup is often much less than it was only a few decades ago.[21] It is much less costly for me to look through emails now than it was in the early 1990s because my emails are indexed for rapid search. We may, on occasion, even determine that external lookup is faster than remembrance.

Gray and Fu[22] provide an analysis of these trade-offs using a rational analysis framework.[23] Improvements in our information tools are likely to further a shift away from reliance on memory and toward reliance on information externally derived, especially from digital data. Even if we can remember the phone number of our favorite pizza place, we may elect to click on the phone number shown on our smartphone screen after a quick lookup of the website. It is just faster than keying in the number.

In many other everyday situations of cognitive processing, we don't decide between lookup and remembrance. Rather, we seek a blend such that external information is structured by the knowledge we have acquired over the years through experience and education. As we do so, we are challenged to combine cognitive abilities associated with both fluid and crystallized intelligence. The relative proportion of each may shift with age.

There may be a compensatory shift toward crystallized intelligence in some measures of cognitive function discussed by Hartshorne and Germine. Even as measures associated with fluid intelligence decline, while measures associated with crystallized intelligence continue to improve, some measures of cognitive function remain relatively constant across a broad range of ages. In figure 2.2 for example, performance on the digit span task, after modest declines for a person in her twenties and early thirties, stays relatively constant through a person's forties and fifties. For this task and in many real-world tasks, there may be a shift with aging such that improvements in crystallized intelligence make up for declines in fluid intelligence. In the case of digit span tasks (i.e., where the person listens to a sequence of digits, spoken one per second, and then repeats this sequence), we know that performance can improve dramatically with practice.[24] Some improvements are made simply by categorizing or "chunking"[25] sequences of digits in the span so that the person is dealing not with a sequence of distinct digits but rather with a consolidated sequence of chunks.[26]

We opportunistically form chunks for a digit sequence based on its happenstance correspondence to numbers we have learned over the years. A chunk may correspond to a telephone country or area code or an address or a friend's birthdate or the year our favorite team won the Super Bowl. A point here is that our candidate pool of familiar digit sequences for purposes of chunking inevitably increases through the years and with experience. Analogous to word vocabulary, we might regard this pool of digit sequences as contributing to crystallized intelligence.

The digit span task can then be seen to draw on a combination of fluid intelligence (i.e., raw processing speed) supporting the maintenance of a larger number of chunks in short-term memory (like the juggling of many balls in the air) and crystallized intelligence supporting the formation of larger chunks. Even as the number of chunks we can keep in short-term memory gradually decreases over the years, the sequence of digits in each chunk goes up so that digit span is roughly constant.

An especially dramatic illustration of the power of crystallized intelligence comes from the study of chess. How does a chess grandmaster differ from a beginning chess player? Research indicates that there is little difference between expert and beginner with respect to number of moves considered, search heuristics, depth of search, or other measures of thought processes.[27] If anything, chess masters consider fewer possible moves than beginning players do. The key difference lies in the "vocabulary" of chess positions. Grandmasters have, as part of their in-the-head knowledge, a long-term memory for many, many more chess positions than do beginners. In a short-term memory test, wherein participants are asked to reproduce a chess position after viewing it for only five seconds, grandmasters perform significantly better than beginning players do. We cannot attribute observed differences to the overall superiority of a grandmaster's memory since when the same chess pieces are placed on the board randomly and not in a position that might occur in an actual chess game, masters do no better than beginners.

Associated with a grandmaster's enormous vocabulary of chess positions is a remembrance for successful move sequences to follow from each. They *remember* to do next what might alternatively be uncovered through a brute force, "fluid" search. In this regard, the play of a grandmaster such as Kasparov is distinctly different from that of a computer program such as Deep Blue, which, although it is endowed with a database of chess positions, can also do a fast systematic evaluation of different move alternatives (over two hundred million chess positions per second).[28]

We are all grandmasters, we might say, in the conduct of our own lives. We're the experts. Our vocabulary for the familiar is countless—the morning routine, the commute, shopping at the grocery store, eating at our favorite restaurant, gathering with friends in the neighborhood, and so on. Anticipation born of experience enables us to complete familiar tasks quickly, with ease and little error—"with our eyes closed."

We have considered two distinctions, fluid versus crystallized intelligence and information versus knowledge. Examples of task completion in familiar situations bring us to a third distinction: bottom-up (data-driven) versus top-down (expectation-based) processing:

- Bottom-up processing works from the raw data of our senses to make perceptions ("Who is that person over there?"), classifications ("Is that a neighbor's dog in the street or a coyote?"), and actions (we slam on the brakes to avoid hitting the deer that has sauntered in front of our car).
- Top-down processing works from our predictions and our expectations where these come from knowledge formed from previous experiences, recent to remote. We quickly determine that Joe is standing over there because we agreed to meet him here at the coffee shop (and "know" what he looks like). We identify that animal scampering across our yard as a coyote partly because of a neighbor's recent email that a coyote has been seen in our neighborhood (and perhaps we even looked up a Wikipedia article on coyotes to refresh our memory concerning what a coyote looks like). We are even faster to see the deer in front of us because we saw the deer-crossing sign a few minutes ago and know that deer frequent this stretch of highway.

The distinction between bottom-up and top-down processing is, like the other two, a great simplification that will nevertheless be useful for our explorations into cognitive issues relating to successful aging: our information processing—our perceptions, our classifications, the actions we take, the decisions we make—is a combination of both bottom-up and top-down processing.[29]

This mixture of bottom-up and top-down processing holds true no matter how old we are; although, just as we may tend to rely more on cognitive facilities associated with crystallized intelligence as we age, we may also come to rely more on top-down processing. I reach out to catch a spoon falling from the dinner table with no problem, notwithstanding my age (sixty-eight as of the writing of this chapter). Great reflexes? Raw speed? Better to attribute this to great anticipation. I know, from much experience, the trajectory the spoon will take and can meet it and catch it just before it hits the floor.

But top-down processing can sometimes be too much of a good thing. The magician's sleight of hand depends on our strong tendency to fill in the gaps, top-down. We assume things that aren't true. We see things that didn't happen. We hear things that weren't spoken.[30] A standard skit has a person, hard of hearing (and typically older), incorrectly repeating what someone else just said to great comedic effect (e.g., "Peas? Why would I forget my peas?"). When we have trouble recognizing a work colleague "out of place" at the grocery store, we might wish for more bottom-up processing.

Another potential downside of excessive top-down processing may be the tendency to categorize or "chunk" our lives away. Today is mostly like yesterday. This weekend is mostly like last weekend. The coming summer vacation is mostly like last summer's vacation. It's hardly surprising if many of us feel that time is telescoping as we age. And it's hardly fair! We would want the opposite! We would want time to slow down!

As human beings, we measure time not in absolute, chronological terms (as by the clock) but rather in terms of the distinct events we experience, recognize, and later remember. Many of us may recall an "endless summer" from our youth—everything was new, and every day was a new adventure. Or perhaps in more recent times, we took an unusual vacation that exposed us to new experiences we couldn't simply chunk away (i.e., into ever larger chunks such as "same vacation as last year with small variations").

In order to slow time down, we might take an exotic vacation, learn a new skill (e.g., learn to dance), try a new restaurant, or even try (although not easy) to be more mindful in our daily lives—make a point of noticing something new and different each day, and perhaps write this down in a journal.[31] Taking this "expose yourself to the new and different" approach to a logical limit, Sorenson argues that, to fight cognitive decline, we should order our lives so that we constantly face new situations and must deal with novel problems.[32]

## Summary

It is useful to group cognitive abilities broadly into two categories of intelligence—fluid and crystallized. Many measures of cognitive ability associated with fluid intelligence begin their decline in early adulthood even as measures of cognitive ability associated with crystallized intelligence continue to improve with age. Some measures, such as for vocabulary and general information, continue to improve as we age through our fifties and beyond.

In many circumstances, there is a complementarity in cognitive abilities associated with the two kinds of intelligence such that declines in fluid abilities can be compensated for by gains in crystallized abilities. Complementarity is more likely to occur to the extent that the current situation is like previous situations so that practice and lessons learned from previous situations can apply.

But what a pity we can't have them both! What a pity we can't function at high levels of both fluid and crystallized intelligence. In project-team situations—work related and not—we may be able to realize high levels of both kinds of intelligence through an age-diverse selection of team members. Age-diverse teams are a potential win-win(-win). Good for the older workers who are included and engaged, good for the team as a whole, and good also for the younger members of the team.[33]

As individuals we might also wish for the best of both kinds of intelligence. What can we do to maintain high levels of fluid intelligence even as our crystallized intelligence continues to improve? In the next section, we consider the decidedly mixed results concerning the efficacy of mental exercise and training to keep our brains in shape.

## THE QUEST FOR THE "INTERACTIONS OF LIFE"

The quest for the "elixir of life,"[34] alternatively defined as eternal life or eternal youth, has been described around the world, across cultures, and under different names. Much that is written about successful aging seeks the latter—eternal youth. Or rather, youthful ability and performance right up to the end of our corporeal lives.

What can be done to slow or even reverse the declines that come with normal aging? There is no elixir at present, although someday we might hope for medicines that can preserve our physical and, most especially, our cognitive facilities as we age.

In the next two sections of this chapter, we consider two other general quests for preserving our youthful cognitive abilities as we age: (1) programs of exercise and training to reduce or eliminate the cognitive declines that typically come with age, and (2) information tools that might function as "cognitive spectacles" to compensate for, or even make irrelevant, age-related declines in cognitive ability.

In the design of each of these—programs of exercise/training and information tools—we are essentially seeking what are, in statistical terms, interactions. Consider figure 2.3, with its two alternate patterns of data from a generic study of aging as affected by some manipulation to "improve." The "improved" condition might represent a better user interface for an information tool, a regimen of exercise and training to stimulate brain health, or something else entirely (e.g., change of diet, smoking cessation, weight loss). The dependent variable (graphed on the Y-axis in figure 2.3) might represent time to complete a task, reaction time, or something else entirely (e.g., error rate, accident rate, or even death rate). A general point for the dependent measure is that lower is better.

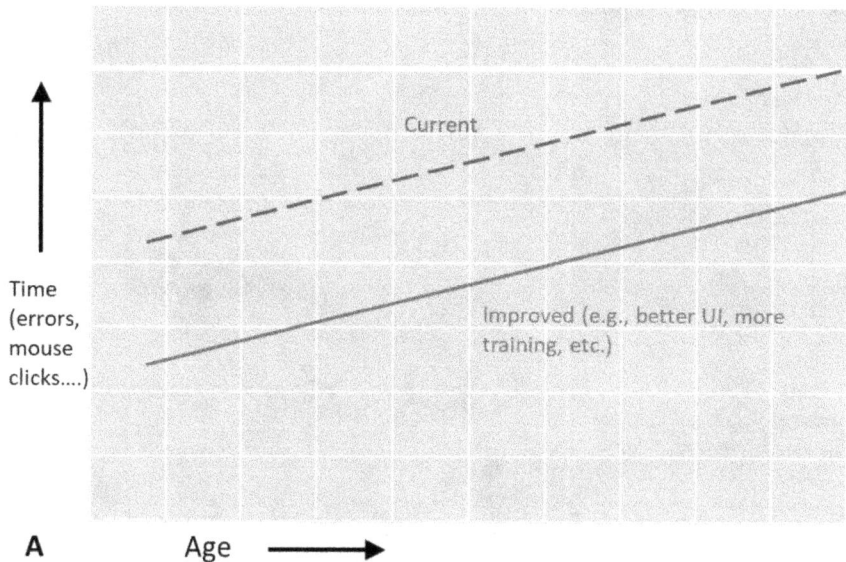

**Figure 2.3A.**  **Main effect for age, main effect for improvement.**
William Jones

"Age," on the X-axis, is represented as a continuous variable, but we could readily replace the X-axis with two or more groupings for age (e.g., young versus old, or ranges such as twenty to thirty-nine, forty to fifty-nine, sixty to seventy-nine, eighty and over).

The data represented in figure 2.3A show a main effect for age and for the "improved" condition versus the "current" condition (commonly referred to as the "control"). Performance is better for everyone, across ages, in the "improved" condition. But in both conditions, performance worsens as age increases (e.g., completion times, error rates, accident rates, and so on increase with age). As we shall see in the upcoming sections, this is very often the pattern observed in studies that look at the benefits that some manipulation might have for older people. Yes, older people *do* see benefits. But so too do younger people so that the overall discrepancy in performance remains. Alternatively, we can say that the rates of age-related decline are the same; only the starting point has changed.

Now look at figure 2.3B. There still appears to be a main effect for age and for the manipulation ("current" versus "improved") as in figure 2.3A. But note that now in the "improved" condition there appears to be no age effect. Older people perform as well as younger people. Alternatively, although everyone has improved performance in the "improved" condition, improvement seems to increase with age.

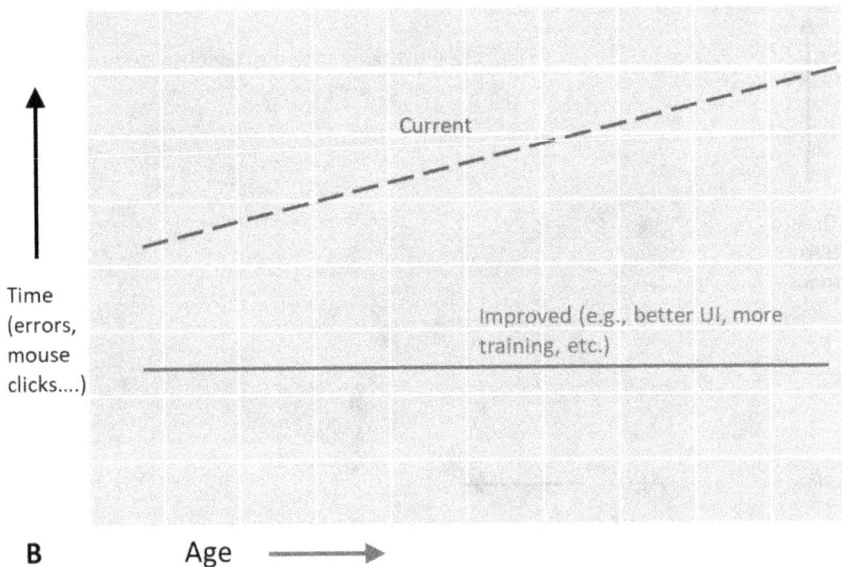

**Figure 2.3B.** Main effects for age and improvement, but also an "emergent" interaction between age and improvement that can't be accounted for by either main effect.
William Jones

This, in statistical terms, is an interaction. We might say that the pattern emerges from an interaction between primary variables such as age and the current versus improved manipulation such that the variance in performance numbers is not fully accounted for by the primary variables alone. Of course, an interaction, if observed, very often goes in the other direction—in other words, if an improvement is better for everyone, regardless of age, it is especially better for younger people who may be able more quickly to adopt (and adapt) an innovation (smartphones, for example) to suit their needs.

Are interactions of life, like "elixirs of life," a thing of legend and fable, not to be found in the real world? We explore this further in the next two sections.

## Keeping Our Brains in Shape

Regular physical exercise is an important part of any program of successful aging. Physical exercise is important not only for the body but also for the brain.[35] If we want to keep our brains in shape, we need to start with a sustainable program of physical exercise.

But what about mental exercise? Muscles atrophy if they aren't used. Following the brain-as-muscle metaphor, does the brain likewise atrophy for lack of use? Several studies suggest the answer is yes. Measures of cognitive function fall sharply, for example, after a person retires.[36] Observed patterns of atrophy for want of activity and engagement give rise to the adage "use it or lose it." Leaving aside the abrupt declines in cognitive abilities that may accompany a major life change such as retirement, as noted in the previous section, measures of cognitive function associated with fluid intelligence decline through our adult lives even as we work and even if we postpone retirement. What can we do? Consider two general approaches:

1. Use it to keep it (longer). This approach follows a brain-as-muscle metaphor. Can mental activity, whether as a natural by-product of lifestyle or because of new mental exercises consciously added (e.g., sudoku, crossword puzzles, reading a challenging book), work to preserve cognitive function as we age?
2. Training to function. With this approach, we follow a cognitive-function-as-skill metaphor and with this metaphor a shift from simple brain exercise to more focused, goal-directed training and practice. We train and practice to get better at golf or playing the piano. Can we consider more basic cognitive abilities (e.g., working memory, executive control, episodic recall) to be skills that can be targeted and trained, if not directly then through tasks that use these abilities?

## The "Use It to Keep It (Longer)" Hypothesis

Salthouse notes the methodological challenges associated with evaluating the hypothesis that mental activity will prevent (or at least slow the rate of) age-related decline.[37] He outlines three essential characteristics for such an evaluation: (1) Random assignment of individuals to the experimental and control groups to minimize effects of preexisting differences (e.g., in cognitive ability or level of education). (2) Rigorous control of the treatment especially with respect to type and amount of mental exercise. (3) Long-term monitoring of the amount of mentally stimulating activity and the level of cognitive functioning.

As an elaboration on the first characteristic, we can add that the control group should be "active." It is well established that participants in a study will sometimes rise to the occasion and perform better than they would normally simply for the appreciation of being under observation.[38] The conditions in the active control group should be such that its members have a reasonable expectation that they are in the experimental group. Even better if the personnel involved with administering the conditions of the experiment also have these expectations—namely, to realize a double-blind situation such that personnel do not inadvertently, even in their gestures or tone of voice, signal that they believe participants are in one group versus the other (the control group versus the experimental group).

The point of such a random assignment between experimental and (active) control groups is, of course, to establish causality (i.e., of mental activity as causal in slowing or stopping the declines of aging), not just correlation. With only correlation data, we are faced with a "chicken or egg" ambiguity. Is mental activity good for mental function (the hypothesis we wish to test) or, conversely, are people more mentally active because they have good mental function in the first place?[39]

Salthouse takes matters a step further through long-term monitoring: "Only if there is evidence that people have differed in their rates of aging does it seem appropriate to characterize them as having 'aged' successfully, as opposed to having been successful at every stage in their lives."[40] In other words, we seek interactions. Main effects are fine; we expect them. We might expect that mental activity is good for everyone regardless of age. But in the context of successful aging, we seek interventions that can slow the declines of age (or alternatively, interventions that have cumulative beneficial effect with advancing age).

The three conditions Salthouse lists are not likely to be achieved in studies involving people. He notes, for example, that "it is impossible (and unethical) to randomly assign people to groups who would maintain the same lifestyle for a substantial proportion of their lives."[41] In assessments of the "use it or lose it" hypothesis (what we refer to here as the "use it to keep it" hypothesis), therefore, researchers must settle for studies "based on approximations to the ideal, with each category of research lacking one or more of the critical characteristics."[42] Salthouse reviews a wide range of research relating measures of cognitive function to age for various groups of people operating at higher levels of cognitive activity (mental exercise). Some studies involved expert players in games such as chess and Go. Other studies looked at occupational groups such as college professors, architects, pilots, and physicians. Yet other studies involved self-reports of various mentally stimulating activities, such as teaching or attending a class, working on crossword puzzles, or playing bridge.

A general result that emerges across these studies is that measures of mental activity correlate with measures of mental ability and in the ways we might predict. Architects performed significantly better than nonarchitects on measure of spatial visualization, for example.

But alas, "very few studies have found an interactive effect of age and mental activity on measures of cognitive functioning."[43] Experts and people with generally high levels of mental activity may maintain superior levels of performance on selected measures of cognitive ability (e.g., reasoning, spatial visualization, processing speed) when compared to people with more average levels of mental activity when matched by age. However, rates of cognitive decline are essentially the same. There is no interaction between levels of mental activity and age such that the more mentally active are any less subject to the cognitive declines of age. All of us who are fortunate enough to age normally (i.e., free from a major loss of function from illness or accident) are subject to roughly the same rates of cognitive decline.

A rejoinder is to "take the main effect and be happy." Join the book club. Do crossword puzzles or sudoku. Learn a new language or a new dance or a new musical instrument. While causality has not been established, there is reason to believe that these and other mentally challenging activities will produce boosts in at least some measures of cognitive ability. If declines still come with advancing age, we may at least be starting from a higher level of functioning. As Salthouse concludes,

> Although my professional opinion is that at the present time the mental-exercise hypothesis is more of an optimistic hope than an empirical reality, my personal recommendation is that people should behave as though it were true. That is, people should continue to engage in mentally stimulating activities because even if there is not yet evidence that it has beneficial effects in slowing the rate of age-related decline in cognitive functioning, there is no evidence that it has any harmful effects, the activities are often enjoyable and thus may contribute to a higher quality of life.[44]

## The "Training to Function" Hypothesis

We turn now to the second approach, "training to function," as inspired by the cognitive-function-as-skill metaphor. In doing so we move to a consideration of the big and growing industry of "brain training" programs and then to the very big issue of skill transfer.

Considering an activity for which performance (e.g., speed and error rate) can be measured, research[45] tells us that with deliberate practice our performance, our skill at this activity, will steadily improve. The very good news is that this is true no matter how old we are. Our brains retain sufficient plasticity to learn new skills right up to the day we die.

But research also tells us that transfer of a performance improvement to other activities—even activities seemingly related to the practiced activity—is very limited. Earlier, we considered the case of chess grandmasters who showed remarkable ability to reproduce board positions for chess games. But this ability was specific to chess game positions that might be realized in a game. As another example of the extreme limits of skill transfer, Ericsson and Polson studied the extraordinary abilities of a highly experienced waiter, JC, to remember dinner orders.[46] However, on other memory tasks not involving dinner orders, JC's memory was no better than that of control subjects.

All the methodological conditions discussed in the previous subsection still apply as we assess the efficacy of brain training programs. But brain training programs face an additional challenge: they must justify the costs in money and time of their use, especially with respect to the opportunity cost of not doing something else instead. We may happily play bridge or participate in a book club discussion or complete a crossword puzzle for the intrinsic pleasure of doing so. Are we equally willing to pay a price, in money and time, to complete the brain training exercises offered by a company such as Lumosity[47] if not for some expectation, if only implicitly suggested, that the skill we hone will have broader application?

The efficacy of brain training programs, especially with respect to transfer, is a hotly debated topic among scientists doing research in the area. Differences surfaced, rather dramatically (by academic research standards) in two open letters published in 2014.

The first open letter, published on October 20, 2014, under the auspices of the Stanford Center on Longevity and the Berlin Max Planck Institute for Human Development, represented a consensus achieved by over seventy of "the world's leading cognitive psychologists and neuroscientists."[48] The letter allows that the brain remains "malleable, even in old age." People are never too old to learn a new skill. And any "mentally effortful new experience, such as learning a language, acquiring a motor skill, navigating in a new environment, and, yes, playing commercially available computer games, will produce changes in those neural systems that support acquisition of the new skill." However, "it is not appropriate to conclude that training-induced changes go significantly beyond the learned skills, that they affect broad abilities with real-world relevance, or that they generally promote 'brain health.'"

On a more positive note, the letter did allow that some "isolated" reports inspire additional research. For example, the letter acknowledges some studies indicating that certain forms of training in reasoning and speed of processing are associated with improved driving in older adults and reduction in accident rates.

The letter goes on to say, however, that findings do not provide a sound basis for the claims made by commercial companies selling brain games.[49] The letter also notes a bias in that studies reporting positive results are more likely to be published than studies reporting no effect. Moreover, the letter reminds us of the opportunity costs associated with brain training programs: "Time spent playing the games is time not spent reading, socializing, gardening, exercising, or engaging in many other activities that may benefit cognitive and physical health of older adults."

Some months later another group of scientists (133 in total) published a rejoinder letter arguing that "a substantial and growing body of evidence shows that certain cognitive training regimens can significantly improve cognitive function, including in ways that generalize to everyday life."[50] This second letter emphasizes the considerable common ground that exists between the authors of the two letters and, more generally, in the research community. I paraphrase:

- Claims should not be made that a product has scientific support when there is little or no scientific evidence.
- Training programs should be evaluated in peer-reviewed, randomized, controlled trials.
- Evidence is stronger if evaluations are run at multiple sites and run and funded independently of the company or organization standing to benefit from a positive evaluation.
- Many companies claiming products that promote brain fitness have not subjected these products (or the training exercises of these products) to peer-reviewed study to demonstrate efficacy.
- And, in fact, claims promoting brain games are "frequently exaggerated, and are often misleading."

The second letter continues by noting agreement concerning evaluative criteria: Does the improvement encompass a broad array of tasks that constitute a particular ability, or does it just reflect the acquisition of specific skills? Do the gains persist for a reasonable amount of time? Are the positive changes noticed in real-life indices of cognitive health? What role do motivations and expectations play in bringing about improvements in cognition?

This last point concerning motivations and expectations brings up again the importance of having active controls (wherein participants have every reason to believe they are in an experimental group) and a double-blind situation (in which personnel administering the conditions also don't know experimental from control).

The second letter even agrees with the five concluding points of the previous letter, repeating these in more succinct form:

1. "More research needs to be done."
2. "Physical exercise is good for physical health and brain health."
3. "A single study generally is not conclusive and needs to be integrated into a larger body of evidence."
4. "No study, to date, has demonstrated that brain training cures or prevents Alzheimer's disease."
5. "Cognitively challenging activities have not been shown to work like one-shot treatments or vaccines."

Where, then, is the disagreement? The first letter concludes that "the promise of a magic bullet detracts from the best evidence to date, which is that cognitive health in old age reflects the long-term effects of healthy, engaged lifestyles." The second letter concludes with a call for more research, arguing that "dozens of randomized, controlled trials published in peer-reviewed journals . . . document specific benefits of defined types of cognitive training." The second letter also provides a reminder of another scientific consensus, long held and only recently overturned, that brain plasticity ends with childhood (i.e., the proverbial notion that "old dogs can't learn new tricks"). This previous consensus, now proven wrong and abandoned, surely held back progress in public health. Touché.

Simons and colleagues, noting the divergent conclusions in the letters, set about understanding how two teams of highly qualified scientists could study the same published research and arrive at such conflicting viewpoints concerning the effectiveness of brain training regimens.[51] They provide a meticulous review and analysis not only of current brain training literature (as of 2016) but also of the brain training industry, theories of training transfer (extending back to the seminal work, over a hundred years ago, by the famous psychologists William James and Edward Thorndike), and methodological considerations relating to "best practices in intervention design and reporting."

The article reaffirms the "gold standard" of a double-blind, placebo-controlled, randomized clinical trial before arguing further that all experiments should be registered prior to the start of data collection with this preregistration to specify target sample size, the characteristics of the tested population, the nature of each intervention group, the technique for randomly assigning participants to conditions, the rules for excluding data, a list and description of all outcome measures, a full description of the a priori hypotheses, and a complete analysis plan for testing those hypotheses. The preregistration should even include testing materials and experimental scripts used to conduct the study. Essentially all the information in the "Method" section of the final report—and more—should be specified in the preregistration. And then the final report should include *all* the study's results, not just the "positive" results. The article also notes that the levels for statistical significance should be adjusted in accordance with the number of tests that are planned—this to maintain a fixed, and acceptably, low rate for false positives. (The more tests of significance we make, the more likely at least one will be falsely significant.)

After a careful review of brain training studies, including those listed on the Cognitive Training Data website,[52] the article concludes that "in sum, despite a large number of published papers reporting tests of the effects of brain-training interventions, the evidence that training with commercial brain training software can enhance cognition outside the laboratory is limited and inconsistent" and that "practicing a cognitive task consistently improves performance on that task and closely related tasks, but the available evidence that such training generalizes to other tasks or to real-world performance is not compelling."[53]

Studies, metastudies, and analyses done more recently mostly affirm Simons and colleagues' conclusions. For example, in an experimental study of working memory training in 142 healthy, older adults (sixty-five to eighty years) with participants randomly assigned between training condition and active control, Guye and Von Bastian conclude that there is an absence of transfer to untrained working memory tasks, "near" or "far" (related or unrelated) to the task trained for and that, in general, working memory training is not an effective way to improve general cognitive functioning.[54] Similar conclusions were reached by Melby-Lervåg and colleagues and, more recently, by Sala and Gobet, who also observed that between-study variability is explained by "design quality and statistical artefacts."[55]

But then, also in 2019, a more upbeat article on the future of brain training research was coauthored by forty-eight academic researchers, noting that "in many ways then, the question 'Does brain training work?' is akin to the question 'Do drugs work?'."[56] It would be better to ask, "Which programs, which approaches, are most promising?" More recently still is a result from the Neuroscape laboratory indicating that virtual reality training in older adults (average age 68.7) transfers to a general enhancement in the fidelity of long-term memory, offsetting age-related declines, so that study participants reached levels of performance reached by younger participants in another experiment.[57]

Researchers, it would seem, have only just begun to explore the enormous space of possibilities for programs of brain training. For any program we learn about, the review of previous methodological considerations gives us a set of questions to ask. Improvements in the immediate skill (e.g., the task or the game being played) is not the issue. We expect people of all ages will get better at the targeted skill with practice and training. But to what other skills does this improvement transfer? Do these skills have practical, real-world application? As demonstrated through methodologically rigorous, empirical study?

Additional questions then occur: What is the magnitude of the improvement in the transferred skill? An improvement may be statistically reliable, but is it practically significant—in other words, is the improvement big enough for us to care with respect to our everyday lives? Does more training produce even more performance gains in transferred skills, or do gains level off at some point (i.e., a diminishing return on our investments in time and money)? For how long do improvements in a transferred skill last? A year? A month? A week? If gains are short-lived but practically significant, we may happily subscribe to a program of periodic, and possibly lifelong, training, but we should know what to expect.

And then, finally, as for "brain exercise" activities we might do on our own (e.g., playing bridge, doing crossword puzzles), we can also ask for brain training programs: Does training result in what here have been termed "interactions of life" (i.e., Does training slow the rates of cognitive decline for a given skill over time?)? Or does training merely provide a boost in current ability? Many of us might happily settle for the latter (i.e., for a boost in current ability). But we do so with the understanding that rates of age-related decline in this ability will still be comparable to those for people of our age who never did the training. We are only starting at a higher level, and our performance may very well fall to the levels for other "nontrained" people should we stop our training.

## Summary and Some Suggestions

In this section we've considered two approaches to keep our brains "fit" as we age, each motivated by a metaphor as applied from other situations.

Use it to keep it (longer) follows a brain-as-muscle metaphor. Can the heightened mental activity—where this may follow from an active lifestyle, possibly as enhanced by new mentally challenging activities (e.g., bridge, dancing, playing a musical instrument)—work to preserve cognitive function in older age?

After a wide-ranging review of relevant research, Salthouse concludes that "there is currently little scientific evidence that differential engagement in mentally stimulating activities alters the rate of mental aging."[58] He suggests that staying active is good for us, even so, for its own intrinsic reward and perhaps for placing our mental function at a higher level even as our cognitive functions decline at the same rates as those for our less-active counterparts.

Training to function follows from a cognitive-function-as-skill metaphor and with this metaphor a shift from simple brain exercise to more focused, goal-directed training and practice. Just as we train and practice to get better at golf or playing the piano, can we train to improve more basic cognitive abilities such as working memory, executive control, or episodic recall? We're never too old to learn a new skill. Our brains retain the plasticity needed for such learning right up until the day we die. Alas, the evidence is still limited and inconsistent that improvements in a trained-for skill transfer to other skills or to the activities of everyday living.

What to do in our lives? To paraphrase Salthouse, we should engage in mentally stimulating activities even so. Do so for the intrinsic reward of these activities and to "stay in the game," so to speak. Some of us might even choose a subscription to a brain training program but primarily because the training is fun. For example, gamification of training can make the training itself fun and even social (as when we share our results with other people in the spirit of friendly competition).

We might train to improve skills that are intrinsically useful and enjoyable. Then any transfer that will (or likely won't) happen is icing on the cake. Here are some possibilities:

- Learn a new language. There is no evidence that learning a foreign language in older age improves memory or intelligence.[59] But do it anyway! Learning a new language is intellectually stimulating and can open new opportunities for friendship and travel.
- Learn a new dance. Do it for fun and then feel good about the ancillary benefits.
- Try an improvement such as making an effort to remember people's names better as you're introduced to them. I made this effort recently after getting tired of hearing myself repeat the same lame excuse for not remembering someone's name over the years ("I'm just not good with names."). I tried instilling the following two-step habit: (1) Always repeat the person's name out loud and possibly even verify that I have the pronunciation right. Doing so, at the very least, keeps the name in short-term memory a little longer. (2) Make a comment, even a good-natured joke, about the name. Make connections. Doing so promotes the long-term preservation of the name. I often don't remember to do these steps, but when I do I'm much better at remembering a person's name. This is good for my self-confidence and a plus for socialization.

- Keep a journal as a way of noticing and remembering the events of the day. The journal is a record and may encourage us to be more attentive in our daily lives.[60]

As a riff on the term *multitasking*, I have suggested a *multigoaling* approach to activity selection.[61] Do just one activity (mostly) rather than attempt a rapid switching between several, but look for activities that can serve several purposes at once. Table 2.1 provides a simple multigoaling analysis of potential benefits for different activities I might choose to do. Line dancing wins! And research supports this verdict.[62] I find it to be mentally challenging (i.e., the sequence of moves can be quite intricate and difficult to memorize), a good cardiovascular workout, and, of course, also a very social activity.

Table 2.1.   A Multigoaling Analysis of Activities and Their Benefits

|  | Mental | Cardiovascular | Social |
| --- | --- | --- | --- |
| Sudoku | X |  |  |
| Walking with a friend |  | X | X |
| Line dancing | X | X | X |

## A CASE FOR COGNITIVE SPECTACLES

One approach considered in the section "Keeping Our Brains in Shape" is inspired by a brain-as-muscle metaphor. In this section, we consider a second sense in which our experiences with the physical can inspire our efforts with the cognitive. The physical declines that come with increasing age are readily apparent. We look older, of course, but changes are more than skin deep. Beginning in our early forties, many of us will experience problems seeing clearly at close distances. About one in five of us over the age of sixty-five will develop cataracts. Our knees and hips will fail. And so on.

Not so long ago, these physical infirmities would have drastically curtailed the activities of an otherwise healthy person. A person with presbyopia, the inability to focus on things nearby—a condition most people develop as they age into their forties and beyond—could no longer read the text of a standard document. A person with severe cataracts could hardly see at all. A person whose knee or hip failed might never again lead an active life.

### We Are Already Cyborgs

Fortunately, we now have tools and technologies to help. Cataracts can be surgically removed. Reading glasses help us to see text. Knees and hips can be replaced. We may think of cyborgs[63] as the stuff of a science-fiction future, but that future is already here for many of us in the form of artificial body parts and extensions. This present future has been a long time coming. The first eyeglasses were thought to have been made in Pisa, Italy, about 1290.[64] The first metallic hip replacement was made in 1940.[65] The first knee replacement occurred in 1968.[66]

Tools and technologies in support of our physical bodies have had a profound impact not only on those who benefit directly but also on the collective impressions of the physical disabilities so corrected. Without the person telling us, we might hardly know that a person's knee or hip is artificial or that she now sees normally because of cataract surgery. Wearing glasses, by young and old, is now commonplace. And those who wish further to disguise this "disability" might wear contact lenses or even opt for corrective surgery. When some 75 percent or more of us have corrected vision,[67] we hardly think that corrected vision is even a consideration, let alone a disqualification, in decisions of employment.

Comparable to the physical declines in various forms that come with aging are declines in mental ability. Short-term memory capacity (the number of things we can keep in mind—the digits of a phone number, for example, or items to buy at a grocery store) declines gradually with normal aging. More generally, working memory capacity—characterized as the ability to keep a problem representation active as we endeavor to solve it[68]—is in gradual decline beginning in our twenties. Raw processing speed decreases.[69] We are less able to recall episodic detail: "Where are my car keys?" And then later, "Where did I park the car?"

Where are the cognitive eyeglasses? Can we reach a point where age-related declines in working memory, processing speed, episodic memory, and the like are no more a hindrance, nor a consideration in matters of selection (e.g., for employment), than age-related declines in the ability to focus on nearby objects without reading glasses?

We may think of a cyborg future in which we wear reality augmenting headsets or even cranial implants that dramatically extend our abilities to think and process information. But the future is here already—not only in physical prosthetics but also in our information devices.

We have our laptops, our tablets, and our smartphones. We have wireless earbuds—for noise cancellation, sound amplification, and hands-free communication, not only with other people but even more so with virtual assistants such as Siri.[70] We have the web for ready lookup of information; we "mine" our own inboxes and our collections of digital photos in support of our memories for personal, episodic information. What is the name of their newborn daughter? Look for the announcement sent in email. If we can't recall what the person we talked to at yesterday's party said about his line of work, we can look up the information on Facebook or LinkedIn. If we need to remember information on a business card, we can take a picture and send it to ourselves.

Alas, many studies do suggest that current information tools, overall, provide further advantage to the young versus the older.[71] But the factor of age is mixed with other factors, most notably that older people generally have less experience with current information tools and possibly have less of a supportive, reinforcing community of friends and colleagues who also use these tools. Moreover, as argued later, research on interactions between age and variations in information tool design is, well, immature.

For a glimpse of what might be coming in the way of information tools working as cognitive spectacles, we look first not to the future but to the past, way back to the early 1980s, when most people still used a terminal for computer access, not personal computers (and certainly not laptops, tablets, or smartphones!). Even full-screen editors were a recent novelty.

## Full-Screen Text Editors as a Memory Aid

Many of us may not remember, nor ever have experienced, a time when full-screen, WYSIWYG ("what you see is what you get") editing was not an everyday reality.[72] But in the early 1980s, full-screen editing was brand-new. The standard of the day was the line-based text editor. (See figure 2.4.)

Studies of line-based text editors had indicated a negative correlation between increasing age and performance, even after influences for other relevant factors (e.g., education level, computing experience) were removed.[73] But in a comparison of results from two different studies, one of performance on a line-based editor (ED) and the other of performance on a full-screen editor (a prototype called TED), Gomez and colleagues reported a dramatic reduction in the effects of age for the standard performance measures of learning time, error rate, and execution time.[74] (Participants were all female, ranging in age from twenty-eight to sixty-two years, mean forty-three.) The text editor (line-based versus full-screen) × age interaction was significant for both execution time and error rate.

We note first that the effect of age is mostly eliminated. For execution time in the full-screen editor condition, there is still a slight upward trend as a function of increasing age that is not significant. For first-try errors there is actually a slight, but not significant, benefit for increasing age in the full-screen editor condition. Moreover, performance using the full-screen editor is overall better, by a factor of nearly two to one, compared to using the line-based editor. In other words, the benefits for older people were not purchased

```
a
ed is the standard Unix text editor.
This is line number two.
.
2i
.
,l
ed is the standard Unix text editor.$
$
This is line number two.$
3s/two/three/
,l
ed is the standard Unix text editor.$
$
This is line number three.$
w text
65
q
```

Figure 2.4. A line-based editing sequence in which "This is line number two." is changed to "This is line number three."
Screenshot from *https://en.wikipedia.org/wiki/Ed_(text_editor).

at the cost of decrements in performance for younger people. The screen-based editor was better for everyone—only especially better for older people.

How might this be? By one explanation, the full-screen editor functioned like a pair of cognitive eyeglasses with respect to the "acuity" of working memory. Certainly, the contrasting line-based editor was demanding of working memory. Those who used it needed, for example, to formulate complex commands (e.g., "3s/two/three") in their heads even as they also endeavored to maintain the state of the document in their heads. (Users could request a listing of lines or regions of a document, but doing so took time.) With the screen-based editor, commands could be expressed more directly (albeit still awkwardly using function arrow keys rather than a mouse). The document and its current state could also be more completely viewed in the screen-based editor.[75]

Study results point to the possibility that in the right information environment and at least on certain tasks, having more youthful cognitive facilities (such as greater working memory capacity) might be no more relevant to performance than having good uncorrected vision is to performance on tasks in today's typical office setting.

Alas, as best I can determine, the study has never been replicated. Certainly, the reason to compare line-based with full-screen editors has passed with the passing of the former and the universality of the latter. Still very relevant, however, are assessments of current variations and innovations in information tool design and, especially, for the potential differential impact these may have on older versus younger people.

Consider all the gains in document processing and in human-computer interaction that have been made since the early days of trial screen-based editing in the early 1980s. We can now use mice, touchpads, and direct screen touch to manipulate the information of a document. We can use a side navigation pane to stay oriented (the less to keep in our minds). We even have features that help us to reestablish a working context when we reopen a document later (e.g., a "Welcome back!" prompt that offers to take us back to the place in a document where we were last). Might at least some of these advances be shown to further reduce the performance decrements of age? Or do some of these innovations work in the other direction—that is to say, as differentially benefiting younger people? Either way, it is important to know.

## From Document Processing to Finding Information on the Web

We take a big twenty-five-year jump in time, from 1983 to 2008, to consider our next case study involving a design alternative and age. The performance of older adults in information retrieval tasks is frequently poorer than for younger adults. Pak and Price note that most of the retrieval tasks under study involved some variant of a hierarchical or taxonomic navigation (e.g., web page navigation via hyperlinks or help menu navigation) and that these tasks placed a considerable burden on a participant's ability to stay spatially oriented.[76] We can suspect that a participant's working memory was also burdened. Both spatial ability and working memory capacity are associated with fluid intelligence. Pak and Price reason from the fluid/crystallized distinction to consider an alternate tag-based information retrieval interface that might better engage a participant's vocabulary for search terms. Vocabulary, an aspect of crystallized intelligence, continues to expand with age.

The difference between the two information retrieval interfaces is represented in figure 2.5. Fifty younger adults (twenty-three men, eighteen to twenty-three years in age) and fifty older adults (twenty-three men, fifty-five

| Condition | Example | Description |
|-----------|---------|-------------|
| Taxonomy | Health & Safety <br> ↳ Before you leave <br> ↳ Vaccinations <br> ↳ Influenza Vaccine | The desired page, Influenza Vaccine, is located in a single location: within the vaccinations subcategory. The page is not accessible from any of the higher-level categories (just as a document placed in a subfolder is not directly accessible from a higher-level folder). |
| Tag based | Vaccinations <br> Before you leave → Influenza Vaccine <br> Health & Safety | The desired page, Influenza Vaccine, was labeled with three different tags ("Vaccinations," "Before you Leave," and "Health & Safety"), so clicking on any of these labels will display the Influenza Vaccine page. |

**Figure 2.5. Illustration of taxonomy vs. tag-based conditions for information retrieval. (Table 2 in Pak & Price, 2008)**

to seventy-eight years in age) were randomly assigned to either the taxonomy or tag-based condition. Orientation and instruction in the two conditions were comparable. Guided completion of one task (e.g., "How much luggage can you take on a cruise ship?") was followed by practice solo completion of a second task. All participants then completed thirty experimental tasks and were measured, per task, for completion time, number of mouse clicks, and number of errors.

The essential findings of the study are as follows: (1) Young people performed significantly better than older people overall, resulting in a significant main effect of age on a composite performance measure (averaging completion times, number of errors, and number of mouse clicks). (2) However, this effect of age was expressed in the taxonomy condition but not in the tag-based condition. Age-group performance differences in the tag-based condition were not significant. For two performance measures (mouse clicks per task and error rate), older participants performed slightly better than younger participants (although these differences were not significant). (3) The interaction of condition (taxonomy versus tag-based search) with age group was significant.

As with word processing, so too with information retrieval: a variation—an innovation—in the user interface served to dramatically reduce, even eliminate, the effects of age. We have our "interaction of life"!

We can note that cognitive processes depicted by Pak and Price for the tag-based condition can be regarded as a variation of those we do every day through a search service such as Google—in other words, form a goal or intention, convert to a search term, and then, in their experiment, select the appropriate tag. By contrast, of course, we type directly into a search box (or speak) to get results from a service like Google. But, increasingly, we also see and accept suggested completions to the term we begin to specify so that we are essentially selecting a tag suggested by the search service. (A service such as Google has a vast amount of data to work with—from our own past queries and those of billions of other users—to suggest search term completions.) Even as we may continue to navigate through taxonomies in the form of menus in our applications and the hyperlinked pages of a website, initial access to web information is via search: type in (at least the beginning of) a search term, (possibly) accept a suggested completion, click to access a web page represented in the results listing, repeat. Some of us can possibly remember, from long ago, using the Yahoo menus as a fundamentally taxonomic way to access web information. Those days are long gone.[77]

Finally, it should be noted that a preference for search as a means of finding public information on the web (and its potential role in reducing the effects of aging) stands in stark contrast to a persistent preference for navigation as the preferred, primary means of access to the files we keep locally on our computer.[78] Here, too, Bergman observes an effect for age such that study participants over fifty years old were four times more likely to use search (instead of navigation) as a means of return to personal files than participants in their twenties.[79] Bergman's analysis indicates that navigation is a faster, more efficient method of return to personal files and that older participants are more likely than younger participants to use search on occasion because they are more likely to have forgotten where the file was initially placed. But it is also possible that older study participants selected search even if they knew how to reach the target file by means of navigation (e.g., older participants may have determined that for them search was the faster method of return).

Returning to retrieval of public information from the web, the past two decades have seen considerable innovation in the support for search via services such as Google, Bing, and DuckDuckGo—including, for example, suggesting search term completions, suggesting related searches (typically at the bottom of the results page), and even bringing information forward into the results page for immediate consumption so that further clicking is frequently obviated. Will this lead to even less reliance on navigation as means of access to public information on the web? Even within websites? Will this, in turn, lead to further reductions in the performance gap between younger and older users? The answer is one of the most popular lines to include in a research paper: "further research is needed."

I can offer a personal anecdote in favor of a further shift toward the use of search that I think is coming—for everyone but especially older people, and then, most especially, for the access of information whose organization we don't directly control. I recently opted for a Google search to find out how to access a command in Microsoft Word that I was unable to find through the ribbon menu interface or through the help system in Word. Search—even a global search outside the context of the application for which I needed the help—bested local navigation.

Again, I emphasize that my comments concerning increasing use of (and support for) search versus navigation apply to efforts to *find* public information (e.g., on the web or relating to the applications we use) and not efforts to *refind* private files on a personal computer. The enduring preference for navigation as a primary means of access in the latter case may have a neurological basis insofar as navigation to personal files appears to engage some of the same spatial abilities we use to navigate in the physical world.[80] It is also the case that we can place files in and directly control the structure of folders in our personal filing system. In line with primacy effects widely observed in studies of human cognition,[81] our remembrance of a desired personal file later may be closely tied to our remembrance for where we placed the file initially.[82]

In cases of information retrieval of public information, the performance gap in favor of youth may disappear or even be reversed. While I researched for this chapter using Google Search and, especially, Google Scholar, I suspected that I might not be as fast now—at sixty-eight years of age—as a younger person might be. But possibly I make up for this gap with greater background knowledge concerning what to look for and what search terms to use.

## Summary and Some Suggestions

We've considered two past innovations: (1) full-screen document processing, and (2) direct-access (search- or tag-based) retrieval of information from the web. In both cases, interactions were observed between the variable of age and the innovation: full-screen versus line-based editing in one case, tag-based (search-based) versus taxonomic navigation in the other. In both cases, the innovation removed or greatly reduced the disadvantages of advancing age. In information tool innovations, we may have what we were unable to find in the last section's review of mentally challenging activities and brain training programs—an "interaction of life."

But caution is strongly advised. Neither of these two studies reporting interactions between the factor of age and information tool innovations have been replicated. Moreover, we can question whether either would meet the high methodological standards set by Salthouse, Simons and colleagues, and others as discussed in the last section.

A larger point is to argue for increasing the number of studies that create an opportunity for such interactions, if they exist, to show themselves. A great deal of research has been carried out on the challenges older people face as they use computer-based information tools (e.g., smartphones and smartphone applications, web browsers and web applications).[83] Studies generally conclude with implications for design improvements, the better to meet the needs of older people.

These studies, as they identify problems in the way older people use information tools and potential remedies, may be only a short step away from studies to validate these remedies. Consider, for example, a study by Dommes and colleagues that compares the performance of older and younger participants in the use of a search engine (Google) and concludes that observed performance deficits for older participants were due to a decline in "cognitive flexibility."[84] We might relate this to notions that people come to rely more on their expectations (top-down processing) as they age and that this can sometimes result in a rigidity in interpreting the results of a search and appreciating their potential relevance.

Dommes and colleagues suggest that "search engines should provide search-refining suggestions from the homepage in a more systematic, perceptible and comprehensible way."[85] The authors do note that Google Search already provides search suggestions at the bottom of the results page but that very few participants, of any age, used these suggestions or—we might suspect—were even aware of their existence or potential utility to their search tasks.

One "low-hanging fruit" manipulation might then be simply to give the participants in an experimental condition some minimal training on the existence and possible uses of these search suggestions. Do we then observe an interaction such that discrepancies of age are significantly reduced when people are able to use system-provided search suggestions more effectively?

## Older Age as the Canary in the Coal Mine

As noted earlier, considerable research has been done on the challenges older people face as they use computer-based information tools. Studies generally conclude with implications for design improvements, the better to meet the needs of older people. Some studies go a step further with prototypes providing demonstrated improvements.[86]

Studies that include age as a factor—if not directly in study design to define participant groups, then at least in subsequent analyses of variance—have the potential to do more. Such studies may uncover "interactions of life" in information tool innovations such as the two noted previously in this section—in other words, where the innovation is not only of general benefit but also removes some of the performance disadvantages that older people face.

Moreover, research targeting older people can potentially identify information tool improvements with general benefit across age groups. For example, Chadwick-Dias and colleagues, in a pair of studies, compared the experiences and performance of participants ranging in age from twenty-two to eighty-two as they completed tasks relating to the use of a company retirement website.[87] The problems older participants (fifty-five and older) experienced in Study 1 led to a new version of the website, which was tested in Study 2 with a new group of participants (also ranging in age).

No interactions between website (original versus new/improved) and age were observed. Significant performance differences, in favor of younger participants, persisted in Study 2. However, the new site resulted in significant performance improvements for *both* younger and older participants. In other words, the experiences of the older participants in Study 1 helped to identify improvements of benefit to everyone. A possible explanation is that younger participants with higher levels of fluid intelligence were better able to adjust to and bypass flaws in the original website even if these flaws still had an impact on their performance. Problems in the website were more readily apparent to and identified by older people operating without such a surplus of fluid intelligence.

## Age as a Continuous Factor in Explorations of Information Tool Design

During my informal review of research relating to age and older people in the Association for Computing Machinery digital library, a considerable proportion of the research I found dealt with the needs of the "older old" (i.e., people in their late seventies and into their eighties and beyond). Some study participants lived independently, but many were in assisted living. Salthouse argues for the inclusion of an intermediate group, which we might call the "younger old."[88]

I've argued for a focus on the needs of people in a pivotal age group, which currently coincides roughly with the baby boomers in the United States.[89] People in this pivotal age group face many major life decisions and changes: they are approaching retirement or are recently retired; they are often still a primary caretaker for both their grown-up children (who sometimes may be living at home) and their elderly parents, but they may have become empty-nesters and be considering downsizing. The needs of this group, especially with respect to information tools, is underresearched. As boomers continue to age, they will shift into the "older old" group, but they will be replaced by a new pivotal age group.

Taking things a step further, why not routinely include age as a continuous, independent variable to be used for the variance it explains in the performance data of studies of information tool design? And then also sample more continuously from a range of adult ages in the selection of participants? Of course, similar arguments can and should be made for other demographic factors, such as gender and ethnic background.

My sense is that researchers have only just scratched the surface in the exploration of potential interactions between information tool design and age. For some of these interactions, as for those discussed earlier for full-screen editing and tag-based information retrieval, we may have the happy circumstance that a design variation is better for everyone but especially better for older adults. Perhaps more often we will see the opposite—in other words, even if an innovation is good for everyone (it makes our lives easier or more productive), it will be differentially better for the young. This is good too. Whichever group they benefit most, we should at least know of these interactions and their magnitude.

Consider, for example, continuing improvements in voice-to-text technology. On my smartphone, voice-to-text sometimes works very well and sometimes is laughably bad. It will get better. I'm pretty sure I can talk as fast as a twenty-year-old. But when keying to text, I'm all thumbs in the bad way. I doubt I'll ever be as fast as a twenty-year-old. Suppose there were a study of texting speeds that contrasted high-quality voice-to-text transcription (perhaps even simulated for purposes of the study) with thumbs as a means of input? I am confident the study would produce an interaction between the factor of age and mode of input such that people of my boomer age are likely to be worse than people in their twenties at thumb input but nearly the same with voice-to-text input.

## Building a Better Personal Space of Information

We've considered information "out there" to complement and sometimes substitute for knowledge "in the head." We've considered information tools and tool variations such as full-screen editing, voice to text, and indexing in support of fast search. These tools might, on occasion, level the playing field with respect to age—that is to say, by reducing the demands an information tool places on cognitive facilities known to decline gradually with age, such as working memory, or by taking better advantage of facilities known to improve throughout our adulthood, such as vocabulary.

A point of distributed cognition[90] is that our ability to do smart things, indeed, to function at all, is very much a function of our extended selves—extended to include the information we have access to or are affected by "out there" as well as the tools we use to work with this information. Information and information tools combine to form a personal space of information (PSI).[91] We each have a PSI unique to us. Part of our PSIs are our connections to information (e.g., the internet, the local library) and our various sources of information, including, perhaps most importantly, the people whose company we keep, such as family, friends, work colleagues, and even casual acquaintances.

Our PSIs play a critical role in our ability to manage information to get things done in our daily lives.[92] The loss of our smartphone, an interruption in internet connectivity, or even, simply, a misplaced document—these disruptions in the landscape of our PSI can profoundly affect our ability to get things done and to function.

There is increasing awareness of the importance of building our PSIs not only for the present but also for the long run to support us as we age and for our loved ones with our passing.[93] Elsewhere, I write of steps we can take to improve our PSI.[94] We begin by taking an inventory. How many devices? How many email accounts? How many social media accounts? How many web stores? Do we need them all? Can we simplify? What constellation of information, information tools, and information sources will best age gracefully with us? And then what do we want to bequeath (with account information and requisite passwords) to our next of kin with our passing? Cleaning our PSI both for our future selves and for our posterity can be likened to the cleaning and possible downsizing of our physical spaces in anticipation of later life.

## CONCLUSIONS

This chapter has focused on cognitive concerns and considerations of successful aging. Cognitive facilities associated with fluid intelligence (e.g., relating to working memory, spatial ability, and speed of processing) begin to decline in early adulthood (as we reach our twenties) even as measures of crystallized intelligence (e.g., for general world knowledge, experience, and vocabulary) continue to improve.

In some cases, improvements in crystallized intelligence may compensate for declines in fluid intelligence. Top-down processing as informed by our internal knowledge (including expectations) can make up for age-related slowdowns in our ability to process incoming information. This compensatory shift to crystallized intelligence is likely less successful in less familiar situations where our expectations are less valid. But in group situations, from work teams to whole societies, age diversity offers a potential to realize the best of both—the raw energy and fluid intelligence of younger people combined with the experience and wisdom of older people.

The search is ongoing for ways to slow the decline in measures of fluid intelligence. The good news is that we are never too old to learn a new skill or to improve an existing one. This holds true whether the skill in question is an ability to play a musical instrument, speak a foreign language, perform a brain training exercise, or play a video game. The not-so-good news is that evidence for transfer of skill improvements to other skills and, most especially, to everyday activities is, at best, mixed. Leaving aside questions of skill transfer, there is no evidence to indicate that our efforts—whether in the form of mentally demanding activities or training—will slow the rates of cognitive decline that accompany normal aging.

But research continues! Brain training programs can differ substantially from one another on a great many dimensions (e.g., activities performed, abilities targeted, nature of feedback, reward system, sensory engagement). Research is only beginning to explore the space of possibilities. Which programs, which approaches, are the most promising? If we eventually return to an assessment that the best training programs are not appreciably better than the mediocre programs or better than what we might otherwise do with our time, then so be it.

Even brain training programs providing proven benefit will need to be assessed for opportunity cost. What other potentially cognitively healthy activities might the time (and money) have been spent on instead? Assess an activity not only for the underlying generality of the skills it develops but for other benefits that may also accrue and then especially for benefits that contribute to successful aging. Does the activity involve physical exercise? Does it foster social connection? Does the immediate skill targeted have practical value independent of skill transfer? Getting better at remembering people's names, for example, or becoming more attentive to and remembering the day's events (possibly as aided by a journal) are practical skills of value in their own right. Most important, is the activity sustainable over time? Do we enjoy the activity? If research on the successful aging benefits of brain training programs and other forms of cognitively engaging activity is still in its infancy, research into the potential for information tools to ameliorate the cognitive declines of aging is a newborn.

Many studies indicate that older people sometimes use information tools in ways that are qualitatively different from the ways younger people use them. Older people may also, but not always, need more time to complete tasks using these tools, and they may make more errors. However, we need to keep in mind that some of these differences may better be attributed to cohort than age (i.e., older people have spent much more of their lives without access to the information tool in question). Most of these studies conclude with implications concerning design improvements that might better accommodate people as they age.[95] Some studies go a step further with prototypes providing demonstrated improvements.[96]

But a systematic search for tools and tool variations that might level the playing field with respect to age has barely begun. There is a need and a tremendous opportunity to include, more consistently, more systematically, the effects of aging in studies of information tool design—namely, across studies of tool design in general and not just studies whose primary purpose is to target the needs of older people.

Of special interest in the context of successful aging are variations in information tool design that are better in general for everyone regardless of age but that are especially good for older people. Such an interaction might occur, for example, through innovations that reduce the demands on cognitive facilities such as working memory, shown to be in decline for *all* of us in adulthood. Conversely, this might happen through user interfaces that better exploit facilities such as vocabulary—an aspect of crystallized intelligence that is known to improve for *all* of us as we age. Either way, such innovations hold the promise of providing general improvement, only especially so for older people. The result is what this chapter has termed an "interaction of life."

For researchers, a more systematic, consistent study of aging effects would mean, at a minimum, ensuring that a broad range of ages (e.g., from eighteen to seventy and beyond) are sampled in the selection of study participants and that age, as a continuous independent variable, is included in analyses of the data collected. A step further would be to include age as a between-subjects manipulation in study design, not just "young" versus "old" but rather as three or more groupings with respect to age (e.g., young—twenty to thirty; older young—thirty-one to fifty; younger old—fifty-one to seventy; and older old—seventy-one and up).

Successful aging is a matter of concern for all adults, regardless of our age. Successful aging is also a matter of concern for us collectively as our societies continue to age. In an ideal of successful aging, we are actively engaged with life, have little or no disease or disability, and maintain physical and cognitive function until very near the end of our lives. We are all aging, and, if we are fortunate, we will live to be old. There's no time like the present to start aging successfully.

# NOTES

1. This chapter is dedicated to K. Anders Ericsson (https://www.nytimes .com/2020/07/01/science/anders-ericsson-dead.html). Anders's passing is a great loss not only to his family but to the world at large and most especially to those, in and outside of academia, who over the years have been inspired by an enduring message of Anders's work—that talent and skill are not something mystical, God-given, but rather something potentially accessible to us all through "deliberate practice."

2. I thank the following people for their helpful comments on earlier versions of this book chapter: Kate Williams, James Cortada, Clara Caldeira, William Aspray, Steven Poltrock, Jeff Canin, Allen Sussman, Vijay Mital, Björn Hovstadius, Scott Stolnack, Tom DeGroot, and, most especially, my wife, Maria Staaf, whose careful, detailed feedback has led to significant improvements in so many of the articles, book chapters, and books that I've written over the years. These reviewers deserve the credit for the many corrections and improvements I've made because of their efforts and none of the blame for the flaws that remain.

3. J. W. Rowe and R. L. Kahn, "Successful Aging," *The Gerontologist* 37, no. 4 (1997): 433–440; and J. W. Rowe and R. L. Kahn, "Successful Aging 2.0: Conceptual Expansions for the 21st Century," *The Journals of Gerontology: Series B* 70, no. 4 (2015): 593–596.

4. A. Bowling and P. Dieppe, "What Is Successful Ageing and Who Should Define It?" *British Medical Journal* 331, no. 7531 (2005): 1548–1551.

5. Rowe and Kahn, "Successful Aging," 433.

6. D. A. Heller, U. de Faire, N. L. Pedersen, G. Dahlen, and G. E. McClearn, "Genetic and Environmental Influences on Serum Lipid Levels in Twins," *New England Journal of Medicine* 328, no. 16 (1993): 1150–1156.

7. Rowe and Kahn, "Successful Aging 2.0," 594.

8. Adam Shirley, "These Are the World's Oldest and Youngest Countries," World Economic Forum, May 2, 2016, https://www.weforum.org/agenda/2016/05/worlds -oldest-and-youngest-countries/#:~:text=Around%2020%25%20of%20people%20 in,by%20the%20Pew%20Research%20Centre.

9. S. J. Olshansky, D. Perry, R. A. Miller, and R. N. Butler, "Pursuing the Longevity Dividend," *Annals of the New York Academy of Sciences* 1114 (October 2007): 11–13.

10. M. Roig, S. Nordbrandt, S. S. Geertsen, and J. B. Nielsen, "The Effects of Cardiovascular Exercise on Human Memory: A Review with Meta-analysis," *Neuroscience and Biobehavioral Reviews* 37, no. 8 (2013): 1645–1666; F.-T. Chen, J. L. Etnier, K.-H Chan, P.-K. Chiu, T.-M. Hung, and Y.-K. Chang, "Effects of Exercise Training Interventions on Executive Function in Older Adults: A Systematic Review and Meta-analysis," *Sports Medicine* 50 (2020): 1451–1467.

11. M. P. Lawton, M. Moss, C. Hoffman, R. Grant, T. T. Have, and M. H. Kleban, "Health, Valuation of Life, and the Wish to Live," *The Gerontologist* 39, no. 4 (1999): 406–416.

12. J. K. Hartshorne and L. T. Germine, "When Does Cognitive Functioning Peak? The Asynchronous Rise and Fall of Different Cognitive Abilities across the Life Span," *Psychological Science* 26, no. 4 (2015): 433–443.

13. Adapted from Hartshorne and Germine, "When Does Cognitive Functioning Peak?," 15.

14. "Digits 1–3 are each paired with a symbol. Given list of symbols, write down corresponding digit as fast as possible." From Hartshorne and Germine, "When Does Cognitive Functioning Peak?," 15.

15. Although Hartshorne and Germine indicate a focus on "cognitively unimpaired" individuals, we cannot rule out the possibility that some of the data may have come from individuals with some cognitive impairment and perhaps in the early stages of dementia. This might, for example, account for the steepness of declines depicted in the figure for the two working memory measures ("digit span" and "visual").

16. R. B. Cattell, "Theory of Fluid and Crystallized Intelligence: A Critical Experiment," *Journal of Educational Psychology* 54, no. 1 (1963): 1.

17. J. L. Horn, "Intelligence: Why It Grows, Why It Declines," *Transaction* 4, no. 1 (1967): 23–31; see 54.

18. T. A. Salthouse, "The Processing-Speed Theory of Adult Age Differences in Cognition," *Psychological Review* 103, no. 3 (1996): 403–428, http://rpadgett.butler .edu/ps320/coursedocs/Salthouse96.pdf.

19. The concept of working memory, which comes from the field of cognitive psychology and cognitive science (see A. D. Baddeley, "Is Working Memory Still Working?," *European Psychologist* 7, no. 2 [2002]: 85 for a discussion of its lineage), figures prominently in discussions of successful aging. Measures of working memory capacity are seen as a primary indicator of fluid intelligence. R. W. Engle, S. W. Tuholski, J. E. Laughlin, and A. R. Conway, "Working Memory, Short-Term Memory, and General Fluid Intelligence: A Latent-Variable Approach," *Journal of Experimental Psychology: General* 128, no. 3 (1999): 309; Z. Shipstead, T. L. Harrison, and R. W. Engle, "Working Memory Capacity and Fluid Intelligence: Maintenance and Disengagement," *Perspectives on Psychological Science* 11, no. 6 (2016): 771–799; N. Unsworth, K. Fukuda, E. Awh, and E. K. Vogel, "Working Memory and Fluid Intelligence: Capacity, Attention Control, and Secondary Memory Retrieval," *Cognitive Psychology* 71 (2014): 1–26, https://doi.org/10.1016/j.cog psych.2014.01.003; K. Yuan, J. Steedle, R. Shavelson, A. Alonzo, and M. Oppezzo, "Working Memory, Fluid Intelligence, and Science Learning," *Educational Research Review* 1, no. 2 (2006): 83–98. Many of us may be more familiar with the concept of short-term memory and its close identification to the digit-span measure of capacity (famously 7+/- 2). G. A. Miller, "The Magical Number Seven, Plus or Minus Two: Some Limits on Our Capacity for Processing Information," *Psychological Review* 63, no. 2 (1956): 81. Working memory can be usefully thought of as the short-term memory store plus an executive capacity to manipulate the information in this store. Engle, Tuholski, Laughlin, and Conway, "Working Memory, Short-Term Memory," 309, describe working memory capacity as the ability to keep a representation active—that is, for purposes of manipulating information to do "work" (e.g., to test hypotheses, make decisions, make predictions).

20. M. Bar, "Visual Objects in Context," *Nature Reviews Neuroscience* 5, no. 8 (2004): 617–629; A. Oliva and A. Torralba, "The Role of Context in Object Recognition," *Trends in Cognitive Sciences* 11, no. 12 (2007): 520–527.

21. I write about a *clerical tax* that we "pay" to access information. W. Jones, *Building a Better World with Our Information: The Future of Personal Information Management, Part 3* (San Rafael, CA: Morgan and Claypool, 2015), http://www.morganclaypool.com/doi/10.2200/S00653ED1V01Y201506ICR042. This includes all the time, effort, and money required to access information and is separate from our cognitive work to read and make sense of this information once we have it. Clerical tax for information access has fallen dramatically in the past few decades. I am able, for example, to access articles relating to this book chapter via the web in a matter of seconds. Comparable access back in the early 1980s (when I worked to complete my doctoral dissertation) would have taken hours with possibly days or weeks of waiting (e.g., to get access to an article not "housed" at my college library).

22. W. D. Gray and W.-T. Fu, "Soft Constraints in Interactive Behavior: The Case of Ignoring Perfect Knowledge In-the-World for Imperfect Knowledge In-the-Head," *Cognitive Science* 28, no. 3 (2004): 359–382, https://doi.org/10.1016/j.cogsci.2003.12.001; W. D. Gray and W.-T. Fu, "Ignoring Perfect Knowledge In-the-World for Imperfect Knowledge In-the-Head," *Proceedings of the SIGCHI Conference on Human Factors in Computing Systems* (2001): 112–119, https://doi.org/10.1145/365024.365061.

23. J. R. Anderson, *The Adaptive Character of Thought* (Mahwah, NJ: Lawrence Erlbaum Associates, 1990).

24. K. A. Ericsson, W. G. Chase, and S. Faloon, "Acquisition of a Memory Skill," *Science* 208, no. 4448 (1980): 1181–1182, https://doi.org/10.1126/science.7375930.

25. H. A. Simon, "How Big Is a Chunk?: By Combining Data from Several Experiments, a Basic Human Memory Unit Can Be Identified and Measured," *Science* 183, no. 4124 (1974): 482–488.

26. Evidence indicates that the average person can keep about three or four chunks at a time in short-term memory (see A. Baddeley, "The Magical Number 7: Still Magic after All These Years," *Psychological Review* 101, no. 2 [1994]: 353–356; D. E. Broadbent, "The Magic Number Seven after Fifteen Years," *Studies in Long Term Memory* [1975]: 3–18.) where the size of these chunks can vary with underlying component items (e.g., digits, letters, animal names, grocery items). The famous short-term memory capacity of seven plus or minus two (Miller, "The Magical Number Seven") is actually specific to digits.

27. W. G. Chase and H. A. Simon, "Perception in Chess," *Cognitive Psychology* 4, no. 1 (1973): 55–81; and A. D. De Groot, "Thought and Choice in Chess," *The Hague* (1965).

28. https://en.wikipedia.org/wiki/Deep_Blue_(chess_computer)#:~:text=Deep%20Blue%20takes%20an%20approach,positions%20in%20its%20game%20database.

29. I write this with the acknowledgment that some—most notably J. J. Gibson and E. J. Gibson—argue that information derivable from the environment alone is sufficient for us to act appropriately and so there is no need for top-down processing. J. J. Gibson and E. J. Gibson, "Perceptual Learning: Differentiation or Enrichment?," *Psychological Review* 62, no. 1 (1955): 32.

30. J. N. de Boer, M. M. J. Linszen, J. de Vries, M. J. L. Schutte, M. J. H. Begemann, S. M. Heringa, M. M. Bohlken, K. Hugdahl, A. Aleman, F. N. K. Wijnen,

and I. E. C. Sommer, "Auditory Hallucinations, Top-Down Processing and Language Perception: A General Population Study," *Psychological Medicine* 49, no. 16 (2019): 2772–2780, https://doi.org/10.1017/S003329171800380X.

31. C. Elsden, A. C. Durrant, and D. S. Kirk, "It's Just My History Isn't It?: Understanding Smart Journaling Practices," *Proceedings of the 2016 CHI Conference on Human Factors in Computing Systems* (2016): 2819–2831, https://doi.org/10.1145/2858036.2858103.

32. H. Sorenson, *Adult Abilities* (Minneapolis: University of Minnesota Press, 1938).

33. M. Schneid, R. Isidor, H. Steinmetz, and R. Kabst, "Age Diversity and Team Outcomes: A Quantitative Review," *Journal of Managerial Psychology* 31, no. 1 (2016): 2–17, https://doi.org/10.1108/JMP-07-2012-0228; J. Wegge, F. Jungmann, S. Liebermann, M. Shemla, B. Ries, S. Diestel, and K.-H. Schmidt, "What Makes Age Diverse Teams Effective? Results from a Six-Year Research Program," *Work: A Journal of Prevention, Assessment and Rehabilitation* 41, no. 1 (2012): 5145–5151, https://doi.org/10.3233/WOR-2012-0084-5145.

34. https://en.wikipedia.org/wiki/Elixir_of_life.

35. C. H. Hillman, K. I. Erickson, and A. F. Kramer, "Be Smart, Exercise Your Heart: Exercise Effects on Brain and Cognition," *Nature Reviews Neuroscience* 9, no. 1 (2008): 58–65; D. Lieberman, *Exercised: Why Something We Never Evolved to Do Is Healthy and Rewarding* (New York: Pantheon, 2020); Roig, Nordbrandt, Geertsen, and Nielsen, "The Effects of Cardiovascular Exercise on Human Memory"; P. J. Smith, J. A. Blumenthal, B. M. Hoffman, H. Cooper, T. A. Strauman, K. Welsh-Bohmer, J. N. Browndyke, and A. Sherwood, "Aerobic Exercise and Neurocognitive Performance: A Meta-analytic Review of Randomized Controlled Trials," *Psychosomatic Medicine* 72, no. 3 (2010): 239.

36. E. Bonsang, S. Adam, and S. Perelman, "Does Retirement Affect Cognitive Functioning?," *Journal of Health Economics* 31, no. 3 (2012): 490–501, https://doi.org/10.1016/j.jhealeco.2012.03.005.

37. T. A. Salthouse, "Mental Exercise and Mental Aging: Evaluating the Validity of the 'Use It or Lose It' Hypothesis," *Perspectives on Psychological Science* 1, no. 1 (2006): 68–87; see p. 71.

38. https://en.wikipedia.org/wiki/Hawthorne_effect.

39. A variation of this question is relevant for the previous discussion concerning the declines in mental ability that are often observed to come with a person's retirement. Was retirement and a presumed decline in mental activity that accompanied retirement responsible for declines in mental ability, or, conversely, did declines in mental ability prompt the person to seek retirement? If we have longitudinal data, we can begin to get a better picture. For example, if declines in mental ability were only observed after retirement, we are more inclined to implicate retirement as a causal culprit. Even here, however, we're on shaky ground since unobserved declines in mental ability might have been gradually building up prior to a person's retirement and only become measurable after retirement.

40. Salthouse, "Mental Exercise and Mental Aging," 70.

41. Salthouse, "Mental Exercise and Mental Aging," 71.

42. Salthouse, "Mental Exercise and Mental Aging," 72.

43. Salthouse, "Mental Exercise and Mental Aging," 68.

44. Salthouse, "Mental Exercise and Mental Aging," 84.

45. A. Ericsson and R. Pool, *Peak: Secrets from the New Science of Expertise* (New York: Houghton Mifflin Harcourt, 2016).

46. K. A. Ericsson and P. G. Polson, "An Experimental Analysis of the Mechanisms of a Memory Skill," *Journal of Experimental Psychology: Learning, Memory, and Cognition* 14, no. 2 (1988): 305.

47. https://en.wikipedia.org/wiki/Lumosity.

48. "A Consensus on the Brain Training Industry from the Scientific Community," Max Planck Institute for Human Development and Stanford Center on Longevity, accessed July 2021, http://longevity3.stanford.edu/blog/2014/10/15/the-consensus-on-the-brain-training-industry-from-the-scientific-community/.

49. Indeed, the company that created the Lumosity "brain training" program agreed to pay $2 million to settle Federal Trade Commission charges of deceptive advertising. https://www.nbcnews.com/business/consumer/lumosity-pay-2m-settle-ftc-charges-over-brain-training-ads-n490571.

50. See the site titled "Cognitive Training Data," https://www.cognitivetraining data.org/the-controversy-does-brain-training-work/response-letter/.

51. D. J. Simons, W. R. Boot, N. Charness, S. E. Gathercole, C. F. Chabris, D. Z. Hambrick, and E. A. Stine-Morrow, "Do 'Brain-Training' Programs Work?," *Psychological Science in the Public Interest* 17, no. 3 (2016): 103–186.

52. www.cognitivetrainingdata.org is the source of the second rejoinder letter mentioned earlier.

53. Simons, Boot, Charness, Gathercole, Chabris, Hambrick, and Stine-Morrow, "Do 'Brain-Training' Programs Work?," 173.

54. S. Guye and C. C. Von Bastian, "Working Memory Training in Older Adults: Bayesian Evidence Supporting the Absence of Transfer," *Psychology and Aging* 32, no. 8 (2017): 732.

55. M. Melby-Lervåg, T. S. Redick, and C. Hulme, "Working Memory Training Does Not Improve Performance on Measures of Intelligence or Other Measures of 'Far Transfer' Evidence from a Meta-analytic Review," *Perspectives on Psychological Science* 11, no. 4 (2016): 512–534; G. Sala and F. Gobet, "Cognitive Training Does Not Enhance General Cognition," *Trends in Cognitive Sciences* 23, no. 1 (2019): 9–20, https://doi.org/10.1016/j.tics.2018.10.004, see p. 9.

56. C. S. Green, D. Bavelier, A. F. Kramer, S. Vinogradov, U. Ansorge, K. K. Ball, U. Bingel, J. M. Chein, L. S. Colzato, and J. D. Edwards, "Improving Methodological Standards in Behavioral Interventions for Cognitive Enhancement," *Journal of Cognitive Enhancement* 3, no. 1 (2019): 2–29, see p. 7 for quotation.

57. P. E. Wais, M. Arioli, R. Anguera-Singla, and A. Gazzaley, "Virtual Reality Video Game Improves High-Fidelity Memory in Older Adults," *Scientific Reports* 11, no. 1 (2021): 2552, https://doi.org/10.1038/s41598-021-82109-3.

58. Salthouse, "Mental Exercise and Mental Aging," 84.

59. See, for example, R. Berggren, J. Nilsson, Y. Brehmer, F. Schmiedek, and M. Lövdén, "Foreign Language Learning in Older Age Does Not improve Memory or Intelligence: Evidence from a Randomized Controlled Study," *Psychology and Aging* 35, no. 2 (2020): 212–219, https://doi.org/10.1037/pag0000439.

60. L. Nyberg and S. Pudas, "Successful Memory Aging," *Annual Review of Psychology* 70, no. 1 (2019): 219–243, https://doi.org/10.1146/annurev-psych -010418-103052.

61. W. Jones, "Transforming Technologies to Manage Our Information: The Future of Personal Information Management, Part 2," *Synthesis Lectures on Information Concepts Retrieval and Serices* 5, no. 4 (2013): 1–179, https://www.morganclaypool com/doi/abs/10.2200/S00532ED1V01Y201308ICR028; Jones, *Building a Better World.* Multi-goaling relates, of course, to the proverbial notion that we can sometimes "kill two birds with one stone."

62. See, for example, C. G. Bennett and M. E. Hackney, "Effects of Line Dancing on Physical Function and Perceived Limitation in Older Adults with Self-Reported Mobility Limitations," *Disability and Rehabilitation* 40, no. 11 (2018): 1259–1265, https://doi.org/10.1080/09638288.2017.1294207; and also https://social dance.stanford.edu/syllabi/smarter.htm, https://www.countrydancingtonight.com/ is-line-dancing-good-for-seniors/, https://www.theborneopost.com/2016/08/13/line -dancing-offers-many-health-benefits/, http://glasgowlinedancing.co.uk/benefits-of -line-dancing/, https://pubmed.ncbi.nlm.nih.gov/28485643/.

63. https://en.wikipedia.org/wiki/Cyborg.

64. https://en.wikipedia.org/wiki/Glasses#Precursors.

65. https://en.wikipedia.org/wiki/Hip_replacement#History.

66. https://orthoinfo.aaos.org/en/treatment/total-knee-replacement/#:~:text= Knee%20replacement%20surgery%20was%20first,procedures%20in%20all%20 of%20medicine.

67. http://www.glassescrafter.com/information/percentage-population-wears -glasses.html#:~:text=According%20to%20the%20Vision%20Council,42%25%20 of%20men%20wear%20glasses.

68. Engle, Tuholski, Laughlin, and Conway, "Working Memory, Short-Term Memory," 309.

69. Salthouse, "The Processing-Speed Theory," 403–428.

70. https://en.wikipedia.org/wiki/Siri.

71. N. Charness and W. R. Boot, "Aging and Information Technology Use," *Current Directions in Psychological Science* 18 (2009): 253–258; A. Chevalier, A. Dommes, and J.-C. Marquié, "Strategy and Accuracy during Information Search on the Web: Effects of Age and Complexity of the Search Questions," *Computers in Human Behavior* 53 (2015): 305–315, https://doi.org/10.1016/j.chb.2015.07.017; M. Sanchiz, A. Chevalier, and F. Amadieu, "How Do Older and Young Adults Start Searching for Information? Impact of Age, Domain Knowledge and Problem Complexity on the Different Steps of Information Searching," *Computers in Human Behavior* 72 (2017): 67–78; and M. Sanchiz, J. Chin, A. Chevalier, W.-T. Fu, F. Amadieu, and J. He, "Searching for Information on the Web: Impact of Cognitive Aging, Prior Domain Knowledge and Complexity of the Search Problems," *Information Processing and Management* 53, no. 1 (2017): 281–294.

72. https://en.wikipedia.org/wiki/WYSIWYG.

73. D. E. Egan and L. M. Gomez, "Characteristics of People Who Can Learn to Use Computer Text Editors: Hints for Future Text Editor Design and Training," *Proceedings of the ASIS Annual Meeting* 19 (1982): 75–79.

74. L. M. Gomez, D. E. Egan, E. A. Wheeler, D. K. Sharma, and A. M. Gruchacz, "How Interface Design Determines Who Has Difficulty Learning to Use a Text Editor," *Proceedings of the SIGCHI Conference on Human Factors in Computing Systems* (December 1983): 176–181, https://doi.org/10.1145/800045.801605.

75. Although Gomez and Egan seemed to discount this more complete WYSIWYG view of the document as a factor (Gomez, Egan, Wheeler, Sharma, and Gruchacz, "How Interface Design").

76. R. Pak and M. M. Price, "Designing an Information Search Interface for Younger and Older Adults," *Human Factors: The Journal of the Human Factors and Ergonomics Society* 50, no. 4 (2008): 614–628, https://doi.org/10.1518/001872008X312314.

77. G. Press, "Why Yahoo Lost and Google Won," *Forbes*, July 26, 2016, https://www.forbes.com/sites/gilpress/2016/07/26/why-yahoo-lost-and-google-won/.

78. D. Barreau and B. A. Nardi, "Finding and Reminding: File Organization from the Desktop," *ACM SIGCHI Bulletin* 27, no. 3 (1995): 39–43; O. Bergman, R. Beyth-Marom, R. Nachmias, N. Gradovitch, and S. Whittaker, "Improved Search Engines and Navigation Preference in Personal Information Management," *ACM Transactions on Information Systems* 26, no. 4 (2008): 1–24, https://doi.org/10.1145/1402256.1402259; O. Bergman and Y. Benn, "A Neuro-cognitive Explanation for the Prevalence of Folder Navigation and Web Browsing," in *Information Systems and Neuroscience* 25, ed. F. Davis, R. Riedl, J. vom Brocke, P. M. Léger, and A. Randolph (New York: Springer International, 2018), 93–99; S. Fitchett and A. Cockburn, "An Empirical Characterization of File Retrieval," *International Journal of Human-Computer Studies* 74 (2015): 1–13, https://doi.org/10.1016/j.ijhcs.2014.10.002.

79. O. Bergman, T. Israeli, and S. Whittaker, "Search Is the Future? The Young Search Less for Files," *Proceedings of the Association for Information Science and Technology* 56, no. 1 (2019): 360–363.

80. Y. Benn, O. Bergman, L. Glazer, P. Arent, I. D. Wilkinson, R. Varley, and S. Whittaker, "Navigating through Digital Folders Uses the Same Brain Structures as Real World Navigation," *Scientific Reports* 5, article no. 14719 (2015), https://doi.org/10.1038/srep14719; Bergman and Benn, "A Neuro-cognitive Explanation."

81. U. Neisser, *Cognitive Psychology* (New York: Appleton-Century-Crofts, 1967).

82. See W. Jones, A. Wenning, and H. Bruce, "How Do People Re-find Files, Emails and Web Pages?," *iConference 2014 Proceedings*, iConference 2014, Berlin, Germany, http://hdl.handle.net/2142/47300, for an explanation for how the primacy effect might explain a person's preference for navigation as a primary means of return to the files of a personal filing system.

83. A. Dommes, A. Chevalier, and S. Lia, "The Role of Cognitive Flexibility and Vocabulary Abilities of Younger and Older Users in Searching for Information on the Web," *Applied Cognitive Psychology* 25, no. 5 (2011): 717–726; M. Sanchiz, F. Amadieu, and A. Chevalier, "An Evolving Perspective to Capture Individual Differences Related to Fluid and Crystallized Abilities in Information Searching with a Search Engine," in *Understanding and Improving Information Search: A Cognitive Approach*, ed. W. T. Fu and H. van Oostendorp (New York: Springer Interna-

tional, 2020), 71–96, https://doi.org/10.1007/978-3-030-38825-6_5. Previous studies showed that older adults experienced difficulties when reformulating queries, when navigating the web (A. Aula, "User Study on Older Adults' Use of the Web and Search Engines," *Universal Access in the Information Society* 4, no. 1 [2005]: 67–81, https://doi.org/10.1007/s10209-004-0097-7; A. Chevalier, A. Dommes, and J.-C. Marquié, "Strategy and Accuracy during Information Search on the Web: Effects of Age and Complexity of the Search Questions," *Computers in Human Behavior* 53 [2015]: 305–315, https://doi.org/10.1016/j.chb.2015.07.017) and when browsing websites (Aula, "User Study on Older Adults' Use of the Web" and Chevalier, Dommes, and Marquie, "Strategy and Accuracy during Information Search"). Also see H. van Oostendorp and S. Karanam, "Supporting Information Search by Older Adults," *Proceedings of the European Conference on Cognitive Ergonomics*, article no. 12 (2016): 1–8, https://doi.org/10.1145/2970930.2970943; K. K. Allah, N. A. Ismail, and M. A. Mohamad, "Web Search User Interface for Elderly: A Systematic Literature Review," *International Journal of Grid and Distributed Computing* 13, no. 1 (2020): 744–772; Z. Xing, X. Yuan, and L. Vizer, "The Age-Related Differences in Web Information Search Process," ArXiv Preprint (2020), https://arxiv.org/abs/2010.13352.

84. A. Dommes, A. Chevalier, and S. Lia, "The Role of Cognitive Flexibility and Vocabulary Abilities of Younger and Older Users in Searching for Information on the Web," *Applied Cognitive Psychology* 25, no. 5 (2011): 717–726.

85. Dommes, Chevalier, and Lia, "The Role of Cognitive Flexibility," 725.

86. M. Sanchiz, F. Amadieu, P.-V. Paubel, and A. Chevalier, "User-Friendly Search Interface for Older Adults: Supporting Search Goal Refreshing in Working Memory to Improve Information Search Strategies," *Behaviour and Information Technology* 39, no. 10 (2020): 1094–1109; A. F. Newell, A. Dickinson, M. J. Smith, and P. Gregor, "Designing a Portal for Older Users: A Case Study of an Industrial/Academic Collaboration," *ACM Transactions on Computer-Human Interaction (TO-CHI)* 13, no. 3 (2006): 347–375. But see also R. Nori, M. Palmiero, F. Giusberti, E. Gambetti, and L. Piccardi, "Web Searching and Navigation: Age, Intelligence, and Familiarity," *Journal of the Association for Information Science and Technology* 71, no. 8 (2020): 902–915, https://doi.org/10.1002/asi.24314; M. Crabb and V. L. Hanson, "An Analysis of Age, Technology Usage, and Cognitive Characteristics within Information Retrieval Tasks," *ACM Transactions on Accessible Computing (TACCESS)* 8, no. 3 (2016): 1–26; A. Chadwick-Dias, M. McNulty, and T. Tullis, "Web Usability and Age: How Design Changes Can Improve Performance," *ACM SIGCAPH Computers and the Physically Handicapped* 73–74 (2002): 30–37.

87. Chadwick-Dias, McNulty, and Tullis, "Web Usability and Age," 30–37.

88. Salthouse, "Mental Exercise and Mental Aging."

89. W. P. Jones, "'As We May Think'?: Psychological Considerations in the Design of a Personal Filing System," in *Cognitive Science and Its Applications for Human-Computer Interaction*, ed. R. Guindon (Mahwah, NJ: Lawrence Erlbaum Associates, 1988), 235.

90. See https://en.wikipedia.org/wiki/Distributed_cognition. See also, https://en.wikipedia.org/wiki/Extended_mind_thesis, https://en.wikipedia.org/wiki/Situated_

cognition, https://en.wikipedia.org/wiki/Social_cognition, and https://en.wikipedia
.org/wiki/Embodied_cognition.

91. W. Jones, *Keeping Found Things Found: The Study and Practice of Personal Information Management* (Amsterdam: Elsevier, 2008), https://doi.org/10.1016/B978-0-12-370866-3.X5001-2; W. Jones, *The Future of Personal Information Management, Part I: Our Information, Always and Forever* (San Rafael, CA: Morgan and Claypool, 2012), https://www.morganclaypool.com/doi/abs/10.2200/S00411ED1V01Y201203ICR021.

92. https://en.wikipedia.org/wiki/Personal_information_management.

93. W. Jones, V. Bellotti, R. Capra, J. D. Dinneen, G. Mark, C. Marshall, K. Moffatt, J. Teevan, and Van M. Kleek, "For Richer, for Poorer, in Sickness or in Health . . . : The Long-Term Management of Personal Information," Proceedings of the 2016 CHI Conference Extended Abstracts on Human Factors in Computing Systems (2016): 3508–3515, https://doi.org/10.1145/2851581.2856481.

94. Jones, *Building a Better World*.

95. A. Dommes, A. Chevalier, and S. Lia, "The Role of Cognitive Flexibility and Vocabulary Abilities of Younger and Older Users in Searching for Information on the Web," *Applied Cognitive Psychology* 25, no. 5 (2011): 717–726; M. Sanchiz, F. Amadieu, and A. Chevalier, "An Evolving Perspective to Capture Individual Differences Related to Fluid and Crystallized Abilities in Information Searching with a Search Engine," in *Understanding and Improving Information Search: A Cognitive Approach*, ed. W. T. Fu and H. van Oostendorp (New York: Springer International, 2020), 71–96, https://doi.org/10.1007/978-3-030-38825-6_5; Oostendorp and Karanam, "Supporting Information Search by Older Adults," 1–8; K. K. Allah, N. A. Ismail, and M. A. Mohamad, "Web Search User Interface for Elderly: A Systematic Literature Review," *International Journal of Grid and Distributed Computing* 13, no. 1 (2020): 744–772; Xing, Yuan, and Vizer, "The Age-Related Differences in Web Information Search Process."

96. See Sanchiz, Amadieu, Paubel, and Chevalier, "User-Friendly Search Interface for Older Adults," 1094–1109; Newell, Dickinson, Smith, and Gregor, "Designing a Portal for Older Users," 347–375. Age matters. But see also Nori, Palmiero, Giusberti, Gambetti, and Piccardi, "Web Searching and Navigation," 902–915; Crabb and Hanson, "An Analysis of Age," 1–26; A. Chadwick-Dias, McNulty, and Tullis, "Web Usability and Age," 30–37.

## Chapter Three

# One Senior Citizen's Information Ecosystem and Infrastructure

## James W. Cortada

Our purpose in this book is to understand how seniors engage with information, because they are extensive users of all manner of facts and experiences. They have parlayed wisdom to contribute to the welfare of their families, communities, and personal well-being for centuries. The moral authority of the grandmother is not to be challenged in any society, and these ladies know it.[1] Much has been made of the use (or not) of information technologies by this cohort, often also referred to as older adults, while scholars have long noted how enthusiastically they have used libraries and that they are "book people" who also read magazines, consume TV news, and are addicted to radio. In this chapter, we study one senior's activities as emblematic of her generation's information consumption, using methods that have previously been employed to understand the role of information in large corporations and professions (e.g., lawyers, engineers) as well as by ethnographers and anthropologists. We explore this topic by describing one person's world of information, called here an "information ecosystem," to explain what facts are used and who is involved.[2] That activity requires an infrastructure, such as ways to obtain information and its artifacts (e.g., books or email), so that is also described. What this exercise teaches us about how to understand the role of information usage and needs among seniors concludes our discussion.

Describing the activities of one individual makes it possible to conduct a detailed study that at its core is specific, as this chapter demonstrates. The value of such an approach is that if the subject is typical of a cohort, this sampling exercise sheds light on what others are doing. Our candidate, Jane, was chosen out of a cohort of a dozen of her peers who behaved in a similar manner and who, based on studies cited later, reflected much of the common behavior of their generation. Their educational backgrounds were similar (shared American K–12 and university schooling), professional careers common to women of their generation of the 1970s to 1990s (interrupted in each case by childrearing), and successful marriages to individuals who were in such professions as business and medicine. All shared common social experiences, such as favoring the same music, foods, entertainment, and lifestyles. While emblematic to a great extent, keep in mind that every individual is also unique. So, while the passion of one member of the cohort may be glass-making art, our subject's might be cooking, and yet another embraced knitting. But they all had their passions and were willing to build an information and social ecosystem in support of these and their ongoing responsibilities as parents, members of a larger family, and community.

Because this case is specific to one individual, a bit more information about the context of her life, and by extension that of her cohorts cited previously, can help to understand her behavior. Jane is White, Virginia-raised but spent the majority of her adulthood outside the state, middle class, of Scotch-Irish-English heritage, and Protestant. She grew up in an agricultural county in Central Virginia on a working farm. She has fond memories of this life because "it was safe, secure, happy, and stable. My parents reflected those characteristics. . . . It was a happy childhood with loving family in an unchanging environment." She lived through the civil rights era and was perhaps shaped by that exposure to accept African Americans and other racial minorities as part of her world, reinforced by living in communities that were more "accepting" than Central Virginia. Politically liberal all her life, this represented a gentle break from the worldviews of her more conservative family. Travel to Europe and Mexico extended her worldview of various cultural norms, which she finds "fascinating to see how other people live their lives. I could relate to a farmer in Spain, for example, even though I could not speak the language, because my background was so similar. . . . I found it fun to go to food markets and see how everyday food preparation was done in different countries. . . . I have nurtured empathy for the less fortune, a reminder of how blessed I have been." Traveling also stimulated her interest in history and in understanding how other societies and cultures worked.

Finally, we should note that she was never poor. Life growing up on her parents' farm can be characterized as distinctly middle class circa mid-twentieth-century America, while she lived her adult years moving from solid middle class to perhaps upper middle class without shedding the values of her childhood. Jane cherishes those early values, which, as she said, she instilled in her two daughters. These included "liking down-to-earth people, acceptance of many different lifestyles." Jane has lived long enough to see her values lived by her daughters as adults with children of their own.

Why do we care? They are a large and energetic cohort active in their largely postcareer, postparenting phases of life, pursuing active retirements;

their educational levels demonstrate long familiarity with information and its ephemera, tools, and ways of using it. A second concern of this chapter is this cohort's interaction with information technology, inasmuch as a lingering impression remains that they are inadequate to the task.[3] We are interested in those elders, here, in their midseventies; our case study is of a woman age seventy-three. Two-thirds of her cohort had home broadband, 82 percent of this same group graduated from college, and 92 percent had access to the internet (a rate of usage exceeding that of the population at large). Just over half of her cohort own a tablet, a third an e-reader. Roughly a third of all seniors used social media in 2017, 42 percent in her age group, 56 percent among her age group with a college education.[4]

But they still faced difficulties using these technologies. Many experienced frustration with how to navigate such devices as smartphones and e-readers. They did not always understand the language of the technology, let alone what user manuals were explaining, despite the fact that they were spending more than half their daily leisure time (four hours a day) with TVs, computers, tablets, smartphones, and similar devices. By 2019, some 73 percent were accessing the internet. Their lower technology literacy did not hold them back; survey data indicated they were "eager to learn."[5] Their generation's relative prosperity since the 1980s, when compared to that of earlier cohorts, facilitated the active retirements exemplified by our case study.[6]

What do seniors think of public libraries? They are extensive users of these resources, finding them trustworthy and reliable.[7] So, while seniors in their seventies had become extensive users of digital sources of information, they had not given up on their lifetime use of public libraries.[8]

Ethnographers, anthropologists, and sociologists have provided questions to explore relevant to people in their seventies in the 2020s. For example, in the early 1970s, Clifford Geertz set an agenda for a generation of scholars by suggesting that people's behavior be situated within the notion of culture, "the total way of life of a people . . . the social legacy the individual acquires from his group . . . a way of thinking, feeling, and believing . . . about the way in which a group of people in fact behave," a "storehouse of pooled learning," and "learned behavior," among other notions.[9] In our case study of one individual, we see those themes played out. Geertz's list became a guidebook to ethnographic studies. This chapter links his ideas to concepts of information ecologies and infrastructures by the example studied here. The method is essentially his, to observe in detail one's behavior, to provide a "thick description." But it also aligns with another theme: that old age can be divided into two categories, first of a postcareer yet healthy period often called the "third age," and then the "fourth age," during which cognitive and physical feebleness and ill health are more prevalent.[10] Our subject lives in the third age.[11]

## HOW WE CAN LEARN MORE

To understand many of the underlying information behaviors that support the statistical profile of seniors cited earlier, we explore the information world of one person in a qualitative manner. Her pseudonym is Jane. In 2020—when this study was conducted—she was seventy-three years old. Jane has an undergraduate degree in home economics, a master's degree in adult education, and periodically took courses at her local university. She considers her health excellent and takes long walks every day. She is the mother of two grown daughters and grandmother of three grandchildren ages twelve, ten, and three, the first two boys. Jane has been married for forty-nine years and lives in a house filled with books, TVs, radios, a laptop, PC, iPad, and one e-reader. Because she grew up on a farm, she easily participated in 4-H education programs as a child; she worked as a home economist for nine years before taking time off to raise her two daughters, then returned to the workplace in the 1990s at a telecommunications firm. She retired in 2011 at age sixty-three to assist in raising her grandsons, as their parents had full-time jobs. Jane enjoys traveling in Europe and the United States, paying particular attention to the history of these regions. Her main passion (hobby), what scholars call "serious leisure," is cooking.[12] She spends several hours each day on cooking matters and has integrated that interest into her travel and reading practices.

We reconstruct her information world using the same methods applied to the institutional studies mentioned earlier. We demonstrate that the same approach can be used to explore a unit of one—a person. We explore Jane's motives and views of her various activities. Our core hypothesis is that people, like organizations, are largely information-handling social constructs and that the bulk of their activities involve the collection, storage, analysis, and application of facts. There has long been a debate about the differences between data, facts, information, and wisdom, a discussion we do not engage with here.[13] The collection and use of information occurs within a context, which is increasingly being viewed holistically as an ecosystem, analogous to what one sees in nature. In a forest one finds that animals, vegetation, geographical features, and weather interact with each other. All living matter remains codependent on each other and on their shared environment to survive. Living matter senses what is occurring by consuming information and responding in ways that preserve its life and meet its objectives. The same analysis applies to human behavior and society.[14] To thrive, humans must understand the realities of their environment and what is happening in real time. A subservient idea that applies here, long discussed in many disciplines, is the idea of networks in which information is taken in (feedback from the environment) and responded to by people, animals, and fauna in some routinized manner.[15]

Elsewhere, I have argued that it is useful to think of infrastructures as consisting of two parts: a collection of physical components, such as a combination of stores and postal services to make it possible, for example, to deliver a book to a person, and a content component, such as the information in that book, report, spreadsheet, or other physical object.[16] The combination of ecosystems and infrastructures makes it possible to move from general comments about what information, say, a senior uses to very specific listings of these. We can construct a clearer understanding of information's relative value and consumption while identifying motives for their use by specific cohorts, such as other seniors. In short, we move from generalized comments to more specific explanations. The approach is useful because its increased precision leads to a greater understanding of the role of information.[17] Finally, information is seen as objects, and by most as a tool, even if it is enjoyed, as proponents of viewing information usage as a hobby, a pleasurable activity, or leisure activity would argue.[18]

In earlier writings, I applied this concept to how a nation (the United States) approaches information, then to the smaller example of a company (IBM), professions (diplomats, computer scientists, sales personnel), even to groups that did not necessarily have to interact with each other (farm wives in one community).[19] Here, we explore how that method works when focusing on just one individual. Think of that person much like an atom, a living cell, a tiny creature in a vast information ecosystem—the jungle suggested earlier. Biologists and sociologists taught us that all activity of an organized form is made up of smaller units (living creatures) interacting with each other, building on similar and dissimilar activities and behaviors that affect each other, that shape the definition and destiny of an ecosystem.[20] Think of Jane as one of those small components, a building block of human society. This approach also centers on solving problems using information. Some research suggests other motives: pleasure and curiosity providing meaning to life.[21] Asked what motivated her, Jane said, "both solving problems and enjoying life." Like other seniors, she reads a great deal and searches for information over the internet.[22] She did not see herself as participating in an information-seeking role; rather, she enjoyed the experience of uncovering new facts.[23] She sought information to fix problems (e.g., a broken refrigerator, a medical problem), enjoy her passions (e.g., cooking, traveling), and improve her volunteering activities (e.g., finding online classes for grandchildren, mirroring behavior of friends and neighbors).[24] In her words, "I like to find answers so I can decide how to proceed."

Looking at Jane through the lens of an information-seeking creature will jar some scholars. Political scientists see people as interested in and motivated by politics, sociologists argue that people are essentially social beings, psychologists view people as extensions of their brains, and economists view the world with their famous neoclassical model *homo economicus*. Yet biologists would be sympathetic, as they have been arguing for decades that all living creatures seek out and send "signals" that make it possible for them to live. But I ask the reader to avoid engaging in an academic bar fight, although your author could probably count on the biologists and computer scientists to help out. Let us explore the reality, which Jane says exists for her, that she is enveloped in an information ecosystem and the reality that she has established an information infrastructure to support it. Then scholars can return to their useful paradigms with possibly new perspectives to inform their own work.

## INTRODUCING A SENIOR'S INFORMATION ECOSYSTEM

Why does Jane live in an information ecosystem? She chose to build an information ecosystem that aligned tightly with her necessary and desired interests in life: family, health, cooking, travel, and gardening. Jane's husband has his own ecosystem that reflects his interests, which are substantially different from hers. One of her daughters is interested in equestrian activities and owns four horses; her information ecosystem is heavily oriented in support of that interest as well as her family and banking career. When observing Jane in her own information ecosystem, it appears she optimized it to meet her needs by acquiring the kind of information she wants, in a timely manner, in a way that she can apply. As a result, information comes in, is stored, and is appropriated in a seemingly effortless way with few complaints. When complaints do occur, it is because technology is not working properly, the facts are out of date or incomplete, or some data is categorically wrong or irrelevant.

Much of Jane's information ecosystem is defined by her primary sources of information. These are displayed in figure 3.1. Central to this collection are her priorities, with family interests dominant. All other groups serve as a constellation around this priority, although some serve as primary agents within secondary interests, such as cooking (hobby), political interests (issue), and social pleasures of friends. Note that participants can be a combination of people, suppliers (e.g., Amazon, public library), and organizations that both supply and serve social purposes (e.g., news, social media, church). Information ecosystems of friends are tapped for a specific query, such as through a college friend to find out about yet another colleague's activities since their school days. She less elegantly calls these "a phone call."

Figure 3.2 drops down into a more explicit level of detail but continues to situate Jane as the central hub of the ecosystem. Within each box we see her more focused areas of interest and sources of related information. For example, members of her "birthday club," comprising a half dozen women of

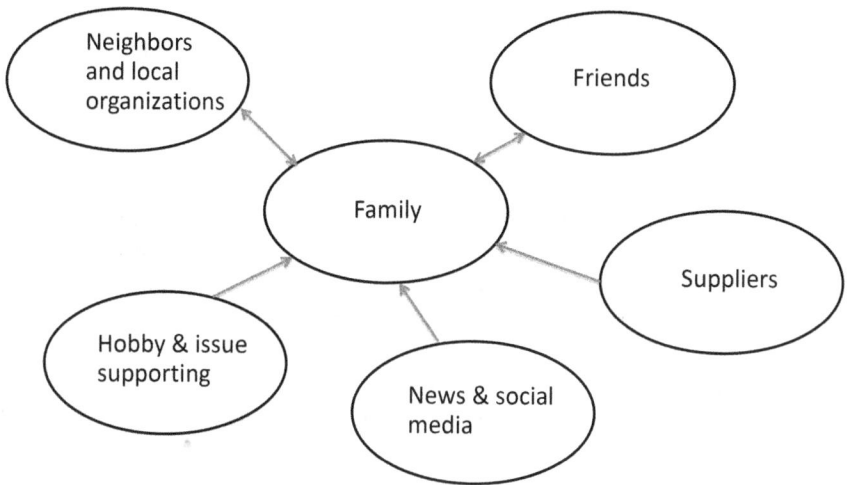

**Figure 3.1. Primary Sources of Jane's Ecosystem for Information.**
James W. Cortada

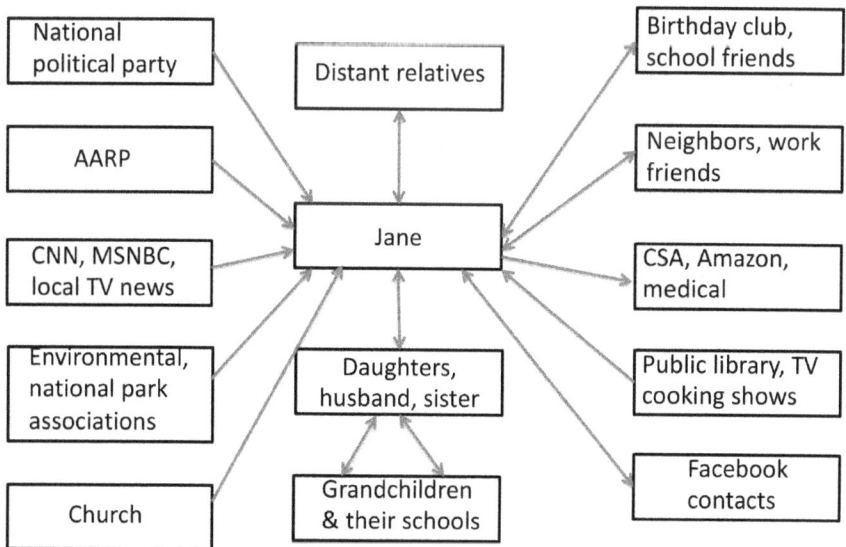

**Figure 3.2. Participants in Jane's Information Ecosystem.**
James W. Cortada

similar socioeconomic and educational backgrounds, discuss family, health, community, and politics as both information exchanges and as entertainment. Jane thinks of these members of her cohort as sources of both information and improved quality of life. Psychologists would agree with her.[25] Her community-supported agriculture farmer provides both fresh vegetables and, through a website, detailed information about food.[26] Her doctors, of course, share information with her, while Facebook allows her to stay engaged with more distant friends and relatives. The directions of the arrows indicate which way the bulk of information flows. For instance, a minister preaches to her; she does not preach back. Family members exchange information and opinions back and forth in equal measures. Newsletters from environmental and national park organizations inform her about their activities; she does not inform them about her interests in them. Everything to the left of Jane's box is largely intended to be unidirectional transmission to her with her per-mission—that is to say, because she turns on the TV or reads a newsletter. However, her TV can be on in the background, which introduces topics that she did not choose yet from which she learns new facts. Newsletters can be uni- and bidirectional as well, although to a lesser extent. More certainly, however, almost everything to the right is bidirectional, as she welcomes pro-actively back-and-forth dialogue, with a partial exception of the local farmer, Amazon, and medical participants, from which she wants more information than she provides.[27] TV and radio cooking programs remain on all day long in her kitchen when she is cooking, along with periodic changes to cable and local news and PBS programming. About a third of the time is devoted to each of these categories (cooking, news, and PBS). Table 3.1 takes us down yet another level of detail.

**Table 3.1.  Relations Among Friends, Information, and Sources**

| Types | Information | Sources and Locations |
|---|---|---|
| Birthday Club (six members) | Family events, politics, medicine and health care, community events, food, housekeeping, travel | Face-to-face, restaurants, home parties, email, texting |
| Neighbors (two dozen individuals) | Same topics as above, neighborhood events and issues | Neighborhood association meetings, local news media, face-to-face, Nextdoor, phone |
| Work alumni (five or six people) | Work gossip and status, politics, community issues, family, travel | Face-to-face, restaurant, less often by phone, email, or texting |
| College friends (four or five people) | Family, deaths, but no college issues | Telephone, occasional face-to- face |

Much has been made of Jane's culinary activities; however, it is insightful to briefly describe her work with travel. Prior to the COVID-19 pandemic stopping travel, Jane in her retirement years strived to go to Europe annually as well as to at least three destinations in the United States—one or more of which had to be linked to visiting her granddaughter in Colorado. Over the years, she had taken the lead in planning trips and had traveled on these trips to Spain and France twice, Germany, Italy, Sweden and Norway, Switzerland, England also twice, Scotland, and Ireland, and to various American national parks and cities. Historians of vacations think in terms of two types: one to have fun, sit on the beach, visit friends and relatives; the other more educational, to be exposed to new cultures and history, and to visit museums and famous landmarks.[28] Jane engages largely in the latter but combines those trips with the former when possible.

Her planning process is rigorous, honed at work, and applied in the same way at home. She acquires a travel book on the target country or area of the United States, reads a history of the region or country (e.g., about World War II and Normandy before vacationing there) to be exposed to its recent history, and conducts online research regarding culinary facts of an area. Once in the country, she visits open-air farmers markets, grocery stores, and specialized food shops; eats at restaurants that serve specific items she is keen on trying; and occasionally acquires a small cooking hand tool or a container of some local spice. Primarily, she collects experiences.

Her planning is thorough (e.g., a hotel reservation for every night in the country and tickets for every leg of the trip acquired in advance). She develops typed lists to track key events and expenses paid for in advance, and she always prepares an itinerary to share with both those traveling and the family remaining at home. She prepares these in the same format and level of detail as one does for a senior government or company official. Upon returning from a trip, photographs are printed and identified, some shared electronically. She and her husband put together a scrapbook that documents the trip and that facilitates storing ephemera, such as tickets and brochures. These are consulted if a subsequent trip is made to the area. Her approach to organizing trips reflects her training at work in both project management and planning, including arranging trips and meetings for senior management. This is an example of a direct transfer of information-handling practices from one phase of life to another.

In Europe she favors visiting historic sites and neighborhoods and, of course, culinary points of interest, including farms. She engaged Viking tours to experience Central Europe and Greece, although the COVID-19 pandemic caused the latter trip to be canceled in 2020. But, as a result of these exercises, Viking River Cruises and Road Scholar send her literature about other possible trips roughly once a month. One emphasizes visiting historic sites, the second national parks. Some sources of information are usually less important to her. For example, Jane expresses little interest in English art galleries but is consumed by the Louvre in Paris. When in a museum, she is in the habit of reading every annotated description next to every object. On one occasion, a member of her birthday club accompanied her to London to see an exhibit of the queen's dresses, then to trace where the members of the Beatles grew up and developed their careers. Their husbands, aware that both ladies would spend twice or more time in museums of no interest to them, suggested that the women go to London on their own, and they did. Jane knew a great deal about the current queen of England and her family, while her friend was deeply immersed in all manner of Beatle information and had an impressive collection of ephemera and books about them. The hunt for information shaped their experience.

What does Jane do with these various collections of information? Two information experts, Jarkko Karl and Jenna Hartel, have proposed a way to catalog such information that, when shown to her, Jane said mostly applied to her. These two scholars suggest that part of understanding the context of information is to recognize that people seek, store, use, conceptualize, create, describe, destroy, exchange, organize, process, and provide information.[29] That list is consistent with the model I developed for exploring information activities of organizations.[30] Jane pushed back on the idea that she spent much time destroying facts, but she clearly did all the rest. Regarding destruction of facts, she spends little time debunking what she ignored but initiates discussions about what she perceives as misinformation or her lack of knowledge about a subject.[31] Her questions are obvious: "Why is something the way it is?" "What is that?" Jane is more of a collector of information that she has vetted, such as a recipe she has tried and that works as promised by a cookbook's author. She has collected three fat three-ring binders of recipes, kitchen-testing them as she was taught to do in college and in her first job; annotating them; often sharing that information with friends and relatives. Her recipes are organized by topic and are conveniently available. (See figure 3.3.) To reinforce a point made by the two scholars, all her actions require physical and intellectual activities, an important point to take into account with seniors, whose health can be a significant factor affecting their ability to carry out these tasks.

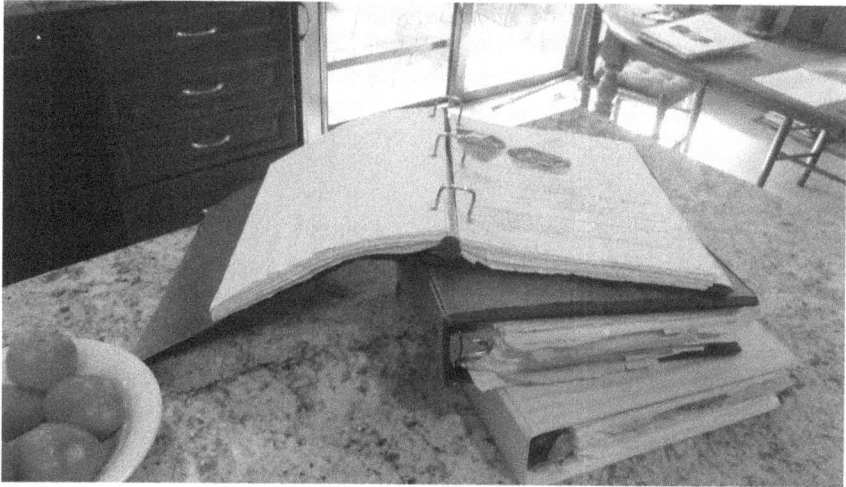

**Figure 3.3. Jane's Recipe Binders.**
James W. Cortada

## HOW JANE'S INFORMATION
## INFRASTRUCTURE SUPPORTS HER ECOSYSTEM

Jane needs an information infrastructure to support her informational activities. That infrastructure consists of two parts: a collection of physical objects and resources, and the information itself. Figure 3.4 conceptually illustrates her infrastructure. Her physical support system is akin to a business supply chain: manufacturers of information, products, delivery services, and tools. Jane must synchronize each, as all are necessary components of her information ecosystem. Publishers of content must exist and stay profitable so as to provide her with information, such as about cooking or travel agents to acquire those complicated-to-buy European train tickets. The postal system and private delivery services bring her books and kitchen tools. Television producers and TV sets are critical components for delivering news, history, and cooking information to her. Her laptop gives her access to the internet, and so she moves it from one room to another each day as needed, using it frequently. The purpose of the physical side of her infrastructure is to provide the tools, ephemera, and information she requires in a timely and cost-effective manner. As the figure illustrates, the physical side is diverse, extensive, and complicated. Jane is in charge of making it all work together, a major task since she asserts that more than half her time spent interacting with information involves its acquisition.

Both components comprising
Information Infrastructure

| Physical | Content |
|---|---|
| Mail, UPS, Federal Express | Publications: magazines, books, catalogs |
| Grocery stores, farmer's markets | CSA & environmental e-newsletters, blogs |
| Public libraries (2) | History, fiction, nutrition, cooking & recipes |
| Television, radio, laptop, smartphone | History, travel, cooking, nutrition, nature |
| Books, magazines, 3-ring binders | History, travel, cooking, children's education |
| Kitchen | Cooking and news shows on TV and radio |
| Home office | Cooking, health & travel books, magazines |

Both components required to sustain each other

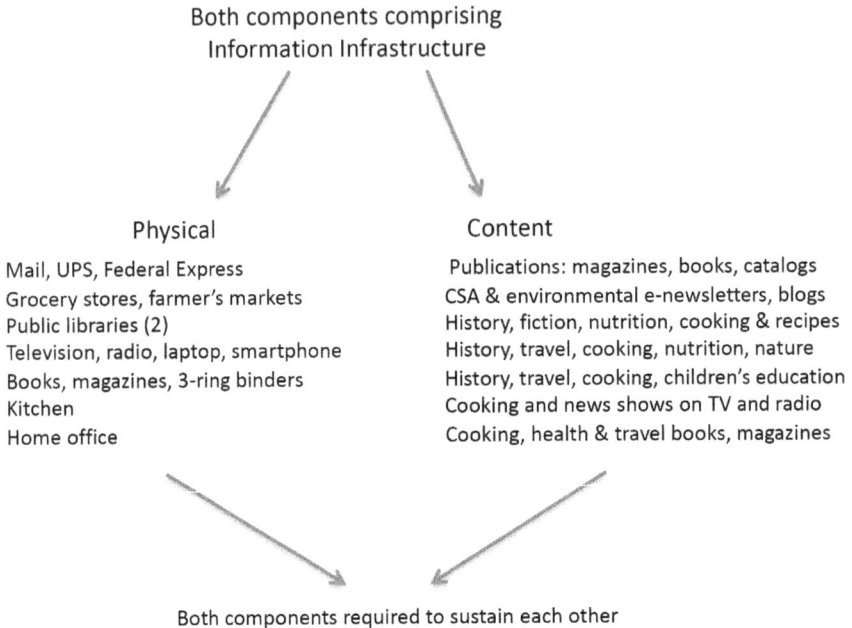

**Figure 3.4.   Two Sides of Jane's Information Infrastructure.**
James W. Cortada

The right-hand side of the figure depicts the more ephemeral parts of her world: the information itself. But that too has physical qualities, such as a recipe card, a book, or digital or paper newsletters. But the intent on the right is to show the content—the data itself—some of which is ephemeral in the true sense of the word in that once it is listened to or seen, it is essentially lost unless remembered, written down, recorded, or retrieved. Television news and radio programs fit into this category of information, so too e-books "borrowed" from the public library. The content presented in this figure are major types of information that Jane routinely seeks out and uses. Both components of her information infrastructures are in constant use. Jane reports that the left side is tapped into at least once daily, while more of the content on the right-hand side is accessed many times each day.

Each of the pieces in the information infrastructure can be dissected even further, and when this is done, the dissection reveals yet another level of detail in this complex network of goods and information and their movement about her world. Table 3.2 catalogs her major providers of information, the physical locations where exchanges of information occur, and her estimates as to the frequency with which these activities take place. The first two col-

**Table 3.2.   Organizations and Physical Locations in Jane's Information Ecosystem and Infrastructuere**

| Information Providers | Locations for Exchanging Information | Frequency |
| --- | --- | --- |
| Family | Family homes, Zoom, email | Daily, weekly |
| Friends (birthday club) | Wisconsin, Colorado, Virginia | Weekly or quarterly |
| Neighbors | Madison, Wisconsin | Weekly |
| CSA | Dane County, Wisconsin | Bimonthly |
| Grocery stores | Madison, Wisconsin (four stores) | Every several days |
| National political party | Mail-only communications | Quarterly |
| Environmental, national park | Publications | Biannually |
| Books | Local public library, Amazon | Weekly |
| Magazine subscriptions (3–5) | US Mail | Weekly to quarterly |
| National print and electronic news | Subscription, NPR, CNN, MSNBC PBS | Daily |
| Food and cooking providers | TV cooking programs, Amazon | Daily |
| High school and college friends | Virginia, Facebook | Several times a year |
| Public library | Madison, Wisconsin | Monthly |
| AARP | Home through membership | Monthly |
| Church | Madison, Wisconsin church, recently Zoom | Weekly |
| Medical doctors, dentists | Madison, Wisconsin, websites | Weekly searches, once per month visits |
| Catalogs for clothing, cooking, and travel | US Mail, Facebook advertisements | Individually once a week, in total sometimes daily |
| Travel agents | Virtual, phone, email, websites | Quarterly |

With the advent of COVID-19 in early 2020, many of these information exchanges shifted to online, such as the use of Zoom, Amazon, and other websites. The frequency of information consumption remained the same, so too the quantity consumed and the time spent on these.

umns are self-explanatory and are simply presented to demonstrate the variety involved, which Jane does not see as a complex orchestration on her part, because all fit together in the way she acquires and uses its content.

More interesting is the third column—frequency—because it is complicated and dense. Earlier we touched on the debate concerning the role of leisure activities, better known as hobbies. Jane's frequency appears similar in the level of activity—think intensity and cadence—one might experience in a job. Some events occur daily at the same time (e.g., preparation of an evening meal), others at an almost regularly scheduled time weekly (e.g., delivery of food), but others are based on the time it routinely takes, say, to read a book. Some are more ad hoc, such as what to do when a food processor breaks down and a workaround has to be researched and applied, or she does not have a key ingredient and so must find a substitute that will work. But even these require responding exactly as done in a paying job with research. The point is, just because someone is not being paid to deal with all these forms of information-handling activities, which are called collectively a hobby or parenting, does not mean they are not treated the same way by a senior. In this instance, Jane manages her information infrastructure just as she did in both her postcollege job and in the positions she held in her second round of salaried work.

To draw even closer parallels with work practices that seniors carry over into their private lives, there is the central issue of the office as a workspace. Clearly, Jane is both a knowledge worker and a knowledge retiree. The fact that her income today comes from a pension and Social Security rather than from a payroll office in a company is irrelevant, because she behaves similarly in both situations. Jane's workspace consists largely of her kitchen, but she also has her own office at home. The kitchen, remodeled to her specifications, looks like many modern middle-class versions, with modifications that only another "foodie" would appreciate: a special drawer designed only to hold spices, cabinet shelves that roll out like drawers in an office filing cabinet, three-pronged electrical outlets for appliances, and internet access, among others. All materials used are chosen based on what a professional test kitchen might use or are fashionably attractive. Lighting is similar to that in a professional test kitchen, so too the sink and access to water. This is another example of a direct transfer from Jane's work experience to her home information handling, in this case infrastructure.

Then there is her office, a room that has a desk, large activity table, floor-to-ceiling bookcases, a metal filing cabinet, containers filled with runs of cooking magazines, and the kinds of wall hangings one might find at work, including her university diplomas and awards from her prior job. She uses her laptop here as in the kitchen, and she has a telephone and a scanner. The office is cluttered, and to the untrained eye it looks like a mess. However, it is exactly like those of other knowledge workers. In a now famous study of the workspaces of computer scientists at leading Silicon Valley firms, two information scholars noted that everyone had stacks of papers on the floors and on every table surface. Diskettes were mixed with piles of papers and publications. Notes were taped to personal computers. To prove their point, they published photographs of these chaotic workspaces in their book.[32] These photos resemble Jane's home office (figure 3.5).

**Figure 3.5. Jane's Home Office.**
James W. Cortada

Yet Jane, like the computer scientists, knows exactly what each pile of ephemera contains, why they are in those piles, and how to get to what she needs. Her bookshelves seem better organized: by type of food book (e.g., cookbooks versus scientific treatises on food and nutrition), travel books apart from cooking, a whole section of community cookbooks from the part of Virginia where she grew up that she continues to add to, another two shelves devoted to Spanish cookbooks, and separate shelves for history and even biographies of her favorite country western musician, Willie Nelson. To her, the room is rationally organized to support her activities exactly as she would have done at work.

Does she need all those books? It appears she has as many as full-time professionals might have to support their work. A professor at a research university would conclude that she had at least a minimal number of needed materials: works of reference, basic overview texts, specialized monographs, and exotic items that only an expert in a field would appreciate. Like a professor, when asked did she need all those books, she said, "Of course not." But they accumulate the same way as those in a scholar's home or department office: purposeful acquisitions, gifts from friends and relatives, serendipitous accumulations, and lost souls that somehow made it onto her shelves. She has periodically culled the collection, donating unneeded materials to charities and library sales, otherwise the number of books alone would have been 50 percent greater in number. By her nature she is not a collector, such as one would envision of a hobbyist working with stamps, rare books, or porcelain figurines. Hers is a working library and inasmuch some items are consulted frequently, and most others are not but are there when needed. An example of the former includes volumes on the science and chemistry of cooking (a recent interest) and of the latter, travel books to places already visited. Neighborhood telephone directories and guidebooks to her city and state are consulted episodically; she could not say how frequently.

But even this office is not enough to support her needs. In the basement of her home, she has a small room about the size of a half bathroom. On three sides are deep shelves on which she stores extra plates (e.g., for use during holiday seasons), large cooking pots, and various other cooking appliances for which there is either no room in her kitchen or that are rarely used. After all, her kitchen is more than her research lab for new ways to prepare meals, as operationally it must also be efficient to prepare meals on a regular basis, as any normal family would expect. Her basement room is essentially what one might call "offsite storage" in a business. She does not store any information in that room. If a recipe collection is not needed in the kitchen, it goes to a shelf in a coat closet within feet of the kitchen or to her office, located some twenty feet away from the kitchen. A member of her birthday club has as her hobby making glass art. She has a building separate from her home in the backyard where she melts glass and has blowtorches and other equipment so that she can in her "retirement" have fun and purpose by making art objects, some of which she occasionally sells at art fairs. But make no mistake, she sees this work as a hobby, a pleasurable pursuit, but one that requires both artistic skills and scientific knowledge.[33] Both women observe what the other does, learning about new ways of, say, using laptops and their phones to acquire new information, such as how to download apps or how to access podcasts. These conversations are as much about information handling as they are about their specific passions.

Missing from our figure illustrating Jane's information infrastructure is an important comment about how she prefers to work with information, as do other seniors. Specifically absent from the model is oral communication as a way of transmitting and receiving information. The only hint we have of that facet of her interaction with information is that she has a landline telephone and smartphone, and she participates in Zoom calls on her computer. In a now classic ethnographic study of how nurses interacted with patients, many of whom were elderly, Karen E. Pettigrew[34] pointed out a feature of senior life that is as relevant today to Jane and her cohort as when the original study was done in the 1990s, when little was known about how the elderly communicated their needs and interests.[35] Pettigrew observed nurses working with people whose average age was seventy-eight (median seventy-eight, range sixty-five to ninety-one), two-thirds female, one-third college graduates. All had worked outside their homes.

Pettigrew observed that when seeking information, while they might use libraries, these were sources of last resort (today with Google and the internet in general, this finding might be dated). More pertinently, she observed that, "for personal, everyday problems people prefer face-to-face communication; that people seek out sources that are most accessible; that informal, interpersonal sources are preferred over formal, institutional resources."[36] Jane often prefers to engage in verbal conversation to discuss a medical problem with a nurse, doctor, or "trusted friend" rather than through an exchange of email or reading a book. It was easier and faster to talk than to log onto her doctor's secure website and carefully construct an email message, then wait for responses, followed by additional questions, and so forth. For less serious matters, or for ones that require less interactive give-and-take exchange of information, she will spontaneously turn to a Google search, such as for biographical information about someone she is discussing with a friend or family member. As an update to Pettigrew's presmartphone-era observation, often when wanting to have a telephone or face-to-face conversation, Jane will text the other party to see if they are available or to set a time for such a dialogue.

## ROLE OF THE INTERNET

The central component of Jane's physical infrastructure—and one might argue, the other half—is the internet. Between 2011 (when she ended salaried work) and 2020, her use of the internet grew from an estimated one to two hours daily to over two hours scattered throughout the day. The lockdown due to COVID-19 in 2020–2021 led her to use the internet for over 90 percent of her data searches, setting aside trips to public libraries and bookstores, for example, which were closed. Shopping (an information query activity) increasingly had shifted to online by 2018 and nearly to 100 percent in 2020 (farmers markets were the exception, occasionally grocery stores). Key sources queried online include Amazon (purchases), Google (specific facts, such as medical, historical), and major online news sources (*New York Times*, *Washington Post*, CNN, local newspaper, BBC, hometown newspaper in Virginia). She uses email to communicate with family, friends, and medical personnel and to make inquiries. Everything described so far in this paragraph is done using an Apple laptop that moves back and forth from kitchen to office but is primarily accessed from a kitchen table.

She is a facile user of her smartphone, which she uses mostly to communicate with friends and family. She speaks with her two daughters approximately once daily and conducts three or four other conversations daily with the same device. She has become skilled at texting, often preferring its use with her daughters for the same reasons as young adults: it is convenient, quick, and less intrusive than a verbal conversation. She largely uses it with members of her family and friends. In addition, she tracks the number of steps she takes using a Fitbit function on her smartphone and occasionally checks weather forecasts and GPS instructions for directions to a physical locality. She conducts serious information gathering and viewing of videos with the laptop. Jane does not play digital games nor watch full-length movies on either device; for movies she uses her television. However, she uses her laptop to connect to specific programs, such as historical dramas accessed through Netflix, which are exhibited on her large television screen. She anticipates that her next television will be directly internet-connected and dependent on various streaming services rather than on cable channel programming.

Earlier we mentioned that seniors have faced challenges with information technology; Jane was no exception. However, she willingly learned new ways to interact with the technologies. She expressed her frustrations, however: "It takes me a lot longer than it should to use my computer." But she overcomes these with friends and relatives incrementally teaching her how to use new tools and applications.[37] An example concerns the transfer of family photographs from one device or another and the subsequent expenditure of what she considers an inordinate "amount of time sorting and archiving these pictures."[38] Once or twice a year, she and her husband bring into their home an expert on personal computing to update their software, teach them how to use new functions, reorganize files and photographs, and ensure that the physical and operating systems are synchronized and operating as they should. In short, this is a service similar to what a salaried worker would have available in their job from the IT Help Desk. This service consumes about three to four hours each time and requires periodical intermittent "just-in-time" conversations of fifteen minutes or so, two or three times a year. These conversations are focused largely on infrastructure issues (e.g., printer fails to print, an unclear request to update a software package). Her internet service is reliable and "up" 99 percent of the time and sufficiently quick to support the speed with which she interacts online.

## IMPLICATIONS AND CONCLUSIONS

Jane's experience with information has much to teach us about seniors. To begin with, even though American society tends to think of people as old (i.e., more feeble) generally after the age of sixty-five, and ageism holds that older people are not as capable as younger people to learn new things—let alone even want to—Jane's experience challenges such assumptions, indeed prejudices.[39] Her friends and the literature on seniors belie the image of declining capabilities in handling information. However, American humor reinforces stereotypes Jane's experience contradicts: "Retirement is just a never-ending vacation," "Why do retirees smile all the time? Because they can't hear a word you are saying!" "The world's longest coffee break is often referred to as retirement." But on the flip side there are comments by retirees repeated constantly on their websites: "Now you can do the things you did not have time to do before," "My best days in retirement are when I give back to the community," or "Enjoy working at living, rather than living at work." Jane's observation: "I can pursue my interests," which for her are, in order of priority, engaging with family and friends, cooking, travel, and reading history and novels.

Like many retirees, she controls how she spends her time. Facilitating her way of living is the collection and use of information; indeed, she calls this "crucial." Jane and other members of her cohort feel young and vigorous when in good health. Comedian George Burns is reported to have quipped that "retirement at sixty-five is ridiculous. When I was sixty-five, I still had pimples." Critical, however, is that she gets to do what she wants and has the economic and cognitive capabilities to do so. That is an image contrary to the one widely held, and so her example suggests that as older Americans live longer, healthier lives, the old jokes no longer reflect reality; comedian George Burns was right! With the increasing call for seniors to take on society's ills, apply their experience, and invest their time in improving the lives of others, how they interact with information becomes a suitable, indeed important, urgent task. If Jane's experience can be validated as also that of millions of other seniors of similar and differing educational and social/ethnic backgrounds, then we know they will contribute less with muscles and more with cognitive capabilities—with information-handling skills.[40] Jane's example illustrates how that might happen.

The scholarly literature on aging is filled with discussions about self-images and others crafted by sociologists and others about what old age involves. Many are around notions of feebleness, third and fourth ages, and so forth. There is more than a hint that seniors identify with some of these characterizations. Jane does not think in those terms. She is comfortable functioning more or less in the same ways as she did in her fifties and sixties. While she grows wiser and more informed about various matters over time, she argues that her behavior and interests have not changed so much because of any generational or age identity. "I feel and think as if I were a fifty-year-old." The reason for her behavior, she says, is because "I fortunately am very healthy and don't have a lot of aches and pains that many seniors endure." Jane also believes that living in a university town "provides many stimulating

experiences that keeps me on my toes." One might argue that she has a growing interest in medical issues as she gets older, but she would also posit that,
as new issues come up, "I pursue those too," such as the activities and perspectives of whoever is the current American president. So, academic notions
of transitions from one phase of life to another, while useful exercises, may
be overstated when seen through the eyes of a participant, so too notions of
identity and imagery.[41] This observation might especially apply in the circumstance where medical or other disabilities have not impeded her intellectual
and physical routines.

Then there is the issue of time to consider. William Shakespeare famously
reported that "all the world's a stage / And all the men and women merely
players," followed by his description of the "seven ages" of one's life. The
life Jane lives in is his number five, "full of wise saws and modern instances
and so plays his part." He would have made a good sociologist for offering
up a framework—seven stages of life—with observations on the behavior of
each. Today, students of life's stages still do the same, useful for our case
study. Recall that Chris Gilleard and Paul Higgs offered two explanations
for how people approach their social structuring in later life. Like Jane, their
examples demonstrate that seniors make a break from prior uses of their time,
working for a salary or raising children, while they still have their cognitive
wits about them and sufficient health—what Gilleard and Higgs call the
"third age" (i.e., translation for Shakespeare's fifth "age").[42] They were not
alone in defining a new age for postwork seniors made evident by how they
allocate their time and activities.[43]

The first two observers note that sociologists and other students of seniors
still do not know how they spend their time—an objective to explore in our
case study of Jane—although they argue that the youthful experiences of
Jane's cohort, baby boomers, shaped what they did: anti–Vietnam War and
the civil rights movement protests, sexual liberation, self-help initiatives in
the 1980s, and continuing self-identification as youthful, thereby in the process confusing the definition of old age in the twenty-first century.[44] They
suggest boomers are not clear as to whether they identify as a cohort; Jane
does not. They point out that only in the United States is there such a clear
delineation of a group as boomers, because elsewhere there were not specific
intense surges in births as occurred in the United States between 1946 and
1964. Marketing to that American generation led to its identification as a
cohort; however, Jane and her circle of friends do not identify that way. They
identify weakly with a nebulous sort of generational divide between their own
parents and their own children, the latter now in their late thirties or early
forties. What these two observers point out about Jane's cohort, confirmed
by how she uses her time, is that "the cultural capital of the third age derives

from the effective use of leisure," which another sociologist described as the "busy ethic," marked by a focus on activity, exercise, travel, dining out, and attention to physical and medical care.[45] To put a fine point on the matter of Jane's use of time, "work and leisure have become disconnected." Cultural capital (from Jane) flows more powerfully from the use and quality of individual leisure time than from what work is done or how money is earned.[46]

Her opportunities for personal choice are augmented, but also influenced, by her education, experiences, and financial stability. If Shakespeare were writing his play *As You Like It* in the 2000s instead of around 1600, he might have defined her stage "both by the continuities of choice and the discontinuity of old age."[47] Scientists and sociologists conclude, as does Jane, that when formulating plans for a postwork "retirement," she and members of her cohort recognize that there are specific behaviors required in order to experience a positive "aging process." The greatest of these is to remain "socially engaged," and in her world that often means the extensive use of intellectual—information-centered—uses of her time.[48] Like sociologists, economists want to understand how her generation spends its time and lament the lack of hard data, which our case study helps to provide in a small way.[49] What is known about seniors is based on pre-COVID-19 behaviors, including how much time they spend reading, watching television, and socializing.[50] Jane's experience suggests allocations of time roughly the same before and after the pandemic began affecting people's activities, but with more face-to-face activities now absorbed into greater uses of the internet. Additional studies will be required to affirm that observation.

Jane's case demonstrates that information-handling skills gained in the workplace at the front end of her adult life, probably also as a full-time mother with her trips to public libraries with her daughters, then back in the workforce after the arrival of PCs, the internet, and smartphones, could be and were applied in retirement. As humor and retiree website comments reiterate, life beyond work is a continuation of activities but with fewer "bosses."[51] Seniors are routinely found to be happier than younger people for many reasons.[52] Being in charge of their time and destinies brings joy. Empirical studies on the role of joy suggest so; humor documents that one often has to wait until retirement to implement that reality.[53]

Jane's experience suggests that a positive human-information relationship is complicated, yet achievable, and can be managed and directed toward purposeful activity. She chose information as her primary tool with which to craft her postwork life. Imagining an alternative path, almost any activity one can imagine for a senior to do requires information. Nursing home residents often play card games that arguably do not require the infusion of additional information, say, from the internet, but other residents would prefer hearing a lecture by a retired professor or a community leader. But Jane chose information as her tool to shape her activities. That offers up the possibility that demarcations of salaried employment/retired epochs in human life are artificial. Her case suggests there is a continuum at work. She has applied cooking practices, for example, since she was in 4-H as a preteen. Jane has commented that many of the cooking and household practices she still carries out were taught to her by both her mother and the home economist running the 4-H programs in her community nearly three-quarters of a century ago, respectfully still "Mrs." Virginia Crigler, who a half century after her death is still discussed by women now in their seventies as having taught them how to use cooking and homemaking information, applying scientific methods of information handling.[54]

Coming full circle to where we started, with Clifford Geertz's admonitions to link one's behavior to a social culture, like he suggested happens across entire societies, one can come to understand that "a people's culture exposes their normalness without reducing their particularity."[55] Jane reflects the behaviors, rituals, and aspirations of her White middle-class American contemporaries, but at the same time does so in her particular way. These twin ideas make her more accessible, better understood, while adding a specific building block in the construction of Geertz's concept of a culture. The approach allows us to interpret Jane's motivations and actions, activities that are both linked to, yet distinct enough within, the context of a culture, of an information ecosystem. Jane's activities demonstrate "how cultural forms find articulation," to borrow from Geertz's insight.[56] For example, Jane continues to behave in her postsalaried work period of life as if still in an office, such as by identifying with a professional way of living, even establishing subconsciously her self-worth in terms shaped by modern concepts of what constitutes activities of an educated person, their use of today's information tools, and the time-defined routines of salaried work.[57]

We began this chapter with a salute to the authority of grandmothers; this was not a casual or humorous slide into our discussion but instead a signal respected by anthropologists that Jane navigates through her world facing such realities as power, change, faith, work, interests, authority, love, religion, and prestige among others. Many of these issues were only touched on here; a fuller biography of Jane would require filling in more details, but our case study suggests the power of a deep dive into one instance, giving us insight about broader cultural behavior by interpreting a few actions of one person. In the end, the links identified through applying our approach to the study of information ecosystems and infrastructures makes a contribution to the broader anthropological interests in what comprises a culture, a society, and how these are held together.

As to the methodology proposed at the start of this chapter for understanding better how seniors handle information, its starting hypotheses is affirmed. The method used to study the use and management of information in large government agencies and corporations and among professions and groups of people interested in a specific discipline or topic can assist in helping us to understand what seniors do. Of course, we picked a sweet spot—people in their seventies—a cohort experiencing good health and who have been out of their professions long enough to develop other interests but not so long out that they abandoned work practices drawn from their careers. As they age, as their numbers increase, and as medical developments extend their quality of life, more people will probably live the way Jane and her cohort do. Asked if she will change her behavior in years to come as her physical and cognitive abilities diminish, she responded unequivocally: "I'm going to do these things as long as I can." A business management expert who lived and worked into his nineties, W. Edwards Deming, spoke of the same power of "constancy of purpose."[58] He taught young people in their forties and fifties of its effectiveness. Japan awards an annual management prize in his name.[59]

Jane probably does not know about Deming, but she does take note of what active older adults do and their contributions to society. Long gone are the days when women her age focused solely on family affairs, although these remain important topics of interest: "There is so much to engage with, because there is a lot going on that interests me. I am so busy that I cannot get everything done that I need to." When asked what always remains to be "done," she pointed to several books yet to be read checked out from her public library and dealing with World War II, additional episodes of *The Crown* to view, and time to read more news stories, all while CNN or PBS broadcasts through her countertop TV. Deming had the same complaints but by the end of his life understood the limits of human energy. Jane is still pushing her physical boundaries.[60]

## NOTES

1. An AARP survey of grandparents conducted in 2018 reported that over half of grandparents saw themselves as sources of wisdom and transmitters of family heritage, culture, and history to their relatives and perceived that other individuals saw them as "valued elders." A third saw themselves as teachers to the next generation or as mentors and as "conveyors of family legacy," P. David and B. Nelson-Kakulla, *2018 Grandparents Today National Survey: General Population Report* (Washington, DC: AARP Research, April 2019).

2. For examples, see S. L. Brown and W. D. Manning, "Family Boundary Ambiguity and the Measurement of Family Structure: The Significance of Cohabitation,"

*Demography* 46 (2009): 85–101; M. J. Cox and B. Paley, "Families as Systems," *Annual Review of Psychology* 48 (1997): 243–267; L. M. Padilla-Walker, S. M. Coyne, and A. M. Fraser, "Getting a High-Speed Family Connection: Associations between Family Media Use and Family Connection," *Family Relations* 61, no. 3 (2012): 426–440; H. Russell Bernard, *Research Methods in Anthropology: Qualitative and Quantitative Approaches* (Lanham, MD: Rowman and Littlefield, 2018): 83–144, 196–253, 323–353.

3. A. Berenguer, J. Goncalves, S. Hosio, D. Ferreira, T. Anagnostopoulos, and V. Kostakos, "Are Smartphones Ubiquitous?: An In-Depth Survey of Smartphone Adoption by Seniors," *IEEE Consumer Electronics Magazine* 6, no. 1 (January 2017): 104–110.

4. M. Anderson and A. Perrin, "Tech Adoption Climbs among Older Adults," Pew Research Center, May 17, 2017, https://www.pewresearch.org/internet/2017/05/17/tech-adoption-climbs-among-older-adults/.

5. R. S. Jefferson, "More Seniors Are Embracing Technology. But Can They Use It? UCSD Researchers Suggest Asking Them," *Forbes*, June 28, 2019, https://www.forbes.com/sites/robinseatonjefferson/2019/06/28/more-seniors-are-embracing-technology-but-can-they-use-it-ucsd-researchers-suggest-asking-them/#1e43fe832323.

6. I. R. Jones, M. Hyde, C. R. Victor, R. D. Wiggins, C. Gilleard, and P. Higgs, *Ageing in a Consumer Society: From Passive to Active Consumption in Britain* (Bristol, UK: Policy Press, 2008).

7. A. W. Geiger, "Most Americans—Especially Millennials—Say Libraries Can Help Them Find Reliable, Trustworthy Information," Pew Research Center, August 30, 2017, https://www.pewresearch.org/fact-tank/2017/08/30/most-americans-especially-millennials-say-libraries-can-help-them-find-reliable-trustworthy-information/.

8. W. A. Wiegand, *Part of Our Lives: A People's History of the American Public Library* (New York: Oxford University Press, 2015).

9. C. Geertz, *The Interpretation of Culture: Selected Essays* (New York: Basic Books, 1973), 3–30, quoted material, 4–5.

10. P. Higgs and C. Gilleard, *Rethinking Old Age: Theorising the Fourth Age* (London: Palgrave, 2015), 10–12. The first two are childhood and early adulthood.

11. Upon being informed that she was a member of that cohort, Jane's reaction reflected the enthusiasm of her age group: "Yay!"

12. Hobbies and information have been the subject of growing interest and debate, with attention often centered on amateur versus professionalism. The more serious one took a hobby, the more it was labeled "serious leisure," with the word leisure often ill-defined but clearly activity for which one was not being paid as an employee. For an introduction to the debate, see A. M. Cox, B. Griffin, and J. Hartel, "What Everybody Knows: Embodied Information in Serious Leisure," *Journal of Documentation* 73, no. 3 (2017): 386–406; R. Savolainen, *Everyday Information Practices: A Social Phenomenological Perspective* (Lanham, MD: Scarecrow, 2008); R. A. Stebbins, *Amateurs, Professionals, and Serious Leisure* (Montreal, QC: McGill-Queen's Press-MQUP, 1992).

13. I have explained the differences and documented the debate elsewhere: J. W. Cortada, *Information and the Modern Corporation* (Cambridge, MA: MIT Press, 2011); J. W. Cortada, *All the Facts: A History of Information in the United States since 1870* (New York: Oxford University Press, 2016), 1–10; J. W. Cortada, Building Blocks of Society: History, Information Ecosystems and Infrastructures (Lanham, MD: Rowman and Littlefield, 2021); L. Floridi, *Information: A Very Short Introduction* (Oxford: Oxford University Press, 2010).

14. A central theme of Cortada, *Building Blocks of Society*, but see also its bibliographic citations.

15. F. Webster, *Theories of the Information Society*, 3rd ed. (London: Routledge, 2006); Y. Benkler, *The Wealth of Networks: How Social Production Transforms Markets and Freedom* (New Haven, CT: Yale University Press, 2006); R. Subramanian and E. Katz, eds., *The Global Flow of Information: Legal, Social, and Cultural Perspectives* (New York: New York University Press, 2011); M. Castells, *Communication Power* (Oxford: Oxford University Press, 2013), and for a short, tightly constructed discussion, see M. Buckland, *Information and Society* (Cambridge, MA: MIT Press, 2017).

16. For my most recent comments, see Cortada, *Building Blocks of Society.*

17. This is becoming very relevant in a study I am conducting on how information changed over the past 150 years: J. W. Cortada, "Discovering Information: How It Evolved in Modern Times" (forthcoming).

18. Cortada, *All the Facts*; information studies scholar Jenna Hartel has studied extensively the role of information and cooking and as leisure activity, for examples see J. Hartel, "Serious Leisure," in *Theories of Information Behavior: A Researcher's Guide*, ed. K. Fisher, S. Erdelez, and L. McKechnie (Medford, NJ: Information Today, 2005), 313–317, which includes an extensive bibliographic discussion, "Information Activities and Resources in an Episode of Gourmet Cooking," *Information Research* 12, no. 1 (October 2006); "Leisure and Hobby Information and Its Users," in *Encyclopedia of Library and Information Sciences*, 3rd ed., ed. J. D. McDonald and M. Levine-Clark (New York: Taylor and Francis, 2011), 3263–3274, and "An Interdisciplinary Platform for Information Behavior Research in the Liberal Arts Hobby," *Journal of Documentation* 70, no. 5 (2014): 945–962.

19. J. W. Cortada, *All the Facts; IBM: The Rise and Fall and Reinvention of a Global Icon* (Cambridge, MA: MIT Press, 2019), and *Building Blocks of Society.*

20. G. E. Allen, *Life Science in the Twentieth Century* (Cambridge: Cambridge University Press, 1975); S. J. Gould, *The Structure of Evolutionary Theory* (Cambridge, MA: Belknap Press of Harvard University Press, 2002); L. M. Magner, *A History of the Life Sciences*, 3rd ed. (New York: Marcel Dekker, 2002); J. Sapp, *Genesis: The Evolution of Biology* (New York: Oxford University Press, 2003).

21. I. Dilman, "Psychology and Human Behavior: Is There a Limit to Psychological Explanation?," *Philosophy* 75 (2000): 183–201; J. Kari and J. Hartel, "Information and Higher Things in Life: Addressing the Pleasurable and the Profound in Information Science," *Journal of the American Society for Information Science and Technology* 58, no. 8 (2007): 1131–1147; M. E. P. Seligman and M. Csikazentmihalyi, "Positive Psychology: An Introduction," *American Psychologist* 55, no. 1 (2000): 514.

22. For the idea of "flow," in which one involved surfing the internet finds pleasure in their total involvement in the activity, see H. Chen, R. T. Wigand, and M. Nilan, "Exploring Web Users' Optimal Flow Experiences," *Information Technology and People* 13, no. 4 (2000): 263–281.

23. C. S. Ross, "Finding without Seeking: The Information Encounter in the Context of Reading for Pleasure," *Information Processing and Management* 36, no. 6 (1999): 783–799.

24. Which is seen as transcending traditional discipline and professional boundaries, S. Gibbs and R. Linley, "'A Bit of a Mess?': Training and Education for Information Workers in the Voluntary Sector," *Education for Information* 18 (2000): 155–167.

25. In modern times, but still over three-quarters of a century ago, this was pointed out by A. H. Maslow, "A Theory of Human Motivation," *Psychological Review* 50, no. 4 (1943): 370–396, and more fully in *Motivation and Personality* (New York: Harper and Brothers, 1954).

26. Crossroads Community Farm, https://crossroadscommunityfarm.com/, accessed August 15, 2020.

27. There is a growing body of research around these issues that is both informative and practical to apply. See, for example, R. Salvolainen, "Everyday Life Information Seeking: Approaching Information Seeking in the Context of 'Way of Life,'" *Library and Information Science Research* 17, no. 3 (Summer 1995): 259–294, and his "Information Behavior and Information Practice: Reviewing the 'Umbrella Concepts' of Information-Seeking Studies," *The Library Quarterly* 77, no. 2 (April 2007): 109–132. The latter has an excellent bibliography on the subject.

28. On the differences of vacationing, Cortada, *All the Facts*, 212–218, 309–401.

29. Kari and Hartel, "Information and Higher Things in Life," 1142.

30. Cortada, *Building Blocks of Society.*

31. She reported that her level of confidence in knowing when she is confronting lies or misinformation has increased with age and experience, providing her with a tacit sense of when something should be challenged or probed. If of little interest to her, she ignores the actual or suspected falsehood because it is irrelevant to her. She is not into fighting windmills.

32. A. J. Sellen and R. R. Harper, *The Myth of the Paperless Office* (Cambridge, MA: MIT Press, 2001).

33. Interview with Jane, September 12, 2020.

34. Now writes under the name of Karen Fisher and teaches at the University of Washington.

35. K. E. Pettigrew, "Lay Information Provision in Community Settings: How Community Health Nurses Disseminate Human Services Information to the Elderly," *The Library Quarterly: Information, Community, Policy* 70, no. 1 (January 2000): 47–85, see her bibliography on the lack of studies in the 1980s–1990s, p. 48.

36. Pettigrew, "Lay Information Provision in Community Settings," 76.

37. A behavior shared widely. M. Bakardjieva, *Internet Society: The Internet in Everyday Life* (Thousand Oaks, CA: SAGE, 2005): 98–102.

38. Interview with Jane, September 17, 2020.

39. Recent research by others reaffirms this finding. Higgs and Gilleard, *Rethinking Old Age.*

40. On the benefits of volunteer work for cognitive health, see G. Yannick et al., "Can Volunteering in Later Life Reduce the Risk of Dementia?," *Plos One*, March 16, 2017, https://journals.plos.org/plosone/article?id=10.1371/journal.pone.0173885.

41. This idea is beginning to receive attention among scholars. Higgs and Gilleard, *Rethinking Old Age*, 11–12.

42. C. Gilleard and P. Higgs, "The Third Age and the Baby Boomers," *International Journal of Ageing and Later Life* 2, no. 2 (2002): 13–30.

43. The modern conversation on this issue was begun by P. Laslett, *A Fresh Map of Life: The Emergence of a Third Age* (London: Weidenfeld and Nicolson, 1989).

44. Gilleard and Higgs, "The Third Age and the Baby Boomers," 19.

45. For first quote, Gilleard and Higgs, "The Third Age and the Baby Boomers," 25; for second quote, D. J. Ekerdt, "The Busy Ethic: Moral Continuity between Work and Retirement," *The Gerontologist* 26 (1986): 239–244.

46. Gilleard and Higgs, "The Third Age and the Baby Boomers," 25.

47. Gilleard and Higgs, "The Third Age and the Baby Boomers," 26.

48. For measures of that use of time, see R. Krantz-Kent and J. Stewart, "How Do Older Americans Spend Their Time?," *Monthly Labor Review* (May 2007): 8–26; J. P. Robinson and G. Y. Godbey, *Time for Life: The Surprising Ways Americans Spend Their Time* (University Park: The Pennsylvania State University Press, 1997).

49. Krantz-Kent and Stewart, "How Do Older Americans Spend Their Time?," 8–26.

50. Krantz-Kent and Stewart, "How Do Older Americans Spend Their Time?" In most instances relies on well over a decade old data.

51. Senior humor websites, such as Kelly Roper, "20 Funny Jokes about Turning 60," Love to Know, accessed July 26, 2021, https://seniors.lovetoknow.com/Turning_60_Jokes; "The Best Corny Jokes (Great Jokes for Senior Citizens)," Suddenly Senior, accessed July 26, 2021, https://www.suddenlysenior.com/tag/jokes/; but also closed Facebook retiree sites, such as for retirees from IBM, GM, and other corporations, open only to fellow retirees.

52. C. Peterson, W. Ruch, U. Beermann, N. Park, and M. E. P. Seligman, "Strengths of Character, Orientation to Happiness, and Life Satisfaction," *The Journal of Positive Psychology* 2, no. 3 (2007): 149–156; volunteering, I. Saz-Gil, A. I. Gil-Lacruz, and M. Gil-Lacruz, "Active Aging and Happiness: European Senior Citizen Volunteers," *Sociologia* 51, no. 3 (2019): 290–312; and by a social psychologist, K. Esty, *Eightysomethings: A Practical Guide to Letting Go, Aging Well, and Finding Unexpected Happiness* (New York: Skyhorse, 2019).

53. M. Cabanac, "Pleasure and Joy, and Their Role in Human Life," in *Creating the Productive Workplace*, ed. D. Clements-Croome (Oxon, UK: Taylor and Francis, 2006), 3–13; D. A. Hershey, J. M. Jacobs-Lawson, and K. A. Neukam, "Influences of Age and Gender on Workers' Goals for Retirement," *International Journal on Aging and Human Development* 55, no. 2 (2002): 163–179; E. Calvo, K. Haverstick, and S. A. Sass, "Gradual Retirement, Sense of Control, and Retirees' Happiness," *Research on Aging* 31, no. 1 (2009): 112–135; R. A. Easterlin, "Happiness of Women and Men

in Later Life: Nature, Determinants, and Prospects," in *Advances in Quality-of-Life Theory and Research*, ed. M. J. Sirgy, D. Rahtz, and A. C. Samli (Dordrecht, Germany: Springer, 2003), 13–25.

54. Cortada, *Building Blocks of Society*, 131–179.

55. Geertz, *The Interpretation of Culture*, 14.

56. Geertz, *The Interpretation of Culture*, 17.

57. These are descriptions of her motives and behaviors that seemed alien to her, as not consciously embraced by her, but obvious to an observer.

58. W. E. Deming, *Out of the Crisis* (Cambridge, MA: MIT Center for Advanced Engineering Study, 1982), 28, 83.

59. For the official description of the Deming Prize by the Union of Japanese Scientists and Engineers, see "Deming Prize," Union of Japanese Scientists and Engineers, accessed August 16, 2020, https://www.juse.or.jp/deming_en/.

60. Not discussed in this chapter is how she takes care of her physical self with activities informed through scientifically reliable insights. She is careful with her diet and understands much of the new scientific and chemical information informing current culinary practices and their relationship to exercise. In her early seventies, she would walk two to three miles per day; at the time of this study, she had nearly doubled that distance. Results included higher levels of energy, a bit of weight reduction, but also a growing desire to do more things, many of which involve her information ecosystem.

# Chapter Four

# AARP and Its Competitors as Information Providers

## William Aspray

The worst thing is that, soon after your 50th birthday, you get The Letter. You older individuals know what letter I'm talking about: It's the one inviting you to join the AARP, which stands for "American Association of Retired Persons Who Are Always Ahead of You in Line Asking If They Get a Discount."[1]

—Dave Barry

Obama, on his own 50th birthday, told a 2011 campaign fund-raiser audience that "by the time I wake up, I'll have an email from AARP asking me to call President Obama and tell him to protect Medicare."[2]

—Julie Pace

The nation's 50+ population is an extremely diverse lot, socially, culturally, economically, even generationally. How can one organization unite some 38 million people with so many different points of view? The short answer, given by AARP itself and based on their member surveys, is that people join for the products and discounts, and renew for the advocacy and social missions, as well as the information and publications.[3]

—Christine Day

There are numerous places where older Americans go to find information related to their everyday lives. The main focus of this chapter is on one such organization: AARP. It is the largest membership organization in the United States, outside of the Catholic Church, and is the subject of the first three sections of this chapter, covering its history and its political and informational activities.[4] However, not everyone is satisfied with the AARP, and it has generated a number of competitors. We describe its main competitors in the next three sections, based on whether they are primarily a political organization, a religious organization, or a combination of political service and membership benefit organization (as AARP itself is).[5] We close with some general conclusions.

The organizations studied in this chapter are primarily focused on issues of particular interest to older Americans. These organizations reach a large portion of Americans over age fifty.[6] There are low barriers to membership in these organizations, and the information they provide is made available for free or for a small membership fee.[7] In many cases, the quality of the information is high, and it addresses not only political issues but more generally the wide spectrum of issues of concern to American seniors.

All the organizations discussed here have Social Security and Medicare as principal topics. This is not surprising. Older Americans need to know how to navigate these large government bureaucracies and understand what to expect in terms of government-provided income and health care coverage and costs. Both systems are complex. With Social Security, for example, the payout varies from person to person, dependent on lifetime earnings and age of retirement. With Medicare, the basic health coverage is not sufficient for most people, so individuals have to decide about add-ons such as drug and vision coverage and other Medicare supplementary programs. Given that Social Security and Medicare are expensive programs whose financial solvency is uncertain as the percentage of the population who are elderly continues to grow, these programs are subject to regular political scrutiny, and older Americans want to know about prospective changes to these lifeline programs. However, there are also a number of other issues that concern people as they grow older, including maintaining a high quality of life, deciding where to live, interacting with younger generations, leaving a legacy, and many more. Several of the organizations discussed next, including AARP (formerly the American Association of Retired Persons), the Association of Mature American Citizens (AMAC), and Christ Above Politics (CAP), go beyond Social Security and Medicare to address this wider range of issues of concern to older Americans.

By examining the largest of these organizations (AARP), we can get a better sense of the range of issues these organizations address. Textbox 4.1 provides a sample of the issues that AARP covers in its publications directed at its millions of members.[8]

While all these issues are covered by AARP, and most of the organizations discussed here cover political issues, issues such as work, housing, poverty, and law are covered by only a few of these organizations.

## TEXTBOX 4.1. ISSUES
## ADDRESSED BY AARP (EXAMPLES)

- Health and Wellness
  - Specific conditions and treatments: COVID, hearing loss, cancer, salmonella in the food supply, flu shots, hand sanitizers, hearing loss, telehealth
  - Healthy living: weight loss, exercise, cooking, diet, lifestyle changes to prevent diseases, meditation, anxiety, stress
  - Health insurance, including Medicare
  - Staying sharp: puzzles, games, information about brain health
- Family Caregiving
  - Local resources, information about Alzheimer's, adult day care, elder law resources, support groups, evaluating nursing homes, home health aides and COVID, problems of isolation, medical diagnoses and treatments, costs, insurance coverage for home health care
- Social Security and Medicare
  - Eligibility, differences between original Medicare and its alternatives, making choices of plans, things not covered, medical and insurance vocabulary, when and how to claim Social Security and how it affects benefits, estimating benefits, relation to SSI and SSDI, ability to work while on Social Security
- Work and Jobs
  - Job search, working when older, working from home, work-life balance, age discrimination, career change, available education opportunities, challenges of perceived overqualification, perceptions about technical skills and other skill sets, harnessing experience and other assets, starting a business
- Having Fun
  - Entertainment, games, quizzes, sweepstakes, travel
- Housing
  - Safety, affordability, community living, aging in place, varieties of assisted living, making decisions about other places to live, property taxes
- Driver Safety
- Poverty and Hunger
- Legal Issues Faced by the Elderly
  - Elder abuse, legislation

- Political Action
  - Current legislation that may affect older Americans, AARP lobbying activities, how an individual can become involved
- Information for Specific Communities
  - Asian, Black, Hispanic, LGBTQ, Native American

## AARP YESTERDAY AND TODAY

Because AARP is the largest of these organizations, and the one these other general member organizations react to, we will consider AARP first. It was founded in 1958 by Ethel Percy Andrus and Leonard Davis.[9] Andrus was a school principal in California who, concerned about the living conditions of retired teachers, created the National Retired Teachers Association (NRTA) in 1947. Davis was an insurance executive who founded the Colonial Penn family of insurance and related companies. When they came together in 1958 to form the American Association of Retired Persons, NRTA was merged into AARP. The reason for the new organization was that other people over age fifty who were not teachers wanted access to the NRTA programs addressing economic concerns and health insurance needs. Over time, AARP broadened its membership requirements to allow anyone over fifty to be a member, not just retirees; at that time, they stopped using the full name, which included the word *retired*, and simply used the letters AARP as their official name. Indeed, today, only about half of the members are retired, and a much smaller percentage are retired teachers.

It should be recognized how large an operation AARP is. Current membership is approximately thirty-eight million, which makes it the second-largest membership nonprofit organization in the United States—after the Catholic Church and roughly equal in size to the membership of the American Automobile Association. The annual operating revenue is more than $1.5 billion, with more than $900 million coming from its affiliation with commercial service and product providers who use the AARP name and marketing muscle. The other major revenue resources for AARP are membership dues and selling of advertising in its publications and other products. AARP is widely regarded as a highly effective lobbying organization in the United States, focused on policies that affect older Americans.

Since its founding, AARP has been a complex organization. It provides information and programs that help older Americans live richer and more productive lives, but it also has an enormous business that sells insurance and financial products[10] as well as a very active lobbying effort at the national and state levels. At least for some older Americans, AARP's involvement in purchased services and lobbying represents a conflict of interest with its other activities to enrich the lives of older Americans, and a number of members have resigned their memberships or chose not to join AARP because of these conflicts of interest. (These issues are described in more detail later.)

Disaffection with AARP over conflicts of interest with its commercial joint ventures in insurance and health products was especially acute from the late 1960s into the 1980s, but these concerns remain salient today. The initial products offered in the late 1950s and early 1960s by NRTA and AARP were a good deal for members—often the only such products available to them. For example, Davis designed a mail-order health insurance plan that was heavily subscribed to by retired teachers, and in 1958 Andrus and Davis created the first mail-order pharmacy service, Retired Persons' Services.

However, things changed for the worse after Andrus died in 1967 and during the first two decades following her death, when Davis and his colleagues at the Colonial Penn companies were in complete control over the activities of AARP.[11] For example, AARP was subject to highly negative investigative reporting by *Consumer Reports* in 1976 and in 1978 by Andy Rooney on the widely watched television program *60 Minutes*.[12] They found, for example, that AARP's health insurance offerings—all of which were being provided by Colonial Penn—had very high expenses associated with them. These insurance sales made Davis a multimillionaire and Colonial Penn one of the most profitable companies in America while paying out at noncompetitive rates on insurance claims made by AARP members.

In the 1990s, AARP continued to come under scrutiny. High-profile congressional hearings were held in 1994, led by Senator Alan Simpson (R-WY), looking into AARP's tax-exempt status.[13] These investigations led to AARP paying fines to the IRS (over unrelated business income) totaling more than $200 million between 1994 and 1999 and a fine of more than $5 million to the US Postal Service for using its lower tax-exempt mailing rates when sending out mailings for its insurance and other commercial products.

These problems began to be rectified in the 1980s, however, when AARP established the practice of competitive bidding to offer its insurance and financial products and services,[14] but even today there are concerns expressed about the relationship between AARP's nonprofit activities and its offering of commercially sponsored products and services. This issue is likely always to be present because AARP's business model is primarily to fund its main activities through revenue from these products and services, not through charitable donations.[15]

These concerns have continued until recent years. For example, in 2011, a group of House Republicans created a report entitled "Behind the Veil: The

AARP America Doesn't Know."[16] In 2018 and 2019, there were class-action suits over AARP's for-profit Medicare supplementary insurance business.[17] However, unlike in the Colonial Penn–dominated years, AARP's health insurance plans today are highly competitive. For example, AARP's Medicare Supplement plans, offered by UnitedHealthcare (the largest health care provider in the United States), are widely listed as among the best plans available to seniors.[18]

## AARP AS A POLITICAL ORGANIZATION

While American seniors are widely interested in having affordable, quality health care available to them, they are not of one mind on which policies to implement to achieve that goal. AARP lobbying on health care has taken a center-left approach, which has received criticism from both conservatives and liberals.[19] As one scholar has noted, "AARP is sufficiently pragmatic in its politics to be both a valued coalition partner and an adversary to groups on both the right and the left."[20] Conservatives are concerned that AARP supports socialized medicine. Liberals are disappointed that AARP has not lobbied strenuously for a single-payer health care system. These criticisms have arisen at numerous times in AARP's history. AARP notes the challenge in finding the right political positions to take for its members but has settled on a small number of key issues to address: "AARP represents the needs of nearly 38 million members with lifestyles and political views as diverse as any group in the United States. Developing public policy recommendations that serve such diversity is a formidable task. We concentrate on the issues most important to those in the 50+ community as they age: economic security; health care; access to affordable, quality long-term care; creating and maintaining livable communities; consumer protections; caregiving; and ensuring that our democracy works better for all."[21]

In two major respects, AARP is a traditionally liberal political institution.[22] First, it has lobbied for federal government spending in a number of areas: health care programs, expansions of Medicare and Medicaid, food stamp programs, housing assistance, and gerontological research. Second, it has lobbied for enhanced government regulation in several areas: age discrimination, rights of the disabled, private retirement plans, funeral practices, and drug pricing.[23]

Consider three examples of AARP lobbying efforts. In 1993, President Clinton proposed a health security plan to fix a lack of affordable health care for the middle class and provide access to health care for the lower class, which was intended to be a moderate proposal and a compromise between the market-based reforms proposed by the political right and the regulation-based reforms of the political left. The population was largely favorable, moderate Republicans agreed to work with Clinton, and the AARP supported this plan. However, the success of the Republicans in the midterm elections of 1994 killed any hope of passing legislation that looked like Clinton's plan.[24] In 2005, AARP was on the winning side when it worked to thwart President George W. Bush's plan to reform Social Security, including the call for investing some of individuals' Social Security contributions in personal retirement accounts.[25] In 2010, AARP supported President Obama's Patient Protection and Affordable Care Act (popularly known as Obamacare), which was passed with some compromises, though Republicans have been dismantling it piecemeal since 2016.[26]

AARP also produces scorecards that track state-level progress on long-term services and support for older adults. These scorecards enable policy makers and others to "benchmark performance, measure progress, identify areas for improvement, and improve lives."[27] AARP's lobbyists are regarded as among the most powerful in Washington.[28]

Every two years, AARP publishes a policy book[29] and a companion priorities book.[30] These two books define how AARP intends to set its policy (both process and general beliefs) and present specific positions the organization is taking consistent with these policies. The current policy books contain separate chapters on policies concerning government integrity and civic engagement, budget and the economy, taxation, savings and retirement security, employment, low-income assistance, health, long-term services and support, livable communities, utilities (telecom, energy, and other services), and financial services and consumer products. Priorities concern shoring up Social Security financially, making it easier for older workers to find jobs, making the health care system more affordable and more accessible, and making housing and transportation work better for seniors. It is beyond the scope of this chapter to discuss these policies and priorities in detail. The positions, however, are consistent with AARP's long-term center-left orientation. For example, these policy documents show that AARP is an ardent supporter of the Affordable Care Act.

AARP also runs a public policy institute that does public policy research, analysis, and development.[31] It employs experts in such areas as financial and health security. It jointly runs the Center to Champion Nursing in America with the Robert Wood Johnson Foundation. It writes reports, such as "Caregiving in the US 2020,"[32] which was jointly produced with the National Alliance for Caregiving. It holds events, such as webinars, to bring together experts to discuss issues of relevance to seniors, such as caregiving and innovations in affordable housing.[33] It collects data on issues of interest to seniors and provides an interactive visualization tool that lets members explore the data either at a national level or for any particular state.[34]

AARP maintains a web page on politics and society linked to its home page.[35] This politics and society page contains a mixture of neutral news articles under categories titled Government and Elections and Events and History (e.g., a comparison of the positions held by Trump and Biden in their presidential campaigns, or the latest news about the spread of COVID-19) as well as a set of advocacy articles under the titles Advocacy and Government Watch. The latter is where one will find letters from AARP to legislators and regulators advocating on behalf of its members' interests.[36] Textbox 4.2 gives examples of specific AARP lobbying efforts.

---

### TEXTBOX 4.2.   SPECIFIC AARP ADVOCACY ISSUES, AS OF SEPTEMBER 2020 (SAMPLE)

- Import of prescription drugs from Canada
- Legislation against price gouging by drug companies
- Making it easier for seniors to vote in elections
- Urging the postmaster general to maintain services to enable the timely delivery of medications and ballots
- Improvements in the laws about nursing homes (e.g., better testing, protective gear, virtual visitation, greater transparency and account-ability)

---

Of critical importance to AARP's political activity is the involvement of its members in advocacy efforts. At the bottom of its landing page (www.aarp. org), AARP has a link for people who want to get involved in these efforts. About five million members write or call legislators each year in response to AARP's call, and some seventeen thousand make visits to legislator offices.[37] AARP's power is not only in its large membership but also in its almost universal (98%) brand recognition in the United States.[38]

## AARP AS AN INFORMATION ORGANIZATION

We have discussed AARP's activities in the advocacy area. That material is a blend of persuasive writing, arguing its case for particular positions on specific issues, and political education (e.g., laying out the positions of

Democratic and Republican presidential candidates without advocating for either). However, AARP's informational activities are much broader than that; the goal is to provide information about any topic of wide interest to people over age fifty. AARP uses multiple media for this purpose. The AARP website (www.aarp.org) is extremely information rich. But the organization also provides a variety of print publications, email alerts, radio and television programs, and several kinds of in-person events (at least in the time before COVID-19).

AARP has separate web pages for a wide range of topics: coronavirus, health, staying sharp, family caregiving, work and jobs, scams and fraud, retirement, Social Security, travel, money, home and family, entertainment, politics and society, auto, videos, podcasts, games, and food.[39] We won't go through and describe each of them, but let us consider the coronavirus page as an example.[40] It has links to approximately twenty-five articles, ranging over many topics: advertisement of an AARP town hall tele-meeting about the pandemic, the status of vaccine trials, traditions such as Halloween trick-or-treating that are being disrupted by the virus, smartwatches for monitoring your health, and multiple stories about grieving, entertainment while at home, and traveling during the pandemic (on planes, trains, and cruise ships), as well as six inspiring stories of everyday heroes—about caregivers, bus drivers, and sanitation workers. The page also has links to information about COVID-19's connections to twenty-five other topics, such as the 2020 Census, insurance coverage, nursing homes, travel, unemployment, and utilities. Most of these pages have a combination of current events, practical information and guidance, and human-interest stories. It is beyond the scope of this chapter to provide more detailed description and analysis of these pages.

AARP has specific web pages for the Asian, Black, Hispanic, LGBTQ, and Native American communities.[41] For example, on the page for the Hispanic community, there are more than twenty-five articles, ranging from the push for a Latin American national museum to a series of stories about the pandemic as it specifically affects Hispanics, several stories about veterans, and some articles about "diversions" such as recipes, mother-daughter relationships, and cut-flower arrangements.[42]

In addition to the individual web pages for such topics as coronavirus and travel, as mentioned earlier, AARP has grouped together collections of web pages about four overarching topics that are of particular interest to members and given links to them on the bottom of its landing page: health and wellness, Social Security and Medicare, family caregiving, and work and jobs.[43] For example, under the health and wellness category, there are links to separate pages on health conditions and treatments, healthy living, health insurance, and staying sharp.[44] Most of these pages include twenty or more articles. For example, the health conditions and treatments page includes articles about effective face masks, flu shots, various details about the coronavirus, and information about vision problems, hearing loss, and prostate cancer. Some of these articles can also be found on other pages, but AARP repeats them to make it easier for its members interested in a specific topic, such as health and wellness, to readily find all the related articles.

AARP's website also makes it easy to find other information (see figure 4.1). At the bottom of the landing page is a category of links for people who are looking for fun diversions (entertainment, games, quizzes, sweepstakes, and travel) and another category entitled Information for You, intended for readers who have a specific information goal. There are links to AARP in Your City, AARP in Your State, Driver Safety, Fighting for Your Health, Fraud Watch Network, Government Watch, Tax Aide, and Where the AARP Stands.

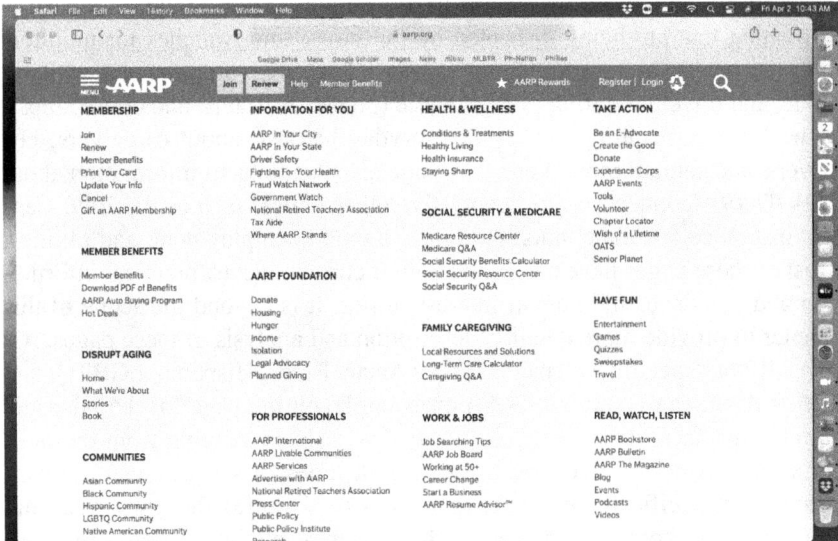

**Figure 4.1. Screenshot of Part of the AARP Home Page.**
William Aspray

In addition to the AARP's information-rich website, the organization publishes and automatically mails to members its monthly bulletin and its bimonthly magazine.[45] There is also an online daily newsletter (*The Daily*) that members can sign up for, which provides a simple list of stories to click on without the layout and design framework provided in *AARP The Bulletin* and *AARP The Magazine*. *AARP The Bulletin* focuses on presenting members with up-to-date news on issues of relevance to them, such as new developments with Medicare or Social Security, relevant pending or passed legislation, or new health issues or scams that might affect seniors.

*AARP The Magazine* has its origins in an earlier AARP publication, *Modern Maturity*, which was first published in 1958. *AARP The Magazine* took its current form in 2002, with a focus on active seniors. It is intended to be inspirational, as well as informative and entertaining, to people of age fifty-plus.[46] Its tagline is "Feel Great. Save Money. Have Fun." There are feature articles, including many profiles of well-known Americans who are still showing a vitality in their later lives. Recent cover stories with this inspiring meme discuss Kevin Costner, Alan Alda, Marlo Thomas, Phil Donahue, Shania Twain, and Annette Bening.[47]

In 2018, AARP launched a new digital newsletter, *Sisters*, targeted at African American women. As one AARP staff member stated, "*Sisters* from AARP is created specifically for Gen X and Boomer black women to offer fashion, health, career, and relationship advice in a fun, relatable voice that speaks to them."[48] AARP has also published on topics of interest to its members—on Medicare, Social Security, yoga, getting a job in later life, and so on—in the popular For Dummies book series.

In addition to the print and online publications, AARP also has a blog, sponsored events, podcasts, videos, radio and television programming, and an online bookstore. The blog includes public policy analyses and advocacy pieces, news releases and other official communications from AARP, and news, feature stories, and practical advice on topics of interest to members, such as work and livable communities.[49] At the time of this analysis, AARP had three active podcasts: *The Perfect Scam*, *Take on Today*, and *Closing the Savings Gap*.[50] Most of the videos available are only about a minute long, like a feature article on television news, on topics such as quarantining of airline passengers and properly cooking frozen food. A few of the videos are as long as ten minutes, for example on back stretching and workouts.[51]

AARP has a weekly radio show, *On the Air*, where individuals who have something interesting to say to seniors are interviewed. These programs are marketed at the state level and appear on local radio stations throughout the country.[52] AARP produces *AARP Live* on RFD-TV, a paid television network that focuses on rural issues.[53] Also, on its website, AARP has a regular feature entitled *TV for Grownups*, which suggests shows to watch and has information about smart televisions and streaming.[54] AARP had an active schedule of local events across the United States prior to the need for social distancing, and currently the events are online, such as a series of couch concerts.[55] AARP also has regularly published books on a number of topics, in the form of print books, e-books, and free downloads, and these books are available at a discount through the AARP bookstore. The bookstore is organized into the following topics: money, work, and retirement; health, food, and cooking; home, family, and caregiving; personal time; technology; and puzzles.[56]

AARP is also a creator of information through research that it conducts. It employs a staff of sixty people who conduct polls, surveys, and research. These researchers carry out three hundred polls or surveys each year and an additional seven hundred studies that involve reviewing relevant literature. Topics of research problems include the role of grandparents as caregivers, the negative portrayal of older people in advertisements, the extent of age discrimination and worker rights, home and community preferences of older adults, and reviews of the literature on brain health.[57]

## POLITICALLY FOCUSED COMPETITOR ORGANIZATIONS

We now turn to the alternatives to AARP. We first consider organizations that are primarily focused on political activities. The 60 Plus Association, founded in 1992 and headquartered in Alexandria, Virginia, describes itself as a "nonpartisan organization working for death tax repeal and advocating for seniors. The organization is also committed to saving Social Security and Medicare, affordable prescription drugs, and lowering energy costs, while adhering to less government, less taxes approach and the Constitution."[58]

The organization's issues page has approximately three hundred stories about political issues of expected interest to its members. Examples are provided in textbox 4.3.

Another page on 60 Plus's website is entitled Saul's News, which contains approximately fifty news stories. Some of its more recently posted news stories include one touting President Trump's record at delivering on his 2016 campaign promises; a story using the 9/11 anniversary as a reminder of the needed vigilance for law and order and a criticism of Biden's platform concerning the riots in America; assertions that the Obama-era FBI spied on the Trump campaign; and a new call for a school voucher program. The 60 Plus Association's website only contains political information, not other kinds of information about health or lifestyle, for example.

Who is involved with the 60 Plus Association? The chairman of the board is Jim Martin, a retired marine who was formerly chief of staff to Senator Edward Gurney (R-FL). Martin was the person who coined the term "the death tax" for the government taxation of estates, and the 60 Plus Association has a web page devoted to this issue. Singer Pat Boone is a spokesperson for the organization, and he has argued against Obamacare on Fox News, for example.[59] In the 2012 presidential election, 60 Plus ran a $3.5 million ad

## TEXTBOX 4.3.   STORIES ON THE
## 60 PLUS ASSOCIATION WEBSITE (SAMPLE)

- Avowing that President Trump will protect Social Security and Medicare
- Speaking out against the Irish tech company Neodron, which they believe is threatening the continuation and growth of telemedicine through its expansive patent infringement claims, and the small US federal agency known as the International Trade Commission, which is taking Neodron's claims seriously
- Speaking in favor of an alliance that is opposing the House's Moving Forward Act, which would extend tax credits to the solar and wind industry for five more years
- Supporting pending health care legislation by two Republican senators (Cassidy and Wicker) addressing surprise medical billing without using government rate setting and price controls[1]
- Proposing expanded access to health savings accounts in upcoming COVID-19 legislation
- Criticizing AARP, CVS, and UnitedHealthcare for increasing prescription drug prices for seniors
- Criticizing House Speaker Nancy Pelosi's proposed legislation that they claim will involve "heavy-handed tactics, confiscatory taxation and retroactive penalties" and lead to "the socialization of the pharmaceutical industry."[2]

### NOTES

1. The proposed bills are S. 1531 STOP Surprise Medical Billing Act and S. 4185 End Surprise Medical Bills for Air Ambulances Act.
2. "Issues," 60Plus: American Association of Senior Citizens, accessed September 16, 2020, https://60plus.org/category/issues/.

campaign that claimed that Obama was going to cut and otherwise restrict Medicare benefits; the *Washington Post* claimed that these ads provided false and misleading information.[60] The main donors to the 60 Plus Association are the conservative billionaire businessmen Charles and David Koch.[61] Other large donations have been made in the past by such organizations as the Center to Protect Patents Rights, the American Petroleum Institute, and the Alliance for America's Future.[62]

In this section, we will also briefly discuss two other organizations, the Seniors Coalition and the United Seniors Association. These two, together with the 60 Plus Association, were all formed primarily for lobbying purposes. Direct-mail entrepreneur Richard Viguerie was involved in the founding of all three of these organizations.[63]

The Seniors Coalition was formed in 1990 as a public advocacy organization to fight the Medicare Catastrophic Coverage Act,[64] but over time it has broadened its scope to include a variety of policy issues related to seniors.[65] The web page highlights its advocacy activities.[66] There are a few benefits, such as discounts on hotel rooms and car rentals, but the number of these offerings pales in comparison to those offered by other seniors organizations. For a while, the spokesperson for the Seniors Coalition was a character named Grandma Green, who traveled across the United States in her RV, the StraightTalk Express.[67] *Mother Jones* magazine described the eighty-two-year-old Flora Green as a grandmother of twenty-seven with a fiery disposition and a toughness from a former job as a debt collector in Utah.[68]

From reading the Seniors Coalition website, it appears to be just another nonprofit serving the broad needs of seniors. However, investigative reporting has shown a darker side to this organization. Its founders were Viguerie and Dan Alexander, a Mobile, Alabama, school board member. The Center for Media and Democracy has reported that Alexander "had been convicted of extorting kickbacks on school construction projects and later served four years of a 12-year prison term. For some of the time Alexander was in prison, he and his wife drew $23,000 a month in 'consulting' fees from the Seniors Coalition while their teenage daughter served as its president."[69] Financing for the Seniors Coalition comes primarily from the Pharmaceutical Research and Manufacturers of America (PhRMA). Thomas Moore served simultaneously as the director of operations for the Seniors Coalition and as director of federal affairs for PhRMA.[70] The Seniors Coalition has been investigated by the New York State Attorney General's Office for fraud and by Congress for mail fraud.[71]

The United Seniors Association was founded in 1991, also as a lobbying organization. It was most active in the period of its founding through 2005. Today, it continues to exist, but it does not have an active website. It is more commonly known today as USANext, which was one of its projects. Like several other organizations, it explicitly calls itself a conservative alternative to AARP. Its primary interests have been in tax cuts, balanced federal budgets, and Social Security privatization.[72] For example, it actively supported President Bush's 2004 efforts to privatize Social Security. It has worked closely with the advertising agency that created the infamous swift boat ads in opposition to John Kerry's presidential bid.[73] Funding appears to come primarily from the pharmaceutical industry, and the lobbying efforts at times have strayed from seniors issues to other conservative causes (e.g., in favor of Arctic drilling and in opposition to gay marriage). The organization was fined more than $500,000 for two misleading mailings. The Center for American Progress has called USANext a "mercenary 'grassroots' group."[74]

AARP has published materials about all three of these politically oriented organizations: the United Seniors Association, the Seniors Coalition, and the 60 Plus Association.[75] AARP's criticisms have included the following:

- While claiming to be nonpartisan, they have only supported Republicans.
- Direct-mail entrepreneur Richard Viguerie has been active in the founding and ongoing activities of these organizations.
- They have been associated with questionable fundraising practices.
- Almost all their funding comes not from membership dues but instead from the pharmaceutical industry, which has a record of using front groups to lobby for its agenda. For example, Martin of 60 Plus worked for Viguerie for four years, and it has been reported that the group's contract with Viguerie's firm enabled it to use 60 Plus's contributor list "in any manner, for any purpose, for its own account" at least until 2003.[76]
- The organization also ran into trouble for using envelopes with official-looking symbols and language that seemed designed to make recipients believe they were urgent government documents.[77]

## RELIGION-FOCUSED COMPETITOR ORGANIZATIONS

There is one major religion-focused organization that represents itself as an alternative to AARP: Christ Above Politics (headquartered in Grapevine, Texas). It describes itself as a members benefits organization for Christians age fifty-plus.[78] CAP was formed to provide an alternative to AARP for Christians who wanted an organization espousing Christian values but who did not want to be actively involved in lobbying or other political activities. It is similar to the other alternatives to AARP in that it espouses conservative values but unlike the others in that it eschews all political activity. It touts itself as "the Christian alternative to AARP" and tells its readers that the organization will help them "save time, money, and improve your life while supporting the body of Christ."[79] Members are asked to attest to a statement of faith.

Where did CAP come from? In 1993, two Chicago men, Billy A. Melvin and Frank D. Nicodem, were upset by articles they were reading in AARP's

*Modern Maturity* magazine, and they decided to create a new organization for Christian seniors. Joined by Roland Johnson, they created a new nonprofit organization that came into operation in 1994 under the name the Christian Association of PrimeTimers (the original source of the acronym CAP).[80] The organization was owned over the years by several media companies (The Total Living Network, Jones Publishing, and JP Media) before it was bought in 2018 by Rene Girard, the owner of Hesed Insurance, one of CAP's service partners, and renamed Christ Above Politics.[81] Its purpose and direction statement indicate that it is a religious organization, not a political one, and that it will not lobby or fund politicians or political parties.

The membership (fifteen dollars per year) pitch calls for members to receive discounts on products and services while supporting Christian businesses and Christian ministries.[82] The organization offers "discounts on an ever growing array of products and services. Financial services. Honest, no-hassle quotes on insurance. A forum to interact with other members around the country. Exclusive articles written by Christians for Christians." It takes a jab at AARP when it notes that it offers insurance from multiple companies, and it asks, "Will AARP pray for you?"[83] Member benefits include business services, eldercare plans and books, a search engine for Christian jobs, PureFlix (a Christian alternative to Netflix), financial services, health care apps and technologies, home warranties, telephone services, insurance services (dental, corporate, health, life, long-term care, medical supplements), magazines (e.g., *Christianity Today*), access to ministry organizations, Christian music (e.g., Soulbreather), discounts on mortgages and movers, car and hotel discounts, and access to a Christian travel agent and travel insurance.[84]

In addition to information provided in connection with these products and services, CAP once had a print newsletter, *CAP Connection*, sent through the mail and running about fifteen pages. Forty percent of the newsletter spelled out member benefits. Each issue had at least one article about products or services of interest to members.[85] The newsletters also included additional ads for Christian businesses, such as Today's Christian Living Online Store, Christian Family Eldercare, and an RV work ministry called SOWERS (Servants on Wheels Ever Ready). There were other feature articles, such as one on National Grandparents' Day of Prayer.[86] Each issue had a page or two of diversions, such as humorous stories, recipes, quotable quotes, or puzzles.

The print newsletter has been replaced by an online monthly newsletter for members. The newsletters contain updated lists of member benefits, information about Bible donations and giveaways, scriptural readings and interpretations, plus a few articles such as one on the treatment of coronavirus.[87]

## MEMBERSHIP-BENEFIT PLUS ADVOCACY ORGANIZATIONS

A third group of seniors organizations that present themselves as alternatives to AARP have both active programs offering products and services to seniors and lobbying efforts. Thus, they are the competitors that are most like AARP in their range of activities. They are unlike the 60 Plus Association, the Seniors Coalition, and the United Seniors Association, described previously, in that the organizations described in this section try to offer tangible member benefits to seniors and not just use their organization for political advocacy. We will explore the largest association in this group, the Association of Mature American Citizens (AMAC), in some detail, followed by more abbreviated coverage of the American Seniors Association (ASA) and the National Association of Conservative Seniors (NAOCS).

The Association of Mature American Citizens was founded in Bohemia, New York, (membership offices now in Florida) in 2007 by Dan Weber, a veteran who had founded a family-run insurance business.[88] According to the AMAC website, "Excessive taxation, out-of-control governmental spending, and increasing interference in the lives of citizens are evidence that our country is going through a period of drastic change—change that is eradicating our traditional values. These concerns, along with a growing recognition that our country's older citizens need more effective advocacy in Washington,

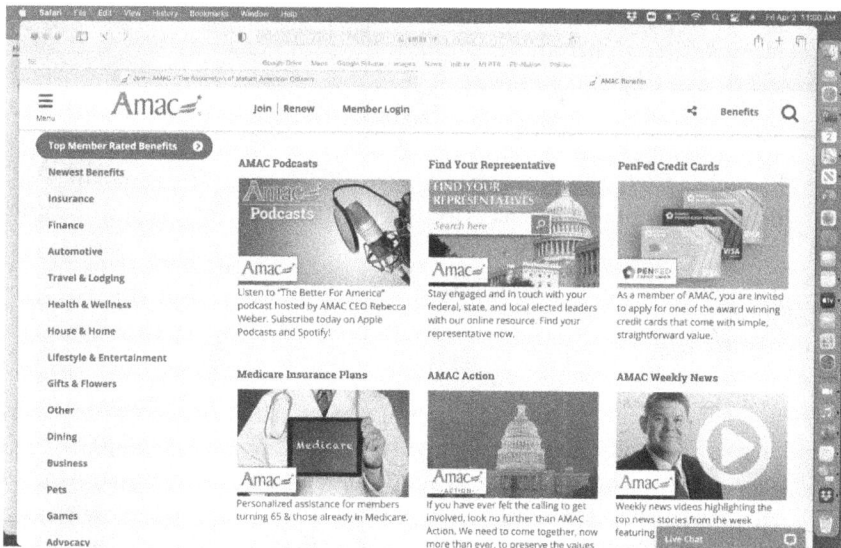

**Figure 4.2.  Screenshot of the AMAC Home Page.**
William Aspray

were driving forces in Dan's 2007 decision to launch AMAC."[89] Like most of these other conservative groups, AMAC explicitly identifies itself as an alternative to AARP.[90]

AMAC provides advice to its members on Medicare (Senior Resources Network), Social Security (Social Security Advisory Services), and financial planning (RoseMark Advisors). It covers active advocacy issues relevant to its members (AMAC Action). It provides consumer benefits to its members, such as credit cards, retail and travel discounts, travel planning, and insurance products (e.g., dental, medical, vision, and prescription plans), and senior living services.[91] AMAC also provides information to its members through its website and social media and through its members-only bimonthly magazine, *AMAC Magazine*.

AMAC's policy activities provide conservative coverage of many of the issues facing older adults: "Concretely, AMAC speaks up for what matters—for Americans' First, Second, Fourth, Sixth, Ninth, Tenth and other constitutional rights, for tradition and moral compass, fiscal responsibility, federal solvency, and accountability in government. AMAC defends the guarantees of social security, Medicare, sanctity of life at all ages, and quality healthcare in the context of limited government, rule of law and a secure nation."[92] Textbox 4.4 lists AMAC's primary policy positions.[93]

In addition to having full-time lobbyists in Washington, AMAC has an ambassador leadership program that organizes members to help the advocacy effort by talking up the organization to other members and prospective mem-

## TEXTBOX 4.4.   AMAC'S PRIMARY POLICY POSITIONS

- Repeal of Obamacare, favoring free-market competition and choice
- Preservation of Social Security and its financial solvency without raising taxes
- Veterans' issues, including access to quality health care, as a national priority
- Pro-life issues
- Support for the Second Amendment
- Reduction in individual and corporate tax rates
- Support for legal immigration with a requirement that immigrants learn English; opposition to illegal immigration, including no benefits for those in the country illegally
- Protection of free enterprise, especially support for small business as an important driver of our economy

bers, giving talks to local civic organizations, getting people to sign AMAC petitions, and helping AMAC to identify policy issues and member services that the organization should address.[94] The delegate program, which aims to have a delegate in each congressional district, enhances advocacy activities at the local level, for example by visiting local congressional offices and holding town hall meetings. Its speakers bureau enlists members as volunteers to speak to seniors groups on issues of interest to AMAC.[95]

AMAC provides information to its members in several forms. Its advocacy information takes two forms. On the AMAC website, the news pull-down menu provides a separate category for advocacy news, apart from the other news it provides to members. The news/advocacy site serves as the primary web page for AMAC Action, the advocacy arm of AMAC. The site provides semiannual activity accounts of the AMAC Action staff, presents news about pending legislation, describes positions that AMAC Action is taking and alliances it has created to support or oppose particular pieces of legislation, and lists AMAC appearances in the media.

The news/politics web page provides stories about current political issues that affect seniors, including Senate races to watch and the latest coronavirus news. The news/veterans' news web page provides news stories about veterans and also has a strong advocacy tone. There is a separate web section for AMAC Action News, which repeats some of the advocacy items mentioned earlier but also gives information about specific political issues of particular interest to AMAC, such as H. R. 856 Physician Pro Bono Care Act and the AMAC Social Security Guarantee.[96]

Another way in which AMAC addresses advocacy information is through its six featured columnists.[97] Articles written by Bob Carlstrom, Daniel Weber, and Robert Charles are focused on political action, while articles by D. J. Wilson, Diana Erbio, and John Grimaldi are a mix of human-interest stories on humor, history, values, and other topics of interest to the membership—with an occasional article specifically about politics.

Independent reviews of AMAC's political claims are not favorable, although the record is not large. PolitiFact's two factchecks on AMAC include one rating in each of the two bottom categories: false (about Planned Parenthood) and pants on fire (about Obamacare).[98]

Nonadvocacy news appears primarily in two places. On the news page in the subpages on health and wellness, home and family, and money, one will find articles on Medicare, senior living, stages of aging, home budgets, Social Security, and the stock market. Some of these articles have a political dimension to them, but others are primarily about bringing seniors up to speed on government programs and other institutions and on programs seniors have to negotiate as part of their everyday lives. The tools and resources web page has a link to *AMAC Magazine*, which appears every two months.[99] Reviewing the first four issues of 2020, for example, the magazine contained feature stories about politics (six); coronavirus (three); heroes and remembrance (Buzz Aldrin, George Washington, D-Day, Melania Trump, first responders); feature stories (national parks); problems with the media, jobs, and economics (three); health and wellness; and adoption (two). There are also regular columns on leisure activities (nostalgia, puzzles), money issues, Social Security, military news, advocacy, and political editorials. The magazine has a strong conservative orientation in both politics and values.[100]

The American Seniors Association, headquartered in Bradenton, Florida, was founded in 2005 under the name National Association for Senior Concerns. Like several of the other competitors, it calls itself "the conservative alternative to AARP." The reference to AARP is clear although unstated on the ASA website when it says, "We believe that you deserve choices when selecting who best represents your interests in Washington, D.C.; and we believe you deserve choices when selecting benefits that help you live a healthier and wealthier life."[101] ASA has lobbied in favor of no cuts to Social Security or Medicare and for a number of Republican plans for reforming the system: rebuilding national values, focusing on the freedom and safety of the individual as well as making choices unfettered by government regulation; a reform of Social Security allowing individuals to choose self-funded private investment accounts; reforming Medicare by offering more choice; simplifying the income tax code; and controlling spending in Washington.

In carrying out its policy education, the ASA provides three types of information:

- identifies 120 bills currently in Congress of interest to their members
- tracks what percentage of votes of individual legislators in House and Senate aligned with the Republican Party
- identifies 150 potential political appointments

In particular, ASA contrasts itself with AARP on three major issues: President Clinton's push to build a large expansion of government involvement in health care, Republican efforts to put Social Security on a sounder financial foundation, and Obamacare. ASA claims (unsubstantiated) that AARP's position on Obamacare caused it to lose approximately three hundred thousand members, and ASA took advantage of this disaffection by offering "to anyone who cut their AARP card in half that we'd give them a year's free membership. . . . We had to stop [the promotion] early. I had too many 55-gallon trash bags full of AARP cards cut in half."[102]

ASA offers a wide range of member benefits. In the health area, it offers prescription drug savings cards, licensed agents who help members select an appropriate Medicare Advantage plan, dental and vision plans, cancer insurance, health plans for people under sixty-five, long-term care plans, discounts and help with eldercare and funerals, and life and final expense insurance. It offers more than a dozen plans to help with car and hotel discounts and travel planning. It has several programs to help members buy or lease a car and insure it. It also has several offerings in the financial area, such as tax and investing programs, debt advice, and home and relocation services. It provides programs to give members security from identity theft and physical falls. It provides member discounts with a number of vendors including groceries, wireless phone service plans, office products, and more.

While the ASA website includes a dozen articles[103] intended to provide political education to its members (all written by former hedge fund manager and real estate investor Steve Hirsch), it has only a brief web page describing Medicare, and almost all the remaining articles are about fishing, scuba, or watersports.[104]

The National Association of Conservative Seniors, formed in 2012 and headquartered in Mooresville, North Carolina, has attempted to compete with AARP in two ways: improving on benefits it offers to its members and, for higher-tiered members, having a Click-to-Call button on its website that enables members to make calls directly to elected officials, including the White House, cabinet members, the Supreme Court, their senators and members of Congress, and their governor.[105] Additional member benefits include "travel deals, discounts to their favorite restaurants and other businesses, healthcare and wellness offerings, Medicare benefits, financial services and automotive benefits. NAOCS partners with leading companies in various industries, including Wyndham hotels, Budget Rent-a-car, WebMD, Senior Reverse Mortgage, and many others."[106] The NAOCS website also provides "access to numerous online resources, including top news stories that affect American seniors, links of assistance to families of fallen veterans and online voter registration."[107] There is reference of NAOCS actively working as late as 2018,[108] but this author can find no references to NAOCS activity since then, and the website (www.naocs.us) was not operable as of September 2020.

## CONCLUSIONS

AARP provides an extraordinary collection of information of interest to older Americans in many forms, including print, online, and in person. The coverage is very wide—not just politics, Medicare, and Social Security but seemingly any topic that would interest Americans of age fifty and up, whether retired or not. In an era when magazine subscriptions have suffered, AARP's continues to be successful, and *AARP The Magazine* is the most circulated magazine in the United States. While there have been major criticisms of AARP's political stances and of conflict of interest over the sale of their insurance plans, there has been no significant criticism of the quality, quantity, or relevance of information that AARP provides.

None of AARP's competitors are even remotely similar in the amount or range of coverage in their information provided to seniors. Several of AARP's competitors have followed after AARP's model: low membership dues, offerings of membership benefits (insurance, travel services, etc.), advocacy activities, and information—although one eschews advocacy (Christ Above Politics), while several others are thin on information. AARP competitors typically differentiate themselves from AARP in one of two ways: espousing more conservative values (which carries over into their advocacy efforts) or providing a choice in benefit providers rather than selecting a single one to affiliate with (as AARP does, for example, with UnitedHealthcare in the Medicare supplement insurance area). There was good reason to criticize AARP's business practices twenty-five years ago, but these problems have largely been fixed, and the organization is much less subject to reasonable criticism today.

The three competitors focused on politics offer little to no real information. To the extent that they provide any kind of information, it is about how to become an advocate. Where there is content material about specific issues or general policies, it is about persuading to their cause. There is no political education (e.g., laying out positions devoid of advocacy) on these sites, whereas AARP engages in political education as well as advocacy.

Perhaps the most successful competitors to AARP are Christ Above Politics and the Association of Mature American Citizens. CAP makes an honest effort to provide services and conservatively oriented information to its members, and its time and funding are not diverted from these benefit and informational issues by advocacy efforts. AMAC is the largest competitor of AARP—though still tiny in comparison—and it is doing the best job of all the competitors of having a full range of benefit, information, and advocacy programs. However, it is hard to see any of these competitors displacing AARP as the authoritative information source for adults over age fifty.

AARP still has opportunities to take advantage of the technological affordances of social networking. It currently acts mostly in the traditional role of information broadcaster rather than taking full advantage of social media to make it an interactive site that can create an information community in which the organization and its millions of members fully share in providing information to one another.

## NOTES

1. D. Barry, *Dave Barry Turns 50* (New York: Ballantine Books, 1998), 161.

2. J. Pace, "Obama Celebrates 50th Birthday at White House," *Seattle Times*, August 4, 2011, http://www.seattletimes.com/seattle-news/politics/obama-celebrates-50th-birthday-at-white-house/.

3. C. L. Day, *AARP: America's Largest Interest Group and Its Impact* (Santa Barbara, CA: Praeger, 2017), 34.

4. AARP has thirty-eight million members according to its 2019 annual report ("AARP 2019 Annual Report," AARP, accessed August 31, 2021, https://www.aarp.org/content/dam/aarp/about_aarp/annual_reports/2019/2019-annual-report.pdf. The Catholic Church had over seventy million members in the United States as of 2017 (*The Official Catholic Directory* [New Providence, NJ: P.J. Kenedy and Sons, 2016]).

5. See, for example, D. C. Lade, "Anti-AARP Groups Looking to Woo New Retirees," *Sun-Sentinel*, January, 14, 2013; L. Johannes, "AARP Faces Competition from Conservative-Leaning Groups," *Wall Street Journal*, March 30, 2014, https://www.wsj.com/news/articles/SB10001424052702304704504579433343359189 1948; J. Slife, "Searching for an Alternative to AARP? Here Are 6 Options," *Sound Mind Investing*, July 27, 2017, https://soundmindinvesting.com/articles/view/seven-alternatives-for-seniors-fleeing-aarp; J. Miller, "Finding an Alternative to AARP," *The Bargain Hunter*, August 6, 2019, https://thebargainhunter.com/news/col-jim-miller/finding-an-alternative-to-aarp; D. Sundblad, "Senior Citizen Organizations that Oppose AARP," LoveToKnow, accessed September 24, 2020, https://seniors.lovetoknow.com/senior-citizen-organizations-that-oppose-aarp.

6. It is hard to obtain reliable, verifiable membership numbers for these organizations, especially for the AARP competitors that are primarily focused on political action, because they want to report their numbers as high as possible in order to increase their lobbying clout. For example, The Seniors Coalition claims to have 2.9 million supporters nationwide (https://www.senior.org), but are these actual dues-paying members? AARP claims to have about thirty-eight million members ("AARP 2019 Annual Report," AARP, accessed September 25, 2020, https://www.aarp.org/content/dam/aarp/about_aarp/annual_reports/2019/2019-annual-report.pdf). AMAC, with approximately two million members, is AARP's largest competitor. See, for example, Report, Democratic Caucus, US House of Representatives, Ways and Means Committee, https://waysandmeans.house.gov/sites/democrats.waysandmeans.house.gov/files/documents/AMAC.pdf, accessed September 25, 2020. The other alternative organizations to AARP are smaller.

Compare this to the overall older population in the United States. As of 2010, there were 58.8 million people ages fifty to sixty-four, 21.7 million ages sixty-five to seventy-four, 13.1 million ages seventy-five to eighty-four, and 5.5 million ages eighty-five or older. Indeed, 34 percent of the American population was fifty or older in 2010, and the trend is for an aging population. (Report, Joint Center for Housing Studies, Harvard University, 2014, https://www.jchs.harvard.edu/sites/default/files/jchs-housing_americas_older_adults_2014-ch2_0.pdf, accessed September 25, 2020).

7. These organizations have annual basic membership dues ranging from eight to twenty dollars, in most cases with lower costs if one signs up for multiple years. For most of these organizations, the spouse of a member receives free membership.

8. This table was compiled by looking informally at AARP's website in August 2020 and 2019 and 2020 issues of the *Bulletin* and *Magazine*. It would be possible to do a more formal content analysis, which would involve systematic coding and classification of a carefully chosen and specified set of AARP products. This would better enable an analysis, for example, of the relative frequency of various topics or the differences in presentation, say, between AARP's English- and Spanish-language publications. However, this more formal content is not needed to simply present an overview of topics covered by AARP. For a more comprehensive list of topics of interest to older Americans, see, for example, National Library Service for the Blind and Print Disabled, Library of Congress, "Resources for Senior Citizens and Their Families," accessed September 2, 2020, https://www.loc.gov/nls/resources/general-resources-on-disabilities/resources-senior-citizens-families/.

9. For an excellent history of AARP, see C. Day, *AARP: America's Largest Interest Group and Its Impact* (Santa Barbara, CA: Praeger, 2017), chapter 2.

10. As of 2017, approximately seven million people held AAQRP-branded health insurance. (Day, *AARP: America's Largest Interest Group and Its Impact*, 36).

11. Davis solidified his control by creating a new law firm (Singer, Miller, and Brickfield) and awarded them the contract to be AARP's external legal counsel and created a new Colonial Penn company under the name CPG Data Inc., which controlled AARP's mailing list, which was essential to both its product marketing and lobbying efforts.

12. See A. A. Rooney, *Sincerely, Andy Rooney* (New York: Public Affairs, 1999). Also see the criticism of Colonial Penn's mail-order life insurance products in a 1974 Senate investigation and a criticism of Colonial Penn's Medicare supplement plan in 1975.

13. US Senate Subcommittee on Social Security and Family Policy, Committee on Finance, *Business and Financial Practices of the AARP* (Washington, DC: US Government Printing Office, June 13, 1995), https://www.finance.senate.gov/imo/media/doc/Hrg104-109.pdf. Also see J. MacDonald, "Senate Investigation Has Critics Setting Sights on AARP," *Hartford Courant*, June 10, 1995, https://www.courant.com/news/connecticut/hc-xpm-1995-06-10-9506100193-story.html.

14. Today, AARP is represented by three main organizations for tax and legal purposes: AARP, which is a 501(c)(4) nonprofit, which is tax-exempt, has unlimited lobbying privileges, and to whom contributions are not tax-deductible; the AARP Foundation, its charitable arm, which is a 501(c)(3) nonprofit, which is tax-exempt, can politically educate but not lobby, and to whom contributions are tax-deductible; and AARP Services, Inc. (often known as ASI), which is responsible for its products and services, which runs as a for-profit, taxable business.

15. Donations to the AARP Foundation are used strictly for charitable purposes, for example, to help support indigent seniors.

16. US House of Representatives, Committee on Ways and Means, "Behind the Veil: The AARP America Doesn't Know," investigative report prepared by Repre-

sentative Wally Herger and Representative Dave Reichert, March 29, 2011, https://waysandmeans.house.gov/UploadedFiles/AARP_REPORT_FINAL_PDF_3_29_11.pdf.

17. 17-09041 DDP (PLAx), US District Court, C. D. California, November 2, 2018, Simon Levay, Judith Willis, and Lionel Brown v. AARP, Inc. et al.; 376 F. Supp. 3d 1 (2019) Helen Krukas v. AARP, Inc. et al. The background is given in P. Barnes, "Same Facts but Different Findings in Lawsuits Alleging Insurance Fraud by AARP," *Forbes*, February 10, 2020, https://www.forbes.com/sites/patriciag barnes/2020/02/10/same-facts-but-different-findings-in-lawsuits-alleging-insurance -fraud-by-aarp/#609d1f7274ed.

18. For example, Paying for Senior Care and Boomer Benefits rank their plans among the top ten in the nation (https://www.payingforseniorcare.com/best-medi-care-supplement-plans, updated August 18, 2020; D. K. Roberts, "Top 10 Medicare Supplement Companies in 2020," Boomer Benefits, accessed October 5, 2020, https://boomerbenefits.com/top-10-medicare-supplement-companies/). The Senior List awards the AARP plan the one with the best coverage options (A. Clark and C. Smith, "Best Medicare Supplement Plans in 2020," The Senior List, accessed October 5, 2020, https://www.theseniorlist.com/medigap/best/). Retirement Living listed the AARP plans among the top nine and noted their "great service" ("Best Medicare Supplement Plans and Companies," Retirement Living, updated October 2, 2020, https://www.retirementliving.com/best-medicare-supplement-plans-companies.)

19. On the history of AARP coming to adopt a center-left approach in the policy area, see chapter 5 and especially chapter 6 in Frederick R. Lynch, *One Nation under AARP* (Berkeley: University of California Press, 2011).

20. Day, *AARP: America's Largest Interest Group and Its Impact*.

21. https://www.aarp.org/about-aarp/policies/?intcmp=FTR-LINKS-PRO-PP -EWHERE, accessed September 28, 2020.

22. For a more detailed discussion of AARP as a political organization, see Day, *AARP: America's Largest Interest Group and Its Impact*, chapters 4 and 5.

23. See the discussion in Charles R. Morris, *The AARP*, New York: Times Books, Random House, 1996, pp. 61, 62.

24. See, for example, T. Skocpol, "The Rise and Resounding Demise of the Clinton Plan," *Health Affairs* 14, no. 1 (1995), https://www.healthaffairs.org/doi/full/10.1377/hlthaff.14.1.66.

25. W. A. Galston, "Why the 2005 Social Security Initiative Failed, and What It Means for the Future," Brookings, September 21, 2007, https://www.brookings.edu/research/why-the-2005-social-security-initiative-failed-and-what-it-means-for-the -future/.

26. S. Rosenbaum, "The Patient Protection and Affordable Care Act: Implication for Public Health Policy and Practice," *Public Health Reports* 126 (January–February 2011), https://journals.sagepub.com/doi/pdf/10.1177/003335491112600118.

27. AARP, Long-Term Services and Supports State Scorecard, http://www.long-termscorecard.org, accessed September 28, 2020.

28. For example, Nancy LeaMond, an executive vice president of AARP, was acknowledged by *The Hill* as one of Washington's top lobbyists (The Hill Staff,

"Top Lobbyists of 2015: Grassroots," *The Hill*, October 28, 2015, https://thehill.com/business-a-lobbying/top-lobbyists/258317-top-lobbyists-2015-grassroots). That same year, JoAnn Jenkins, AARP's CEO, was recognized to be in the top fifty in power and influence (P. Clolery, "Power and Influence Top 50 in '15," *The Non-Profit Times*, August 1, 2015, http://www.thenonprofittimes.com/wp-content/uploads/2015/07/8-1-15_Top50PI.pdf).

29. AARP, *AARP Policy Book 2019–2020*, https://policybook.aarp.org, accessed September 28, 2020.

30. AARP, *The Priorities Book: Building a Better Future, 2015–2016*, https://www.aarp.org/content/dam/aarp/about_aarp/aarp_policies/2015-05/AARP-Priorities-Book-2015-2016.pdf, accessed September 28, 2020.

31. AARP, AARP Public Policy Institute, https://www.aarp.org/ppi/, accessed September 28, 2020.

32. AARP, *Caregiving in the United States*, May 2020, https://www.aarp.org/content/dam/aarp/ppi/2020/05/full-report-caregiving-in-the-united-states.doi.10.26419-2Fppi.00103.001.pdf, accessed September 28, 2020.

33. Events, AARP Public Policy Institute, 2020, https://www.aarp.org/ppi/events/, accessed September 28, 2020.

34. Data, AARP Public Policy Institute, 2020, https://dataexplorer.aarp.org, accessed September 28, 2020.

35. Politics and Society, AARP, https://www.aarp.org/politics-society/?intcmp=GLBNAV-PL-POL-POL, accessed September 28, 2020.

36. Government Watch, AARP, https://www.aarp.org/politics-society/advocacy/government_watch/, accessed September 28, 2020.

37. Day, *AARP: America's Largest Interest Group and Its Impact*, p. 41.

38. Day, *AARP: America's Largest Interest Group and Its Impact*.

39. These were the active pages listed on the main page of the AARP website (https://www.aarp.org) as of September 29, 2020.

40. AARP, Coronavirus, https://www.aarp.org/coronavirus/?intcmp=GLBNAV-PL-CRNA, accessed September 29, 2020.

41. At the very bottom of the landing page for the AARP website (https://www.aarp.org) there are links to the pages for each of these communities.

42. AARP, Hispanic Heritage, https://www.aarp.org/home-family/voices/hispanic-heritage/?intcmp=AE-HF-VOIC-TERTNAV-HISP, accessed September 29, 2020.

43. Links to these categories are found at the bottom of the AARP landing page (https://www.aarp.org).

44. AARP, Conditions and Treatments, https://www.aarp.org/health/conditions-treatments/?intcmp=FTR-LINKS-HEA-CT-EWHERE, accessed September 29, 2020.

45. There is also an iPad app for delivery of *The Bulletin*. As of 2017, *The Bulletin* was reaching 29.7 million people and *The Magazine* was reaching over 37 million, making it the largest mass circulation magazine in the United States. (S. Husni, "AARP The Magazine: Relevant, Vibrant and Still the Largest Circulation Magazine in the Country with Over 37 Million Readers," *Mr. Magazine*, January 9, 2017, https://mrmagazine.wordpress.com/2017/01/09/aarp-the-magazine-relevant-vibrant

-still-the-largest-circulation-magazine-in-the-country-with-more-than-23-million -readers-the-mr-magazine-interview-with-shelagh-daly-mille/.)

46. See A. A. Newman, "A Magazine Now Tailored to the Not Necessarily Retired," *New York Times*, August 23, 2010. Contrast with the account of *Modern Maturity*, which wanted to "show the positive side of getting older" but was nevertheless focused on retirees of an older age than the current version of the magazine, with such topics as loose dentures and leaving one's body to science: A. Johnson, "Magazine or Older Readers Looking Robust," *Los Angeles Times*, November 3, 1991. Both publications have been highly successful in terms of circulation and advertising revenue.

47. AARP, *AARP The Magazine*, https://www.aarp.org/magazine/, accessed September 28, 2020.

48. AARP Press Room, "AARP Launches Sisters from AARP Digital Newsletter Celebrating Gen-X and Baby Boomer African American Women," AARP, August 8, 2018, https://press.aarp.org/2018-8-8-2018-AARP-Launches-Sisters-From-AARP -Digital-Newsletter-Celebrating-GenX-BabyBoomer-AfricanAmerican-Women.

49. AARP, AARP Blogs, https://blog.aarp.org/?intcmp=FTR-LINKS-RWL -BLOG-EWHERE, accessed September 29, 2020.

50. AARP, Podcasts, https://www.aarp.org/podcasts/?intcmp=FTR-LINKS-RWL -PODCAST-EWHERE, accessed September 29, 2020.

51. AARP, Videos, https://videos.aarp.org, accessed September 29, 2020.

52. See, for example, the story about the North Carolina broadcast network for On the Air: G. Bridges, "Listen Up: AARP Radio Show," May 1, 2014, https://states .aarp.org/nc-listen.

53. See, for example, AARP, AARP Live on RFD-TV, https://states.aarp.org/ aarplive, accessed October 2, 2020, where there are AARP programs on prescription prices during the pandemic, social security, personal finance during the pandemic, making small towns great, playing it safe online, estate planning, protecting our veterans, reining in robocalls, and the dark web.

54. AARP, Entertainment, TV for Grownups, https://www.aarp.org/entertainment/ television/, accessed October 2, 2020.

55. AARP, AARP Events, https://www.aarp.org/about-aarp/events/?intcmp=FTR -LINKS-RWL-EVENTS-EWHERE, accessed September 29, 2020.

56. AARP, AARP Bookstore, https://www.aarp.org/entertainment/books/ bookstore/?intcmp=FTR-LINKS-RWL-BOOK-EWHERE, accessed September 29, 2020.

57. "The Truth about You: AARP Research's Goal: Understanding Aging Today," *AARP Bulletin* 61, no. 9 (November 2020): 42. Also see "About AARP Research," AARP Research, accessed April 2, 2021, https://www.aarp.org/research/about/.

58. 60 Plus, American Association of Senior Citizens, Our Mission, https://60plus. org/about-60-plus-association/, accessed September 16, 2020. The 60 Plus Association does earn some funds from life insurance programs for its members, but this is clearly secondary.

59. P. Abowd, "Nonprofit Profile: 60 Plus Association," The Center for Public Integrity, June 21, 2012, https://publicintegrity.org/politics/nonprofit-profile-60-plus-association/?gclid=EAIaIQobChMIoNPh7vDt6wIVhYbACh24sgQtEAAYASAAEg

KNxvD_BwE. Another person familiar to seniors, Art Linkletter, has also appeared in political advertising campaigns for these conservative groups.

60. G. Kessler, "More 'Mediscare' Hooey, GOP Version," *Washington Post*, March 14, 2012, https://www.washingtonpost.com/blogs/fact-checker/post/more -mediscare-hooey-gop-version/2012/03/13/gIQAcDC89R_blog.html.

61. On the Koch brothers' political activities, see T. Skocpol and A. Hertel-Fernandez, "The Koch Network and Republican Party Extremism," *Perspectives on Politics* 14, no. 3 (2016): 681–699; A. Hertel-Fernandez and T. Skocpol, "Business Associations, Conservative Networks, and the Ongoing Republican War over Medicaid Expansion," *Journal of Health Politics, Policy and Law* 41, no. 2 (2016): 239–286; and J. Mayer, *Dark Money: The Hidden History of the Billionaires Behind the Rise of the Radical Right* (New York: Doubleday, 2016).

62. The Center for Public Integrity, Nonprofit Profile: 60 Plus Association, https://publicintegrity.org/politics/nonprofit-profile-60-plus-association/?gclid=EAIaIQobC hMIoNPh7vDt6wIVhYbACh24sgQtEAAYASAAEgKNxvD_BwE, accessed September 16, 2020; also see OpenSecrets.org, Outside Spending, https://www.opense crets.org/outsidespending/contrib.php?cmte=60+Plus+Assn&cycle=2014, accessed September 16, 2020.

63. Viguerie built up a direct-mail practice in his unsuccessful effort to get Barry Goldwater elected as president, and he continues to employ his mailing lists and mailing techniques to support conservative causes. He claims, in an autobiographical note, to have sent out more than two billion pieces of direct mail for these political purposes over the years. (ConservativeHQ, About Conservative HQ, http://www .conservativehq.com/article/43-about-conservative-hq, accessed September 17, 2020). There is a long Wikipedia article about his life and work (https://en.wikipedia. org/wiki/Richard_Viguerie, accessed 31 August 2021).

64. The Medicare Catastrophic Coverage Act became law in 1988. Its goal was to reduce the risk of large financial losses for seniors. However, the law was repealed only one year later because of the high costs to individual seniors. See W. E. Aaronson, J. S. Zinn, and M. D. Rosko, "The Success and Repeal of the Medicare Catastrophic Coverage Act: A Paradoxical Lesson for Health Care Reform," *Journal of Health Politics, Policy and Law* 19, no. 4 (Winter 1994): 753–771.

65. The Seniors Coalition, About the Seniors Coalition, https://www.senior.org/about-tsc, accessed September 17, 2020.

66. The Seniors Coalition, landing page, https://www.senior.org, accessed September 17, 2020.

67. Sourcewatch, https://www.sourcewatch.org/index.php?title=SourceWatch, accessed September 17, 2020.

68. M. Scherer, "The Artful Codger," *Mother Jones*, July–August 2005, https://www.motherjones.com/politics/2005/07/artful-codger/.

69. The Center for Media and Democracy, "Senior Coalition," Sourcewatch, accessed September 17, 2020, https://www.sourcewatch.org/index.php/Senior_Coali tion. Sourcewatch points the reader to the following article in evidence, which this author has been unable to access: "Drug Industry–Financed Seniors Coalition Mails Warning Against Imported Prescription Drugs," *Business World*, June 18, 2003.

70. Sourcewatch, https://www.sourcewatch.org/index.php?title=SourceWatch, accessed September 17, 2020.

71. Sourcewatch, https://www.sourcewatch.org/index.php?title=SourceWatch, accessed September 17, 2020.

72. B. T. Dreyfuss, "Poison Pill: How Abramoff's Cronies Sold the Medicare Drug Bill," *Washington Monthly*, November 2006, http://www.washingtonmonthly.com/features/2006/0611.dreyfuss.html.

73. For background information on the swift boat ads, see D. Buckaloo, "Swift Boat Veterans for Truth," The Election of 2004 web page, Center for Presidential History, accessed April 5, 2021, http://cphcmp.smu.edu/2004election/swift-boat-veterans-for-truth/.

74. USANext, https://en.wikipedia.org/wiki/USA_Next, accessed September 17, 2020.

75. B. Hogan, "Pulling Strings from Afar," *AARP Bulletin Today*, July 3, 2006, https://archive.is/20100114024354/http://bulletin.aarp.org/yourworld/politics/articles/pulling_strings_from.html. Also see other criticisms of these three organizations: M. Ivins, "For Whom Are They Balancing the Budget?," *Progressive Populist*, revised October 29, 1995, http://www.populist.com/11-95.Ivins.html; and from a Communist perspective, see P. E. Benjamin, "The Nation's Health and Workers Safety, Seniors: Focal Point of Struggle," *People's Weekly World*, March 25, 1995, http://www.hartford-hwp.com/archives/45/027.html.

76. Hogan, "Pulling Strings from Afar."

77. Hogan, "Pulling Strings from Afar."

78. CAP: Christ Above Politics, Frequently Asked Questions, https://christabovepolitics.com/faq, accessed September 15, 2020.

79. CAP: Christ Above Politics, landing page, https://christabovepolitics.com, accessed September 15, 2020.

80. CAP: Christ Above Politics, https://christabovepolitics.com/cap-s-past, accessed September 15, 2020.

81. CAP: Christ Above Politics, Learn About CAP: History to the Future, https://christabovepolitics.com/about, accessed September 15, 2020.

82. CAP: Christ Above Politics, Learn About CAP: History to the Future, https://christabovepolitics.com/about, accessed September 15, 2020.

83. CAP: Christ Above Politics, Frequently Asked Questions, https://christabovepolitics.com/faq, accessed September 15, 2020.

84. CAP: Christ Above Politics, Member Benefits, https://christabovepolitics.com/benefits, accessed September 15, 2020.

85. For example, the September–October 2016 issue had a full-page ad and an article about the LifeFone Medical Alert System, which is a CAP sponsor; and the spring 2017 issue has an article from another sponsor answering frequently asked questions about long-term care insurance. Thanks to the owner of CAP for providing copies of the newsletter to review.

86. CAP: Christ Above Politics, *CAP Connection*, September–October 2016.

87. This description of the newsletter is based on an examination of the June, July, August, and September 2020 newsletters, which the owner of CAP, R. Girard, kindly provided to me in October 2020.

88. For a testimonial on the death of Weber, see The National AMAC Leadership Team, "The Powerful Legacy of Dan Weber, Founder of the Association of Mature American Citizens," *The Gilmer Mirror*, February 7, 2020, http://www.gilmer mirror.com/view/full_story/27699931/article-The-Powerful-Legacy-of-Dan-Weber --Founder-of-the-Association-of-Mature-American-Citizens?.

89. AMAC: Association of Mature American Citizens, Meet the AMAC Team, https://amac.us/about-us/meet-the-amac-team/, accessed September 23, 2020.

90. For an analysis of AMAC's competition with AARP—not just on advocacy but also on insurance benefits for members—see A. Markow, "AMAC vs. AARP: Fighting for the Hearts and Minds of Seniors," *Independent Voter News*, June 17, 2012, https://ivn.us/2012/06/17/amac-vs-aarp-fighting-hearts-minds-seniors. Markow's conclusion is harshly critical of AMAC: "Rather than providing a useful alternative for information to seniors, AMAC adds to the further splintering of American politics along partisan, ideological lines." Like the Seniors Coalition and the United Seniors Association, AMAC also has a connection to big pharma. See S. Peterson, "Big Pharma Is Boosted by PADS Alliance with Association of Mature American Citizens," Checks and Balances Project, October 25, 2019, https://checksandbalances project.org/big-pharma-pads-amac/.

91. AMAC: Association of Mature American Citizens, Benefits, https://amac.us/ benefits/, accessed September 23, 2020.

92. AMAC: Association of Mature American Citizens, About Us: Overview, https://amac.us/about-us/, accessed September 23, 2020.

93. AMAC: Association of Mature American Citizens, Our Stance on Key Issues, https://amac.us/about-us/our-stance-on-the-issues/, accessed September 23, 2020.

94. AMAC: Association of Mature American Citizens, AMAC Ambassador, https:// www.amac.us/amac-ambassador-leadership-program/, accessed September 23, 2020. On AMAC's annual lobbying expenses, see Center for Responsive Politics, "Client Profile: Association of Mature American Citizens," OpenSecrets.org, 2020, https:// www.opensecrets.org/federal-lobbying/clients/summary?cycle=2018&id=F210231.

95. AMAC: Association of Mature American Citizens, Frequently Asked Questions, https://amac.us/about-us/frequently-asked-questions/, accessed September 23, 2020.

96. AMAC: Association of Mature American Citizens, landing page, https://amac .us, accessed September 24, 2020.

97. AMAC: Association of Mature American Citizens, AMAC Columnists, https://amac.us/columnists/, accessed September 24, 2020.

98. Politifact, The Poynter Institute, Personalities, https://www.politifact.com/per-sonalities/association-mature-american-citizens/, accessed September 24, 2020; also see Politifact, The Poynter Institute, Fact Checks, https://www.politifact.com/fact checks/2012/dec/02/association-mature-american-citizens/association-mature-amer ican-citizens-says-under-af/, accessed September 24, 2020. Media Bias/Fact Check summarizes its analysis of AMAC as follows: "Overall, we rate AMAC Right Biased based on political positions and story selection that favors the conservative right. We also rate them Mixed for factual reporting due to the use of poor sources that have failed fact checks." (https://mediabiasfactcheck.com/amac-association-of-mature -american-citizens/, accessed September 24, 2020).

99. AMAC: Association of Mature American Citizens, AMAC Magazine, https://amac.us/magazine/, accessed September 24, 2020.

100. In addition to political action in favor of its conservative views, AMAC occasionally protests and boycotts, as it did in 2017, when it threatened to boycott movie theaters if the Academy Awards ceremony turned into a Trump-bashing event by celebrities including Meryl Streep, Jimmy Kimmel, and ten others AMAC named. See P. Bedard, "Oscars Warned: 'Diss Trump and Face a Theater Boycott," *Washington Examiner*, February 23, 2017, https://www.washingtonexaminer.com/oscars-warned-diss-trump-and-face-a-theater-boycott. AMAC filed a complaint with the Federal Communications Commission over CNN's reporting of Russian hacking. (I. Mason, "Exclusive—Seniors Group Files FCC Complaint Against Very Fake News CNN," *Breitbart*, June 30, 2017, https://www.breitbart.com/politics/2017/06/30/exclusive-seniors-group-files-fcc-complaint-against-very-fake-news-cnn/).

101. American Seniors Association, landing page, https://americanseniors.org/page.aspx?id=3, accessed September 18, 2020.

102. Sound Mind Investing, Seven Alternatives for Seniors Fleeing AARP, https://soundmindinvesting.com/articles/view/seven-alternatives-for-seniors-fleeing-aarp, accessed September 18, 2020.

103. See, in particular, the critique of AARP: "AARP—A Social Welfare Organization?," American Seniors, accessed October 5, 2020, https://americanseniors.org/articles/aarp/is-aarp-a-social-welfare-organization/.

104. See American Seniors Association, Articles, See https://americanseniors.org/articles/, accessed October 5, 2020.

105. R. Stott, "New Senior Association Takes on AARP," Associations Now, October 8, 2012, https://associationsnow.com/2012/10/national-association-of-con servative-seniors-aarp/.

106. "The National Association of Conservative Seniors Now Offers Extra Benefits to New Members," CISION PRWeb, press release, April 11, 2013, https://www prweb.com/releases/2013/4/prweb10612692.htm.

107. "National Association of Conservative Seniors Offers Americans Alternative to AARP," PR Newswire, press release, November 11, 2012, https://www.cnbc.com/id/100126203.

108. See, for example, Spectrum Retirement Communities, [About] Association for Seniors, https://spectrumretirement.com/associations-for-seniors/, accessed September 21, 2020.

## Chapter Five

# Age and Technology in Action

## Claudia Grisales Bohorquez, Marilyn Kay, Noah Lenstra, and Kate Williams

In the United States and globally, people of all ages can be dedicated technology learners and users. This includes people over sixty-five ("old") and over eighty-five ("old old"). They are motivated to connect with family and friends and to participate in culture and society. These elders have been studied in detail, as they should be, since they are a growing portion of humanity. Today, online communication is second only to face-to-face communication and may even be first in richer pandemic-stricken countries with adequate digital infrastructure. Much like the 1970s Gray Panthers' slogan, "Age and Youth in Action," our chapter title conveys how active and engaged elders are with technology. Active engagement with technology includes complaining about it, which, by the way, we all do.

We have been helping people use technology, and studying that process, for twenty-five years. One of us, Marilyn Kay, has been helping people read for at least fifty years. Older people have been a special focus of ours, not least because they tend to get technology help in more public settings, such as libraries, seniors centers, and group living facilities. The rest of us tend to rely on tech help at work or in school or the university, where help is paid for, naturalized into the day, and harder to study. And, of course, most of us also get along with a little help from our friends. They are among those Bakardjieva calls the "warm experts."[1] But we think big advances are possible from understanding how elders use technology.

We are also involved in training people to give tech help. This involves a lot of stereotype shattering and really rethinking the whole process. New concepts are key here. Naming something makes it real and guides our thinking. So, this chapter is organized by the eleven concepts that our research and teaching have brought to light. Whether you are getting or giving help—and many people do both—we hope you too will arm yourself with these concepts. First, we review five crucial concepts from our past research: the digital divide, informatics moment, ageism, informatics life course, and "each one teach one." Then we explain six more concepts as they emerged in our fieldwork: agents not users, strategic patience, building digital maze-ways, shaping community-based information infrastructure, nonjudgmental awareness, and experts-together. Whether you are a senior using technology or helping one, operating with these concepts is a guide to success. Help, of course, is very much the issue. Seniors by definition are mostly not in school or at work, where technology help is built in. The truth is no one uses technology by themselves, as these eleven concepts demonstrate.

## DIGITAL DIVIDE

The digital divide is a concept that has evolved and stayed in use for close to three decades, but it first came to light in the 1990s as the gap between those who used computers and those who did not became apparent.[2] Overcoming the social exclusion that deepened when human life migrated online has often been an uphill battle. Centuries ago (and in many agricultural societies today), if you couldn't read or write, you turned to the community scribe. Still more recently, if you didn't have a phone, there was a pay phone you could use. But then came the home computer: expensive, elite, and complicated. And still later came the smartphone and the tablet. Depending on the viewpoint, these may still be expensive, elite, and complicated. And for many, they even replace the home computer. "Digital divide," "digital inequality," "digital inclusion"—there are many ways to describe the gap and the efforts to overcome it.

The digital divide was such a rallying cry that, in the 1990s, people across the United States—many of them volunteers—created an estimated hundred thousand public access computer labs.[3] The Department of Commerce started surveying the country's population as to their digital access and use. The phrase launched a wave of public and private money to support—and some would say capture—this movement. Its binary simplicity soon accommodated the moving-target aspect of digital tools. We moved from home modem to WiFi, from computers to smartphones, from asking "Do you use technology?" to "Do you even want to?" The digital divide has been measured in countless ways. It's familiar to many, and it can be overcome. In the United States, the public library has stepped in to provide public computing, which has made a huge difference.

What is great about the term *digital divide* is that it externalizes the problem. People do not have to blame themselves for this broad social problem.

By contrast, we now have the insidious and false concepts of the smartphone, smart home, and smart community, which imply that the have-nots or the have-lesses are dumb.[4] The digital divide is a two-way bridge where there is human intelligence on both sides.[5]

## INFORMATICS MOMENT

Following the concept of the digital divide is the idea of the informatics moment.[6] This is when you seek and get help from someone to resolve some technological obstacle facing you. It is a short or long helping interaction that, at its best, ends with clear sailing toward the task at hand. Every time you are trying to do something with technology that is not working for you, you are ripe for an informatics moment. Where the digital divide signals a problem, the informatics moment signifies a solution, and it puts human agency in the center of the image.

At a more abstract level, the informatics moment is also something all of humanity, every society and every sector, is passing through. Where cashiers used to use arithmetic to make change, now they need a feel for the quirks of the card reader appended to their register. Or where customers formerly used their math skills to check the cashier's doings, now they need to feel confident at a self-checkout kiosk. The transition from one to the next is an informatics moment en masse.

This chapter considers the informatics moment in both its empirical and abstract meanings. Empirically, informatics moments are events in which people seek and receive help using digital technologies. More abstractly, an informatics moment can also refer to "a phase in the transition of a society or social sector to the information age, with all the dislocations and transformations that are entailed in introducing digital tools and infrastructure."[7]

Cybernavigator is a related concept, a new job title invented by the Chicago Public Library in 1998 to identify the computer helper. As one of these staff members told us, "With books came the librarian, and with computers came the cybernavigator, you know?"[8] The phrase *informatics moments* just turns our gaze from the helper (cybernavigator) to the helping interaction between the two parties.

The informatics moment is often an emotional ride from frustration and anxiety to relief and laughter. Worldwide, humanity is mostly in the anxiety phase, not least because technology does not stand still. Market competition drives constant updates: tweaking, "mission creep," and marketplace confusion. Sometimes as soon as you're used to one version of something, a device or an app will force a new one on you. But with enough successful informatics moments and the mastery that results, our sense is that better days are coming.[9]

## AGEISM

It is true that those a little older have tended to have a little more difficulty incorporating digital technology into everyday life. The Pew Research Center shows that those over sixty-five are most likely to need help using new electronic devices.[10] But what does that fact mean? Some interpret these data and assume there is something inherently deficient about the minds or bodies of older adults. We instead read this finding as a reflection of the structural inadequacies of our current digital infrastructure. In other words, computer help is there for some and not for others. Although it is true that older adults are more likely to need tech help than the general population, the numbers in table 5.1 suggest that we *all* need help with technology. We all have informatics moments. And because ageism is readily internalized, age and technology in action benefits from a helper who can affirm someone's abilities and explicitly reject the stereotypes.

Table 5.1. Percentage of US Adults, by Age, Who Say the Statement "When I get a new electronic device, I usually need someone else to set it up or show me how to use it" Describes Them Well or Somewhat Well

| Age | Very Well | Somewhat Well |
|---|---|---|
| 18–29 | 6 | 12 |
| 30–49 | 18 | 18 |
| 50–64 | 37 | 25 |
| 65+ | 48 | 25 |

*Note*: Survey data from 2015. Monica Anderson and Andrew Perrin, "Tech Adoption Climbs among Older Americans," Pew Research Center, May 17, 2017, https://www.pewresearch.org/internet/2017/05/17/tech-adoption-climbs-among-older-adults/.

A study of how technology help operates in public libraries and seniors centers found that in these spaces the agency and expertise of older adults is not always respected, or even acknowledged, by the staff and administrators responsible for structuring the provision of technology help services.[11] Policies favor younger tutors for older learners, which is not always the best combination. Institutional structures render older adults invisible. Nonetheless, despite institutional invisibility, older adults exert their agency in technology support services in multiple ways, including by insisting on respect for their experience and seeing older people as contributors to their communities—in the present moment as well as in their earlier decades.

Part of the challenge of understanding technology help among older adults is that we all so often fall prey to ageist ideas about technology and learning. With fine-grained analyses of older adults using technology in community spaces, scholars like Bowen, and Sayago and Blat, remind us that we all can learn a lot about new technology and the digital divide by seeing the information society from the perspective of seniors.[12]

But who is attending to what older people do with technology? A recent article in *Forbes* magazine is titled "More Seniors Are Embracing Technology. But Can They Use It? UCSD Researchers Suggest Asking Them."[13] Unfortunately, it is still rare for us to see older adults as the experts they actually are about the experience of aging in an information society. Our research contributes to the dismantling of ageist ideas.

## INFORMATICS LIFE COURSE

We dismantle ageism in part by attending to the diverse and heterogeneous ways in which older adults adopt and make technology part of their lives over time. We call this the informatics life course: how a person learns technology throughout the stages of their life.[14] Studying the informatics life courses of a diverse group of older adults in East Central Illinois revealed a multitude of life trajectories with technology, including a number of individuals who had engaged in mainframe computing in the 1960s and 1970s only to find themselves on the wrong side of the digital divide as the technological universe changed from under them and as they found themselves cut off from workplace-based technology support in retirement.[15]

Close attention to the heterogeneous ways older adults learn technology and practice digital literacy over time reveals a critical lesson about technology development and the hidden biases that shape it. First, disruptions in the informatics life course, and the digital divide among older adults, is caused by society, not by older adults themselves. We hear this in the stories of older adults who feel like technology has changed over the course of their lives from something over which they had mastery to something more like a foreign language. This shift may in part relate to the fact that technology designers typically target young people as their audience. If technology companies and other researchers studied older adults and their technology practices rather than biasing and basing their work on what younger people do, the constant thrill of revised tools might be laid aside. An oft-referenced example of this is how the physically more efficient DVORAK keyboard never replaced the QWERTY one because millions of us had already mastered QWERTY over its fifty prior years of usage.

## EACH ONE TEACH ONE

"Each one teach one" is an African American epigram that arose in the freedom struggles of either the 1800s or the 1960s (historians disagree). Each of these periods saw an explosion of informal learning. The first was when it was illegal to teach an enslaved person to read; the second was when Black people were de jure and de facto excluded from adequate public schooling.

By the 1990s, informal learning had exploded once again. But instead of conventional literacy, the concern was computer literacy. And quickly it was also about all kinds of knowledge across the internet. The Tunisian French Canadian philosopher Pierre Lévy saw the emerging internet as a beehive of information sharing and proposed the concept of "collective intelligence."[16]

Each one teach one and collective intelligence are closely related. The digital age called for these concepts in two ways. First, computing and the internet were such giant leaps that formal education could not keep up. Computers sat in classrooms in their shipping boxes. Overworked teachers couldn't stop to unpack and learn them. Few tech helpers were on the way. But meanwhile hobbyists started their own user groups to solve problems and play with computers. Their activity, and informal learning in general, represents each one teach one in action. Second, the internet itself connected one-to-one (and one-to-many) in ways previously unimaginable: Usenet, bulletin board services, chat, email, LISTSERVs, texting, and later corporate social media and an unimaginable number of apps. Wikipedia crowdsourced highly reliable entries on myriad topics of both "high" and "low" culture.

Seniors at the residential community we have studied have picked up on each one teach one too. In our 2015 survey of seventy-six households, of those who averaged eighty-five years old, 42 percent reported helping others with technology.[17] Clearly, this generation has been wrongly stereotyped as tech know-nothings. After all, the process of each one teach one is as old as human culture. For how do we learn language itself? Each one teach one— collective intelligence.

The earliest written document we have found in the United States on how to teach someone to use a computer recognizes this: "Knowledge lives in communities, not individuals. A computer user who's part of a community of computer users will have an easier time than one who isn't."[18]

**Figure 5.1.** Graduate student Sam Suber and resident Shirley Mahaffey collaborate at Clark-Lindsey Village.
Photo courtesy of the authors.

## TOWARD OUR SIX NEW CONCEPTS

To present our newer concepts, we now turn to our most recent fieldwork and analysis. This work was done at the Clark-Lindsey Village seniors community and the Urbana Free Library, both in Urbana, Illinois. While our work built on years of service and research, it was the creative adaptation of that routine by a student and an elder, coauthors here: Claudia Grisales Bohorquez and Marilyn Kay.

In 2007, from the then–library school at the University of Illinois, Kate Williams found a service opportunity in the library of the Clark-Lindsey Village seniors community. It was and is an all-volunteer library constituted from selections from the book collections of incoming residents. Kate and her students started as volunteer librarians. But the library was managed with circulation software, plus it featured four computer workstations for residents. Students quickly became cybernavigators. This took the shape of Friday Tech Help, an hour of help that has continued for fourteen years, interrupted only by COVID-19. In 2018, the village and the Urbana Park District supplemented this, creating their own fifty-fifty shared cybernavigator staff person called the age-friendly program coordinator. One semester we connected villagers with peers in China via Skype. And we helped establish a similar volunteer service at the Urbana Free Library that serves all ages.

Noah Lenstra's doctoral dissertation on seniors and technology took shape alongside the fieldwork of many students in Kate Williams's community informatics course. One product of the course was a demographic survey of the digital divide in the village.[19]

Most recently, a doctoral student who provided tech help (Claudia) and a retired educator and literacy specialist who asked for tech help (Marilyn) developed six new concepts to guide the vast number of us, seniors and others, who get and give tech help. These concepts arose in conversations and collaborations between Claudia and Marilyn. So now this chapter shifts to Claudia's voice, where it stays.

## CLAUDIA TELLS THE STORY

I first saw Marilyn as I walked into the library at Clark-Lindsey Village. It was my third time volunteering as a technology support provider, which was part of a course I took during spring 2019. My professor had assigned us to serve as cybernavigators, following the practice of Chicago Public Library.

Marilyn was holding her phone as she walked up to the small group of volunteers; she was expecting to get help resetting the fingerprint recognition feature on her phone. I started walking her through the process of getting into the settings menu and scanning the fingerprints she wanted to use. When her fingerprints had been scanned, and we were unsure if the process had worked, I suggested that she lock her phone. Marilyn looked at me and asked, "What was that word you used?" When I answered, "Lock?" she said, "You know, I learn better when you young people use the same, most basic words to teach me." I smiled and asked Marilyn to let me know any way she thought I could help her better.

That was the beginning of our learning path toward what we've called *experts-together* or (more formally) *collaborative expertise*: a set of collective knowledge, skills, and motivations that emerges when two or more people come together to achieve a common goal, and that is more than just the sum of individual expertise.

From our very first meeting, Marilyn grounded me in identifying six new concepts, some of which have been hinted at before.[20] Along with the first five concepts explained earlier, they make the difference between providing help in a traditional way and providing help in a community informatics style.[21] They are lessons developed in our encounters at Clark-Lindsey Village. So, this section draws insights from our conversations and the complementary volunteer work that I also performed in Champaign Public Library during spring 2019 to explain these concepts.

The trauma often evoked by informatics moments in the study by Williams resonates with Mindy Thompson's description of root shock: the traumatic stress reaction to the destruction of one's ecosystem or to losing the set of patterns we use for navigating the external environment.[22] But Marilyn and I shared experiences that neither of us would define as traumatic. How can we reconcile this contradiction as to the emotions of the informatics moment? Can informatics moments actually mend the cracks that the agitated transition to the information age has caused?

We hope this account of a particular experience of informatics moments will illuminate possible answers to these questions. Most of all, we propose collaborative expertise as a means to overcome the trauma brought about by the common myths in mainstream technological discourses.

As an educator, Marilyn has cultivated a particular awareness of the process of learning. As the story of our first meeting relays, from the start, she has given me guidance on how to support her learning and use of technology. We think that being able to provide better information technology support in practice relates to our understanding of informatics moments as embedded practices in society. We now relate our experience to present six new concepts to add to the five earlier. We think these ideas will improve the way we support older adults working with technology and the way elders seek help. The concepts are agents not users, strategic patience, building digital mazeways, shaping community-based information infrastructure, nonjudgmental awareness, and experts-together.

## Agents, Not Users

I started visiting CLV, as it is also called, on Fridays after my first meeting with Marilyn. She would often be waiting for me, holding a sheet of paper on which she had written the tasks we would go over that day. These tasks included changing the picture on her screensaver, managing antivirus protection, accessing accounts, sending messages on her phone, and using Excel. Our relationship was built around technology, but it quickly grew from chance and kindness, as we learned that one of her sons now lives in my home country of Colombia.

At the library, I witnessed similar experiences of patrons seeking familiarity. They would introduce themselves or ask for my name; sometimes they would approach the volunteer stand and start a conversation, smile, or wave at me. We may understand these interactions as social capital building, which is a relevant factor for sustainable technology use in community settings.[23]

As we worked on the tasks Marilyn had devised for the day, we would get into stories from which I could understand why these tasks were important to her. By listening closely and paying attention to the mood of our interactions, I tried to determine the moments in which it was best to allow her to practice or discover things by herself and those in which she needed me to just do something on her phone or computer for her. In my field notes on my work at the library, I wrote, "I thought it was sometimes better to let patrons figure things out rather than to point at the mistakes right away. But I also think you have to balance this with the frustration that might be building."

My conversations with Marilyn helped me understand the insight that I later read in Lenstra,[24] that older adults are active agents in their communities and not mere users of technology. Moreover, as Shoshana Zuboff points out, the term *users* is a vague and almost insulting term that highlights the asymmetric relationship between technology providers and consumers.[25] It places the latter as objects susceptible to experimentation and exploitation. People as agents conveys the idea of having power to act. It also includes people's ties to place and community that put them in front of a technological artifact in the first place. People as users only recognizes their relationship to the artifact. It isolates people from place and community but not from the market. A number of researchers in the field of human-computer interaction, particularly in Scandinavia, are recognizing this without abandoning the word. They advocate and practice "user-centered design." Understanding agents, not users—and I mean really understanding it—should shape the way in which we provide older adults the technology support they need.

## Strategic Patience

Marilyn has dedicated her life to helping children and adults cope with dyslexia. She has developed unique methods to help people with this reading disorder, which she understands well, having faced it herself. When instructing other teachers on working with dyslexic children, Marilyn uses the term *pregnant pause* to refer to the practice of not expecting something to follow and instead just letting things sink in. We have crystallized this insight, together with the understanding of older adults' agency, into what we think is a needed habit for volunteer technology helpers: strategic patience.

Marilyn related a negative experience to stress the importance of strategic patience: "That one helper's style was very different: very fast talking and he took charge of the situation. After working with him, I felt inadequate and that's not a good feeling." He did not get to know her or create space for bidirectional learning. Frustration was felt all around.

By strategic patience, we mean the ability to tell when to intervene and when to allow space for making mistakes and discoveries. It consists of limiting your own impulse to provide immediate solutions. This enables people to identify their own actions, remember, explore options, or just rest their minds. If our minds are set on supporting people as agents, we will learn that this can involve (1) supporting people with instruction, insisting that they perform tasks themselves; (2) working together to get a task done; or, rarely, (3) doing something for them.

## Building Digital Mazeways

Information and communication technologies are filled with redundancies. Having many ways to accomplish a task using computers and other digital devices can allow people to build their own strategies to deal with technology without needing to completely "master the entire technological environment."[26] Moreover, these strategies are embodied forms of people's multiple learning paths; they are embodied informatics moments from the past!

A simple experience with one of the first patrons I helped at the library exemplifies this. My field notes read:

> She reached out timidly from her working station and putting her hand over her face she said: "Could you help me? I'm just old." I came to her station and she said that she wanted to send a spreadsheet to herself. I asked if she had an e-mail address and when she said yes I started giving her all the instructions to access it and attach the file. However, I realized that she had done this herself before, as she already knew which link to click when she looked for "university of Illinois mail" on the search engine. Actually, I told her to click on a different link (which I thought would be faster) and she said "I always click on this other one, let's see . . . right, but I'm not a student . . ," so she did it the way she knew how, which made me realize I should have said "Go to your mail" instead of starting from scratch.

What Noah Lenstra called the informatics life course is an ongoing cycle of learning, using, adapting, and shaping technology, supported by *community-based information infrastructure*, a term he coined. In her book *Root Shock*, Mindy Thompson describes how people build a way of navigating the environment "based on individual and collective trial-and-error experiences with the maze-like possibilities offered by the surrounding world." She calls the selected pattern of movement "a way to run the maze of life" or a *mazeway*.[27] We can draw an analogy between the physical and social environment and the digital world, or even place the digital world within that environment, which we must also learn in order to navigate the information age. In their informatics life courses, people build their own ways of navigating the digital world—they build their own digital mazeways. Like the emotional ecosystems that support our sense of place in the material world, our digital mazeways allow us to feel oriented in the digital world by enabling our agency.

Marilyn has used a technique to help her reading students gain confidence in themselves during their learning processes. She highlights events in which they use their own thinking to solve a problem or face a task. "Did you notice?" she will say. "You are your own best teacher." In a similar way, older adults have been learning throughout their entire lifetimes, and so it is safe to assume that they too are their own best teachers. This means they know best how they learn, and most of the time they will be able to communicate this to the people helping them—if the opportunity is provided.

Our lesson for volunteer technology-help providers here is to support people building their digital mazeways. These are different for everybody. They may involve only digital skills, or they may also involve analog practices such as taking notes or asking for help. They may want an explanation of the big picture, or they may just want to follow the specific path they're on. Be aware of the diversity and richness in forms of digital learning and literacy, and talk to the people you are supporting about the process as well as the technology. The stereotype that young people know more about technology than older people is simply the ageist belief that the digital mazeways of young people are somehow superior to those of older adults. Recognize a particular informatics moment as a point in a long series of learning practices. Ask questions like "How could I support your learning better?" or "What has worked for you in the past?" This lesson also echoes the idea of agency and contributes to flattening the hierarchies between so-called computer experts and supposedly helpless users.

## Shaping Community-Based Information Infrastructure

The informatics moment is defined as the seeker-helper interaction but also as a phase that all of society is passing through. What if the success or failure of all our small informatics moments determines how traumatic is a society's transition to the information age? The field of community informatics has proven to be much more than an emergency measure for the digitally "left-behinds." The field strives to shape what the information age means and what technologies and infrastructure supporting it should be like if they are to meet community needs and aspirations equitably.

Marilyn started The Reading Group in 1972, together with two educators with years of experience working with students, children and adults, with dyslexia, attention and memory problems, and fine motor problems. Initially working one-on-one in children's homes, The Reading Group became a not-for-profit corporation in 1978. Its first headquarters was in a church in Urbana, and it now has its own place of operations in Champaign, Illinois. Thanks to a grant, some of their material was placed and used in twenty-five public libraries across Illinois. Marilyn relayed to me how excited she is that The Reading Group will soon be able to collaborate more closely with the African American community in Champaign-Urbana. We talked about the conditions that have kept this community from effectively addressing reading disabilities among youth and children. She now trusts that current staff of The Reading Group will continue to create the needed bonds and solidarities to be able to assist the African American community in this process.

The Reading Group was also one of the first programs in the United States to implement computer-aided reading software and one-on-one personal support to help children with dyslexia. Marilyn told me how she came to know the local scholar David Zola and the work he and other researchers were doing at the university. Zola introduced computer technologies to The Reading Group as an aid in the work of getting past reading difficulties. An article in the *Chicago Tribune* describes the use of new software in one of the rooms of The Reading Group,[28] and Zola's work is archived at the university's digital repository, IDEALS (http://ideals.library.illinois.edu).

Weekly accounts of her activities quickly convinced me that Marilyn has always been an active member of her community at CLV. In partnership with other older adults, as well as with people in other sectors who care about and collaborate with them, Marilyn has helped shape the community-based information infrastructure around her. Social capital has been a relevant factor that has amplified Marilyn's influence in her community.

The technology program at CLV has been running for fourteen years. Recently, the retirement community decided to hire a person to host office hours and provide technology support during the week. According to the current volunteer program coordinator and senior coordinator for informatics education programs at the university, this has reduced the demand for tech help on Fridays, which has been good, given the limited number of volunteers available recently. However, the Friday volunteer program has not ended. Residents continue to sign up for instruction. Every Friday there are regulars who have developed a learning bond with specific volunteers and enjoy working with them. Sometimes there are adults with specific problems with their technology that cannot wait until Monday. This has given most Friday volunteer sessions a different nature. They have shifted toward patron-driven technology learning sessions, taking charge of their own informatics moments to the extent of scheduling them in advance and tackling them in small groups rather than one-on-one.

At CLV, volunteers keep a loose record of the type of help patrons request, which then informs the content of the "Getting Started with Tech" workshops the library provides. In this way, the interactions of patrons and older adults with the existing community-based information infrastructure continue to shape it. Moreover, these interactions take place in public, in a community, and so the experience becomes community and people centered rather than user and tech centered as one might see in an Apple store.

This is also why the local community broadband initiative to bring broadband to underserved areas in Champaign-Urbana is so important, and it relates to the multiple encounters that cybernavigators have at public libraries in which they help people apply for jobs. These encounters have a deep impact on cybernavigators, as related in Williams's article "Informatics Moments."[29] Indeed, what we are encountering are society's class structure and the limited capabilities we have built to deal with its inequalities.

## Nonjudgmental Awareness

Persistent class structure is why, as Noah Lenstra wrote in his dissertation, there is a noticeable difference between public and private facilities within the community.[30] From our modification to Marilyn's handbook for helping the reluctant learner—a single page containing a list of tips with the title "10 Ways to Help the Reluctant Learner," which she pulled out of her records to fuel our conversation—we draw an additional lesson for community informatics volunteers and practitioners: nonjudgmental awareness. When working with her students, Marilyn tries to help them realize—and verbalize—what their difficulties are without judging themselves or calling themselves dumb. Instead, difficulties just call for work and support. Translating this concept to community informatics means cultivating awareness of the multilayered factors that converge in an informatics moment and attempting accurate identification of the race, gender, class, or age factors that bring cybernavigators and help seekers together in a particular space and time. This awareness will allow us to think about the best possible strategies, whether individual or collective, to address inequalities and improve on best practices.

## Experts-Together

It is common to be called an expert when helping older people with technology. In our course, we learned to respond with something like "We are not geniuses!" and to complain about the technology ourselves, thus contributing to breaking the smart/dumb dichotomy set up by tech-corporation marketing.

It would often happen that I was not able to help someone at the library or at Clark-Lindsey. On several of these occasions, I could go to the library staff or to other volunteers and ask them for help. If the problem was too cumbersome, we would all try to figure it out together, using different strategies, including consulting internet forums and support sites. Of course, some patrons didn't feel happy about this situation. Frustration would start building up as the informatics moment appeared to drift to an unsuccessful end. But however complicated the problem was, if there were enough of us, we would be able to figure it out eventually.

Several studies have found that older adult digital literacy emerges from a network of distributed expertise among family and friends as well as support provided in community technology centers, including peer-to-peer support.[31] (In fact, this is not unlike the group cognition that Edwin Hutchins observed in ship navigation.[32])

Marilyn taught me teaching skills. From my work with her and at Champaign Public Library, I learned about the local community and its people. This specific knowledge was very important for me as an international student building my mazeway in a new place.

These observations relate to Pierre Lévy's description of collective intelligence. Lévy writes, "Nobody knows everything, everyone knows something, all knowledge resides in humanity." I would add that all knowledge is harnessed somehow, and the how matters.[33] Observing the situations in which several actors gather to solve a specific technology problem at the library or the seniors center reminded me of the piranha-effect metaphor that Andrew Lih used to describe the creation and evolution of Wikipedia.[34] What he meant was that people see something exciting getting done on Wikipedia and they join in, creating a buzz of productivity. The only unfortunate aspect of his concept is the hideous name; in fact, this is collaborative expertise in action. Community technology centers foster similar dynamics offline, and community-based information infrastructure helps communities make use of their distributed expertise.

Our lesson for technology support on this point is simple: allow yourself to be removed from the expert's high position, acknowledge networked expertise and changing hierarchies—and enjoy the wonders of being experts-together.

## CONCLUSIONS

We have reflected on seniors using technology as witnessed in fieldwork performed at a seniors community, in a public library, and in co-elaborative research with Marilyn, a resident of that community. We drew on five concepts: (1) the digital divide, (2) ageism, (3) informatics moments, (4) informatics life course, and (5) each one teach one. We presented six more concepts for seniors (and others) using technology and their helpers: (6) agents not users, (7) strategic patience, (8) supporting digital mazeway building, (9) shaping community-based information infrastructure, (10) nonjudgmental awareness, and (11) experts-together. These eleven concepts help us better understand both the empirical and the abstract meanings of the term *informatics moment*. They attempt to consciously bring this understanding into the practice of seniors' technology use.

In fact, we learned something new about informatics moments as we wrote this chapter. The Friday sessions moved away from "spontaneous" informatics moments. We recalled that elders discovered (and helpers earned) a higher level of comfort and trust. As that happened, tech problems began to be laid out in advance and informatics moments became a group process rather than one seeker with one helper. We already knew that social capital accelerates any given informatics moment, but now we see that a stable community with a stable volunteer infrastructure can gather its power together to really speed up everyone's learning and mastery. It does not have to be a group assembled for that purpose, as was the legendary Homebrew Computer Club started in California in 1975 or similar early groups.

The eleven guiding concepts presented here work as a complement to Phil Agre's article "How to Help Someone Use a Computer,"[35] which was one of the first conceptualizations of the informatics moment, although not by that name. They also support and extend previous theory and empirical findings relating social capital to sustainability of technology use in community settings.

To recapitulate our six new concepts: The first is *agents not users*. Any senior doing something with technology has agency and is much more than a user. This concept removes technology from the center and places the focus on the person and on the community (i.e., the social and physical environment).

The second is building *strategic patience* as the ability to judge when to intervene and when to allow space for mistake and discovery. This lesson is linked to the recognition of people as agents and not mere users of technology.

The third concept consists of supporting people in *building digital mazeways*. Digital mazeways are selected patterns of movement in the digital world, built from individual and collective trial-and-error experiences and learning practices; they allow people to enact their agency in the information age. Learning processes are long and diverse. A particular informatics moment is only one event within someone's lifetime of learning. This concept mandates talking to people not only about the technology but also about how they like to learn, or at least observing carefully and aligning yourself with their approach.

The fourth concept is that seniors are *shaping community-based information infrastructure*. At work or at school, information technology services are usually in place well before we arrive. At the very least, they have a name. But seniors in communities create their own technology help services by assembling the parts and setting them in motion. This is an invaluable lesson when it appears no help is in sight; the pieces can be found and put together.

The fifth concept is cultivating *nonjudgmental awareness* of the multilayered factors that converge in an informatics moment and acknowledging the race, gender, class, or age factors that bring together cybernavigators and people seeking help in a particular space and time. This awareness will help us devise more effective strategies to provide support, especially when thinking of infrastructure- or policy-scale initiatives.

The last concept is to practice collaborative expertise, or *experts-together*. Remove the helper from the expert position. Collaborative expertise is a set of collective knowledge, skills, and motivations that emerge when two or more people come together to achieve a common goal. This is more than just the sum of their individual skills. Seniors may even develop a self-supporting community with minimal need for outside help. In this way, we may discard the myths around elders and those who help them and celebrate being experts-together.

Marilyn made a comment as we completed this chapter. She was speaking to the other three authors by teleconference, after almost a year of pandemic lockdown, from her apartment at Clark-Lindsey Village. For months, her meals had been brought to her. She had very limited opportunities to do almost everything she was used to doing. And, of course, she was fortunate to have all this support. She said, "We're constantly reminded of things we can't do anymore. So much is done for us. Showing ourselves and others what we can do, for instance with technology, is key to our self-actualization. This gives our lives meaning even in this pandemic." We are all grateful to have gotten to know each other, to have learned so much about technology in actual use, and to share here what we have learned about age and technology in action.

## NOTES

1. M. Bakardjieva, *Internet Society: The Internet in Everyday Life* (London: SAGE, 2005).

2. K. Williams, "Rethinking Digital Divide Research: Datasets and Theoretical Frameworks," in *Main Fronts of Information Science and Information Management:*

*Forum on Information Science and Information Management*, Peking University (情报学与信息管理的主战场:北京大学情报学与 信息管理论坛文集, in English and Chinese), ed. C. Jianlong, S. Jing, Z. Qingshan, and C. Wenguang (Peking: Peking University Press, 2011), 109–127.

3. K. Williams, "Research Note: Across the US, 85,000 to 144,000 Public Computing Sites," *First Monday* 8, no. 4 (April 2003), http://firstmonday.org/ojs/index.php/fm/article/view/1046/967.

4. J. L. Qiu, *Working-Class Network Society: Communication Technology and the Information Have-Less in Urban China* (Cambridge, MA: MIT Press, 2009).

5. R. Eglash, "A Two-Way Bridge across the Digital Divide," *The Chronicle of Higher Education* 48, no. 41 (2002): B12.

6. K. Williams, "Informatics Moments," *The Library Quarterly* 82, no. 1 (2012): 47–73.

7. Williams, "Informatics Moments," 47.

8. Williams, "Informatics Moments," 70.

9. Williams, "Informatics Moments."

10. M. Anderson and A. Perrin, "Tech Adoption Climbs among Older Americans," Pew Research Center, May 17, 2017, https://www.pewresearch.org/internet/2017/05/17/tech-adoption-climbs-among-older-adults/.

11. N. Lenstra, "Agency and Ageism in the Community-Based Technology Support Services Used by Older Adults," *First Monday* 22, no. 8 (August 2017), https://doi.org/10.5210/fm.v22i8.7559.

12. L. M. Bowen, "Rewriting the Aging Body: Literacy, Technology, and History" (PhD diss., University of Illinois at Urbana-Champaign, 2012), http://hdl.handle.net/2142/31001; S. Sayago and  J. Blat, "Telling the Story of Older People E-mailing: An Ethnographical Study," *International Journal of Human-Computer Studies* 68, no. 1 (2010): 105–120. Also see M. Castells, "Grassrooting the Space of Flows," *Urban Geography* 20, no. 4 (1999): 294–302.

13. Robin Seaton Jefferson, "More Seniors Are Embracing Technology. But Can They Use It? UCSD Researchers Suggest Asking Them," *Forbes*, June 28, 2019, https://www.forbes.com/sites/robinseatonjefferson/2019/06/28/more-seniors-are-embracing-technology-but-can-they-use-it-ucsd-researchers-suggest-asking-them/?sh=5f6fddba2323.

14. N. Lenstra, "Designing for the Informatics Lifecourse and Ageing in Place," in *Perspectives on Human-Computer Interaction Research with Older People*, ed. S. Sayago (Cham, Switzerland: Springer, 2019), 155–168.

15. N. Lenstra, "The Community Informatics of an Aging Society: A Comparative Case Study of Senior Centers and Public Libraries," Dissertation, University of Illinois at Urbana-Champaign (2016).

16. P. Lévy, *Collective Intelligence* (New York: Plenum Trade, 1999). First published in French in 1994.

17. Kate Williams, Noah Lenstra, Hui Yan, Karin Readel, Jillian Coy, Travis Faust, Brad Irwin, Chang Liu, Emily Metcalf, Ari Nussbaum, Cameron Riesenberger, and Noah Samuel, "Older Adults and the Informatics Moment" (unpublished manuscript).

18. P. Agre, "How to Help Someone Use a Computer," *The Network Observer* 1, no. 5 (May 1994), https://pages.gseis.ucla.edu/faculty/agre/tno/may-1994.html#how.

19. Williams et al., "Older Adults and the Informatics Moment."

20. Lenstra, "The Community Informatics of an Aging Society."

21. P. Day, "A Brief Introduction to the History of Community Informatics," *AI and Society* 25, no. 3 (2010): 259–263, https://doi.org/10.1007/s00146-010-0286-2.

22. Mindy Thompson Fullilove, *Root Shock. How Tearing Up City Neighborhoods Hurts America and What We Can Do about It* (New York: One World/Ballantine Books, 2004). Also see B. Wellman and B. Leighton, "Networks, Neighborhoods and Communities," *Urban Affairs Quarterly* 14, no. 3 (1979): 363–390.

23. K. Williams, "Informatics Moments," *The Library Quarterly* 82, no. 1 (2012): 47–73, https://doi.org/10.1086/662946; A. Alkalimat and K. Williams, "Social Capital and Cyberpower in the African American Community: A Case Study of a Community Technology Center in the Dual City," in *Community Informatics: Shaping Computer Mediated Social Relations*, ed. Leigh Keeble and Brian Loader (London: Routledge, 2001).

24. Lenstra "The Community Informatics of an Aging Society."

25. Shoshana Zuboff, "The Age of Surveillance Capitalism," talk given at the Institute of Art and Ideas, London, video, 29:10, https://www.youtube.com/watch?v=8HzW5rzPUy8.

26. Lenstra, "The Community Informatics of an Aging Society," 157.

27. Fullilove, *Root Shock*, 211.

28. I. Chang, "Coping with Dyslexia," *Chicago Tribune*, May 13, 1990, https://www.chicagotribune.com/news/ct-xpm-1990-05-13-9002080339-story.html.

29. Williams, "Informatics Moments."

30. Lenstra, "The Community Informatics of an Aging Society."

31. Bowen, "Rewriting the Aging Body"; N. Selwyn, "The Information Aged: A Qualitative Study of Older Adults' Use of Information and Communications Technology," *Journal of Aging Studies* 18, no. 4 (2004): 369–384; T. Kanayama, "Ethnographic Research on the Experience of Japanese Elderly People Online," *New Media and Society* 5, no. 2 (2003): 267–288.

32. E. Hutchins, *Cognition in the Wild* (Cambridge, MA: MIT Press, 1994).

33. Lévy, *Collective Intelligence*, 20.

34. A. Lih, *The Wikipedia Revolution: How a Bunch of Nobodies Created the World's Greatest Encyclopedia* (New York: Hyperion Books, 2009).

35. Agre, "How to Help."

*Chapter Six*

# Health Insurance Literacy and Older Adults

## Emily Vardell

I believe honor thy mother and father is not just a good commandment to live by, it is good public policy to govern by. That is why I feel so strongly about Medicare.[1]

—Barbara Mikulski

For individuals in the United States, their sixty-fifth birthday comes with a letter from the US government informing them of their eligibility (or non-eligibility) for Medicare. Eligibility for Medicare Part A benefits (outlined in a later section) is determined through the payroll taxes a person has paid through their workplace. Individuals may also qualify for coverage through the work record of their current (or in some cases divorced or deceased) spouse. Even if an individual is not eligible to enroll in Part A of Medicare for free, at the age of sixty-five they are nevertheless eligible to enroll in Part B and Part D (also outlined in subsequent sections) by paying premiums just like any other individual over the age of sixty-five. US citizens and legal residents who have lived in the United States for at least five years before applying are eligible. Sixty million adults in the United States have health insurance coverage through Medicare, making it by far the primary source of health insurance coverage for older adults in the United States.

Layered on top of these decision-making points are issues of health insurance literacy, or "the extent to which consumers can make informed purchase and use decisions."[2] Research has shown that the senior population is often characterized by lower levels of health insurance literacy, meaning they may not have the skills necessary to navigate Medicare and other health insurance options effectively and select the options that are most appropriate for their medical and financial needs. In addition, the higher medical needs of aging individuals leads to more frequent interactions within the health care system and reliance on those health insurance literacy skills for which there may be cognitive or other limitations. Medicare Part D, in particular, can present a difficult decision-making scenario for enrollees who instead of selecting from a small subset of employer-sponsored options may instead be deciding between an array of Part D options with few opportunities to ask for clarifications or advice from parties without a vested interest (e.g., insurance companies or insurance brokers).

This chapter explores the history of Medicare and health insurance coverage for older adults in the United States, and the complex Medicare system itself is detailed in the following sections. The aspects of both insurance system structure and individual agency are important to consider when describing the health insurance literacy barriers faced by older adults when interacting with the health care system.

## HEALTH INSURANCE IN THE UNITED STATES

Who gets health insurance? The vast majority of individuals in the United States obtain health insurance coverage through employer-sponsored insurance (ESI).[3] ESI has been the foundation of the US health care system since the 1940s. In the United States, health insurance began during the Great Depression, when hospitals would offer prepayment plans to employment-based groups to ensure that patients would pay their bills.[4] Private health insurance is a mechanism by which individuals can protect themselves from the tremendously high costs of medical care due to severe illness or accident.[5] When an individual has health insurance, the person can use this coverage to subsidize the cost of a visit to their physician. In the case of a physician visit, the insurance company will pay a portion of the cost (sometimes dependent on whether the physician is in the insurance company's preferred network), and the individual will pay the remaining portion (i.e., a copay required by the insurer, generally a percentage of the bill).

ESI is an economically effective system[6] in that it allows companies to insure a diverse group of people (often of mixed ages and health statuses) and provides a convenient risk pool. This reduces administrative costs and allows employees to cancel out each other's risk. Because insurance comes through an employer, health insurance companies also see it as a reliable way to be paid. Premiums paid via payroll deductions are a much more reliable way to fund coverage than requiring each individual to pay for their insurance separately. The ESI system also plays into cultural attitudes in the United States about work. Rather than a national system (such as the systems in Europe) where everyone has coverage regardless of how "deserving" they are of coverage (i.e., whether or not they have paid into the system), the US health care system requires that individuals be employed to receive health insurance coverage.[7]

The most recent major development in the history of US health care reform came on March 23, 2010, when President Barack Obama signed into law the Patient Protection and Affordable Care Act (P.L. 111-148) and the Health Care and Education Reconciliation Act of 2010 (P.L. 111-152), commonly referred to as the Affordable Care Act (ACA). At its core, the ACA (nicknamed Obamacare) aims to extend health care coverage to all people. One of the most significant aspects of the ACA for seniors is that plans may no longer deny coverage to individuals based on a preexisting condition, particularly important for older adults who are more likely to have health conditions. The ACA requires a plan to cover specific preventive services, many of which are relevant to seniors, including colorectal cancer screening, diabetes (type 2) screening, falls prevention for adults sixty-five and older living in a community setting, hepatitis C screening, immunization vaccines, and lung cancer screening.[8] The ACA also funded navigator positions, in which individuals were trained to help consumers look for health insurance coverage options as well as complete eligibility and enrollment forms. These ACA navigators were required to be unbiased and were funded through the ACA as a free service for consumers.

A complementary piece of the puzzle in the US health care system is that of the Veterans Health Administration (VHA), the largest integrated health care system in the United States, which provides health care services to over nine million veterans enrolled in the Veterans Administration (VA) health care program.[9] Almost half (48.7%) of VHA enrollees are over the age of sixty-five[10] and thus qualify for VA benefits for elderly veterans, including aid and attendance, geriatrics care, long-term care, and other home-based and community services.[11] As is the case with all VA benefits, veterans must apply for services and are qualified based on a number of factors, including years of service. The VA recommends veterans with VA health care enroll in Medicare as soon as they are eligible,[12] although there is no coordination of benefits between the two services. Enrollees must use VA coverage in VA facilities and Medicare coverage anywhere else.

## HISTORY OF MEDICARE

When did Medicare begin? While little has changed in the US health care insurance system over the last ninety years or so, there have been a few successful attempts at health care reform, such as Medicare. Political factors, such as timing, political sympathies, partisanship, and special interest group politics, have played a role in defining the success of the 1965 legislation creating Medicare. Perhaps the biggest reason why the Medicare legislation was so successful was that it focused on a very politically sympathetic demographic group: the elderly.[13]

First, older retired Americans were uninsured through no fault of their own; most simply were not eligible for employer-sponsored insurance. The fact that the elderly were uninsured due to age (rather than due to being unemployed, for example) played a key role in Medicare's success as it built on very American political ideas about earning. Instead of being seen as a system that would be giving anything away unmerited, the program had working individuals pay into a Medicare account (building on the model set by Social Security benefits). Then, once they had retired, they would have "earned" coverage. The way this was constructed fought against the idea of government handouts. Since they had paid in, they were eligible for coverage. This aspect appealed to both major political parties and ensured its passage.[14]

It was also closer to true insurance in that, at the beginning, it only covered catastrophic events such as surgeries or hospitalizations. It also required higher deductibles, which resulted in many seniors enrolling in supplemental "Medigap" insurance[15] from health insurance companies (this trend continues today and will be explored further in later sections). Medicare was also particularly politically popular as it relieved the burden on children taking care of their elderly parents' medical expenses.

The legislation that created Medicare also created Medicaid. This legislation was the first example of demographic incrementalism.[16] This technique was used to provide coverage demographic group by demographic group. It started with the elderly (through Medicare), one of the most politically sympathetic groups in existence. It then expanded through Medicaid to the medically indigent (those going bankrupt due to health care costs), people with long-term disabilities (as a result of an expansion of Medicare in 1972), kidney patients, pregnant mothers, and children. It was hard to argue against covering these segments of the population.

Those who feared that Medicare and Medicaid were a slippery slope toward national health insurance may have been right. Ultimately, Medicare became enormously successful with good approval ratings and a nearly 100 percent enrollment rate. It also created a vocal and strong interest group: Medicare enrollees. They like their coverage and will fight to keep it. In many ways the success of Medicare became a warning against further health care reform. Any discussion of health care reform must include Medicare as part of the picture. This creation of a health care juggernaut made many politicians wary of creating further untouchable health care programs.[17]

# THE STRUCTURE OF MEDICARE

How does Medicare work? Medicare is to date the only truly national health care program in the United States and currently helps more than sixty million seniors and people with disabilities pay for their health care.[18] While ESI provided retiree health coverage to three in ten (30%) of traditional Medicare beneficiaries in 2016, this percentage is expected to continue to drop as the number of large firms offering retiree health benefits to their employees continues to decrease (e.g., it was 66% in 1988 and 18% in 2018).[19] The vast majority of individuals aged sixty-five and older obtain their health insurance coverage through Medicare and its associated coverages. In its current state, Medicare is comprised of four parts, which are detailed in table 6.1.

The traditional high deductibles and cost-sharing requirements (e.g., coinsurance) required through Medicare place a financial strain on many retired individuals already living on fixed incomes. In addition to these out-of-pocket expenses, Medicare does not include coverage for many services sought by older individuals, including long-term services, dental services, eyeglasses, and hearing aids. To address the gaps left by the benefits offered through Medicare, "Medigap" policies, also called Medicare supplement insurance, provided supplemental coverage for 29 percent of Medicare beneficiaries in 2016.[20] These plans are sold by private health insurance companies and help to cover cost-sharing requirements and other associated health care costs. Most Medicare beneficiaries (in 2016, 81%)[21] elect some type of supplemental coverage to help cover costs and address benefit gaps, including employer-sponsored insurance, Medigap, Medicaid, and other coverage.

The most popular type of Medicare Advantage plans (i.e., Part C plans) are HMOs (health maintenance organizations).[22] Like traditional HMOs offered through employer-sponsored insurance plans, these plans offer managed care, which generally requires coordination through a primary-care physician for specialty care or other services. HMOs are often geographically limited in their service areas and so may be appropriate choices for some seniors but not work as well for others (e.g., snowbirds who travel between multiple locations or others who travel frequently).

# "MEDICARE AND YOU"

How do eligible citizens learn about their Medicare eligibility and coverage details? Each year the Centers for Medicare and Medicaid Services create a handbook entitled "Medicare and You," which has been mailed out annually to all Medicare beneficiary households since its first printing in 1999 and has

**Table 6.1. Medicare Coverage: Parts A, B, C, and D**

| | |
|---|---|
| **Part A** | • Most people ages sixty-five and over are entitled to Part A if they or their spouse are eligible for Social Security payments.<br>• Most people do not have to pay a premium for Part A if they paid payroll taxes for ten or more years (these payroll taxes are the funding stream that keeps Part A "free" for beneficiaries).<br>• Often described as hospital insurance to distinguish it from medical insurance (Part B).<br>• Covers inpatient hospital stays, skilled nursing facility stays, some home health visits, and hospice care.<br>• Part A benefits are subject to a deductible and require coinsurance. |
| **Part B** | • Requires a monthly premium unless a beneficiary's income is low enough to qualify for state assistance (most people pay a standard premium, $144.60 in 2020).<br>• Often referred to as medical insurance to distinguish it from hospital insurance (Part A).<br>• Covers physician visits, diagnostic and lab tests, outpatient services, preventive services, outpatient mental health care, and some home health visits.<br>• Many Part B benefits are subject to a deductible and a coinsurance (typically 20%).<br>• No coinsurance is charged for many annual wellness visits or preventive services. |
| **Part C** | • Referred to as the Medicare Advantage program.<br>• An optional program in which beneficiaries can enroll in a private health plan and receive all Medicare-covered Part A and Part B benefits and typically also Part D.<br>• Run by private insurance companies, who provide managed care primarily through health maintenance organizations (HMOs) or preferred provider organizations (PPOs).<br>• As of 2018, twenty million beneficiaries enrolled in Medicare Advantage (i.e., 34% of all Medicare beneficiaries). |
| **Part D** | • Outpatient prescription drug coverage through private plans that contract with Medicare.<br>• Optional coverage that requires paying additional premiums.<br>• Includes stand-alone prescription drug plans (PDPs) and Medicare Advantage plans with prescription drug coverage (MA-PDs).<br>• For 2021 coverage, beneficiaries have an average choice of sixty Medicare plans with Part D coverage (including thirty PDPs and twenty-seven MA-PDs).<br>• Part D coverage is the most recent Medicare program, having been initiated in 2006. |

served as a primary information source for many Medicare enrollees since then.[23] The handbook is printed in a larger font size ideal for older readers who may be suffering from vision loss and includes the use of symbols (e.g., showing comparisons between Original Medicare and Medicare Advantage, information about costs and coverage, and information about preventive services) as well as clearly laid out charts and an index of topics at the beginning of the handbook.

There are eleven sections included in the handbook: Signing Up for Medicare; Finding Out If Medicare Covers Your Test, Item, or Service; Original Medicare; Medicare Advantage Plans and Other Options; Medicare Supplement Insurance (Medigap); Medicare Drug Coverage (Part D); Get Help Paying for Health and Drug Costs; Know Your Rights and Protect Yourself from Fraud; Get More Information; Definitions; and Compare Health and Drug Plans in Your Area (which is customized to the geographic location of the recipient).[24] The 2021 handbook was approximately 125 pages long, depending on the customized information at the back of the book. The creators of "Medicare and You" clearly have literacy concerns in mind and so make liberal use of white space, bolding of important information, and laying out significant comparisons in chart format. The definitions chapter is limited (i.e., only four pages long) but does demonstrate an interest in assisting users with complicated insurance jargon. While the publication is mailed out automatically in English, there is a section at the back of the book labeled "Help in Other Languages," with information about the 1-800-MEDICARE number available in sixteen other languages. On the Medicare and You website, several different formats are offered, including English and Spanish PDFs, large-print English and Spanish PDFs, e-book formats including Kindle, an English podcast and a Spanish podcast, and in Braille (available by calling 1-800-MEDICARE).[25] "Medicare and You" is paid for by the Department of Health and Human Services and is one of the few examples of health literacy materials published and distributed in such large quantities across the United States.

Other materials designed to help individuals navigate the Medicare process include the book *Medicare for Dummies*, sponsored by AARP. This title is much more in depth than "Medicare and You" (the fourth edition is over four hundred pages long), and it provides additional definitions and discussions of core terminology as well as more guidance than "Medicare and You" can provide (e.g., it includes chapters on getting help in making Medicare choices and top ten Medicare mistakes).

# HEALTH INSURANCE AFFORDABILITY
# CONCERNS AMONG OLDER ADULTS

How much does health insurance cost? Those transitioning from employer-sponsored insurance to Medicare coverage may very well experience serious concerns about affordability and losing some of the benefits of having coverage through an employer (e.g., higher pharmaceutical out-of-pocket costs for specialty drugs).[26] Transitioning to retirement includes a host of changes in a person's life, and one of the changes that may present many questions is transitioning to Medicare coverage. In a 2018 National Pharmaceutical Association Foundation survey of adults aged fifty to sixty-four, 45 percent of respondents had little to no confidence in their ability to afford health insurance in retirement, which was linked to delaying or forgoing care due to cost concerns.[27] Factors associated with affordability concerns included lower health insurance literacy (as measured through confidence in knowing health insurance terms) as well as fair/poor health.[28] As the authors write, "These results suggest that it may be possible to reduce health insurance affordability concerns and delayed/forgone care by improving adults' confidence in understanding and using health insurance."[29]

# MEASUREMENTS OF HEALTH
# LITERACY AND HEALTH INSURANCE LITERACY

Is understanding health insurance difficult? In 2003, the US Department of Education National Center for Education Statistics administered the National Assessment of Adult Literacy (NAAL) to more than nineteen thousand adults, making the NAAL the largest-scale measurement of health literacy in the United States to date. Adults aged sixty-five and older had lower average health literacy than adults in any other age group (i.e., sixteen to twenty-four, twenty-five to thirty-nine, forty to forty-nine, fifty to sixty-four). Adults who received health insurance through Medicare or Medicaid or had no health insurance coverage had lower health literacy than adults with other types of health insurance coverage (e.g., ESI and military insurance). For adults who received Medicare, a full 27 percent had below-basic health literacy and another 30 percent had only basic health literacy skills. *Below basic* is defined as having "no more than the most simple and concrete literacy skills" with a range of skills from being nonliterate to being able to locate information in short prose texts and simple documents and performing simple quantitative operations (primarily addition). Skills from the intermediate and proficient categories include reading and understanding dense prose texts, locating information in dense documents, locating less familiar quantitative information, integrating multiple pieces of information located in complex documents, and using quantitative information to solve multistep problems.[30] These skills are important to note as clearly more than half of Medicare beneficiaries are not able to perform these tasks and potentially select the most appropriate Part D coverage or effectively navigate the health care system, for example.

In addition, individuals who struggled the most with understanding health care information in the NAAL were more likely to be sixty-five years or older, male, Black or Hispanic, or have spoken a language other than English prior to formal education. These findings are a strong reminder that health literacy skills cannot be generalized to particular populations. While there are demonstrable trends, low health literacy levels can be observed in portions of most populations, and intersectionality—that is, the intersection of multiple points of identity—is an important aspect to consider when exploring the multifaceted nature of health insurance literacy.

In one of the few studies focused exclusively on health insurance literacy and Medicare beneficiaries, McCormack and colleagues created a two-part instrument to assess health insurance literacy, including questions designed to gauge prior knowledge and familiarity with health insurance terminology and questions aimed at assessing proficiency using the Medicare insurance. Based on their findings, these authors developed the Conceptual Framework for Health Insurance Literacy. This framework models age, education, race, and culture all playing a role in financial literacy. Financial literacy, in turn, affects numeracy, health literacy, health care decision making, and use of health care services, which ultimately affects health outcomes. In the terminology section of their study, the terms that were the most misunderstood included *provider network* (41%), *formulary* (44%), and *Medigap* (56%).[31] This indicates a lack of prior knowledge of insurance concepts and supports the need for dictionaries or glossaries in Medicare informational materials, such as the handbook "Medicare and You."

## HEALTH INSURANCE INFORMATION SOURCES

Where can you go for more information about health insurance? While many Medicare beneficiaries might automatically get enrolled in Part A, when it comes to Part C (i.e., Medicare Advantage programs), Part D (prescription drug coverage), and/or Medigap policies, the number of choices can quickly become overwhelming, and many may need to consult information sources for additional guidance. In a study of 1,673 Medicare beneficiaries' ability to make informed choices about fee-for-service and managed care options, survey results indicated that participants use a variety of information sources to learn about health plans, with an average of 2.8 sources each. For both HMO and traditional Medicare enrollees, HMO advertisements were the most common information source for learning about health plans. In addition, "30 percent of beneficiaries know almost nothing about HMOs; only 11 percent have adequate knowledge to make an informed choice; and HMO enrollees have significantly lower knowledge levels of the differences between the two delivery systems."[32] These findings are surprising, given that enrollees had to make an active decision to enroll in HMOs and yet are the least well informed. These findings raise serious concerns as the number of Medicare choices continues to expand and older adults are forced to make hard choices often in the context of lower literacy skills.

In addition, results like these have implications for educating beneficiaries about their expanded choices and highlight the importance of addressing information needs in this population as well as their susceptibility to "aggressive marketing."[33] The authors in that study encourage moving from mere information dissemination to active education. Targeted educational efforts aimed at intermediaries such as patient advocates, consumer health librarians, family members, and health professionals will be needed to enhance their ability to assist seniors in making informed health care choices.

One of the unusual aspects of health insurance is that it is a difficult topic to get assistance with from someone who does not have a vested interest in the results. Even in an employer-sponsored insurance setting, enrollees asking questions of human resources officers might find themselves pointed to the cheapest option as the easiest and most fiscally conservative option available from employers. For those seeking to enroll in the various Medicare programs, there are government and nonprofit organizations available as resources. An example of this type of government assistance is the State Health Insurance Assistance Program (http://www.shiptacenter.org/), which is a Congress-created, state-based program available in all fifty states (as well as Guam, Puerto Rico, the Virgin Islands, and the District of Columbia) where seniors can turn for one-on-one counseling and assistance with Medicare. In addition to these government and nonprofit organizations, there are also insurance brokers devoted to providing assistance to those sifting through the options. When many of the 1-800 numbers lead directly to insurance company call lines, it is challenging for many enrollees to locate unbiased assistance.

AARP, for example, is a source of health insurance information for many Medicare beneficiaries. AARP offers a Medicare Resource Center linked from its home page with articles about reviewing Medicare coverage and a Medicare Q&A tool. Many of the information pages within that section provide authoritative information (in both English and Spanish) without an obvious agenda. However, AARP also offers members Medicare plans through UnitedHealthcare. A Google search of "AARP Medicare" first leads a searcher to sites selling AARP Medicare Plans, from which AARP obtains a good portion of its revenue, presenting a serious conflict of interest in this key information source.

A key piece of the puzzle when considering health insurance information sources is how individuals become aware of programs in the first place. In order to be able to navigate a health care system effectively, one must have an awareness of available resources. In a study of inner-city seniors conducted to determine awareness of pharmaceutical cost-assistance programs, male gender, Black race, inadequate health literacy, and receiving care in a clinic setting (as opposed to private or group practice) were associated with low awareness of cost-assistance programs.[34] Study participants who had heard a live presentation about health insurance were more likely to be aware of such programs. These findings support the "use of live presentations, in addition to health literacy materials and messages, [as] . . . important strategies in promoting knowledge of and enrollment in state and federal pharmaceutical cost-assistance programs for low-income seniors."[35] This study underscores the importance of first knowing that programs exist. A lack of knowledge about such programs, particularly among African Americans and those accessing care in public clinics, could further exacerbate unequal access to health care coverage and access that has already been identified among minority populations.[36]

This issue presents a promising opportunity for libraries and other organizations that provide information services to have a direct impact on health outcomes by building awareness of cost assistance and other Medicare-related programs. Librarians have proven track records in the area of providing much-needed health information to seniors, including MedlinePlus instruction with older Latinos[37] and helping seniors find reliable online information with Senior Navigator.[38] These kinds of successes can serve as models for librarians seeking to assist seniors with locating and using authoritative information on their health insurance plans as well as librarians seeking to connect with organizations that can provide enrollment assistance. Public librarians, for example, can collaborate with community organizations (such as an Area Agency on Aging) to develop and deliver engaging health programming that appeals to, attracts, and serves diverse audiences. Libraries that currently offer engaging programming for older adults may want to consider infusing timely health insurance and Medicare content within their successful outreach efforts.

## HEALTH INSURANCE CHOICE RESEARCH

What have researchers found when they study people's choices in their health insurance? In the limited number of research studies focused on the ability of individuals to make sense of their health insurance choices, many of the studies have, in fact, focused specifically on individuals' ability to select from Medicare Part D prescription drug coverage options.[39,40,41] These studies have demonstrated the multiple factors that researchers can choose to focus on when assessing individuals' ability to choose a health insurance plan, such as presenting a selection of options and asking individuals to indicate which choice best matches their specified coverage needs. It should be noted that many of these studies are structured so that there are "right" and "wrong" answers that do not accommodate for individual preferences (e.g., some people may prefer to overpay for coverage to enhance their peace of mind that health care bills will not bankrupt them, even if it means initially paying more out of pocket). The results overwhelmingly indicate that most individuals are not able to make effective health insurance decisions.

Underpinning health insurance choice research is the idea that individuals should select the health care coverage that matches their anticipated health care utilization. Health insurance companies should, in a fair market, compete to attract subscribers with a financially competitive offering. However, research has indicated that consumers are often unable to select the most financially appropriate option. Consequently, the competition in the market is minimized and "naïve consumers pay prices substantially above marginal cost, and effectively subsidize sophisticated consumers who are able to exploit the mispricing."[42]

When assessing individuals' ability to make health insurance decisions, researchers often concentrate on their ability to ascertain the cheapest health insurance coverage option given their health history and health needs.[43,44] Researchers are also interested in the roles that numeracy, health insurance literacy, demographics, and other individual characteristics might play in people's ability to select the most appropriate option.

For example, many researchers have looked at choice set size (or the number of insurance choices available) as a factor in effective insurance decision-making.[45,46,47] The results suggest that individuals are much more successful in identifying the most appropriate coverage option when they have fewer choices. The more choices offered, the more difficult it becomes for individuals to indicate which option makes the most fiscal sense. This is particularly significant when reflecting on Medicare Part D plans, where individuals must select from somewhere between forty and sixty competing private insurers in their area.[48] While policy makers may have originally assumed that having a wide range of insurance plans would benefit older consumers, research has not borne out that benefit and has instead indicated that the overwhelming number of options instead serves as a barrier for seniors in selecting a coverage option that meets their needs. Medicare has standardized Medigap policies with required basic benefits and a predefined lettering system (e.g., every state must offer a Plan A if they offer any Medigap policy). This is designed to make it easier to compare Medigap policies and is perhaps an attempt by the government to reduce the information burden on the consumer; however, there are still ten possible plans that states can offer (labeled with the letters A, B, C, D, F, G, K, L, M, and N).[49] It should also be noted that while Medicare is a national program, there are state regulators, so some companies' offerings and plan availability may vary by state (e.g., Medigap policies are standardized in different ways in the states of Massachusetts, Minnesota, and Wisconsin).

The overwhelming number of options could without a doubt compromise the ability of individuals to effectively assess the differences between the options available to them and select the best fit for their needs, and, in fact, the results indicate that "many seniors choose Medicare Part D plans offering poorer coverage at greater cost."[50] In a simulated health insurance selection environment, most participants performed at near chance levels and were not able to select the most cost-effective option.[51] These studies demonstrate the financial implications of individuals' ability or inability to select the appropriate health insurance plan for their needs as well as the importance of employing tools or other kinds of assistance to narrow down the options to a smaller set of appropriate choices.

It should be noted that the ability to navigate effectively between available options is "likely influenced by cognitive abilities consumers possess (e.g., numeracy) and the amount of information available in the decision environment."[52] Health insurance providers should consider displaying information using symbolic representations[53] and side-by-side comparisons of plan options.[54] Other commonly used tactics, such as bronze versus gold naming conventions, premium pricing breakdowns (i.e., weekly versus monthly),[55] educational tutorials, and calculation aids are all helpful tools for conveying health insurance information to users.[56]

It is also worth noting that monthly premiums are often not the main consideration when choosing a health plan, but other factors, such as whether a health provider is in network and whether specific medications are covered, can play larger roles.[57] In their pamphlet "Understanding Your Medicare Advantage Plan's Provider Network," the Centers for Medicare and Medicaid Services suggests that enrollees determine whether their providers are in the plan's network,[58] but that can be quite difficult for even the most health literate consumer to ascertain. In addition to the difficulty of determining a plan's network, the often near impossibility of tracking down original procedure costs may make it difficult for individuals to determine specific health care costs (e.g., calculating 20% of a procedure without knowing the original costs). In fact, older adults with chronic diseases are more likely to choose the gold health plan (i.e., the higher-cost, higher-coverage plan) even if they have a higher health insurance literacy level. These types of findings suggest that individuals may, in fact, be acting rationally by buying the most comprehensive coverage and that there is a need for more studies to consider the "peace of mind" factor when assessing people's ability to make what others might deem appropriate health insurance choices.

Simplifying the structure of the Medicare Part D decision environment may assist consumers in making better choices. Suggestions for such simplification include presenting less information about each plan and developing decision aids that can assist older adults.[59] As with all insurance materials, it is imperative that those who develop such tools keep literacy concerns and the unique needs of senior adults in mind when seeking to simplify the decision environment.

## BEYOND LITERACY ISSUES

What are other factors that make it hard to understand health insurance? In addition to the literacy challenges explored in this chapter, additional elements compound the difficulties facing older adults when turning to health insurance coverage. First, individuals may be juggling Medicare coverage, employer-sponsored coverage, and in some cases Medicaid coverage. Figuring out who pays for what and when to sign up for each makes a complicated situation that much more difficult to navigate. In addition, other factors unique to seniors, such as snowbirds who travel between locations and US citizens living outside the United States, may make it difficult to determine which coverage option best suits them geographically (not to mention those who undertake foreign travel and may seek supplementary health insurance to cover any unforeseen issues that happen abroad).

In addition, health insurance decision-making is rarely something that happens in a vacuum; instead, many individuals turn to spouses, family members, friends, and colleagues to provide assistance in determining what the best coverage option is.[60] For older adults, there may be adult children who provide guidance on enrollment options, or they may turn to friends in a retirement facility to help them determine which coverage options work best for their specific needs. It is also possible that older adults may be facing greater isolation with the loss of work colleagues and potentially smaller social networks. These individuals may not have access to the people they would normally turn to for advice on such matters, which may compound the difficulties in selecting health insurance coverage.

## CONCLUSIONS

The issue of health insurance literacy and older adults is becoming more pressing and more expensive as the senior population in the United States increases. Seniors face the real possibility of paying more than necessary for their health care by either selecting a plan with incredibly high premiums that covers more than they need or selecting a plan that does not cover their needs and results in astronomically high out-of-pocket costs. In addition to this financial burden on seniors, adults in the increasingly larger sandwich generation[61] who might be financially supporting their own children as well as their parents may find themselves shouldering the financial burden of covering what their senior parents cannot manage on fixed incomes. As this chapter has indicated, finding assistance with navigating the whole process can be very difficult, as there are so few resources that do not have a financial stake or potential bias in the ultimate outcome. Pressure from insurance and pharmaceutical companies to provide a multitude of expensive options for seniors to choose from is not met with unified opposition. Who will advocate for the needs of seniors—both in terms of literacy and finances—when so many other groups are lobbying to make money where they can?

When it comes to understanding older adults' interactions within the US health care system, it is important to explore the overlapping roles of coverage options (e.g., Medicare, employer-sponsored insurance, Veterans Health Administration, and Medicaid) and health insurance literacy abilities. Consumers often need help sifting through what can be an overwhelming number of options, understanding the unique jargon of health insurance, and getting help. As the number of Medicare choices continues to expand, older adults are required to make difficult choices and may not have access to the necessary tools or skills to make informed decisions. Some of the Medicare infrastructure (e.g., standardizing Medigap policies with a specific lettering system) may be designed to assist in this decision-making process, and yet there are still many more steps that could be taken to assist in this at times unnecessarily complex process. For example, smart systems that would help users narrow down available options by what applies to their circumstances or needs could help trim down the number of choices seniors must sift through. In addition, funding positions where trained individuals could provide unbiased, one-on-one assistance with the enrollment process (building on the success of ACA navigators) may be a path worth considering. Other information professionals, such as public librarians, may consider expanding their health-related outreach to include providing programming for older adults that includes discussions of Medicare and health insurance. Librarians, educators, social workers, and other information professionals can play a role in providing the guidance and support the public requires when navigating health insurance options based on their own individual needs.

## NOTES

1. Barbara Mikulski, US senator from Maryland from 1987 to 2017; US Congress, *Congressional Record* 149, 108th Cong., 1st sess., at 14160–14161 (2003).

2. Jinhee Kim, Bonnie Braun, and Andrew D. Williams, "Understanding Health Insurance Literacy: A Literature Review," *Family and Consumer Sciences Research Journal* 42, no. 1 (2013): 3.

3. "Health Insurance Coverage of the Total Population," Kaiser Family Foundation, accessed September 29, 2015, http://kff.org/other/state-indicator/total-population/.

4. Sherry A. Glied and Phyllis C. Brozi, "The Current State of Employer-Based Health Coverage," *Journal of Law, Medicine, and Ethics* 32, no. 3 (2004): 404–410.

5. "How Private Health Coverage Works: A Primer," Kaiser Family Foundation, accessed October 14, 2015, http://kff.org/health-costs/issue-brief/how-private-health-coverage-works-a-primer/.

6. Ellen O'Brien, "Employers' Benefits from Workers' Health Insurance," *The Milbank Quarterly* 81, no. 1 (2003): 5–43.

7. Jonathan Oberlander, "The Political Economy of Unfairness in U.S. Health Policy," *Law and Contemporary Problems* 69, no. 4 (2006): 245–264, http://www.jstor.org/stable/27592158.

8. "Preventive Care Benefits for Adults," HealthCare.gov, accessed April 29, 2021, https://www.healthcare.gov/preventive-care-adults/.

9. "Veterans Health Administration," Veterans Administration, accessed April 29, 2021, https://www.va.gov/health/aboutvha.asp.

10. Joan Wang, Pavan Dhanireddy, Cynthia Prince, Michael Larsen, Michael Schimpf, and Gerald Pearman, *2019 Survey of Veteran Enrollees' Health and Use of Health Care* (Washington DC: Department of Veterans Affairs, 2020), https://www.va.gov/HEALTHPOLICYPLANNING/SOE2019/2019_Enrollee_Data_Findings_Report-March_2020_508_Compliant.pdf.

11. "Elderly Veterans," Veterans Administration, accessed April 29, 2021, https://www.benefits.va.gov/persona/veteran-elderly.asp.

12. "VA Health Care and Other Insurance," Veterans Administration, accessed April 29, 2021, https://www.va.gov/health-care/about-va-health-benefits/va-health-care-and-other-insurance/.

13. Jonathan Oberlander, "Medicare and Medicaid," in *Oxford Companion to American Politics*, ed. David Coates (New York: Oxford University, 2012), 104–108.

14. Robert M. Ball, "What Medicare's Architects Had in Mind," *Health Affairs* 14, no. 4 (1995): 62–72.

15. As defined by Medicare.gov, a Medicare Supplement Insurance (Medigap) policy is sold by private companies and is designed to help pay for health care costs not covered by original Medicare (e.g., copayments, coinsurance, and deductibles). "What Is Medicare Supplement Insurance (Medigap)?," Medicare.gov, accessed January 28, 2020, https://www.medicare.gov/supplement-other-insurance/medigap/whats-medigap.html.

16. Jonathan B. Oberlander and Barbara Lyons, "Beyond Incrementalism? SCHIP and the Politics of Health Reform," *Health Affairs* 28, no. 3 (2009): w399–w410.

17. Oberlander, "Medicare and Medicaid," 104–108.

18. "An Overview of Medicare," Kaiser Family Foundation, accessed February 13, 2019, https://www.kff.org/medicare/issue-brief/an-overview-of-medicare/.

19. "2018 Employer Health Benefits Survey," Kaiser Family Foundation, accessed October 3, 2018, https://www.kff.org/health-costs/report/2018-employer-health-benefits-survey/.

20. "An Overview of Medicare," Kaiser Family Foundation, accessed January 28, 2021, https://www.kff.org/medicare/issue-brief/an-overview-of-medicare/.

21. "Sources of Supplemental Coverage among Medicare Beneficiaries in 2016," Kaiser Family Foundation, accessed April 26, 2021, https://www.kff.org/medicare/issue-brief/sources-of-supplemental-coverage-among-medicare-beneficiaries-in-2016/.

22. "A Dozen Facts about Medicare Advantage in 2020," Kaiser Family Foundation, accessed April 26, 2021, https://www.kff.org/medicare/issue-brief/a-dozen-facts-about-medicare-advantage-in-2020/.

23. "Medicare & Medicaid Milestones 1937–2015," Centers for Medicare and Medicaid Services, accessed January 28, 2021, https://www.cms.gov/About-CMS/Agency-Information/History/Downloads/Medicare-and-Medicaid-Milestones-1937-2015.pdf.

24. "Medicare & You," Medicare.gov, accessed January 28, 2021, https://www.medicare.gov/medicare-and-you.

25. "Download 'Medicare & You' in Different Formats," Medicare.gov, accessed January 28, 2021, https://www.medicare.gov/forms-help-resources/medicare-you-handbook/download-medicare-you-in-different-formats.

26. Sonal Parasrampuria, Aditi P. Sen, and Gerard F. Anderson, "Comparing Patient OOP Spending for Specialty Drugs in Medicare Part D and Employer-Sponsored Insurance," *American Journal of Managed Care* 26, no. 9 (2020): 388–394.

27. Jamie Luster, Renuka Tipirneni, Erica Solway, Preeti Malani, Jeffery Kullgren, Matthias A. Kirch, Dianne Singer, and Aaron M. Scherer, "Confidence in Health Insurance Affordability and Delayed or Forgone Health Care among Adults Approaching Retirement," *Innovation in Aging* 3, no. 1 supplement (2019): S12.

28. Aaron M. Scherer, Erica Solway, Preeti Malani, Jamie Luster, Jeffery Kullgren, Matthias A. Kirch, Dianne Singer, and Renuka Tipirneni, "Health Insurance

Literacy, Health Status, and Concerns about Affordability of Health Insurance Near Retirement," *Innovation in Aging* 3, no. 1 supplement (2019): S12.

29. Scherer et al., "Health Insurance Literacy."

30. Mark Kutner, Elizabeth Greenburg, Ying Jin, and Christine Paulsen, "The Health Literacy of America's Adults: Results from the 2003 National Assessment of Adult Literacy," US Department of Education NCES 2006-483 (Washington, DC: National Center for Education Statistics, 2006).

31. Lauren McCormack, Carla Bann, Jennifer Uhrig, Nancy Berkman, and Rima Rudd, "Health Insurance Literacy of Older Adults," *Journal of Consumer Affairs* 43, no. 2 (2009): 223–248.

32. Judith H. Hibbard, Jacquelyn J. Jewett, Siegfried Engelmann, and Martin Tusler, "Can Medicare Beneficiaries Make Informed Choices?," *Health Affairs* 17, no. 6 (1998): 181.

33. Ya'akov M. Bayer, "Older Adults, Aggressive Marketing, and Unethical Behavior: A Sure Road to Financial Fraud?," in *Ethical Branding and Marketing: Cases and Lessons*, ed. H. Gringarten and R. Fernández-Calienes (New York: Routledge, 2019), 1–18.

34. Alex D. Federman, Dana Gelb Safran, Salomeh Keyhani, Helen Cole, Ethan A. Halm, and Albert L. Siu, "Awareness of Pharmaceutical Cost-Assistance Programs among Inner-City Seniors," *American Journal of Geriatric Pharmacotherapy* 7, no. 2 (2009): 117–129.

35. Federman et al., "Awareness of Pharmaceutical Cost-Assistance Programs."

36. "America's Health Literacy: Why We Need Accessible Health Information. An Issue Brief from the U.S. Department of Health and Human Services," Department of Health and Human Services, accessed January 29, 2021, https://www.ahrq.gov/sites/default/files/wysiwyg/health-literacy/dhhs-2008-issue-brief.pdf.

37. Virginia M. Bowden, Frederick B. Wood, and Debra G. Warner, "Health Information Hispanic Outreach in the Texas Lower Rio Grande Valley," *Journal of the Medical Library Association* 94, no. 2 (2006): 180–189.

38. Dana L. Ladd, Patricia Sobczak, and Talicia Tarver, "Providing Health Information to Seniors: A Program Overview and Reliable Online Senior Health Resources," *Journal of Consumer Health on the Internet* 23, no. 2 (2019): 113–122.

39. Andrew J. Barnes, Yaniv Hanoch, Melissa Martynenko, Stacey Wood, Thomas Rice, and Alex D. Federman, "Physician Trainees' Decision Making and Information Processing: Choice Size and Medicare Part D," *PLOS ONE* 8, no. 10 (2013): e77096.

40. Florian Heiss, Adam Leive, Daniel McFadden, and Joachim Winter, "Plan Selection in Medicare Part D: Evidence from Administrative Data," *Journal of Health Economics* 32, no. 6 (2013): 1325–1344.

41. Kathleen Kan, Andrew J. Barnes, Yaniv Hanoch, and Alex D. Federman, "Self-Efficacy in Insurance Decision Making among Older Adults," *American Journal of Managed Care* 21, no. 4 (2015): e247–e254.

42. George Loewenstein, Joelle Y. Friedman, Barbara McGill, Sarah Ahmad, Suzanne Linck, Stacey Sinkula, John Beshears, et al., "Consumers' Misunderstanding of Health Insurance," *Journal of Health Economics* 32, no. 5 (2013): 851.

43. Stacey Wood, Yaniv Hanoch, Andrew Barnes, Pi-ju Liu, Janet Cummings, Chandrima Bhattacharya, and Thomas Rice, "Numeracy and Medicare Part D: The Importance of Choice and Literacy for Numbers in Optimizing Decision Making for Medicare's Prescription Drug Program," *Psychology and Aging* 26, no. 2 (2011): 295–307.

44. Chao Zhou and Yuting Zhang, "The Vast Majority of Medicare Part D Beneficiaries Still Don't Choose the Cheapest Plans That Meet Their Medication Needs," *Health Affairs* 31, no. 10 (2012): 2259–2265.

45. Andrew J. Barnes, Yaniv Hanoch, Stacey Wood, Pi-ju Liu, and Thomas Rice, "One Fish, Two Fish, Red Fish, Blue Fish: Effects of Price Frames, Brand Names, and Choice Set Size on Medicare Part D Insurance Plan Decisions," *Medical Care Research and Review* 69, no. 4 (2012): 460–473.

46. Yaniv Hanoch, Stacey Wood, Andrew Barnes, Pi-ju Liu, and Thomas Rice, "Choosing the Right Medicare Prescription Drug Plan: The Effect of Age, Strategy Selection, and Choice Set Size," *Health Psychology* 30, no. 6 (2011): 719–727.

47. Helena Szrek and M. Kate Bundorf, "Enrollment in Prescription Drug Insurance: The Interaction of Numeracy and Choice Set Size," *Health Psychology* 33, no. 4 (2014): 340–348.

48. Szrek and Bundorf, "Enrollment in Prescription Drug Insurance."

49. "How to Compare Medigap Policies," Medicare.gov, accessed April 30, 2021, https://www.medicare.gov/supplements-other-insurance/how-to-compare-medigap -policies.

50. Barnes et al., "One Fish, Two Fish," 461.

51. Eric J. Johnson, Ran Hassin Hassin, Tom Baker, Allison T. Bajger, and Galen Treuer, "Can Consumers Make Affordable Care Affordable? The Value of Choice Architecture," *PLOS ONE* 8, no. 12 (2013): e81521.

52. Andrew J. Barnes, Yaniv Hanoch, and Thomas Rice, "Determinants of Coverage Decisions in Health Insurance Marketplaces: Consumers' Decision-Making Abilities and the Amount of Information in Their Choice Environment," *Health Services Research* 50, no. 1 (2015): 60.

53. Barnes et al., "One Fish, Two Fish."

54. Jessica Greene, Ellen Peters, C. K. Mertz, and Judith H. Hibbard, "Comprehension and Choice of a Consumer-Directed Health Plan: An Experimental Study," *American Journal of Managed Care* 14, no. 6 (2008): 359–376.

55. Peter A. Ubel, David A. Comerford, and Eric Johnson, "Healthcare.gov 3.0—Behavioral Economics and Insurance Exchanges," *New England Journal of Medicine* 372, no. 8 (2015): 695–698.

56. Johnson et al., "Can Consumers Make Affordable Care Affordable?"

57. Joachim O. Hero, Anna D. Sinaiko, Jon Kingsdale, Rachel S. Gruver, and Alison A. Galbraith, "Decision-Making Experiences of Consumers Choosing Individual-Market Health Insurance Plans," *Health Affairs* 38, no. 3 (2019): 464–472.

58. "Understanding Your Medicare Advantage Plan's Provider Network," Medicare.gov, accessed April 26, 2021, https://www.medicare.gov/Pubs/pdf/11941-Un derstanding-Your-Medicare-Advantage-Plan.pdf.

59. Wood et al., "Numeracy and Medicare Part D."

60. Emily J. Vardell, "Health Insurance Literacy: How People Understand and Make Health Insurance Purchase Decisions" (PhD diss., University of North Carolina at Chapel Hill, 2017).

61. Kim Parker and Eileen Patten, *The Sandwich Generation: Rising Financial Burdens for Middle-Aged Americans* (Washington, DC: Pew Research Center, 2013), https://www.pewresearch.org/social-trends/2013/01/30/the-sandwich-generation/.

# Chapter Seven

# Active Aging in
# the Era of Smart Devices

Pallabi Bhowmick, Clara Caldeira, Kay Connelly,
Ben Jelen, Novia Nurain, and Katie A. Siek

I've fallen, and I can't get up!

—Mrs. Fletcher, LifeCall commercial, 1987

Tech companies compete for territory in an already overcrowded youth market; whereas older adults, if considered users at all, are offered little more than fall alarms, activity monitors, and senior-friendly (often lower functionality) versions of existing tools.

—Knowles et al., *The Harm in Conflating Aging with Accessibility*[1]

From "smart" appliances to smartphones to wearable activity monitors, the Internet of Things (IoT) encompasses physical technologies that are connected to the internet. IoT devices are meant to connect with each other to make life easier. For older adults, IoT has been touted as enabling older adults to live in their homes for longer (i.e., aging in place), as common caregiving tasks can be made easier. For the purposes of this chapter, we see as relevant three broad categories of IoT technologies: (1) ambient, typically home-based technologies that include sensors, cameras, displays, and custom-made physical objects that older adults can interact with; (2) portable technologies, such as smartphones, that an older adult can use inside and outside of their homes; and (3) wearable devices that older adults can wear inside and outside of their homes, such as commercial wearable activity monitors. The recent explosion of IoT devices makes them low-cost and accessible to the broader population; however, researchers have been investigating IoT issues and solutions for older adults for over twenty years.

There are two important caveats to the work we present. The first is that while many designs have been explored, there is little large-scale research that demonstrates the efficacy of these designs. Most are deployed on a small scale for short periods, not as clinical trials. This naturally calls for further research to validate whether these designs equitably benefit different older adult populations. Second, there is a legitimate fear among older adults and their advocates that many aging-in-place technologies, meant to help keep older adults independent for longer, will either replace human contact and thus increase social isolation or increase reliance on technology and reduce agency. All solutions meant to "increase independence" or "ease the burden" of human caregivers should be examined for potential negative consequences on social interactions.

In this chapter, we delve into how IoT can go beyond aging in place, with the main goal of preventing or delaying a need to move due to caregiving needs, to support active aging—as defined by the World Health Organization: "the process of optimizing opportunities for health, participation, and security in order to enhance quality of life as people age."[2] Older adults have maintained their independence (i.e., the ability to live in their homes without a caregiver present) by utilizing devices to remember events and surveillance-like systems to assuage caregiver fears. Researchers developed systems to keep older adults safe with automated fall detection and wandering tracking systems to reduce risks associated with accidents. Older adults can proactively manage their health by engaging with apps and systems that help them track their nutrition, exercise, sleep, and chronic illnesses. Although older adults' social networks contract as they age, IoT can provide older adults with the ability to stay socially connected with loved ones and friends and grow their peer networks through remote social events. We recognize that this increased connectedness also brings with it physical and digital security risks that must be addressed to help older adults maintain their autonomy. We describe how technology has affected older adults and identify opportunities to help older adults use technology to their advantage by supporting their well-being while maintaining their agency. We also highlight overarching challenges for IoT technology to support older adults, including accommodating privacy trade-offs, understanding older adults' needs, balancing tensions between surveillance and autonomy, acknowledging that technology is not always the answer, and introducing interventions early to more easily integrate them into their lives in the long term.


## INDEPENDENCE

For older adults, independence often comes down to their ability to make their own choices about how and where they live. Independence is threatened when family members (or the state) feel an older adult is a danger to themselves or others. Activities of daily living (ADLs) are often assessed when determining if an older adult can remain independent in their own home.[3] In addition to ensuring older adults can complete all the ADLs (basic hygiene, going to the bathroom, dressing themselves, preparing and consuming meals, and getting around their home), other common threats to independence include safety risks (e.g., risks of falling) and community mobility (e.g., no longer being able to drive). Early sociotechnical systems focused on surveillance to help caregivers assess how a loved one was doing rather than empowering older adults to maintain their own independence with dignity. In this section, we explore the evolution of these sociotechnical systems, from creating a virtual window for caregivers to view their older adult loved ones to systems that proactively help older adults connect with the people and resources they need.

## Early Independence Systems

The earliest sociotechnical systems to help older adults live independently often were one-way surveillance-like systems that would track the older adult. Initially, wearable emergency call buttons were used; however, these were often reactive solutions to a possible safety event. Then, researchers started using sensor and camera networks throughout an older adult's home to provide information to a caregiver, typically an adult child, on how the older adult was doing that day. For example, with CareNet, adult children are able to see on an ambient, frame-like display if their loved one had a fall, ate, took their medication, was in a good mood, attended any events, or went on any outings. Older adults were willing to share their information, and caregiving participants enjoyed knowing more about their loved one's day and used the information to improve their caregiving.[4] Researchers in the United States[5] and Europe[6] investigated how to automate detection of other ADLs to provide caregivers and loved ones more in-depth insights about their older adult loved one. Although older adults were okay with sharing sensor data, more obtrusive camera-based data was less welcome, so researchers focused more on helping them to preserve their privacy.[7]

As smart home technology and connectivity improved, researchers explored intergenerational, two-way information sharing so that the older adult could also see how their caregiving loved one was doing. An example is the Presence Clock, which was a pair of analog clocks with LEDs around the edges.[8] Whenever motion was detected in the remote home, the LEDs corresponding to the current time would light up. The more activity, the brighter the LED for that time period. Thus, a person could glance at their clock and see when their loved one had awakened, when they were likely cooking, and when they were sitting still or had left their home. Instead of the clock being used to monitor the older adult (such as in CareNet), both parties had a clock and could see the activity levels in their loved one's home. More recently, these reciprocal systems have evolved to empower older adults to check in with a network of trusted loved ones—including older adult friends. One such example is the Check-in Tree in figure 7.1, with which older adults signal how they are doing for the day, and their network of friends and family can decide if they want to follow up with each other.[9]

Researchers have also investigated helping older adults live independently by using reminder systems to help them with ADLs—from ambient prompts

**Figure 7.1.   Check-in Tree privileges older adults with the ability to check in with each other.**
Courtesy of Pallabi Bhowmick

to remind an older adult with cognitive issues of the order of operations to wash their hands,[10, 11] to systems that ensure older adults can cook safely in their home,[12] to systems that can be personalized to remind an older adult about any activity (e.g., medication) through multiple modalities (e.g., an ambient display, sound, tactile vibration, or smell).[13] These reminder systems evolved from simple time-based reminders, where someone preprogrammed the time to remind one of an activity, to utilizing the surveillance-like systems to understand an individual's context with respect to the activity they should do. For instance, a person may not want a reminder to take medication to show up on their television if they are hosting guests.[14] Indeed, researchers have found that the complexity of what people want to remember extends beyond time and context cues.[15] More recently, embedded technology has become so small that researchers have placed it in everyday objects (e.g., pill boxes, as shown in figure 7.2) to not only provide reminders but also track possible decline in doing everyday activities (e.g., the dexterity to open a pillbox).[16]

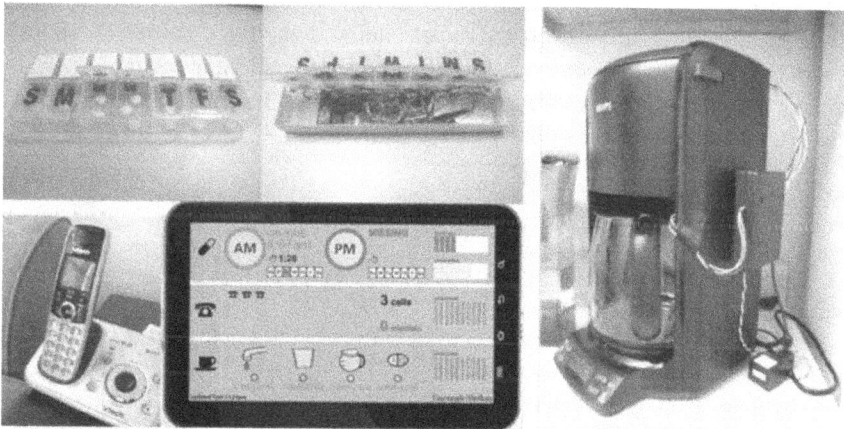

**Figure 7.2.** Example of dwell Sense—a system where everyday artifacts, such as a pill box, phone, or coffee pot, are electronically enhanced to identify how an older adult is living within their home.
Courtesy of Matthew L. Lee

## Modern Independence Systems

As technology has advanced, so too have independence systems. Commercial IoT, such as smart thermostats and appliances, has become more affordable, opening up opportunities for older adults to integrate such technology into their everyday, independent lives. Voice assistants (e.g., Amazon Alexa,

Google Home, Microsoft Cortana) have become increasingly popular for older adults—especially since they easily integrate into one's life and do not require interacting with a physical interface. Research has been divided on how useful voice assistants are—some have found that older adults use voice assistants mostly for finding information, especially health information, but have some concerns about the reliability of other functions (e.g., reminders).[17] Whereas other researchers have found older adults think of voice assistants more as toys but still use them for music, alarms, weather, and news.[18] One theory is that one's perception of usefulness may be based on how one thinks about the voice assistant—Does the older adult consider the voice assistant as a piece of technology or an anthropomorphized digital companion?[19]

Initially, most aging-in-place technologies to facilitate independence were focused on the home, but as technology has become smaller and more ubiquitous, we see how it is used to help older adults navigate their community. We expect this trend will continue as smart cities evolve and stakeholders advocate to ensure everyone can access community resources. Similar to early in-home surveillance systems, many systems exist to track older adults in their everyday lives outside of their home—an especially important functionality for older adults who are experiencing dementia. People can choose to use smartphone software that reports on one's location or wearable, stylish bands that proactively monitor and alert caregivers of an older adult's location (e.g., CareBand[20] in figure 7.3).

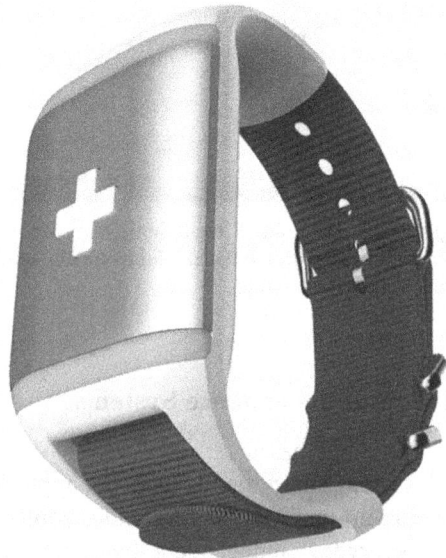

**Figure 7.3.   CareBand, a wearable device to help caregivers track older adults' locations.**
Courtesy of CareBand

For older adults who are *not* experiencing dementia, we know they are more likely to walk, share rides, and use motorized scooters and public transport in their community when getting food.[21] Researchers have outfitted older adults with a wearable sensor to understand how built environments may cause stress (e.g., at an unsafe intersection or a sidewalk without a curb cut).[22] Ultimately, these data could be used by local governments to improve accessibility for older adults in their built communities.

## Opportunities to Support Older Adults' Independence

When considering systems to help maintain an older adult's independence, one should determine the goal for the check-in. Is the goal to see if a loved one is safe? That they moved around the house some today? That they are fulfilling ADLs? Early systems to "support" older adult independence were typically one-way systems in which caregivers could check on a loved one quickly; however, future systems must respect older adults' agency by allowing them to define what kind of information is shared, when, and with whom. For example, knowing how often an older adult consulted with a voice assistant may be sufficient to know if someone was active in their home instead of knowing what questions were asked. Likewise, people who are considering monitoring older adults' independence should consider what information they are willing to relinquish to provide a reciprocal, two-way experience. Two-way systems can prompt cross-generational discussions that are broader than the specific metric being tracked.

In cases where older adults need to drive to maintain autonomy, self-driving cars have been hailed as a future technology that could help older adults maintain their independence. Researchers have noted, however, that older adults may want different types of information when using self-driving cars;[23] thus more work must be done to ensure older adults are involved in technology design processes. Indeed, researchers have shown that assistive technology for older adults must be more than just useful—it must be usable, affordable, accessible, compatible, and reliable and allow older adults to use it confidently.[24]

## SAFETY

Safety and security are complementary concepts, where the source of the concern is what differentiates them. While safety is the protection of an older adult from *themselves* (i.e., something they might do to themselves unintentionally), security focuses on physical and digital protection of an older adult from *others* (i.e., an outside, ill-intentioned actor). Safety narratives around older adults are often dominated by technology helping to handle physical and cognitive declines that can come with aging, but technology security narratives often center on physical security (e.g., break-ins) and protecting older adults from scams (e.g., financial scams).[25]

As older adults have even modest physical and mental declines, they are at higher risk of common safety hazards such as falling, becoming unable to call for help during illness, taking the wrong doses of medications, driving unsafely, and getting lost when walking or driving outside the home (i.e., wandering). Ensuring older adults' safety is important because they are most at risk, suffer the most severe injuries, and have the highest mortality rate of any age group.[26] Addressing the safety needs of older adults can help both themselves and their families have a better quality of life. In this section, we address two of the most common safety hazards: falling and wandering. Although relevant to safety, we address medication adherence in the health section and driving support and technologies for contacting help in the independence section.

## Falls

One-third to one-half of people older than sixty-five years are prone to falling.[27,28] More than two-thirds of people who have experienced a fall are likely to fall again.[29,30] Physical injuries and psychological problems often lead to decreased mobility and independence among older adults.[31]

The first fall monitoring system, introduced in 1975, was a manual system that relied on the user to press a button that would then send out an alert message.[32] There are many devices like this still available today (e.g., MyNotifi[33] and AutoAlert).[34] Few of these devices allow for the user to cancel an alert (e.g., iVi Intelligent Pendant)[35] to reduce false alarms from accidental button presses. One possible issue with user-initiated fall detection systems is that an older adult may not be able to reach the wearable if they experience a fall.[36]

The 1990s brought about research in automatic fall detection,[37] with systems designed to not only detect falls but also monitor daily activities with the goal of preventing falls. Fall prevention systems analyzed fall patterns and long-term fall condition trends to predict when a person may be in need of a preventative intervention.[38] Here, we explore three types of IoT-based automatic fall detection systems: sensor-based systems in smart home environments, video analysis systems, and wearable devices.

Sensor-based fall detection systems monitor older adults in a nonintrusive and passive way. Early commercial systems simply used motion sensors throughout the home and triggered an alert if someone spent too much time in a particular location (e.g., the bathroom). More sophisticated systems used different types of sensors (acoustic[39, 40] and floor vibration)[41] throughout the home to detect falls in real time.

Video fall detection systems[42, 43, 44, 45, 46] provide real-time fall detection by monitoring older adults' posture using video surveillance in the home environment.[47, 48] Video-based systems have adoption privacy issues, since older adults often do not want video surveillance in their homes. Two promising privacy-preserving techniques are using silhouettes[49] or collecting depth image and skeleton data instead of full video like what the discontinued Microsoft Kinect used.[50, 51, 52, 53]

Wearable systems, typically watches[54, 55, 56] or pendants,[57] detect falls using internal motion sensors and communicate the information to predetermined phone numbers via a phone call, text message, or web portal. Recent commodity versions of smartwatches, such as those sold by Apple and Garmin, display an alert after detecting hard falls. The user is given the option to confirm the fall occurrence and to decide whether to contact emergency services.[58]

Finally, there are systems that combine home-based and wearable sensors into a single system, with the goal of increasing accuracy and coverage.[59, 60, 61] For example, the HOme health care sentiNEl sYstem (HONEY) system for home-based fall detection leveraged sensors and home-area networks.[62] A fall was detected based on the combined data of users' movements, speech recognition, and on-demand video. When a fall occurred, an alarm email was delivered to a medical professional or a caregiver.

A major drawback of these wearable fall-detection devices is that the older adult must be wearing the device at the time of the fall. Older adults often take off wearable devices for reasons of comfort and stigma (i.e., shows they might be frail),[63] leaving them vulnerable to an undetected fall while their caregivers may believe *any* fall will be detected. Further, the placement of sensors on the body and external noises may also affect the system's performance and accuracy.

## Wandering

Wandering is losing the ability to effectively navigate and is regarded as one of the first manifestations of Alzheimer's disease and dementia.[64] Traditional methods to prevent wandering include imposing restraints (e.g., locking doors) and medication; however, these methods are not always effective for protecting wanderers because physical restraints cause several physical or psychological problems,[65, 66, 67, 68, 69] and medications[70] have side effects.

More recently, interventions used to manage, rather than prevent, wandering indicate a shift toward assisting safe walking.[71, 72, 73] Intervention methods include motion tracking, behavioral intervention, cognitive rehabilitation, and modifications of the living environment. With the increasing proliferation of sensing technologies, monitoring human movement is not only technically feasible but also financially viable. Researchers designed assistive systems to detect wandering trajectories from real-time GPS readings embedded in shoe inserts,[74] badges,[75] and ankle tags[76] to prevent older adults from walking outside a predefined safe zone. Instead of requiring something new for older adults to wear, researchers attached RFID tags on older adults' personal items; thus, when an older adult left their home, the system would send a notification to caregivers.[77]

With the advent of the smartphone, several phone-based technologies have emerged to tackle wandering concerns of older adults. For example, iWander uses GPS location data from the smartphone to estimate the probability that the user is wandering and can automatically take actions to help the person navigate to a safe location, notify caregivers, and provide current location.[78] Instead of estimating wandering, other systems provide caregivers with the ability to predefine a zone where an older adult can walk—when the older adult moves beyond that zone, the caregivers are notified.[79]

## Opportunities to Support Older Adults' Safety

Although there has been significant work done for fall detection of older adults, researchers use simulated fall data, oftentimes with younger adults pretending to fall.[80] This can lead to both false positive and false negative results. Too many false positives can lead to alert fatigue and distrust in the system, resulting in a slower response to alarms and eventual discontinuation. False negatives lead to an older adult not being helped in their time of need. A future area of work is to gather a larger corpus of real fall data from older adults[81] by instrumenting environments in which falls are likely to happen (e.g., communities of older adults transitioning from independent to assisted living may provide data representing a variety of abilities).[82]

While fall detection is crucial, fall prevention would better improve older adults' safety. It is always better to predict or anticipate the incidence of a fall before the fall actually happens.[83] Some researchers have created fall reaction systems—augmenting fall detection systems with wearable airbags to protect the user from the body-ground impact when a fall occurs.[84, 85] The power of machine learning could also be harnessed to predict higher risk of falls or wandering[86] based on one's longitudinal data to predict individual declines instead of reacting to them.

## HEALTH

Health management among older adults has much in common with health management for other populations, as it involves everyday habits around sleep, nutrition, medication, and physical activity. Health management also involves preventing or managing diseases; however, this is more critical as people age, when considering older adults are more likely to have chronic illness (85% for older adults versus 60% for younger demographics) or multiple chronic illnesses (60% for older adults versus 40% for younger demographics).[87, 88] Older adults' health and perspectives can differ enough from younger age groups that technology created for a more general population might not work well for them. In this section, we share how older adult–focused health technologies address nutrition, sleep, exercise, chronic conditions, and general health technologies.

### Nutrition

Older adults can benefit from carefully managing their diet with help from technology. Dietary habits are part of preventing and managing health conditions that tend to be more common in old age, particularly when there are risk factors such as family history.[89] Technology involving older adults and family members can help create awareness of eating habits and support diet management. For example, keeping a food diary over a few days or weeks[90] can help people find patterns that could be addressed. Older adults can identify nutrition habits they want to change, whereas caregivers can identify issues with specific food-related activities (e.g., grocery shopping). Periods of change, such as the diagnosis of a new condition, might result in recommendations from clinicians for dietary changes. These situations in particular represent an important opportunity to support diet management through technology.[91] Using sensors in appliances (e.g., rice cooker or microwave) and collecting data about when they are used can also create awareness around mealtimes and routines for older adults and caregivers.[92] At the same time, data on dietary habits, such as what food was consumed, can be perceived as sensitive, since people might prefer not to share with family members for fear of judgment.[93]

Access to food is another important factor for adequate nutrition. Older adults with mobility restrictions may use a variety of food sources, including grocery stores, food banks, restaurants, convenience stores, or delivery services (e.g., Meals on Wheels). They may face barriers to food access due to distance (e.g., in food deserts), available transportation, cost, and lack of accessibility (e.g., heavy doors).[94] IoT could be used to track what food is located in places frequented by older adults and combine data with older adult reviews to help local communities improve access.

## Sleep

While getting enough sleep is essential for the health of older adults, they are more likely to experience issues such as insomnia and lack of deep sleep.[95] Wearable devices such as smart bands or smartwatches often have the ability to measure sleep duration and quality. Older adults tend to find sleep-tracking technologies useful for a short period for the purpose of gaining awareness, but after learning about their sleep patterns, they tend to find little benefit to their continued use. Despite the lack of sustained use, older adults can benefit from short-term use, changing sleep habits in response to the feedback received.[96,97] Abandoning a wearable after having learned enough about one's habits also happens among younger populations. Still, users retain and benefit from knowledge and skills acquired during use.[98]

## Exercise

Independent of age, adults are encouraged to get at least 150 minutes of moderate-intensity exercise each week;[99] however, older adults are warned to be more mindful of their activity in relation to their physical abilities. Wearable activity trackers can assist older adults in monitoring their activity by passively measuring exercise habits, helping older adults to gain awareness of their physical activities and pursue specific goals.[100] Technology such as exergames can support exercising indoors.[101] Still, there are several aspects of exercise technology that are specifically needed by or beneficial for older adults. For example, activity trackers can also be used for exercising safely, such as preventing overexercising, dehydration and overheating, and maintaining heart rate within a safe range (e.g., for an older adult with heart disease). In addition, including other family members by having them use a physical activity technology together with an older adult is beneficial for engagement with the system.[102]

Many barriers exist to effectively using these systems, in part because older adults are often unintended users. For example, step counting can be rejected by older adults who find the common goal of ten thousand daily steps unattainable.[103] Exercise trackers also tend to be less accurate for older adult users since their gaits are different, particularly those who walk slowly or use mobility aids.[104, 105] Older adults also prefer passive tracking, such as using wearables that collect data without the need for manual entry. Wearables can be less cumbersome for keeping track of exercise in comparison with devices such as smartphones.[106] Evidence-based strategies used to support behavior change in technology design (e.g., increasing exercise levels) have been shown to be less effective for older adults.[107] While older adults value exercise as a way to maintain their health and mobility, middle-aged individuals (thirty to sixty-four) approach exercise as a means to improve health and meet personal goals, and younger individuals (eighteen to twenty-nine) focus primarily on fitness and prevention. Older adults expect that wearable technologies will take into account everyday activities that require physical effort, such as gardening, and allow the inclusion of user-defined activities and goals.[108] They can also benefit from linking their health data with the concrete benefits of exercise they experience, such as pain reduction.[109] However, many of these functionalities that are particularly useful for older adults are not common in commercial exercise technology, which is more aligned with fitness-related goals.

## Chronic Conditions

Chronic illness management is an important issue for older adults because prevalence increases with age.[110] Technology that allows older adults to measure blood sugar, blood pressure, pain, or heart rate can help older adults identify patterns in their symptoms and seek help from health care providers when the data are worrisome.[111, 112] Collecting long-term data on symptoms can register and detect changes over time in severity of degenerative conditions, such as Parkinson's disease.[113] Certain conditions are most common among older adults and warrant particular attention from health technology, such as heart disease[114] and diabetes.[115]

Older adults also go through rehabilitation to recover from health events such as a fall, surgery, or stroke. Technology can be used to support rehabilitation, increasing access to services such as physical therapy, by lowering costs and not requiring transportation to a clinic when they have access to resources that support therapy at home (e.g., video guides or game-based exercises).[116] Technology can be used during rehabilitation activities themselves (e.g., physical therapy session).[117, 118] In addition, technology can help to monitor older adults during their daily lives to measure and motivate use of the body part under rehabilitation (e.g., arm) during everyday activities.[119]

Managing multiple chronic conditions, an issue that is common among older adults, might be particularly challenging. In addition to a higher burden for self-care, different illnesses might involve conflicting recommendations or treatments. For example, physical exercise is recommended to manage diabetes, but its feasibility could be limited due to another condition, such as chronic pain.[120, 121, 122] Since most consumer-facing health technology focuses on specific chronic conditions, there is a lack of tools available to help people address the specific challenges experienced by those who have chronic conditions with conflicting treatments. Still, several tasks involved in chronic illness management are shared by many conditions. For example, treatments could include a combination of increasing self-knowledge and health literacy, making adjustments to self-care or treatment, learning from others with similar conditions,[123] and managing medication intake.[124] Medication management can be a particularly challenging aspect of self-care since it can vary over time, and known strategies to facilitate remembering, such as establishing a routine, are not as effective for sporadic medications (e.g., weekly or monthly prescriptions). Technology that supports these common self-care activities, rather than focusing on specific illnesses, can be useful for older adults with diverse health contexts.

## Opportunities to Support Older Adults' Physical Health

Despite the benefits, older adults' adoption of health data technology is low in comparison to other age groups.[125] They prefer to use technology that is not targeted at older populations;[126] however, they face several barriers because these tools are not aligned with their needs, less accurate for them, and burdensome to maintain (e.g., daily charging). The short-term and fluctuating use of health technology indicates a need to support varying levels of engagement rather than only focusing on increasing engagement.[127]

Older adults particularly value the ability to monitor their health and communicate data to health care providers holistically by taking into consideration different symptoms, conditions, constraints, values, and preventative goals together rather than approaching different aspects of their health separately.[128] Technologies designed for the health of older adults can have holistic benefits, even if they focus on specific conditions or activities. For example, exergames can affect several important aspects of health for older adults, such as cognition, social interaction, and fun.[129]

Older adults can experience gradual or sudden changes in health that require changes in their own or caregivers' behavior and workflow. Technology could be used to detect and address such changes through wearable and smart home technologies that analyze data over the long term. Supporting these periods through technologies can make a substantial impact by helping people to overcome particularly challenging periods for their health.[130] For example, sleep management is particularly underexplored, especially when considering that older adults have more interrupted sleep and might experience "sundowning" as a symptom of dementia.[131] Recognizing gradual assistance needs early can help older adults and caregivers determine when to introduce more assistance, such as moving in with family members or adopting new technology designed to extend independence. Technology could provide substantial benefits to older adults' quality of life by helping them and potentially their families make informed decisions based on tracked health data.

## SOCIAL CONNECTIONS

Social isolation and loneliness are frequently experienced by older adults due to their retirement, reductions in their own mobility (as sometimes happens with aging), and/or their social circle narrowing because of death or limited mobility of spouses and friends. Social isolation and loneliness are risk factors for declines in physical health (including premature death), increased rates of dementia, and increased prevalence of mental health disorders.[132] Because of these serious consequences, the design of technologies to build social connections is a ripe area of research.

Technological approaches to decrease social isolation fall into a few broad categories. One approach is to make existing communication (e.g., email, texting, smartphone) and social networks (e.g., Facebook, Twitter) more accessible to older adults, who may have limited technology experience or may be experiencing physical ailments that make using commercial technologies more difficult (e.g., declining eyesight). Another approach is to create new technologies that enable frequent and intimate interactions with close family members, which often includes an aspect of caregiving. A third approach is to increase communication with friends, which focuses on friendships and mutual aid as opposed to caregiving. A final approach is to design technologies that either explicitly or as a side effect enable socialization outside of an older adult's existing social networks. We provide a brief overview of each of these approaches, with specific examples for further exploration.

### Accessibility of Existing Technologies

Perhaps the most straightforward approach to using technologies to increase older adults' social connections is to make popular commercial technologies more accessible to this population, which tends to have less experience with technology and is likely to experience physical declines, which in turn make using such technologies difficult. There has been considerable work on how to help older adults access email and the internet in general.[133, 134]

Some work on improving existing social networking sites has resulted in recommendations that focus on easier-to-use interfaces, which can benefit all users.[135] For older adults who do not want to get on a computer or smartphone, early research shows how social network data could be fed to ambient displays so older adults could consume their friends' content without ever interacting with the site itself.[136] At the time of writing, there are numerous commercial "smart frames" that allow pictures from social networking sites to be sent directly to an electronic photo frame. These are often marketed to family members of older adults as an easy way to keep older adults connected with loved ones, without loved ones changing their own digital sharing work-flows.

Finally, some technologies are becoming more accessible to older adults as they become more accessible to everyone. Facetime, for example, evolved from an idea of how to make online gaming a richer experience[137] but is now used by older adults and children around the world to have richer remote interactions across the generations.[138]

## Existing Family Networks

There have been considerable improvements to connecting the generations through technology, and many systems for older adults have slowly built up to also improve social connectedness. Early commercial monitoring systems, as mentioned in the safety and independence sections, focused on extending typical home alarm systems to monitor older adults and raise alerts for po-tential crises, such as an illness or fall. While the data could be examined by family members, the focus was more on the 24/7 alerts provided by a service and not on decreasing social isolation.

Early work on connecting family members with an older adult loved one also focused on monitoring and caregiving tasks, where socialization was a side effect of the technologies. The Digital Family Portrait (DFP) was the first smart home research that allowed a family member of an older adult to remotely visualize home-based sensor information in an ambient display to determine the well-being of the older adult.[139] The DFP was a digital picture frame with a picture of the older adult in the center and a butterfly around the edge of the frame for each of the preceding thirty days. The size of a butterfly indicated how good of a day an older adult had based on the amount and type of activity one did throughout the home. The goal was to allow caregivers to glance at the display to see how their loved one was doing and prompt them to check in if there were potential problems. This system was extended by Intel in the CareNet display, which included more details (e.g., medication adher-ence and eating behavior) that would be of interest to someone who played a caregiving role.[140] Social connection and impact on mental health were side effects, not an intended design feature. Indeed, these types of systems concep-tualized older adults as the target of care and were inherently disempowering.

Technologists started looking at reciprocity and making older adults equal actors in the system, thus forming deeper connection between the two parties. The Presence Clock,[141] described in the section on independence, is an example of such reciprocity, where both the older adult and their loved one could "see" into the other's home. These types of "presence" technologies were reported to give a comforting feeling to the older adult, both observing the rhythms of their loved one's day and knowing that their rhythms were likewise observed.[142]

## Existing Peer Networks

Technologies can also be used to connect older adults with their peers. While the type of information may be different than when sharing with family members (e.g., older adults may be willing to share information about their health with their family members but not with their friends), the idea of sharing presence information with friends not only increases feelings of connection[143] but can also give older adults a feeling of being needed. For example, the Check-In Tree, mentioned in the independence section, allowed up to eight older adults to check in with each other in the mornings, making each friend an important part of ensuring everyone is okay.[144]

## Growing Peer Networks

Finally, there has been research on how to use technology to enable new social opportunities with people outside an older adult's existing social network. Many times, the social aspect of the activity is a side effect and not the primary focus. For example, virtual exercise groups can be more accessible to homebound older adults. Instead of having a one-on-one session or prerecorded exercise routine, a single health instructor can lead a group of older adults using virtual conferencing technologies.[145] This can lead to older adults interacting with each other during the activity, just as if they had gone to a local recreation center. Alternatively, some researchers have looked at how gamified exercise activities can explicitly increase socialization.[146]

## Opportunities to Support Older Adults' Social Connections

As adults age, their peer social circle often contracts due to relocation to be near family, decreasing independence (their own and their friends'), and death. While there has been significant research into how to maintain and connect within existing peer networks, there is far less work on technology to support older adults in replacing lost connections with new ones and thereby keeping a vibrant social network.

We know that almost a quarter of older adults engage in volunteer work.[147] Researchers have explored the personal importance of civic involvement, social opportunities, and sense of purpose volunteering can provide.[148] There is an opening to help expand an older adult's social connections by using technology to help them find and participate in civic engagement opportunities. This could not only help older adults expand their social connections but could also provide them with a satisfying sense of purpose, which is linked to better mental and physical health outcomes.

A more controversial approach is to replace human contact with technologies. Robotic pets, such as Paro, were initially deployed as a social catalyst in community settings, encouraging older adults to bond in groups around the caring of the pet.[149] We can imagine robotic pets living with older adults in their homes and providing companionship similar to a living pet. Similarly, just as science fiction has envisioned humans bonding with virtual agents, older adults could find socialization in fully automated virtual agents, such as chat bots or embodied agents in virtual reality environments.[150, 151]

# SECURITY

While safety primarily addresses potential harms to oneself, security addresses threats from others. There are growing conversations around older adults' digital security as more older adults are moving online[152] and emerging technologies are less clear about how they treat people's data.[153] Research has attempted to support older adults in maintaining their online independence, while older adults' worries about their digital security has led some to limit or avoid technology altogether.[154] Although not all older adults experience these worries, older adults are unfortunately more susceptible to digital security threats.[155, 156] Their worries about online security often stem from their lack of clarity around what is happening with their data, especially for emerging technologies such as IoT.[157] Older adults are rightfully concerned that their information is being sold[158] or used for malicious purposes, such as plotting physical attacks from their GPS data.[159] In this section, we expand on how IoT and wearable technologies are supporting older adults' physical and digital security.

## Physical Security

Physical security systems focus primarily on helping older adults feel secure in their homes, especially from malicious break-ins and scams. The classic example is a commercial home security system that uses IoT sensing systems to monitor doors, windows, and the surrounding property. The industry is expected to be worth $79 billion by 2025.[160] These systems have also recently started including cameras to show when people approach the front door, even displaying the information on a mobile device, allowing caregivers to check in on older adults.[161] These notifications can be particularly helpful for in-person scams. The FBI warns that older adults are often targeted because they are trusting, have access to significant savings, and are less likely to report fraud since they are worried about caregivers' confidence in their ability to handle their finances.[162] Furthermore, older adult victims of financial scams tend to die three times faster than older adults who have not been victims, making scams a public health crisis.[163] Although these commercial systems are not designed specifically for older adults, they are nevertheless one common solution for protecting older adults' physical security and helping them avoid financial scams.

Researchers have explored home security systems designed specifically for older adults, often emphasizing the support of a privacy-conscious caregiving relationship. DigiSwitch was one such project designed to help older adults and their caregivers navigate the omnipresent camera.[164] Older adults review the data collected on DigiSwitch's touchscreen-capable digital picture frame and turn the collection feature on or off. Older adult participants could temporarily turn off data collection, such as when they were planning a surprise party for the caregiver at their home. With systems such as DigiSwitch, older adults can feel better about how they are being supported by caregivers, especially with more transparency and control of their data. Some older adults still view home systems as an intrusion of their privacy.[165, 166] Furthermore, researchers have noted how these home monitoring systems can reduce the social interaction between older adults and their caregivers.[167]

Some systems also include physical security at the community level, similar to Neighborhood Watch programs. Commercial systems (e.g., neighborhood social networking sites, such as Nextdoor)[168] and security camera systems (e.g., Nest)[169] have started networking people together to help them create safer communities. Similarly, a German research team designed a neighborhood web portal for a community of older adults.[170] Tenants accessed the system via private devices at home and public displays in front of their residences, where they were inclined to share pictures, well wishes, and community-wide events. Participants developed concerns about sharing information that might affect their privacy and security, so the research team encouraged participants to choose how visible they were online.[171] Taking inspiration from an analog Neighborhood Watch, researchers studied the possibility of digital neighborhood watches through home security cameras.[172] They found that people were comfortable sharing the camera data in specific instances (i.e., an incident) but still had concerns about sharing continuous data. More recently, commercial camera systems have started networking together cameras from multiple homes, allowing police to pull footage from the network for a fee; however, this approach has multiple privacy concerns.[173]

## Digital Security

While less obvious than physical threats, protecting older adults' digital lives is increasingly challenging as more of our lives are moving online. Unfortunately, older adults are more vulnerable to online threats, such as phishing attacks, than younger groups.[174, 175] These digital threats can put them at financial risk if scammers are able to get access to key accounts or if older adults do not follow secure password practices. Older adults believe they are unlikely to click on phishing attacks, yet they were the most common age group to do so,[176] and they have a more limited understanding of digital security tools.[177] Some of this may be explained by a lack of technology experience, technology consistently evolving, declines in abilities, and their financial or living situation. For example, people living in care communities often shared devices without understanding the risks.[178] These security challenges are even more pronounced for older adults with mild cognitive impairments who, along with their caregivers, want to maintain their independence online, but this care work adds to caregiving demands.[179, 180]

Unfortunately, little work has been done using IoT or wearable technology to protect older adults' digital lives, but there are growing opportunities to support IoT security through current research. A first step has been to better communicate digital risks to older adults, such as with narrative-driven risk communication videos.[181] Another area of interest is to create systems to better protect older adults' accounts online. For example, two-factor authentication tokens are about the size of a dime and have poor instructions to support older adults in better securing their online presence.[182] Furthermore, researchers have investigated how to connect older adults with people who may be better suited to support their digital security than those who are most convenient and available,[183] such as an app for delegating privacy and security decisions to a trusted person.[184]

## Opportunities to Support Older Adults' Security

A key consideration for designs protecting older adults' security is how much privacy they are forced to give up in order to be more secure.[185, 186, 187] If a caregiver is able to see *everything* an older adult does offline and online, they will likely be more secure—assuming the caregiver has the expertise. This trade-off is already being navigated at many continuing care retirement communities[188] and aging-in-place arrangements,[189, 190] where older adults know they are giving up some of their privacy in return for "care surveillance." Outside of caregiving relationships, older adults still face many of the same privacy challenges with their security that younger people face with technology (e.g., companies storing data about them). Addressing those challenges more broadly will benefit older adults too. Regardless, the need to navigate this balance between privacy and security will increase as people adopt more IoT into their lives.

Future technologies have an opportunity to support older adults' physical and digital security by offering more creative ways to take advantage of the ubiquity that comes with IoT and wearable technologies while navigating the privacy challenges. For example, many IoT and wearables are always connected to the internet and could be used as another form of two-factor authentication for older adults. Near-field communication (NFC) is an emerging option for two-factor authentication. Designers could create easy-to-set-up NFC tokens with receivers located around the house to better secure older adults' digital lives. Another option is the idea of a "security caregiver" who would be able to help with security decisions.[191, 192, 193, 194] Older adults already work with convenient and available younger relatives and caregivers to get help,[195, 196] so researchers have started exploring apps that help with delegating that process.[197] IoT and wearable technologies could be used to provide further avenues for communicating those decisions and simplify the decision-making process with caregivers, such as notifying caregivers and older adults through smart speakers and wearables.

## THE FUTURE OF AGING: EVERYTHING CONNECTED?

This chapter has introduced the notion of using IoT technologies to support active aging. Early IoT systems that helped older adults safely maintain their independence were more surveillance oriented to help address caregiver concerns more than older adults' needs. We see how technology itself and the design of interactions has evolved to help empower older adults to maintain their health and develop social connections while also maintaining their digital security. We are encouraged by the significant move in commercial and research systems to be more inclusive of the concerns of older adults, respecting their autonomy and desire to be fully empowered in their lives instead of simply being targets of care. More work needs to be done to ensure that older adults' goals and limitations are fully accounted for in the selection of current technology and the design of future technology.

To this end, we encourage all decision makers to understand older adults' specific needs, since technologies designed for younger people, or even the population in general, are often not well aligned with older adults' contexts and preferences. At the same time, simply creating separate technologies specifically for older adults is not an effective strategy either, since aging is gradual by nature and these devices might be rejected due to associated stigma[198, 199] or because they underestimate the skills and abilities of potential users.[200] There is an opportunity to improve the technology available for older adults through an approach of universal usefulness and usability, where technologies can serve the needs of diverse populations, including older adults with different degrees of independence. For example, designers should make more effort to evaluate their technology with groups of older adults to assess any unintended consequences of their design choices that cater to a particular group.

We should also recognize that technology is not always the answer; many features of health technology for older adults can be accomplished through other means. For example, keeping track of medication can be done with pill organizers, and people can collect and share their health data (e.g., blood pressure) using pen and paper. Although these tools often can be replaced by technology, technology can introduce additional costs, both financial and in management complexity. It is worth considering no-tech or low-tech solutions that might work better for older adults.

Finally, the ultimate vision for technologies to support older adults is that they can be introduced early and increased gradually as physical and mental declines are experienced. We are far away from IoT technologies that can be integrated seamlessly over time and across multiple technology platforms. We need better technologies that can support older adults' independence and autonomy while evaluating the current state of their abilities, predicting the pace of decline in the near future, and suggesting system enhancements appropriate for that individual in a particular time and place. But to do so, we also need older adults, family members, and caregivers to trust the technology and resulting decisions. Anything less will result in older adults trying to deceive the system to avoid unwanted intrusions into their lives.

## NOTES

1. B. Knowles, V. Hanson, Y. Rogers, A. M. Piper, J. Waycott, N. Davies, A. Ambe, et al., "The Harm in Conflating Aging with Accessibility," *Communications of the ACM* 64, no. 7 (2021): 66–71.

2. "Active Ageing: A Policy Framework," World Health Organization, 2002, https://www.who.int/ageing/publications/active_ageing/en/.

3. "Active Ageing," 13.

4. S. Consolvo, P. Roessler, and B. E. Shelton, "The CareNet Display: Lessons Learned from an In-Home Evaluation of an Ambient Display," in *International Conference on Ubiquitous Computing* (Heidelberg, Berlin: Springer, 2004), 1–17.

5. M. Skubic, G. Alexander, M. Popescu, M. Rantz, and J. Keller, "A Smart Home Application to Eldercare: Current Status and Lessons Learned," *Technology and Health Care* 17, no. 3 (January 1, 2009): 183–201.

6. L. Dupuy, C. Consel, and H. Sauzéon, "Self Determination-Based Design to Achieve Acceptance of Assisted Living Technologies for Older Adults," *Computers in Human Behavior* 65 (December 1, 2016): 508–521.

7. K. E. Caine, C. Y. Zimmerman, Z. Schall-Zimmerman, W. R. Hazlewood, L. J. Camp, K. H. Connelly, L. L. Huber, and K. Shankar, "DigiSwitch: A Device to Allow Older Adults to Monitor and Direct the Collection and Transmission of Health Information Collected at Home," *Journal of Medical Systems* 35, no. 5 (October 2011): 1181–1195.

8. L. L. Huber, K. Shankar, K. Caine, K. Connelly, L. J. Camp, B. A. Walker, and L. Borrero, "How In-Home Technologies Mediate Caregiving Relationships in Later Life," *International Journal of Human-Computer Interaction* 29, no. 7 (July 3, 2013): 441–455.

9. I. Arreola, Z. Morris, M. Francisco, K. Connelly, K. Caine, and G. White, "From Checking on to Checking in: Designing for Low Socio-economic Status Older Adults," in *Proceedings of the SIGCHI Conference on Human Factors in Computing Systems* (April 26, 2014): 1933–1936.

10. D. Warnock, M. McGee-Lennon, and S. Brewster, "Multiple Notification Modalities and Older Users," in *Proceedings of the SIGCHI Conference on Human Factors in Computing Systems* (April 27, 2013): 1091–1094.

11. A. Mihailidis, J. N. Boger, T. Craig, and J. Hoey, "The COACH Prompting System to Assist Older Adults with Dementia through Handwashing: An Efficacy Study," *BMC Geriatrics* 8, no. 1 (December 2008): 1–8.

12. Q. T. Tran and E. D. Mynatt, "What Was I Cooking? Towards Deja Vu Displays of Everyday Memory," Georgia Institute of Technology Technical Reports, no. 33 (April, 2004): 1–8.

13. D. Warnock, M. McGee-Lennon, and S. Brewster, "Multiple Notification Modalities and Older Users," in *Proceedings of the SIGCHI Conference on Human Factors in Computing Systems* (April 27, 2013): 1091–1094.

14. Y. S. Lee, J. Tullio, N. Narasimhan, P. Kaushik, J. R. Engelsma, and S. Basapur, "Investigating the Potential of In-Home Devices for Improving Medication Adherence," *3rd International Conference on Pervasive Computing Technologies for Healthcare*, IEEE (April 1, 2009): 1–8.

15. R. N. Brewer, M. R. Morris, and S. E. Lindley, "How to Remember What to Remember: Exploring Possibilities for Digital Reminder Systems," *Proceedings of the ACM on Interactive, Mobile, Wearable and Ubiquitous Technologies* 1, no. 3 (September 2017): 20, https://doi.org/10.1145/3130903.

16. M. L. Lee and A. K. Dey, "Reflecting on Pills and Phone Use: Supporting Awareness of Functional Abilities for Older Adults," in *Proceedings of the SIGCHI Conference on Human Factors in Computing Systems* (May 7, 2011): 2095–2104.

17. A. Pradhan, A. Lazar, and L. Findlater, "Use of Intelligent Voice Assistants by Older Adults with Low Technology Use," *ACM Transactions on Computer-Human Interaction* 27, no. 4 (September 16, 2020): 1–27.

18. M. Trajkova and A. Martin-Hammond, "Alexa Is a Toy: Exploring Older Adults' Reasons for Using, Limiting, and Abandoning Echo," in *Proceedings of the 2020 CHI Conference on Human Factors in Computing Systems* (April 21, 2020): 1–13.

19. A. Pradhan, L. Findlater, and A. Lazar, "'Phantom Friend' or 'Just a Box with Information': Personification and Ontological Categorization of Smart Speaker-Based Voice Assistants by Older Adults," *Proceedings of the ACM on Human-Computer Interaction* 3, CSCW (November 7, 2019): 1–21.

20. "CareBand | Wearable Technology for Seniors Living with Dementia," Care-Band, accessed November 27, 2020, https://www.carebandremembers.com/.

21. D. L. Huang, D. E. Rosenberg, S. D. Simonovich, and B. Belza, "Food Access Patterns and Barriers among Midlife and Older Adults with Mobility Disabilities," *Journal of Aging Research* 2012, no. 231489 (September 26, 2012): 2090–2204.

22. G. Lee, B. Choi, C. R. Ahn, and S. Lee, "Wearable Biosensor and Hotspot Analysis–Based Framework to Detect Stress Hotspots for Advancing Elderly's Mobility," *Journal of Management in Engineering* 36, no. 3 (May 1, 2020): 04020010.

23. S. Li, P. Blythe, W. Guo, A. Namdeo, S. Edwards, P. Goodman, and G. Hill, "Evaluation of the Effects of Age-Friendly Human-Machine Interfaces on the Driver's Takeover Performance in Highly Automated Vehicles," *Transportation Research Part F: Traffic Psychology and Behaviour* 67 (November 1, 2019): 78–100.

24. C. Lee, "Adoption of Smart Technology among Older Adults: Challenges and Issues," *Public Policy and Aging Report* 24, no. 1 (March 6, 2014): 14–17.

25. WHO, "Active Ageing."

26. "Web-Based Injury Statistics Query and Reporting System (WISQARS)," Centers for Disease Control and Prevention, National Center for Injury Prevention and Control [online], accessed November 27, 2020, https://www.cdc.gov/injury/wisqars/index.html.

27. M. E. Tinetti and C. Kumar, "The Patient Who Falls: It's Always a Trade-off," *JAMA* 303, no. 3 (January 20, 2010): 258–266.

28. L. Yardley and J. Lord, "Falls in Older People: Risk Factors and Strategies for Prevention," *Ageing and Society* 28, no. 2 (February 1, 2008): 299.

29. L. J. Baraff, R. Della Penna, N. Williams, and A. Sanders, "Practice Guideline for the ED Management of Falls in Community-Dwelling Elderly Persons," *Annals of Emergency Medicine* 30, no. 4 (October 1, 1997): 480–492.

30. B. J. Vellas, S. J. Wayne, L. J. Romero, R. N. Baumgartner, and P. J. Garry, "Fear of Falling and Restriction of Mobility in Elderly Fallers," *Age and Ageing* 26, no. 3 (May 1, 1997): 189–193.

31. J. E. Walker and J. Howland, "Falls and Fear of Falling among Elderly Persons Living in the Community: Occupational Therapy Interventions," *American Journal of Occupational Therapy* 45, no. 2 (February 1, 1991): 119–122.

32. "What's New in Electronics: Emergency Dialer," in *Popular Science* (New York: Bonnier Corporation, 1975), 104.

33. "Shop All MyNotifi Medical Alert Devices," MyNotifi Automatic Fall Detection, accessed July 27, 2021, https://www.mynotifi.com/product/category&path=74.

34. "Automatic Fall Detection," Philips Lifeline, accessed July 27, 2021, https://www.lifeline.philips.com/medical-alert-systems/fall-detection.html.

35. "iVi Intelligent Pendant," Tunstall, accessed November 27, 2020, https://www.tunstall.co.uk/our-products/product-catalogue/ivi-intelligent-pendant/#.

36. Amie Clark, "The Risks and Limits of Medical Alert Systems," *The Senior List* (blog), December 2, 2020, https://www.theseniorlist.com/blog/risks-limits-medical-alert-systems/.

37. C. J. Lord and D. P. Colvin, "Falls in the Elderly: Detection and Assessment," *Proceedings of the Annual International Conference of the IEEE Engineering in Medicine and Biology Society* 13, no. 1991 (October 31, 1991): 1938–1939.

38. A. J. Majumder, I. Zerin, M. Uddin, S. I. Ahamed, and R. O. Smith, "Smart-Prediction: A Real-Time Smartphone-Based Fall Risk Prediction and Prevention System," *Proceedings of the 2013 Research in Adaptive and Convergent Systems* (October 1, 2013): 434–439.

39. Y. Li, Z. Zeng, M. Popescu, and K. C. Ho, "Acoustic Fall Detection Using a Circular Microphone Array," *2010 Annual International Conference of the IEEE Engineering in Medicine and Biology*, IEEE (August 31, 2010): 2242–2245.

40. Y. Li, K. C. Ho, and M. Popescu, "A Microphone Array System for Automatic Fall Detection," *IEEE Transactions on Biomedical Engineering* 59, no. 5 (February 1, 2012): 1291–1301.

41. Y. Zigel, D. Litvak, and I. Gannot, "A Method for Automatic Fall Detection of Elderly People Using Floor Vibrations and Sound—Proof of Concept on Human Mimicking Doll Falls," *IEEE Transactions on Biomedical Engineering* 56, no. 12 (August 25, 2009): 2858–2867.

42. H. Foroughi, B. S. Aski, and H. Pourreza, "Intelligent Video Surveillance for Monitoring Fall Detection of Elderly in Home Environments," *2008 11th International Conference on Computer and Information Technology*, IEEE (December 24, 2008): 219–224.

43. M. Yu, A. Rhuma, S. M. Naqvi, L. Wang, and J. Chambers, "A Posture Recognition-Based Fall Detection System for Monitoring an Elderly Person in a Smart Home Environment," *IEEE Transactions on Information Technology in Biomedicine* 16, no. 6 (August 22, 2012): 1274–1286.

44. C. Rougier, J. Meunier, A. St-Arnaud, and J. Rousseau, "Robust Video Surveillance for Fall Detection Based on Human Shape Deformation," *IEEE Transactions on Circuits and Systems for Video Technology* 21, no. 5 (March 17, 2011): 611–622.

45. Z. P. Bian, J. Hou, L. P. Chau, and N. Magnenat-Thalmann, "Fall Detection Based on Body Part Tracking Using a Depth Camera," *IEEE Journal of Biomedical and Health Informatics* 19, no. 2 (April 23, 2014): 430–439.

46. J. L. Chua, Y. C. Chang, and W. K. Lim, "A Simple Vision-Based Fall Detection Technique for Indoor Video Surveillance," *Signal, Image and Video Processing* 9, no. 3 (March 2015): 623–633.

47. Foroughi, Aski, and Pourreza, "Intelligent Video Surveillance."

48. Yu et al., "A Posture Recognition-Based Fall Detection System."

49. G. Demiris, D. P. Oliver, J. Giger, M. Skubic, and M. Rantz, "Older Adults' Privacy Considerations for Vision-Based Recognition Methods of Eldercare Applications," *Technology and Health Care* 17, no. 1 (January 1, 2009): 41–48.

50. E. E. Stone and M. Skubic, "Fall Detection in Homes of Older Adults Using the Microsoft Kinect," *IEEE Journal of Biomedical and Health Informatics* 19, no. 1 (March 17, 2014): 290–301.

51. G. Mastorakis and D. Makris, "Fall Detection System Using Kinect's Infrared Sensor," *Journal of Real-Time Image Processing* 9, no. 4 (December 2014): 635–646.

52. S. Gasparrini, E. Cippitelli, S. Spinsante, and E. Gambi, "A Depth-Based Fall Detection System Using a Kinect Sensor," *Sensors* 14, no. 2 (February 2014): 2756–2775.

53. B. Kwolek and M. Kepski, "Human Fall Detection on Embedded Platform Using Depth Maps and Wireless Accelerometer," *Computer Methods and Programs in Biomedicine* 117, no. 3 (December 1, 2014): 489–501.

54. H. Gjoreski, J. Bizjak, and M. Gams, "Using Smartwatch as Telecare and Fall Detection Device," *2016 12th International Conference on Intelligent Environments (IE)*, IEEE (September 14, 2016): 242–245.

55. T. R. Mauldin, M. E. Canby, V. Metsis, A. H. Ngu, and C. C. Rivera, "Smart-Fall: A Smartwatch-Based Fall Detection System Using Deep Learning," *Sensors* 18, no. 10 (October 2018): 3363.

56. E. Casilari and M. A. Oviedo-Jiménez, "Automatic Fall Detection System Based on the Combined Use of a Smartphone and a Smartwatch," *Plos One* 10, no. 11 (November 11, 2015): e0140929.

57. J. Santiago, E. Cotto, L. G. Jaimes, and I. Vergara-Laurens, "Fall Detection System for the Elderly," *2017 IEEE 7th Annual Computing and Communication Workshop and Conference*, IEEE (January 9, 2017): 1–4.

58. "Fall Detection Using Apple Watch," Apple, accessed November 3, 2020, https://support.apple.com/en-us/HT208944.

59. R. Rashya and M. Sindhuja, "An Enhanced & Effective Fall Detection System for Elderly Person Monitoring Using Consumer Home Networks," *International Journal of Research in Engineering and Science* 3 (2015): 50–57.

60. S. Greene, H. Thapliyal, and D. Carpenter, "IoT-Based Fall Detection for Smart Home Environments," *2016 IEEE International Symposium on Nanoelectronic and Information Systems*, IEEE (December 19, 2016): 23–28.

61. Q. Zhang, L. Ren, and W. Shi, "HONEY: A Multimodality Fall Detection and Telecare System," *Telemedicine and e-Health* 19, no. 5 (May 1, 2013): 415–429.

62. Zhang, Ren, and Shi, "HONEY."

63. C. Li, C. F. Lee, and S. Xu Stigma, "Threat in Design for Older Adults: Exploring Design Factors that Induce Stigma Perception," *International Journal of Design* 14, no. 1 (April 1, 2020): 51–64.

64. L. Teri, E. B. Larson, and B. V. Reifler, "Behavioral Disturbance in Dementia of the Alzheimer's Type," *Journal of the American Geriatrics Society* 36, no. 1 (January 1988): 1–6.

65. C. G. Ballard, R. N. Mohan, C. Bannister, S. Handy, and A. Patel, "Wandering in Dementia Sufferers," *International Journal of Geriatric Psychiatry* 6, no. 8 (August 1991): 611–614.

66. D. A. Klein, M. Steinberg, E. Galik, C. Steele, J. M. Sheppard, A. Warren, A. Rosenblatt, and C. G. Lyketsos, "Wandering Behaviour in Community–Residing Persons with Dementia," *International Journal of Geriatric Psychiatry* 14, no. 4 (April 1999): 272–279.

67. D. C. Chan, J. D. Kasper, B. S. Black, and P. V. Rabins, "Prevalence and Correlates of Behavioral and Psychiatric Symptoms in Community–Dwelling Elders with Dementia or Mild Cognitive Impairment: The Memory and Medical Care Study," *International Journal of Geriatric Psychiatry* 18, no. 2 (February 2003): 174–182.

68. T. Hope, K. M. Tilling, K. Gedling, J. M. Keene, S. D. Cooper, and C. G. Fairburn, "The Structure of Wandering in Dementia," *International Journal of Geriatric Psychiatry* 9, no. 2 (February 1994): 149–155.

69. "Electronic Tagging—Enabling or Disabling People with Dementia?," UK Alzheimer's Society, accessed November 18, 2020, http://www.alzheimers.org.uk/site/scripts/news_article.php.

70. C. Ballard and J. O'Brien, "Treating Behavioural and Psychological Signs in Alzheimer's Disease: The Evidence for Current Pharmacological Treatments Is Not Strong," *British Medical Journal* 319 (1999): e138–e139.

71. L. B. Taft, K. Delaney, D. Seman, and J. Stansell, "Dementia Care Creating a Therapeutic Milieu," *Journal of Gerontological Nursing* 19, no. 10 (October 1, 1993): 30–39.

72. W. Coltharp, M. F. Richie, and M. J. Kaas, "Wandering," *Journal of Gerontological Nursing* 22, no. 11 (November 1, 1996): 5–9.

73. J. Cohen-Mansfield and P. Werner, "The Effects of an Enhanced Environment on Nursing Home Residents Who Pace," *The Gerontologist* 38, no. 2 (April 1, 1998): 199–208.

74. "What Is GPS SmartSole?," GTX Corp, accessed November 18, 2020, https://gpssmartsole.com/gpssmartsole/.

75. D. Taub, E. Lupton, R. Hinman, S. Leeb, J. Zeisel, and S. Blackler, "The Escort System: A Safety Monitor for People Living with Alzheimer's Disease," *IEEE Pervasive Computing* 10, no. 2 (April 8, 2010): 68–77.

76. D. Martino-Saltzman, B. B. Blasch, R. D. Morris, and L. W. McNeal, "Travel Behavior of Nursing Home Residents Perceived as Wanderers and Nonwanderers," *The Gerontologist* 31, no. 5 (October 1, 1991): 666–672.

77. C. C. Lin, M. J. Chiu, C. C. Hsiao, R. G. Lee, and Y. S. Tsai, "Wireless Health Care Service System for Elderly with Dementia," *IEEE Transactions on Information Technology in Biomedicine* 10, no. 4 (October 9, 2006): 696–704.

78. F. Sposaro, J. Danielson, and G. Tyson, "iWander: An Android Application for Dementia Patients," *2010 Annual International Conference of the IEEE Engineering in Medicine and Biology*, IEEE (September 2010): 3875–3878.

79. H. Ogawa, Y. Yonezawa, H. Maki, H. Sato, and W. M. Caldwell, "A Mobile Phone-Based Safety Support System for Wandering Elderly Persons," *The 26th*

*Annual International Conference of the IEEE Engineering in Medicine and Biology Society* 2 (September 1, 2004): 3316–3317.

80. M. Kangas, I. Vikman, L. Nyberg, R. Korpelainen, J. Lindblom, and T. Jämsä, "Comparison of Real-Life Accidental Falls in Older People with Experimental Falls in Middle-Aged Test Subjects," *Gait and Posture* 35, no. 3 (2012): 500–505.

81. Stone and Skubic, "Fall Detection in Homes."

82. K. L. Courtney, G. Demeris, M. Rantz, and M. Skubic, "Needing Smart Home Technologies: The Perspectives of Older Adults in Continuing Care Retirement Communities," *Informatics in Primary Care* 16 (2008): 195–201.

83. K. Chaccour, R. Darazi, A. H. El Hassani, and E. Andres, "From Fall Detection to Fall Prevention: A Generic Classification of Fall-Related Systems," *IEEE Sensors Journal* 17, no. 3 (2016): 812–822.

84. T. Tamura, T. Yoshimura, M. Sekine, M. Uchida, and O. Tanaka, "A Wearable Airbag to Prevent Fall Injuries," *IEEE Transactions on Information Technology in Biomedicine* 13, no. 6 (October 20, 2009): 910–914.

85. G. Shi, C. S. Chan, W. J. Li, K. S. Leung, Y. Zou, and Y. Jin, "Mobile Human Airbag System for Fall Protection Using MEMS Sensors and Embedded SVM Classifier," *IEEE Sensors Journal* 9, no. 5 (March 27, 2009): 495–503.

86. Q. Lin, D. Zhang, K. Connelly, H. Ni, Z. Yu, and X. Zhou, "Disorientation Detection by Mining GPS Trajectories for Cognitively-Impaired Elders," *Pervasive and Mobile Computing* 19 (May 1, 2015): 71–85.

87. "Supporting Older Patients with Chronic Conditions," NIH National Institute on Aging, accessed July 27, 2021, https://www.nia.nih.gov/health/supporting-older -patients-chronic-conditions.

88. "Chronic Diseases in America," Centers for Disease Control and Prevention, accessed July 27, 2021, https://www.cdc.gov/chronicdisease/resources/infographic/ chronic-diseases.htm.

89. A. Panicker, K. Basu, and C. F. Chung, "Changing Roles and Contexts: Symbolic Interactionism in the Sharing of Food and Eating Practices between Remote, Intergenerational Family Members," *Proceedings of the ACM on Human-Computer Interaction* 4, CSCW1 (May 28, 2020): 1–9.

90. M. Bojic, O. A. Henkemans, M. A. Neerincx, C. A. Van der Mast, and J. Lindenberg, "Effects of Multimodal Feedback on the Usability of Mobile Diet Diary for Older Adults," in *International Conference on Universal Access in Human-Computer Interaction* (Heidelberg, Berlin: Springer, July 19, 2009), 293–302.

91. J. Sandbulte, J. Beck, E. K. Choe, and J. M. Carroll, "Turning Points: Motivating Intergenerational Families to Engage on Sustainable Health Information Sharing," in *International Conference on Information* (Cham, Switzerland: Springer, March 31, 2019), 741–753.

92. S. M. Fattah, N. M. Sung, I. Y. Ahn, M. Ryu, and J. Yun, "Building IoT Services for Aging in Place Using Standard-Based IoT Platforms and Heterogeneous IoT Products," *Sensors* 17, no. 10 (October 2017): 2311.

93. Panicker, Basu, and Chung, "Changing Roles and Contexts."

94. Huang, Rosenberg, Simonovich, and Belza, "Food Access Patterns."

95. G. S. Brewster, B. Riegel, and P. R. Gehrman, "Insomnia in the Older Adult," *Sleep Medicine Clinics* 13, no. 1 (March 1, 2018): 13–19.

96. "Building a Better Tracker: Older Consumers Weigh In on Activity and Sleep Monitoring Devices," AARP, 2015, https://www.aarp.org/content/dam/aarp/home -and-family/personal-technology/2015-07/innovation-50-project-catalyst-tracker -study-AARP.pdf.

97. K. E. Burton, "Evaluating Activity and Sleep Tracking Technologies for Older Adults" (PhD diss., Georgia Institute of Technology, 2016).

98. D. A. Epstein, M. Caraway, C. Johnston, A. Ping, J. Fogarty, and S. A. Munson, "Beyond Abandonment to Next Steps: Understanding and Designing for Life after Personal Informatics Tool Use," *Proceedings of the 2016 CHI Conference on Human Factors in Computing Systems* (May, 2016): 1109–1113.

99. "How Much Physical Activity Do Older Adults Need?," Centers for Disease Control and Prevention, accessed July 27, 2021, https://www.cdc.gov/physicalactiv ity/basics/older_adults/index.htm.

100. AARP, "Building a Better Tracker."

101. R. Cornejo, D. Hernández, J. Favela, M. Tentori, and S. Ochoa, "Persuading Older Adults to Socialize and Exercise through Ambient Games," *2012 6th International Conference on Pervasive Computing Technologies for Healthcare (Pervasive-Health) and Workshops*, IEEE (May 21, 2012): 215–218.

102. L. H. Barg-Walkow, C. N. Harrington, T. L. Mitzner, J. Q. Hartley, and W. A. Rogers, "Understanding Older Adults' Perceptions of and Attitudes towards Exergames," *Gerontechnology* 16, no. 2 (2017): 81.

103. C. Caldeira, M. Bietz, M. Vidauri, and Y. Chen, "Senior Care for Aging in Place: Balancing Assistance and Independence," *Proceedings of the 2017 ACM Conference on Computer Supported Cooperative Work and Social Computing* (February 25, 2017): 1605–1617.

104. T. A. Floegel, A. Florez-Pregonero, E. B. Hekler, and M. P. Buman, "Validation of Consumer-Based Hip and Wrist Activity Monitors in Older Adults with Varied Ambulatory Abilities," *Journals of Gerontology Series A: Biomedical Sciences and Medical Sciences* 72, no. 2 (February 1, 2017): 229–236.

105. L. A. Simpson, J. J. Eng, T. D. Klassen, S. B. Lim, D. R. Louie, B. Parappilly, B. M. Sakakibara, and D. Zbogar, "Capturing Step Counts at Slow Walking Speeds in Older Adults: Comparison of Ankle and Waist Placement of Measuring Device," *Journal of Rehabilitation Medicine* 47, no. 9 (October 5, 2015): 830–835.

106. C. N. Harrington, L. Wilcox, K. Connelly, W. Rogers, and J. Sanford, "Designing Health and Fitness Apps with Older Adults: Examining the Value of Experience-Based Co-design," *Proceedings of the 12th EAI International Conference on Pervasive Computing Technologies for Healthcare* (May 21, 2018): 15–24.

107. D. P. French, E. K. Olander, A. Chisholm, and J. McSharry, "Which Behaviour Change Techniques Are Most Effective at Increasing Older Adults' Self-Efficacy and Physical Activity Behaviour? A Systematic Review," *Annals of Behavioral Medicine* 48, no. 2 (October 1, 2014): 225–234.

108. D. L. Kappen, P. Mirza-Babaei, and L. E. Nacke, "Gamification through the Application of Motivational Affordances for Physical Activity Technology,"

*Proceedings of the Annual Symposium on Computer-Human Interaction in Play* (October 15, 2017): 5–18.

109. Harrington, Wilcox, Connelly, Rogers, and Sanford, "Designing Health and Fitness Apps."

110. B. W. Ward, J. S. Schiller, and R. A. Goodman, "Peer Reviewed: Multiple Chronic Conditions among US Adults: A 2012 Update," *Preventing Chronic Disease* 11 (2014): 1–4.

111. C. Storni, "Multiple Forms of Appropriation in Self-Monitoring Technology: Reflections on the Role of Evaluation in Future Self-Care," *International Journal of Human–Computer Interaction* 26, no. 5 (April 27, 2010): 537–561.

112. C. Caldeira, M. Bietz, and Y. Chen, "Looking for the Unusual: How Older Adults Utilize Self-Tracking Techniques for Health Management," *Proceedings of the 10th EAI International Conference on Pervasive Computing Technologies for Healthcare* (May 16, 2016): 227–230.

113. S. R. Mishra, P. Klasnja, J. MacDuffie Woodburn, E. B. Hekler, L. Omberg, M. Kellen, and L. Mangravite, "Supporting Coping with Parkinson's Disease through Self Tracking," *Proceedings of the 2019 CHI Conference on Human Factors in Computing Systems* (May 2, 2019): 1–16.

114. J. Maitland and M. Chalmers, "Self-Monitoring, Self-Awareness, and Self-Determination in Cardiac Rehabilitation," *Proceedings of the SIGCHI Conference on Human Factors in Computing Systems* (April 10, 2010): 1213–1222.

115. C. C. Quinn, B. Khokhar, K. Weed, E. Barr, and A. L. Gruber-Baldini, "Older Adult Self-Efficacy Study of Mobile Phone Diabetes Management," *Diabetes Technology and Therapeutics* 17, no. 7 (July 1, 2015): 455–461.

116. R. Tang, X. D. Yang, S. Bateman, J. Jorge, and A. Tang, "Physio@ Home: Exploring Visual Guidance and Feedback Techniques for Physiotherapy Exercises," *Proceedings of the 33rd Annual ACM Conference on Human Factors in Computing Systems* (April 18, 2015): 4123–4132.

117. Y. J. Chang, S. F. Chen, and J. D. Huang, "A Kinect-Based System for Physical Rehabilitation: A Pilot Study for Young Adults with Motor Disabilities," *Research in Developmental Disabilities* 32, no. 6 (November 1, 2011): 2566–2570.

118. S. Ananthanarayan, M. Sheh, A. Chien, H. Profita, and K. A. Siek, "Designing Wearable Interfaces for Knee Rehabilitation," *Proceedings of the 8th International Conference on Pervasive Computing Technologies for Healthcare* (May 20, 2014): 101–108.

119. B. Ploderer, J. Fong, A. Withana, M. Klaic, S. Nair, V. Crocher, F. Vetere, and S. Nanayakkara, "ArmSleeve: A Patient Monitoring System to Support Occupational Therapists in Stroke Rehabilitation," *Proceedings of the 2016 ACM Conference on Designing Interactive Systems* (June 4, 2016): 700–711.

120. T. Ongwere, G. Cantor, S. R. Martin, P. C. Shih, J. Clawson, and K. Connelly, "Design Hotspots for Care of Discordant Chronic Comorbidities: Patients' Perspectives," *Proceedings of the 10th Nordic Conference on Human-Computer Interaction* (September 29, 2018): 571–583.

121. T. Ongwere, G. S. Cantor, J. Clawson, P. C. Shih, and K. Connelly, "Design and Care for Discordant Chronic Comorbidities: A Comparison of Healthcare Pro-

viders' Perspectives," *Proceedings of EAI International Conference on Pervasive Computing Technologies for Healthcare*, PervasiveHealth (2020): 133–145.

122. C. Caldeira, X. Gui, T. L. Reynolds, M. Bietz, and Y. Chen, "Managing Healthcare Conflicts When Living with Multiple Chronic Conditions," *International Journal of Human-Computer Studies* 145, no. 6 (January 2021): 102494.

123. F. Nunes, N. Verdezoto, G. Fitzpatrick, M. Kyng, E. Grönvall, and C. Storni, "Self-Care Technologies in HCI: Trends, Tensions, and Opportunities," *ACM Transactions on Computer-Human Interaction* 22, no. 6 (December 14, 2015): 1–45.

124. Lee and Dey, "Reflecting on Pills and Phone Use."

125. S. Fox and M. Duggan, "Tracking for Health," Pew Research Center, January 28, 2013, https://www.pewresearch.org/internet/2013/01/28/tracking-for-health/.

126. A. Light, T. W. Leong, and T. Robertson, "Ageing Well with CSCW," in *EC-SCW 2015: Proceedings of the 14th European Conference on Computer Supported Cooperative Work* (Cham, Switzerland: Springer, September 19–23, 2015), 295–304.

127. Maitland and Chalmers, "Self-Monitoring, Self-Awareness, and Self-Determination."

128. Harrington, Wilcox, Connelly, Rogers, and Sanford, "Designing Health and Fitness Apps."

129. Barg-Walkow, Harrington, Mitzner, Hartley, and Rogers, "Understanding Older Adults' Perceptions."

130. Panicker, Basu, and Chung, "Changing Roles and Contexts."

131. D. L. Bliwise, "Sleep in Normal Aging and Dementia," *Sleep: Journal of Sleep Research and Sleep Medicine* 16, no. 1 (January 1993): 40–81.

132. National Academies of Sciences, Engineering, and Medicine, *Social Isolation and Loneliness in Older Adults: Opportunities for the Health Care System* (Washington, DC: National Academies Press, 2020).

133. W. Boot, N. Charness, S. J. Czaja, and W. A. Rogers, *Designing for Older Adults: Case Studies, Methods, and Tools* (Boca Raton, FL: CRC Press, 2020).

134. H. Y. Tsai, R. Shillair, S. R. Cotten, V. Winstead, and E. Yost, "Getting Grandma Online: Are Tablets the Answer for Increasing Digital Inclusion for Older Adults in the US?," *Educational Gerontology* 41, no. 10 (October 3, 2015): 695–709.

135. C. Norval, J. L. Arnott, and V. L. Hanson, "What's on Your Mind? Investigating Recommendations for Inclusive Social Networking and Older Adults," *Proceedings of the SIGCHI Conference on Human Factors in Computing Systems* (April 26, 2014): 3923–3932.

136. R. Cornejo, J. Favela, and M. Tentori, "Ambient Displays for Integrating Older Adults into Social Networking Sites," *International Conference on Collaboration and Technology* (Heidelberg, Berlin: Springer, September 20, 2010), 321–336.

137. S. Tibken, "FaceTime Creator Details Its History, Including Code Name," *CNET*, April 22, 2014, https://www.cnet.com/news/apple-engineer-details-facetimes -history-including-original-codename/.

138. K. Gidick, "Grandparents Boost Their Video Chat Skills to Connect with Grandchildren," AARP, 2020, https://www.aarp.org/home-family/friends-family/ info-2020/grandparents-video-chat.html.

139. E. D. Mynatt, J. Rowan, S. Craighill, and A. Jacobs, "Digital Family Portraits: Supporting Peace of Mind for Extended Family Members," *Proceedings of the SIGCHI Conference on Human Factors in Computing Systems* (March 1, 2001): 333–340.

140. Consolvo, Roessler, and Shelton, "The CareNet Display."

141. Arreola et al., "From Checking On to Checking In."

142. Arreola et al., "From Checking On to Checking In."

143. Y. Riche and W. Mackay, "PeerCare: Supporting Awareness of Rhythms and Routines for Better Aging in Place," *Computer Supported Cooperative Work* 19, no. 1 (February 1, 2010): 73–104.

144. Arreola et al., "From Checking On to Checking In."

145. C. Kennedy-Armbruster, L. Lorenzen-Huber, and F. Ona, "Increasing Functional Fitness Using Internet-Based Video Conferencing," *ACSM's Health and Fitness Journal* 13, no. 3 (May 1, 2009): 31–32.

146. Cornejo et al., "Persuading Older Adults."

147. J. A. Kieffer, "Productive Roles in an Older Society: The Older Volunteer Resource," *Institute of Medicine (US) and National Research Council (US) Committee on an Aging Society* (Washington, DC: National Academies Press, 1986).

148. J. Stewart, C. Browning, and J. Sims, "Civic Socialising: A Revealing New Theory about Older People's Social Relationships," *Ageing and Society* 35, no. 4 (April 1, 2015): 750.

149. S. Šabanović, C. C. Bennett, W. L. Chang, and L. Huber, "PARO Robot Affects Diverse Interaction Modalities in Group Sensory Therapy for Older Adults with Dementia," *2013 IEEE 13th International Conference on Rehabilitation Robotics*, IEEE (June 24, 2013): 1–6.

150. Steven Baker, Ryan M. Kelly, Jenny Waycott, Romina Carrasco, Thuong Hoang, Frances Batchelor, Elizabeth Ozanne, Briony Dow, Jeni Warburton, and Frank Vetere, "Interrogating Social Virtual Reality as a Communication Medium for Older Adults," *Proceedings of the ACM on Human-Computer Interaction* 3, CSCW (2019): 1–24.

151. Steven Baker, Jenny Waycott, Sonja Pedell, Thuong Hoang, and Elizabeth Ozanne, "Older People and Social Participation: From Touch-screens to Virtual Realities," *Proceedings of the International Symposium on Interactive Technology and Ageing Populations* (2016): 34–43.

152. M. Anderson and A. Perrin, "Tech Adoption Climbs among Older Adults," Pew Research Center, May 17, 2017, https://www.pewresearch.org/internet/2017/05/17/tech-adoption-climbs-among-older-adults/.

153. A. Frik, L. Nurgalieva, J. Bernd, J. Lee, F. Schaub, and S. Egelman, "Privacy and Security Threat Models and Mitigation Strategies of Older Adults," *Fifteenth Symposium on Usable Privacy and Security*, SOUPS (2019).

154. Frik et al., "Privacy and Security Threat Models."

155. "Elder Fraud," Federal Bureau of Investigations, accessed October 21, 2020, https://www.fbi.gov/scams-and-safety/common-scams-and-crimes/elder-fraud.

156. N. Leiber, "How Criminals Steal $37 Billion a Year from America's Elderly," *Bloomberg*, May 3, 2018, https://www.bloomberg.com/news/features/2018-05-03/america-s-elderly-are-losing-37-billion-a-year-to-fraud.

157. Frik et al., "Privacy and Security Threat Models."

158. S. Banerjee, Y. Chen, K. Nissim, D. Parkes, K. Siek, and L. Wilcox, "Modernizing Data Control: Making Personal Digital Data Mutually Beneficial for Citizens and Industry," Computing Community Consortium, accessed July 27, 2021, https://cra.org/ccc/resources/ccc-led-whitepapers/#2020-quadrennial-papers.

159. Banerjee et al., "Modernizing Data Control."

160. A. Mehra, "Home Security Systems Market Worth $78.9 Billion by 2025," *PR Newswire*, Cision, accessed October 20, 2020, https://www.prnewswire.com/news-releases/home-security-systems-market-worth-78-9-billion-by-2025--exclusive-report-by-marketsandmarkets-301090831.html.

161. J. Duncan, L. J. Camp, and W. R. Hazelwood, "The Portal Monitor: A Privacy-Enhanced Event-Driven System for Elder Care," *Proceedings of the 4th International Conference on Persuasive Technology* (April 26, 2009): 1–9.

162. FBI, "Elder Fraud."

163. M. S. Lachs, C. S. Williams, S. O'Brien, K. A. Pillemer, and M. E. Charlson, "The Mortality of Elder Mistreatment," *Journal of the American Medical Association* 280, no. 5 (1998): 428–432.

164. Caine et al., "DigiSwitch."

165. Caine et al., "DigiSwitch."

166. J. Vines, S. Lindsay, G. W. Pritchard, M. Lie, D. Greathead, P. Olivier, and K. Brittain, "Making Family Care Work: Dependence, Privacy and Remote Home Monitoring Telecare Systems," *Proceedings of the 2013 ACM International Joint Conference on Pervasive and Ubiquitous Computing* (September 8, 2013): 607–616.

167. Vines et al., "Making Family Care Work."

168. Nextdoor, accessed July 27, 2021, https://nextdoor.com/.

169. Nest, accessed July 27, 2021, https://nest.com/.

170. D. Hornung, C. Müller, I. Shklovski, T. Jakobi, and V. Wulf, "Navigating Relationships and Boundaries: Concerns around ICT-Uptake for Elderly People," *Proceedings of the 2017 CHI Conference on Human Factors in Computing Systems* (May 2, 2017): 7057–7069.

171. Hornung et al., "Navigating Relationships and Boundaries."

172. A. B. Brush, J. Jung, R. Mahajan, and F. Martinez, "Digital Neighborhood Watch: Investigating the Sharing of Camera Data amongst Neighbors," *Proceedings of the 2013 Conference on Computer Supported Cooperative Work* (February 23, 2013): 693–700.

173. D. Harwell, "Doorbell-Camera Firm Ring Has Partnered with 400 Police Forces, Extending Surveillance Concerns," *Washington Post*, August 28, 2019, https://www.washingtonpost.com/technology/2019/08/28/doorbell-camera-firm-ring-has-partnered-with-police-forces-extending-surveillance-reach/.

174. V. Boothroyd, "Older Adults' Perceptions of Online Risk" (Master's thesis, Carleton University, Ontario, Canada, 2014).

175. D. Oliveira, H. Rocha, H. Yang, D. Ellis, S. Dommaraju, M. Muradoglu, D. Weir, A. Soliman, T. Lin, and N. Ebner, "Dissecting Spear Phishing Emails for Older vs Young Adults: On the Interplay of Weapons of Influence and Life Domains in Predicting Susceptibility to Phishing," *Proceedings of the 2017 CHI Conference on Human Factors in Computing Systems* (May 2, 2017): 6412–6424.

176. Oliveira et al., "Dissecting Spear Phishing Emails for Older vs Young Adults."

177. Boothroyd, "Older Adults' Perceptions of Online Risk."

178. Frik et al., "Privacy and Security Threat Models."

179. H. M. Mentis, G. Madjaroff, and A. K. Massey, "Upside and Downside Risk in Online Security for Older Adults with Mild Cognitive Impairment," *Proceedings of the 2019 CHI Conference on Human Factors in Computing Systems* (May 2, 2019): 1–13.

180. A. M. Piper, R. Cornejo, L. Hurwitz, and C. Unumb, "Technological Care-giving: Supporting Online Activity for Adults with Cognitive Impairments," *Proceedings of the 2016 CHI Conference on Human Factors in Computing Systems* (May 7, 2016 ): 5311–5323.

181. V. Garg, L. J. Camp, L. Mae, and K. Connelly, "Designing Risk Communication for Older Adults," *Symposium on Usable Privacy and Security*, SOUPS (July 20, 2011): 20–22.

182. S. Das, A. Kim, B. Jelen, L. Huber, and L. J. Camp, "Non-inclusive Online Security: Older Adults' Experience with Two-Factor Authentication," *Proceedings of the 54th Hawaii International Conference on System Sciences*, HICSS (January 5, 2021).

183. J. Nicholson, L. Coventry, and P. Briggs, "'If It's Important It Will Be a Headline': Cybersecurity Information Seeking in Older Adults," *Proceedings of the 2019 CHI Conference on Human Factors in Computing Systems* (May 2, 2019): 1–11.

184. Wan Zhiyuan, Lingfeng Bao, Debin Gao, Eran Toch, Xin Xia, Tamir Mendel, and David Lo, "AppMoD: Helping Older Adults Manage Mobile Security with Online Social Help," *Proceedings of the ACM on Interactive, Mobile, Wearable and Ubiquitous Technologies* 3, no. 4, article 154 (December 2019): 9.

185. Caine et al., "DigiSwitch."

186. Frik et al., "Privacy and Security Threat Models."

187. Mentis, Madjaroff, and Massey, "Upside and Downside."

188. A. Essén, "The Two Facets of Electronic Care Surveillance: An Exploration of the Views of Older People Who Live with Monitoring Devices," *Social Science and Medicine* 67, no. 1 (July 1, 2008): 128–136.

189. Frik et al., "Privacy and Security Threat Models."

190. D. Townsend, F. Knoefel, and R. Goubran, "Privacy versus Autonomy: A Tradeoff Model for Smart Home Monitoring Technologies," *2011 Annual International Conference of the IEEE Engineering in Medicine and Biology Society*, IEEE (August 30, 2011 ): 4749–4752.

191. Das et al., "Non-inclusive Online Security."

192. T. Mendel and E. Toch, "My Mom Was Getting This Popup: Understanding Motivations and Processes in Helping Older Relatives with Mobile Security and Privacy," *Proceedings of the ACM on Interactive, Mobile, Wearable and Ubiquitous Technologies* 3, no. 4 (December 11, 2019): 1–20.

193. S. T. Peek, K. G. Luijkx, M. D. Rijnaard, M. E. Nieboer, C. S. van der Voort, S. Aarts, J. van Hoof, H. J. Vrijhoef, and E. J. Wouters, "Older Adults' Reasons for Using Technology while Aging in Place," *Gerontology* 62, no. 2 (2016): 226–237.

194. Wan et al., "AppMoD."

195. Nicholson, Coventry, and Briggs, "'If It's Important It Will Be a Headline.'"

196. Peek at al., "Older Adults' Reasons for Using Technology."

197. Wan et al., "AppMoD."

198. G. E. White, K. H. Connelly, and K. E. Caine, "Opportunities for Ubiquitous Computing in the Homes of Low SES Older Adults," *Proceedings of the 2012 ACM Conference on Ubiquitous Computing* (September 5, 2012 ): 659–660.

199. Light et al., "Ageing Well with CSCW."

200. M. Crabb and V. L. Hanson, "An Analysis of Age, Technology Usage, and Cognitive Characteristics within Information Retrieval Tasks," *ACM Transactions on Accessible Computing* 8, no. 3 (April 6, 2016): 1–26.

## Chapter Eight

# Telephone-Based Communities for Information and Social Connectedness

### Robin N. Brewer and Mary Janevic

> When you feel like you need someone there
> Feel like no one really cares
> Call me on the telephone
> I'll be there
>
> —Diana Ross, "Telephone," 1984[1]

Older adults (ages sixty-five-plus) are using social media and technologies such as smartphones more than ever before, showing how previous narratives of older adults being unskilled or disinterested in technology are outdated. However, the pervasiveness of screen-based technologies (e.g., computers, smartphones) and online communities (e.g., Facebook) makes it difficult for older adults with disabilities or limited internet access to engage online. Further, research shows that older adults prefer to communicate by speaking on the phone rather than through screen-based technologies.[2,3,4] As such, telephones remain pervasive technologies, with most older adults preferring and feeling more confident using landline phones over cell phones, though these preferences could change as cell phones become ubiquitous among older adults.[5,6] In this chapter, we argue that landline phones and audio interaction can be a more accessible alternative to engaging with others online.

Specifically, we present research on tele-communities. A tele-community is a community that promotes social interaction with other people by telephone. Rather than being screen based, as is the case with many mobile apps on a smartphone, a tele-community is accessible without a screen and uses voice. We will discuss two types of tele-communities—asynchronous and synchronous. An asynchronous tele-community is similar to an answering machine or voicemail where people leave messages for one another and can listen to content without needing to be available in real time. A synchronous tele-community is similar to a teleconference but less structured and encourages more interaction among participants. We will first discuss xPress, an asynchronous tele-community designed to support the social needs of older adults with disabilities. Next, we will discuss the Silver Center, a synchronous tele-community designed to support the needs of urban older adults with limited internet access.

## XPRESS: AN ASYNCHRONOUS TELE-COMMUNITY

### Motivation

Aging and disability are deeply intertwined. As the number of older adults increases globally, so does the number of people whose lives are affected by disability. According to the Centers for Disease Control and Prevention, one in four adults in the United States identifies as having a disability.[7] The likelihood of disability increases with age, as two in five adults over the age of sixty-five are disabled. The United Nations shows a similar connection between aging and disability where 15 percent of the global population has at least one disability, of which more than 46 percent are over sixty years old.[8]

Another pattern related to aging and disability is that of digital use. In what has been described as "the disability divide," older people with disabilities are less likely to own and use computers and the internet compared to younger people and those without disabilities.[9] According to the US Census Bureau, 13 percent of older adults with a disability live in poverty compared to 7 percent of older adults without a disability.[10] As economic mobility affects one's purchasing decisions, lower income connected to disability or limited income in retirement means that many older adults are unable to afford computers, smartphones, and internet access.

This disability divide is not equitably pervasive by disability, with those who are deaf and hard of hearing or with mobility impairments not experiencing significant access challenges. Rather than focus on factors affecting this divide, we extend arguments describing how disability, aging, and information access have a complex relationship.[11] We take a strengths-based approach to designing for these complexities, focusing on values and activities that older adults with disabilities find meaningful, positioning technology as a tool to supplement and support these values and activities.

Prior work shows how social communication and content sharing continue to be popular activities for older adults online.[12,13,14,15] These reports show older adults in the United States have increased their social media use over time. We extend this work by contextualizing beyond binary classifications of use, arguing there is a spectrum of use rather than solely "user" and "nonuser" while studying one specific social activity online: blogging.[16] Findings describe the ways in which older adults find blogging to be a meaningful online activity for sharing lived experiences or using content as a form of age-related activism.[17]

Yet, age-related disability can negatively affect one's perceived ability to engage socially online. For example, prior work on late-life vision loss shows that older adults who experience sudden or gradual blindness face barriers to learning to use assistive technologies. Several of these older adults described "giving up" on computers and online communities because of the time needed to learn and maintain assistive technologies and accessible software.[18]

## Community Description

Motivated by this prior work, we continue this section by describing a case study of a telephone-based online community designed for older adults with late-life vision loss. This tele-community, xPress, was designed to mimic the affordances of assistive technologies for blind people, particularly through the use of audio and tactile interaction as forms of input and output. We include the technical design and system implementation details in prior work.[19] Its design was driven from observations and interviews with older adults in long-term care communities who had easy access to phones but not computers, interviews with older adults experiencing late-life vision loss who found it difficult to learn to use screen readers for computer-based internet access, and interviews with older adult bloggers who describe the value of connecting with others through blogging platforms.[20,21,22]

The primary form of access with the xPress tele-community is by telephone. Leveraging a strengths-based approach of engaging with technology that people already own and are comfortable with, this telephone does not need to be internet enabled, allowing for landline or feature (non-smart cell) phone use. Users dial a toll-free number and interact by listening to others' messages, recording their own message, or commenting on others' messages through audio input. Users hear recordings of others' messages rather than a speech-to-text playback with synthetic audio. In addition, they receive announcements at the beginning of each call notifying them of how many people have commented on their posts since their last community interaction, similar to a notification. While the interaction style is different, the types of interactions are similar to the content creation and sharing options afforded in online communities such as Facebook, Twitter, or Tumblr. Users navigate through different community features using tactile input by pressing buttons on their phone. Informed by preliminary interviews and observations with older adults, being able to use a landline phone and press physical buttons aligns with affordances of touch-based forms of communication (e.g., Braille).[23] The tactile feedback of knowing a button has been pressed is more reliable than using a smartphone with a touchscreen display. In addition, this mode of interaction is similar to customer service phone calls or checking voicemail messages, where the possible actions are clearly associated with an instruction (e.g., press 1 to listen to others' messages). Similar to voicemail messages, interactions in xPress are asynchronous, which removes the pressure of needing to respond instantly or worrying about interrupting another person's routines if calling by phone, a concern outlined in previous literature on aging and social technologies.[24]

The first author of this chapter conducted a pilot deployment of xPress with seven older adults with late-life vision loss for two months.[25] In this deployment, we observed how people enjoyed connecting with new social contacts and sharing vision-related disability advice such as accessible transportation recommendations and voting locations. For example, one participant posted:

> I was sighted and drove a car and actually chose to stop driving because of safety, my concern [being] that I might not see somebody out of my peripheral that I could have hit. . . . I don't live in the city and public transportation is not accessible here. I have a senior transportation service in our community that I have to call and make a reservation for. It's a nuisance. They're not always available or convenient for me. There's no evening hours so ugh. That is the worst part of my vision [loss] so that's my thoughts for now. If you have anything to say or want to continue, we can chat back and forth.

In interviews, they reflected on how their messages in the tele-community could be used to teach or inform people about vision loss, intending to reduce stigma around disability and aging, aligning with older adult bloggers' expectations of their blog posts on a computer.[26] For example, one participant reflected in their post interview: "This would be a good way for them to maybe learn about blindness, or blind people. 'Cause we are just regular people."

For participants, connecting based on shared stigmatizing experiences was cathartic when compared to medicalized, less personal, and more formal conversations about their disability. Overall, people enjoyed being able to hear another person's voice as it gave cues about emotions such as sadness or sarcasm that they described as being harder to interpret when listening to synthetic speech from screen readers that read text on a computer or smartphone.

## Research and Design Opportunities

While participants seemed to value the community for connecting them to people with similar disabilities, there were three primary areas in which the community and interaction aspects of a tele-community could be improved: provide opportunities to learn about their audience, design for listening rather than posting content, and encourage in-depth posts.

First, older adults wanted to learn more about other participants using the tele-community. This is similar to how older adult bloggers and others use readership statistics and user profiles on visual online communities to discover information such as city or state, age, gender, and interests of their audience.[27] Features such as voice profiles with biographies or introduction topic prompts could support this form of community building. Another option could be to schedule regular synchronous group conversations with community members to facilitate relationship development. This combination of synchronous and asynchronous communication can be seen in visual online communities such as Facebook with features like Facebook Live or video calling in Facebook Messenger to supplement status updates and comments, yet it has not been implemented in audio or voice-based communities.

Next, we learned about the value of listening rather than solely posting content. In biweekly phone check-ins with older adult participants, they discussed the content of others' posts in detail. This interest in others' posts was also shown in our data, as our data logs showed participants listened to posts more than creating new posts themselves. While this could be a factor relating to the novelty of the community, it suggests legitimate peripheral participation in which newcomers enter a community of practice by observing, then slowly adjusting and engaging in "active" participation.[28] We argue that active participation can go beyond posts, likes, or comments, which are forms of activity valued in many visual online communities.[29] Instead, listening or observing can be a form of active participation, which can be rendered invisible if system developers prioritize visible forms of interaction. Other researchers have also made this argument in online communities such as Wikipedia and Twitter, arguing for amplifying "nonpublic participation" and valuing listening.[30,31,32,33] In an inherently audio-based tele-community like xPress, listening should remain a core value. As such, content should be paired with a notification of how many people have listened to that post as a form of active engagement.

Lastly, older adults sometimes described wanting more in-depth posts that communicated something beyond mundane tasks, preferences, and hobbies. Being able to speak about topics at length has been described in prior work on active older adults in online communities.[34] Future iterations of xPress should encourage this depth by varying prompt topics to include content such as aspirations, political discourse, and so on that allow for more discussion and involvement.

## Iterating on a Community

In this section we describe a recent iteration of the design of xPress and preliminary use by twenty-two older adults with vision impairments. We intentionally choose not to include detailed usage data or analyze the content of audio posts in this chapter; rather, we focus on motivation to participate and values derived from the first six months of usage.

### Design

In this iteration, the first author of this chapter incorporated the social components above into xPress's design. To promote learning about others in the community, participants were asked to create introduction posts after their initial interview. To emphasize the importance of others listening to content, we added listener analytics. Participants now hear not only how many people have commented on each post but also how many people have listened to that post. To encourage more meaningful posts, prompts were changed to stimulate more reflection and promote conversation. Prompts now include topics such as "What is the most difficult thing you have ever done?," "What is one thing you would change about the world?," and "What do you think it means to be successful?"

### Use

We recruited twenty-two older adults to use xPress for one year (eleven females, eleven males; average age, seventy-nine; minimum age, sixty-five; maximum age, eighty-four; thirteen people with low vision; eight blind people) through a university participant recruitment pool and an email sent to members of the National Federation of the Blind. Prior to the tele-community deployment, older adults participated in preinterviews where the researcher asked questions about their social and digital routines and briefly described how the tele-community works. Training was informal and asynchronous as participants were asked to listen to a post, create a post, and create a comment to learn to use the system within a week of their preinterview, at which point the researcher answered any additional questions about how the system worked by phone or email.

The deployment began in May 2020, within three months of the start of the COVID-19 pandemic and restrictions reducing in-person interactions around the United States. As such, in their responses to preinterview questions, many participants described how they were motivated to take part in this study to prevent or mitigate loneliness. For example:

- "As you age you become more and more isolated and this [service] is a way to be included." (P20)

- "I think it does have value, particularly for people who don't get out much and maybe it has even more value during a pandemic like this. Because we don't get together in person as much." (P1)
- "I understand we're in the middle of a pandemic. There are people out there like myself who are alone, who really kind of want to use it just to call in and kind of say, okay, this is the kind of day I'm having." (P23)

These quotes show how older adult participants were eager to meet and engage with people due to the COVID-19 pandemic. Preinterviews also show how participants were excited to engage with disability-related topics while using xPress. For example:

- "I'd like to hear 'how do people cope'? . . . Here's a simple example for me, I had to figure this one out, tying black shoelaces on black shoes. It sounds like nothing, right, except when you're in a gym and you have to learn to tie your shoes pretty much by feel without even looking at them. . . .

    What are some of the things other people have had to deal with as a way of making me feel a little bit better about all the adjustments that have had to happen in my life. . . . We all moan and groan sometimes. But I would like to hear about the constructive and optimistic things that people are doing to enjoy their lives. And be able to do with their lives the way they would that will make them happy and not make them feel like being a burden on anybody else." (P1)

In this quote, P1 describes the importance of connecting with others who have shared disability experiences, not only to learn about coping mechanisms but also to promote positive well-being and to challenge deficit-based narratives of disability.

Participants joined the research study at different periods, and within the first seven months of the first xPress user being enrolled, participants dialed in 738 times. Of these calls, participants created 104 posts and listened to others' posts 822 times. Users could also interact with others' posts via comments, creating 76 comments and listening to comments 79 times. These statistics emphasize the value of listening to content as a form of active participation rather than solely contributing content, as highlighted in the first author's recent work on older adult Facebook users.[35]

We have transcribed a subset of interviews at the one-, three-, and six-month marks and conducted a preliminary analysis to provide clues as to what older adults value about using an asynchronous tele-community. These values include learning about experiences, establishing and strengthening new friendships, and ease of access.

In the following quotes, three participants share how they enjoy hearing from people in different locations, describing messages as "magical" and as a way to feel connected to others (even if alone physically) and learn about different ways of life:

- "I love hearing from people all over the country. . . . The program is great and I would love to respond to a lot more people." (P11)
- "It helps to pass the time to hear different stories, and some of them are quite magical, the experiences that people have had, I have the pleasure of listening to." (P20)
- "I really liked the whole concept of talking to people all over the country, which is nice. 'Cause you know, you're in [state anonymized] and you really don't know what the rest of the country is doing. And so I've enjoyed listening to the people. . . . I think the whole, the whole concept is great. So sometimes if I'm up at night—I live alone—so sometimes it's nice, sometimes at night I just like to sit down and hear what someone has to say." (P5)

In the following two quotes, participants describe how the tele-community was useful for its potential to make new friends or to use the discussions to supplement relationships with existing connections:

- "You know, the first time I listened to her, I had an impression, let's just say, not a judgment, an impression. Subsequent listenings changed that impression, what a wonderful woman she is and what experiences have occurred in her life and if we lived closer I would love to touch base with her.

  When I do listen to some of the comments but especially ones that came from [name anonymized]. I shared it with my family this weekend. We were at dinner and I said, this is somebody I listen to and we talked about what she had said. And it was a wonderful discussion. So, we all laughed about it." (P20)
- "I don't drive, but I go to a school for the blind, but you don't have contact with other people as much because we can't get around. So I love hearing what other people have done, it kind of encourages you to keep on doing you know or do more . . . it's nice to know there are other people out there that are just like you." (P11)

Lastly, participants appreciated the system's ease of access. For example, P11 appreciated that the system was "approachable" for those not familiar with technology, while P37 enjoyed the "informality" of the community, finding xPress to be a valuable form of communication and connection.

- "I think it has the potential to help people who don't like techie stuff to talk with other people. And also, but more importantly, learn to use some techie stuff themselves. . . . I think there is a fear on a lot of people's parts of anything that's different and this is so slightly different that it's more approachable." (P11)
- "I like . . . the informality of it. It didn't have an agenda to convince anybody of anything. At least the ones I heard didn't try to convince anybody of anything or offer unwanted advice or, heaven forbid, sell anything. It wasn't like that it was just people sharing their stories and experiences. I just think in general that's a valuable way of connecting." (P37)

While several participants seem to enjoy xPress as an asynchronous tele-community, we find that they may merge expectations of a computer-based online community and phone conversation, of which features of both are included but not exhaustive. Because a phone typically affords more continuous conversations, participants expressed a desire for a more continuous and faster conversational flow. In comparison to visual online communities such as Facebook and Reddit, with features such as separate forums and topic-specific groups that encourage conversation, content discoverability remains a challenge in a voice-based setting, particularly for an asynchronous community that archives messages.

In this section, we discussed the design and older adults' use of an asynchronous tele-community. Yet, tele-communities can also offer opportunities for real-time connections. In the following section, we describe the motivation, design, and pilot study of a synchronous tele-community to support older adults with limited in-home internet access.

## THE SILVER CENTER: A SYNCHRONOUS TELE-COMMUNITY

### Motivation

Prior work has shown how telephone-based communities can provide social, emotional, and informational resources to underserved communities that lack internet access. In the second case study in this chapter, we will focus on a program called the Silver Center. The Silver Center is a synchronous telephone community offering seniors center–style health and enrichment classes to older adults in and around Detroit, Michigan. The priority population for the Silver Center consists of older adults who are not able to visit traditional brick-and-mortar centers and who need an alternative way to engage with their community and peers. The motivation for developing the Silver Center is rooted both in digital exclusion patterned by age, location, and socioeconomic position as well as in the critical role seniors centers play in the lives of older adults.

## Digital Exclusion among Older Adults in Detroit

Many older adults in Detroit, Michigan, and the immediately surrounding communities in Wayne County are on the "wrong side" of the digital divide. In the United States, internet access in older age groups continues to lag behind the general population. In 2016, 67 percent of adults ages sixty-five-plus had internet access compared to 90 percent of adults ages eighteen and older. Similar trends exist for in-home broadband: 51 percent of adults ages sixty-five-plus have access compared to 73 percent of adults ages eighteen and up.[36] The US Census Bureau reports that nearly 80 percent of residents in Detroit own a computer, but only 60 percent have in-home broadband access.[37] Cost and infrastructure are the primary reasons underlying this lack of access,[38] particularly in underserved areas of the city (e.g., low-income housing communities). While smartphone adoption continues to increase across all segments of the population, including among older adults, a recent Detroit-based study by Reisdorf and colleagues demonstrated that being able to access the internet solely on a mobile phone does not allow for full participation in social capital–enhancing activities. In other words, smartphone ownership is not a replacement for having broadband access at home in terms of social and informational benefits.[39] In this study, increased age was associated with having fewer ways to access the internet (i.e., public internet access, home broadband, mobile phone data plan). The Detroit Community Technology Project has taken a justice-centered approach to deploy "neighborhood-governed community wireless networks," yet disparity in access persists.[40]

## The Role of Seniors Centers in Promoting Health and Well-Being

Seniors centers are a lifeline for many older adults, providing access to socialization, opportunities for exercise, health screenings, volunteer opportunities, informational resources such as financial planning, enrichment activities, and nutritious meals. They also frequently provide free internet access and technology training for older adults. Unfortunately, the number of seniors centers has not kept up with demand. Even as the US population rapidly ages, budget cuts have forced the closure of seniors centers at an alarming rate; the National Institute of Senior Centers reports that from 2005 to 2018, 37.5 percent of centers closed.[41,42] Similar to other large metropolitan areas in the United States, there are neighborhoods in Detroit with a high density of older residents that lack seniors centers and community centers within a target service area of a 2.5-mile radius.[43] Even when seniors centers are located nearby, many older people are unable to take advantage of them due to inaccessible or unreliable transportation, health and mobility challenges, or caregiving responsibilities. The reliance on the traditional in-person seniors and community center model for providing services to older adults thus leaves an important gap. Creative models are needed to ensure that older adults who are partially or entirely homebound can reap the benefits of seniors centers in terms of health, functioning, and quality of life.

## Target Audience

The Silver Center's primary audience was defined as older adults over the age of sixty who lack access to seniors centers because of geographic location, transportation challenges, health/mobility issues, and/or caregiving responsibilities. At the time of the project's launching, which was prior to the COVID-19 pandemic, the primary audience consisted of older adults living in specific areas of Wayne County, Michigan. Later, due to COVID-19 and the resulting increased need for remote programming for older adults, the target audience expanded to any older adult in the Detroit metropolitan area. Project collaborator Dr. Katrina Ellis further explains the necessity of the Silver Center due to COVID-19, saying,

> The Silver Center (and similar programs) are uniquely positioned to serve as a hub for social connection, resource referral, continued learning, and enjoyment for homebound older adults. This program could also be a nice complement to brick-and-mortar senior centers, helping to meet the needs of older adults with varying levels of mobility. The coronavirus pandemic has highlighted that for some individuals, being homebound and connected with others may vary over time. The Silver Center could be a resource to those who are experiencing being homebound for short (time-limited) or extended periods of time.

## Community Description

The idea for the Silver Center in the Detroit area was originally conceived of by Norvena Wilson, program developer for a nonprofit organization in Detroit. While employed at a large Detroit seniors center, Ms. Wilson noticed that some of the most regular members would stop coming to the center when it was no longer safe for them to drive due to age-related changes. From a survey completed by older adults in the Detroit/Wayne County area (n = 257), results show that a telephone-based seniors center had widespread appeal, with more than half of survey respondents indicating their interest in partici-pating in such a program. Fewer than one-third of older adults surveyed had internet access at home (29%), yet more than half owned a smartphone (66%) or landline phone (54%), revealing a clear need to develop ways to keep older adults engaged and connected from home. Yet, limited technology access and know-how in this group meant that alternatives to online programs were needed. Telephone-based programming for seniors had been successfully used elsewhere and could be used as models for future programs, though none existed in the Detroit area.[44,45,46,47]

## Community Design

### System Design

Informed and supported by the concept survey findings, the Silver Center began to take shape. The goal was to offer a tele-community providing in-formational and social services through a series of classes similar to those at in-person seniors and community centers. Inspired by a conference call format, our research team designed the Silver Center using two platforms: TurboBridge[48] and CallFire.[49] We used TurboBridge's audio conferencing capability to host each class using a toll-free phone number. We used CallFire to send reminder calls for each class and to disseminate audio-based phone surveys periodically throughout the program.

### Silver Center Structure

Silver Center participants were mailed a schedule of courses being offered each month as well as any accompanying handouts needed for the course. Courses were generally offered two mornings a week, with two hours of programming (consisting of two to four individual classes) each morning. At the designated class time, participants dialed a toll-free number and were connected with the instructor and any other attendees so that they could par-ticipate in the class. A paid conference operator, a staff member at the host agency, was present to assist participants as needed with logistical issues and to mute/unmute participants during discussions. By default, all participants were muted and could "raise their hand" to speak by pressing a specific num-ber combination on the keypad (e.g., *9).

### Class Design

Classes offered had a variety of goals. Some were intended to offer cultural or intellectual enrichment, others focused on health and wellness promotion, and others provided useful information or discussed local resources for older adults. Table 8.1 lists examples of Silver Center classes in each of these three categories. Some courses were held once, while others were progressive, rolling out over the course of a few weeks or the length of the pilot. Interaction styles were lecture, discussion, activity-based, or a combination of these formats. For example, the Detroit Institute of the Arts offered a weekly lecture led by a docent who verbally walked participants through a subset of art at the museum. An image of each painting was shared with participants via printed materials sent by mail prior to the session. Participants could ask the docent questions after each art narrative.

**Table 8.1.   Examples of Silver Center Classes**

| Enrichment | Health/Wellness | Informational |
|---|---|---|
| Detroit Institute of Arts: Picturing Music *lecture* | Mindful Meditation course, actively guiding attendees through breathing and meditation exercises *activity* | Achieving Financial Resiliency (AARP) *lecture* |
| Book Club (audio version of book available in companion session) *discussion* | Gratitude Journaling and Emotional Wellness *activity* | Financial Exploitation *lecture* |
| Detroit Historical Society: Remembering Detroit's Newspapers, Detroit's Belle Isle Park, Detroit in the Roaring '20s *lecture* | Diabetes Plate Method *lecture* | How to Identify Fake News *lecture* |
| Basics of Gardening *discussion* | 10 Warning Signs of Alzheimer's *lecture* | Senior Resources and Services *discussion* |
| Five Important Days in Classical Music *lecture* | Elder Abuse Prevention *lecture* | |

Class facilitators were cognizant of the access barriers of the Silver Center's audience and were volunteers, either from local health or social service organizations or cultural institutions (e.g., Detroit Institute of Arts, Detroit Historical Society) or individuals with expertise in a particular area who volunteered their own personal time for this project.

## Use

### Overview

An evaluation of the Silver Center pilot project was conducted, led by Ms. Wilson on behalf of the agency offering the program in conjunction with researchers at the University of Michigan (including the two chapter authors and Dr. Katrina Ellis). The primary goals of the evaluation were to determine whether the Silver Center program was feasible and well received by the target audience, to identify the benefits and challenges experienced by participants and volunteer facilitators, and to learn what should be changed to improve future versions of the program. Mailed surveys were sent to participants upon registering for the six-month pilot program and then again at program's end. In addition, two focus groups were conducted with Silver Center participants to collect more contextualized information about their experience with the program. In this chapter, we provide a summary of who participated and choose not to include specific usage data; rather, we describe the program's impact from the perspective of older adult participants.

### Participants

Brief evaluation surveys, which collected demographic information, were completed by thirty-five Silver Center participants. The average age of respondents was seventy-three years, which is slightly younger than the national seniors center average of seventy-five years, and were about three-quarters female. About two-thirds identified as African American/Black and one-third as White. One-quarter did not have internet access, and 40 percent did not have a computer. One-third of participants indicated they did not participate in any other community activities (e.g., cultural activities, volunteering, church). Almost half lived alone and had scores on a standardized loneliness scale that were higher than the national average. Also, most participants reported at least some difficulty getting around in their home or out of their home.

### Program Impact

Four-fifths of Silver Center participants indicated they enjoyed the Silver Center program "very much." Nine out of ten reported learning something new, and nearly three-quarters reported that it made them feel connected to others. Most participants discussed Silver Center classes with family members, friends, or neighbors and were, at times, joined by another person (family member, friend, or caregiver) at least once for a class session. They also described using a resource in the community or on the internet that they had learned about from a class. Preferences for the different formats (lecture, discussion, or guided activity such as meditation) were evenly distributed.

## Other Feedback

Similar to the xPress asynchronous tele-community, key themes from focus groups were that participants appreciated the diversity of programming, the convenience and connection to the wider world, the fact that the classes gave them something to talk about with family and friends, and that they gained new information and knowledge. Silver Center offerings were noted to be especially helpful during the period when social distancing was required due to COVID-19. Although feedback was predominantly very positive, several challenges were noted in the surveys and focus groups. Because all interactions were synchronous, scheduling conflicts made it difficult for some people to regularly participate (e.g., medical appointments). Also, the format was audio only, so some older individuals with hearing impairments faced challenges listening to content. Finally, some participants reported technical difficulties, such as lost connections or problems with their own telephones. Future iterations of the Silver Center could explore adding video-based content to supplement, rather than replace, audio content for those with hearing loss.

## Access and Potential Impact

The Silver Center tele-community reached a group of older adults who faced mobility challenges, who had above-average levels of loneliness, and some of whom lacked in-home internet access and/or smartphones. It provided older adults with access to information and a way to connect with others outside of their household without needing to purchase a new device or learn how to use new applications/software. Despite the reliance on standard telephones, the program was able to provide a variety of interaction styles (lecture, discussion, activity), and because preferences for these styles varied, we conclude that the classes met a range of needs. Finally, the Silver Center appeared to have ripple effects beyond the individuals who participated, as participants shared information from the classes with others, and the classes provided them with topics to discuss with members of their social network.

## The Silver Center and the COVID-19 Pandemic

The Silver Center was conceived and launched prior to the COVID-19 pandemic. At that time, it was thought to be the only virtual program that offered a variety of classes to older adults in southeast Michigan. However, when pandemic-related restrictions on in-person contact were put into place (during the last ten weeks of the pilot program), the landscape of virtual programming for older adults began to change. More seniors centers started to offer virtual classes, but these were limited and the classes were generally only accessible to those with internet access. Similarly, a few agencies that traditionally offered in-person classes at seniors and community centers, group meal sites, and seniors apartments started to offer a limited number of their classes remotely. Before the pandemic, these agencies relied on those site partners to promote the classes and generate their audience. During the pandemic, they lost access to that ready-made audience. This points to the value of the Silver Center as an accessible platform for reaching an audience of older adults that is not limited to technology users. Finally, we note that the pandemic also had the effect of cutting off internet access to those older adults who previously accessed the internet at seniors centers, highlighting the additional need for telephone-based programming during this time.

## REFLECTING ON TELE-COMMUNITIES

We use the preliminary and pilot data described in this chapter to reflect on the utility of asynchronous and synchronous tele-communities for more equitable and accessible information and social support.

### Future of Asynchronous Tele-Communities

Deploying the xPress community was timely given the COVID-19 pandemic, which significantly affected how blind and low-vision older adults engaged with others. In-person support groups and gatherings were canceled and/or shared transportation services were limited or ceased operation, making it difficult for people to access their in-person networks while physically distanced. While organizations such as the National Federation of the Blind have local chapters that host phone meetings, the synchronous nature of a phone call means that interaction is limited to a specific time period. Asynchronous tele-communities such as NFB's Newsline exist and provide relevant daily information such as news and weather.[50] Yet, a social asynchronous tele-community such as xPress offers new ways to connect to people and build new relationships by prioritizing discussion with other people rather than updates about news and events. We look forward to completing the yearlong deployment of xPress and analyzing whether changes in social well-being (e.g., loneliness, social connectedness) occur. In the meantime, we reflect on the future of asynchronous communities and how they can improve connectedness among aging and disability communities.

First, the "slow" pace of asynchronous tele-communities promotes the value of listening. Prior work has described the pressure older adults feel to contribute and/or consume content in synchronous spaces or visual online communities.[51] Yet, with affordances similar to voicemail and answering machines where people can listen on their own time, we reflect on how older adults enjoyed listening to content. Some dialed in at night or in the morning, reflecting that there is no single time that works well for everyone, an affordance that draws people to screen-based online communities. All participants in the study lived in their own homes, yet we may consider how to extend listening options to older adults in other living environments, such as long-term care communities, with more structured schedules. Asynchronous tele-communities could have broadcast options paired with long-term care communities such as assisted living or skilled nursing facilities where activity coordinators promote "listening circles," encouraging residents to listen to messages created by older adults on the tele-community and reflect through in-person discussion. In this sense, tele-community messages could be plural in nature—promoting interaction with older adults on the phone and in person.

Further, we reflect on what topics older adults enjoyed listening to. They enjoyed posts of those with similar visual experiences, of those with vision impairments that they might experience in the future, and those with different experiences. While all participants lived in the United States, we could consider how such an asynchronous community can expand globally, exposing people to non-Western views on aging and disability. Also, researchers may consider different audience levels of asynchronous tele-communities. The xPress system is a one-to-many community where messages are broadcast to each of the other members, but building community may happen in smaller circles or pairs. Asynchronous tele-community designers and developers can consider implementing a program similar to pen pals—cross-time zone, one-to-one pairings in which users are matched to a new community "buddy" each month. These audio pen pals could also choose to communicate synchronously with options on the platform or using a communication modality of their choosing, similar to how relationships develop with older adult bloggers on a computer.[52] Next, we reflect on the future of synchronous tele-communities through the Silver Center deployment.

## Future of Synchronous Tele-Communities

The COVID-19 pandemic caused most seniors centers around the country to close their in-person operations at least temporarily.[53] At the time of this writing, many seniors centers continue to offer virtual versions of classes and other activities such as health screenings. Even postpandemic, having remote options for seniors center programming is likely here to stay[54] due to the newfound comfort with such offerings on behalf of both center staff and older adults and supported by new initiatives to train older adults in remote technology use like Get Setup Michigan.[55] As program developer Norvena Wilson states, "When the pilot Silver Center program launched in December 2019, most participants had never heard of a conference call or webinar. Due to the pandemic, more seniors have at least heard of Zoom or Facebook Live [video conferencing technologies] or utilized such a system to connect with family and friends." Offering a blend of remote and in-person activities may therefore become standard at many seniors centers and with tele-communities.

Yet, flexibility in these remote options will continue to be essential to ensuring equity in access, as today's cohort of older adults is characterized by wide diversity in technology proficiency and ownership. Therefore, looking to the near future, remote programming options will likely mean offering classes and activities in both low-tech (telephone) and high-tech (online) formats. Most online conference tools allow participants to join classes via phone or video, maximizing reach and appeal to all older residents. Indeed, offering classes by computer may increase accessibility with built-in features such as live transcription for people experiencing hearing loss. Future work should integrate multiple ways of delivering the same content, ensuring that the interaction is equivalent across modalities.

The Silver Center provides an example of how synchronous telephone-based communities can continue to play an important role in supporting the well-being of older adults during an era of rapid change in communication technologies. The COVID-19 pandemic has only accelerated the shift to reimagining how services and information can be provided to older adults. As the older population in this country continues to grow, having a menu of alternatives to traditional in-person seniors centers will ensure that their benefits will be realized by the broadest possible group of older adults. As Wilson says, "The pandemic shined a light on the various service gaps we have in serving our older residents. In addition to the food insecurity, one of the gaps highlighted was how we reach and engage our older population. I feel the pandemic increased the sense of urgency in reimagining the senior center model."

Further, our data show how tele-communities can provide more equitable information access, particularly among those most marginalized in society. Dr. Katrina Ellis reflects on the Silver Center's impact on racial and ethnic health disparities, connecting the tele-community to Baum's metaphor of "cracking the nut" and applying pressure at different societal levels for promoting health equity.[56] Ellis reflects, "The Silver Center provides an opportunity to reach seniors at the individual level but also connect seniors with other agencies and resources at the community level. Future versions of the Silver Center would benefit from building these community partnerships with other agencies and stakeholders early on. As opportunities and needs among Silver Center participants arise, there can be a coordinated and collaborative effort to address these needs."

As such, we not only urge researchers to design and develop tele-communities, in collaboration with organizations and agencies serving older and/or disabled adults, but also urge local and national organizations to consider ways to deploy existing models for access at scale. We note that synchronous tele-communities could be beneficial for a range of populations that face internet access challenges, such as people in rural areas, in long-term care facilities, or disabled people. Therefore, we want to acknowledge two logistical and sustainability considerations of a synchronous tele-community: class coordination and cost. First, while this type of tele-community can leverage existing volunteers, each Silver Center class session was made possible through call coordination provided by a program leader, Norvena Wilson. Wilson sought volunteer class facilitators, introduced each session at the appropriate time, unmuted and muted phone lines for Q&A, and provided technical assistance. As class facilitators benefited from not needing to take on these responsibilities, we recommend any synchronous tele-community include funding for a class coordinator. Second, to sustain a program such as the Silver Center over time, we recommend establishing buy-in from long-term partners such as seniors centers or aging-focused organizations (e.g., AARP) who can fund monthly call hosting fees and a class coordinator on an ongoing basis. Other potential program sponsors are local libraries, Area Agencies on Aging, or local or state health departments.

In summary, we describe how older adults engage with two telephone-based communities: xPress, an asynchronous tele-community for social connection among older adults with disabilities, and the Silver Center, a synchronous tele-community to engage with community resources for older adults who face difficulties accessing a seniors center. We find that both types of communities have great potential to promote information and social equity among older adults. We provide suggestions for how tele-communities can be sustainable and appropriately designed to align with the values of older users.

## NOTES

1. Diana Ross, "Telephone," track 1 side B on *Swept Away*, RCA Records, vinyl.
2. Anabel Quan-Haase, Guang Ying Mo, and Barry Wellman, "Connected Seniors: How Older Adults in East York Exchange Social Support Online and Offline," *Information, Communication and Society* 20, no. 7 (2017): 967–983.

3. Robin Brewer, Raymundo Cornejo Garcia, Tedmond Schwaba, Darren Gergle, and Anne Marie Piper, "Exploring Traditional Phones as an E-mail Interface for Older Adults," *ACM Transactions on Accessible Computing (TACCESS)* 8, no. 2 (2016): 1–20.

4. Shupei Yuan, Syed A. Hussain, Kayla D. Hales, and Shelia R. Cotten, "What Do They Like? Communication Preferences and Patterns of Older Adults in the United States: The Role of Technology," *Educational Gerontology* 42, no. 3 (2016): 163–174.

5. Katherine E. Olson, Marita A. O'Brien, Wendy A. Rogers, and Neil Charness, "Diffusion of Technology: Frequency of Use for Younger and Older Adults," *Ageing International* 36, no. 1 (2011): 123–145.

6. Monica Anderson and Andrew Perrin, "Tech Adoption Climbs Among Older Adults," Pew Research Center, May 17, 2017, https://www.pewresearch.org/internet/2017/05/17/technology-use-among-seniors/.

7. CDC, "CDC: 1 in 4 US Adults Live with a Disability," CDC, August 16, 2018, https://www.cdc.gov/media/releases/2018/p0816-disability.html.

8. United Nations, "Ageing and Disability," United Nations, https://www.un.org/development/desa/disabilities/disability-and-ageing.html.

9. Kerry Dobransky and Eszter Hargittai, "The Disability Divide in Internet Access and Use," *Information, Communication and Society* 9, no. 3 (2006): 313–334.

10. United States Census Bureau, "Mobility is Most Common Disability Among Older Americans, Census Bureau Reports," U.S. Census, December, 2, 2014, https://www.census.gov/newsroom/press-releases/2014/cb14-218.html.

11. Gerard Goggin, "Disability and Digital Inequalities: Rethinking Digital Divides with Disability Theory," in *Theorizing Digital Divides*, ed. Ragnedda Massimo and Glenn W. Muschert (New York: Routledge, 2016).

12. Dobransky and Hargittai, "The Disability Divide."

13. Kerry Dobransky and Eszter Hargittai, "Unrealized Potential: Exploring the Digital Disability Divide," *Poetics* 58 (2016): 18–28.

14. Emily A. Vogels, "Millennials Stand Out for Their Technology Use, But Older Generations also Embrace Digital Life," Pew Research Center, September 9, 2019, https://www.pewresearch.org/fact-tank/2019/04/10/share-of-u-s-adults-using-social-media-including-facebook-is-mostly-unchanged-since-2018/.

15. https://www.pewresearch.org/fact-tank/2019/09/09/us-generations-technology-use/.

16. Robin Brewer and Anne Marie Piper, "'Tell It Like It Really Is': A Case of Online Content Creation and Sharing among Older Adult Bloggers," *Proceedings of the 2016 CHI Conference on Human Factors in Computing Systems* (2016): 5529–5542.

17. Amanda Lazar, Mark Diaz, Robin Brewer, Chelsea Kim, and Anne Marie Piper, "Going Gray, Failure to Hire, and the Ick Factor: Analyzing How Older Bloggers Talk about Ageism," *Proceedings of the 2017 ACM Conference on Computer Supported Cooperative Work and Social Computing* (2017): 655–668.

18. Anne Marie Piper, Robin Brewer, and Raymundo Cornejo, "Technology Learning and Use among Older Adults with Late-Life Vision Impairments," *Universal Access in the Information Society* 16, no. 3 (2017): 699–711.

19. Robin N. Brewer and Anne Marie Piper, "xPress: Rethinking Design for Aging and Accessibility through an IVR Blogging System," *Proceedings of the ACM on Human-Computer Interaction* 1, CSCW (2017): 1–17.

20. Brewer et al., "Exploring Traditional Phones."

21. Piper, Brewer, and Cornejo, "Technology Learning and Use among Older Adults."

22. Brewer and Piper, "'Tell It Like It Really Is.'"

23. Brewer et al., "Exploring Traditional Phones."

24. Siân E. Lindley, Richard Harper, and Abigail Sellen, "Desiring to Be in Touch in a Changing Communications Landscape: Attitudes of Older Adults," *Proceedings of the SIGCHI Conference on Human Factors in Computing Systems* (2009): 1693–1702.

25. Brewer and Piper, "xPress: Rethinking Design."

26. Lazar et al., "Going Gray, Failure to Hire, and the Ick Factor."

27. Brewer and Piper, "'Tell It Like It Really Is.'"

28. Jean Lave and Etienne Wenger, *Situated Learning: Legitimate Peripheral Participation* (Cambridge: Cambridge University Press, 1991).

29. Robin N. Brewer, Sarita Schoenebeck, Kerry Lee, and Haripriya Suryadevara, "Challenging Passive Social Media Use: Older Adults as Caregivers Online," *Proceedings of the ACM on Human-Computer Interaction* 5, CSCW1 (2021): 1–20.

30. Judd Antin and Coye Cheshire, "Readers Are Not Free-Riders: Reading as a Form of Participation on Wikipedia," *Proceedings of the 2010 ACM Conference on Computer Supported Cooperative Work* (2010): 127–130.

31. Kate Crawford, "Listening, Not Lurking: The Neglected Form of Participation," *Cultures of Participation* (2011): 63–74.

32. Kate Crawford, "Following You: Disciplines of Listening in Social Media," *Continuum* 23, no. 4 (2009): 525–535.

33. Blair Nonnecke and Jenny Preece, "Silent Participants: Getting to Know Lurkers Better," in *From Usenet to CoWebs*, ed. Christopher Lueg and Danyel Fisher (London: Springer, 2003), 110–132.

34. Brewer and Piper, "'Tell It Like It Really Is.'"

35. Brewer et al., "Challenging Passive Social Media Use."

36. Anderson and Perrin, "Tech Adoption Climbs Among Older Adults."

37. United States Census Bureau, "QuickFacts Detroit City, Michigan," U.S. Census, https://www.census.gov/quickfacts/detroitcitymichigan.

38. Kaleigh Rogers, "Ignored By Big Telecom, Detroit's Marginalized Communities Are Building Their Own Internet," Vice, November 16, 2017, https://www.vice.com/en/article/kz3xyz/detroit-mesh-network.

39. Bianca C. Reisdorf, Laleah Fernandez, Keith N. Hampton, Inyoung Shin, and William H. Dutton, "Mobile Phones Will Not Eliminate Digital and Social Divides: How Variation in Internet Activities Mediates the Relationship between Type of Internet Access and Local Social Capital in Detroit," *Social Science Computer Review* (2020): 0894439320909446.

40. Detroit Community Technology Project, https://detroitcommunitytech.org/.

41. National Council on Aging, "Facts and Benefits About Senior Centers You Probably Didn't Know," NCOA, February 10, 2021, https://stage2.ncoa.org/national-institute-of-senior-centers/tips-for-senior-centers/senior-center-research-is-the-phrase-an-oxymoron/.

42. National Council on Aging, "Get the Facts on Senior Centers," NCOA, June 4, 2015, https://www.ncoa.org/news/resources-for-reporters/get-the-facts/senior-center-facts/.

43. City of Detroit, "2017 Parks and Recreation Improvement Plan," City of Detroit, January 24, 2017, https://detroitmi.gov/Portals/0/docs/Parks/2017%20Parks%20and%20Recreation%20Improvement%20Plan.pdf.

44. Virtual Senior Centers, http://vscm.selfhelp.net/.

45. Covia, https://covia.org/services/well-connected/.

46. Mather, "Mather Telephone Topics," Mather, https://www.mather.com/neighborhood-programs/telephone-topics.

47. Family Eldercare, "Lifetime Connections without Walls," Family Eldercare, https://www.familyeldercare.org/programs/lifetime-connections-without-walls/.

48. TurboBridge, https://www.turbobridge.com/.

49. CallFire, https://www.callfire.com/.

50. National Federation of the Blind, "NFB NEWSLINE," NFB, https://www.nfb.org/programs-services/nfb-newsline.

51. Lindley, Harper, and Sellen, "Desiring to Be in Touch."

52. Brewer and Piper, "'Tell It Like It Really Is.'"

53. National Council on Aging, "Key Resources About COVID-19 for Senior Centers," NCOA, March 20, 2020, https://www.ncoa.org/news/ncoa-news/national-institute-of-senior-centers-news/covid-19-resources-for-senior-centers/.

54. Susan Stiles, "Virtual Classes for Older Adults: Here to Stay," NCOA, June 12, 2020, https://www.ncoa.org/blog/virtual-classes-for-older-adults-here-to-stay/.

55. GetSetUp, https://www.getsetup.io/michigan.

56. Fran Baum, "Cracking the Nut of Health Equity: Top Down and Bottom Up Pressure for Action on the Social Determinants of Health," *Promotion and Education* 14, no. 2 (2007): 90–95.

## Chapter Nine

# Not Your Grandparents' Family Tree

## *Practices of Privacy in*
## *Genetic Genealogical Networks*

### Judith Pintar

Genealogical and family history research are pastimes often associated with the oldest members of extended families, whose memories reach back to their own grandparents' time and who have in their possession the documents needed to successfully assemble family trees, the data visualization tool of choice for genealogical information. Genealogy is a notoriously time-consuming hobby. It involves tracking down long-lost relatives to request private information from them, taking driving trips to overgrown cemeteries to hunt for lost grave markers, visiting county historical societies to access undigitized collections, and organizing family reunions during which inherited photographs and other memorabilia can be shared and compared. Not surprisingly, serious engagement with these information-gathering, analyzing, visualizing, and communicating tasks are often put off until after retirement. With the advent of the internet, genealogists have been able to communicate more efficiently, trading "look-ups" from their personal collections or local archives. Now they do their own looking up, searching through online repositories of scanned materials and family trees, though much valuable genealogical information was commodified as it was scanned and exists only behind paywalls. Genealogical information still flows freely across regional, personal, and family websites and on social media platforms such as Facebook, where genetic genealogy interest groups operate independent of the for-profit corporations providing genetic genealogical services.

With the appearance of direct-to-consumer genetic testing, younger people now have an appealing gateway to an interest they share with their oldest relations. They may be surprised to discover they can make little progress on the *genetics* side without the *genealogical* information collected by those relatives through traditional means. The knowledge-producing genetic genealogy communities of today benefit greatly from the presence of experienced genealogists. Navigating a modest learning curve, they are well positioned to combine the data produced by new genetic technologies with the crucial information acquired through paper-based and internet-era digital information seeking.

In this chapter I begin by overviewing theoretical approaches to privacy as they provide a framework for understanding information practices within genetic genealogical networks and how our shared cultural notions of kinship affect privacy choices made by genetic genealogists when using these services. After surveying the theoretical landscape surrounding privacy in genetic genealogy, I will explicate the steps needed to accomplish the creation of genetic genealogical knowledge through these services, why someone might choose one website over another, and why serious genetic genealogists may have accounts on many such sites at the same time. I will compare the information services of three of the leading commercial websites (AncestryDNA, ftDNA, and 23andMe) as well as the "grassroots" genetic genealogy website GEDmatch, which became a for-profit service in 2019. Through this comparison, I also explore the motivations behind the strategies these companies employ as they make use of existing cultural understandings of kinship and belonging to both encourage and control the sharing of private genetic and genealogical information.

## INTRODUCTION

Information flows through networks of relations. When it is designated as owned, dangerous, or privileged, information may be impeded in its movement by cultural and sociotechnical barriers such as paywalls or filters that protect children from inappropriate content. Information may, conversely, be requested, expected, or demanded at point of entry into a new social network: when joining a church, when applying for a job, or when downloading a phone app. Every family network also establishes privacy norms, with flows of information determined by kinship ontologies, a sorting of who is more or less related to whom, which might determine who is entitled to be called first, for example, when there is an emergency or a death in the family. Some of these decisions may derive from cultural norms, like the broad distinction between "nuclear" and "extended" family. Other, finer, sorting develops through experience, as certain beloved friends may come to be treated "as family" and trusted to a greater degree than "closer" relatives who are kept at arm's length. In some families, second cousins (who share great-grandparents) and their children (who are third cousins to each other, sharing great-great-grandparents) may feel and act as close to one another as do first cousins (who share grandparents), while in other families second cousins are all but strangers. The idiosyncrasies within any given family also affect the ontology, determining whether close relatives' right to hear about a new pregnancy may be outweighed by their inability to keep a secret. So, patterns of privacy emerge both from traditional ideas about who is "owed" access to truth as well as lived experience about who can be trusted or not.

A distinctly different calculation occurs when a family genealogist cold-calls distant cousins to request the maiden names of their daughters-in-law and the birth dates of new grandchildren in order to update a family tree chart. Genealogists typically exhibit a peculiarly nonjudgmental curiosity regarding illegitimacies, family feuds, and suspicious deaths—exactly the kinds of information that families might desire to conceal. Depending on the privacy norms of the extended family, genealogists may or may not be successful in their data collection if they present themselves to these distant cousins *as relatives*; they don't have a right to the information in those terms. But if the cousin on the other end of the line (or the receiver of an out-of-the-blue email or social media message) accepts the essential premise of the genealogical endeavor, then they become part of a network that connects them to this inquisitive stranger not as family but as *kin*. Within genealogical kinship networks, information sharing flows as a matter of course. As a result, the genealogist in the family may be trusted with secrets about which even close relatives are unaware.

Two decades ago, I sat at a table with various charts and trees beside me, conversing with an assortment of my father's cousins who had gathered together to meet me, granddaughter of their long-lost relative, just arrived from America. Only one of the people at that long table, the wife of my second cousin, spoke English, so the rest of the party waited for her to translate our conversation to them. At one point she broke the flow of her translation, pointing to her mother-in-law, an old woman at the other end of the table. She said to me, in English, "That woman over there, you think she is your cousin's mother, but she is not. Her baby died in the hospital. They gave her the child of another woman who died giving birth that same night. That man there," she pointed at her own husband, "you think he is your cousin, but he is not. He was someone else's child. Nobody at this table knows this, except my husband and me, not even his mother. But I thought you should know the truth." Everyone waited for this to be translated, but she swiftly changed the subject and translated that instead, never mentioning the matter again.

Within a genealogical network, the free flow of private information is a self-evident positive good. Regarding particularly sensitive facts, a genealogist may be directed, as I was, to write down some information but not to add it to the family tree. Presumably in the future the notes would incorporate the information after all the people involved had died. In a sense, I received the painfully private information because I served as a proxy for the far future descendants who are presumed to have a right to know the truth about their ancestors' lives.

This is no different from the disciplinary premises of history and archeology that find self-evident the importance of the knowledge acquired by opening and exploring ancient tombs intended to have been sealed for eternity. A belief in the rights of the future over the past is a culturally constructed value, visible in conflicts between scientists and indigenous peoples, for example, over the treatment of ancient remains.[1]

Since genealogical kinship networks branch backward into the impossibly distant past and forward into the barely imagined future, they are different from family networks, which set their own boundaries for relatedness through tradition and experience. In contrast, within genealogical kinship networks, sharing private information doesn't require any judgment of closeness or trustworthiness; it flows as a result of the *belonging*. In some contexts that belonging may stretch to include anyone who comes from the same geographic region, or who speaks the same language, or practices the same religion, especially if the village is small, the language is endangered, or the group itself is an object of bias or persecution. There is a presumption that people in such cultural groups descend from common ancestors, even when the names of the specific lineal ancestors are unknown. Genealogical tools, which can provide empirical proof of common ancestry, help to extend such belonging-based kinship beyond the record-bound family tree.

## THEORETICAL FRAMING OF PRIVACY AND BELONGING

A broad consensus among scholars concerned with privacy has emerged— that privacy should be considered *in context*, as a set of norms, practices, and values that may only become visible when incompatible contexts collide. Nissenbaum's comprehensive reframing of privacy draws from and synthesizes multiple lineages of thought: legal, psychological, and sociological.[2] The concept of contextual integrity asserts that the right to privacy, when analyzed in its context, is actually the right to have *our expectations* regarding the protections of our privacy met.[3] It follows that these expectations, which exist generally unnoticed when they are collectively shared, become exposed when incompatible privacy norms trigger a "context collapse," producing the affective sensation that privacy has been violated.[4]

In our present era, the very real and growing danger of criminal, corporate, and governmental misuse of personal information (collected, compiled, and mined as big data) has added urgency to the need to make comprehensive sense of multidisciplinary approaches to privacy and to study a range of critical issues related to risk and disclosure.[5] The rapid rise of information and communication technologies has had a significant effect on discussions of privacy because it has placed technology's role in shaping information flow at the center of analysis. What the appropriate unit of that analysis and the corresponding research method should be differs by disciplinary orientation. Psychological approaches, for example, focus on the contradictions between users' beliefs and their behaviors, the so-called privacy paradox.[6] Sociological approaches to studying privacy tend to emphasize the networked nature of the technologies through which information flows. Pushing back against the prevailing individualistic frames favored in legal and psychological studies, Marwick and boyd, for example, have argued that the context surrounding teenagers' attitudes toward privacy must take into account the networked nature of social media.[7] They have introduced the concept of networked privacy, arguing that Nissenbaum's theory of contextual integrity may lead to analysis that mistakenly assumes privacy contexts are stable and discrete rather than dynamic and coconstructed: "Contextual integrity assumes the context is a given, whereas networked privacy takes into account that individuals may interpret context differently, that contexts may be destabilized or collapse, or that other people may have control over the context in ways that are beyond the purview of the individual (e.g., surveillance, information leakage, or data-mining.)"[8] Ochs and Ilyes view networked privacy through the lens of interdisciplinary science and technology studies (STS) and offer the sociotechnical as a promising unit of analysis.[9] They argue that non-STS approaches may decontextualize privacy decisions, stripping practice down to observable "behavioral bits" (such as checking a certain box when setting up an online profile), presuming that such acts have rational motives behind them, though that may not be what's happening at all.[10] In contrast, an STS approach situates practice within the collectivity of what Callon calls sociotechnical "agencements" and Clark and Star refer to as "social worlds."[11] Empirically and analytically, user behaviors, in this view, cannot be studied in isolation from the collectivities within which they are practiced. Notably, a sociotechnical privacy assemblage comprises material as well as human agents. Included in a network to be analyzed would be corporations, users, web interfaces, and the genetic data itself. Actor network theory (ANT) provides a method and a vocabulary for describing how networks are dynamically and continuously recomposed by such heterogeneous actors.[12] ANT has been productively employed to analyze health-based direct-to-consumer genetic testing, genomics and racial health disparities, e-health, and biomedical research, for example.[13] The posthumanist thread in STS has been shaped by

Pickering's empirical observation that human and nonhuman actors within a laboratory perform their relationships with one another.[14] Pickering views the production of scientific knowledge as emergent, arising from the nonhierarchical and nondeterministic performative relationship between these actors. He describes such performances as a kind of tuning. In observing interactions between scientists, their instruments, and the material agencies they are trying to capture, he described a process of resistance and accommodation that becomes a dance between them.[15]

Through a posthumanist STS lens, following Pickering, it is possible to observe how interactions of resistance and accommodation between human and nonhuman actors create a *practice* of privacy through which genetic genealogical knowledge is produced. For example, it is possible to observe the emergent composition of a genealogical network and the tuning that occurs during the transfer of private information. Imagine a conversation between a genealogist and some distant cousins when the data fields in the family tree are not set up to record information relating to nonstandard family relationships. The genealogist will likely fail to convince a family with adopted step-grandparents, problematically unacknowledged half-siblings, and a gay marriage to enroll themselves into the genealogical kinship network. We might say that the tree resists the incompatible data while the family resists the informational request in turn. If, however, the genealogist accommodates the family by altering the tree format, or switching to a different software product, or simply agreeing to write information down that cannot be visually represented in the tree, the family may also accommodate the ill-fitting process, letting go of feelings of resentment caused by the genealogist's seeming lack of interest in nonbiological or nontraditional family relationships. If the tuning between actors is successful, the privacy context shifts, and the personal information is transferred. The flow of information occurs as a result of the family now *belonging* to the genealogical kinship network that has demonstrated its acceptance of them into the family tree, a tangible sociotechnical expression of that belonging.

I won't be discussing privacy as it pertains to legal protections or user agreements offered by genetic genealogy sites; the nature of the risks associated with sharing personal genetic information; the awareness, anxieties, and attitudes of the public toward those risk; nor their privacy behaviors and what might explain or predict them.[16] Nor will I engage with critical issues related to the shaping of personal, cultural, and racial identities (and attendant historical and political meanings) as a result of membership in genetic genealogical networks.[17] My aim is to shed light on the agency of the information technologies themselves while providing readers with some idea of the differences among four of the most popular genetic genealogy websites and why their interfaces, analytic tools, and policies are designed the way they are. Specifically, I will outline the different ways in which web interfaces and online tools practice privacy, mediating the flow of private information necessary for the production of genetic genealogical knowledge.

I understand both genealogy and genetic genealogy to be collaborative practices of data collection that transform protected private history into shared public knowledge. A family tree can be understood as a "boundary object," an informational agent that facilitates such informational collabora-tion.[18] Just as genealogists participate in self-organized, crowdsourced family history, genetic genealogists can be viewed as citizen scientists who collect and analyze private data (their own and that of their genealogical and genetic genealogical kin), producing knowledge that can be attained in no other way.

## THE TASKS OF GENETIC GENEALOGY

The central practice of genetic genealogy is the comparison of genetic seg-ments between two individuals, where similarities or their lack can be used to confirm or challenge genealogical presumptions of ancestry and to provide new leads where a lack of historical records or family history have produced genealogical dead ends. In decades past, this would more often have occurred across a table with a physical family tree laid out on it and being edited with a pencil; now it requires multiple information technologies and is facilitated not only by an extended family genealogist but by proprietary algorithms and powerful strategies of corporate persuasion. Online genealogy services encourage their users to entreat their relatives, both close family members and distant strangers, to send their genetic information to be tested. To be successful in convincing relatives to do this, genetic genealogists need not argue there is no risk but only persuade them that they *already belong* to a genetic genealogical network. If spitting into the vial or swabbing a cheek for DNA-rich cells and sending them off through the mail is understood as a responsibility of that belonging, the need to rationally assess risk becomes all but irrelevant. This is not far different from the decisions teenagers make to join a social media site because their friends use it; accepting the privacy policy unread is an act that strengthens their sense of belonging, just as refus-ing to join because of privacy concerns might weaken it.[19]

After a user's genome is decoded, usually through a direct-to-consumer service, it is compared to those of other users in that service's databases. The first step in "doing" genetic genealogy is to analyze the specific genetic seg-ments shared with other users. Some of these users will be known relatives, and others will be strangers. Sharing the same genetic segment with another person is evidence that both are descended from a common pair of ancestors. The more numerous and the longer those genetic segments are, the more recently the shared ancestors likely lived. Siblings share significantly more and longer genetic segments in common than do first cousins, who share more segments than second cousins, and so on. It is possible to estimate based on the size and number of segments and the percentage of genome shared how many generations one must go back to find a common ancestor between any two users who share identical genetic segments.

Here's the rub: the discovery of a genetic match does not do the work of *identifying* the specific common ancestors shared. Traditional document-based genealogy work is necessary to give names to common ancestors who may have been the conduit for the genetic information passed down through a particular shared segment. I say conduit and not source, since our ancestors inherited their genes from their own ancestors, and it will always be a puzzle to determine from which one they did. In many cases this will be an unsolvable mystery, since beyond fifth cousins most inherited genetic segments become vanishingly small. Some genetic genealogists are interested in identifying genetic segments definitively inherited from more distant forebears. This can only work when there is genetic information about many extended cousins from many different descendant lines who share the same small segments but who *also* have complete and accurate family trees going back far enough in time. When trying to identify a common ancestor with a known first cousin, there are only two grandparents to choose between. For a fourth cousin, there are sixteen different possible sources for the shared genetic information, if you know on which side of the family you connect. If you don't, there are thirty-two possible sources, and this number doubles every generation. The vast majority of genetic matches provided by commercial services are at the fourth to fifth cousin level. Some include matches that are more distant, especially for individuals who come from regions and cultural groups where genetic testing is uncommon; the paucity of close matches is generally due to lack of data, though for some family lines it reflects a history of illness, tragedy, or war that affected their family's reproductive success. It is a common frustration for users of genetic genealogy services that the majority of their cousin matches may be descended from shared ancestors about whom much is already known, and few or none at all from the ancestors about whom they most desire to gain knowledge.

The next piece of bad news is that even the discovery of a correspondence between a shared genetic segment and shared ancestry is not enough to prove that the identified link between specific genetic segments and particular ancestors is accurate. The chances that any two individuals from the same regional or cultural community share *more* than one ancestor within the last four hundred years is very high, particularly if the cultural group is largely homogeneous or historically isolated. Even in a largely mixed genetic population, as in the United States, it is still likely that people whose ancestry goes back to pre-Revolutionary War times, or who have multiple ancestors who immigrated to the United States from the same geographic region, will be genetically related to one another through several ancestral lines, some of which will be genealogically unknown and perhaps unknowable because of a lack of paper records to document them.

Another difficulty is determining whether a small shared segment is "identical by descent" (IBD)—that is to say, it has been inherited from a common ancestor—or if it is "non-IBD," sometimes referred to as "identical by state" (IBS), meaning that the correspondence occurs by chance. Tiny segments may be inherited from extremely distant ancestors more than once, making it genealogical useless, because it is impossible to determine the specific path of its inheritance. This frustrating scenario occurs with confounding regularity even for larger segments when attempting to do genetic genealogy for ancestors who lived in isolated geographic regions with small founding populations and a pattern of endogamous marriage; often-cited examples of such "genetic isolates" include the Amish, Ashkenazi Jews, Afrikaners, and Sardinians among others.[20]

Triangulation is said to occur when at least three individuals share the same genetic segment with each of the others and also have documented genealogical evidence showing descent from the same pair of individuals down different family lines.[21] Triangulation, especially when it is confirmed through connections between many descendants, is considered empirical evidence of a genealogical relationship and passes for proof. Triangulation is the key process through which genetic genealogical evidence is created.

The analytic tools provided by 23andMe, AncestryDNA, Family Tree DNA (ftDNA), and GEDmatch address the task of triangulation differently. In analyzing these differences, I pay attention to the interactions of resistance and accommodation between corporate business plans, web technologies, methods of data collection, the available genetic and genealogical data, and users and their relatives (close, distant, and deceased), processes that are mediated by specific practices of privacy. In my comparison of the four websites and their services, I first examine the data analytic and communication tools provided to help users accomplish triangulation. Specifically, I will assess whether and the extent to which the four services allow users to view (1) the names (pseudonymous or actual) of all genetic matches available in their database; (2) the chromosome, location on the chromosome, and size of the genetic segments shared with genetic matches; (3) the names of the genetic cousins that users and their genetic matches have in common; (4) the location and size of genetic segments that these common cousins share with one another; and (5) the names of their cousins' genetic matches that the users themselves do not happen to match. These five types of information are the data necessary to use genetic genealogy effectively for the identification of distant ancestors.

Following the comparison of data analytic tools, I will look at the communication paths provided by each of the sites to facilitate collaboration between genetic kin, followed by an analysis of the information flow itself—where it is encouraged and where it is impeded. Finally, I will discuss the significance of these differences to elucidate the practices of privacy within genetic genealogy most broadly.

## NAMES OF ALL GENETIC MATCHES

All four services cap the number of matches their software will report to users. The practical effect of such a truncation of available data is that the most distant genetic relatives disappear from lists of matches as more recent cousins are added. As previously noted, not all shared genetic segments are genealogically significant. Each genetic testing site does its own calculations based on the number of shared segments, their individual and collective length, and then sets and resets the thresholds for the size of segment that would indicate a match. The number at which they cap matches varies among services (and has changed considerably within the services over time).

It is important to note that everyone on GEDmatch is also a user of at least one other service, since GEDmatch does not decode genomes but only helps to analyze them after they have been decoded. The largest number of matches available as of January 2021 through GEDmatch using the free version of its analytic tools is three thousand, with ftDNA and Ancestry providing more and 23andMe fewer. Advanced tools on GEDmatch, available for a fee, increase the number of matches to a theoretical maximum of one hundred thousand.

## LOCATION AND LENGTH
## OF MATCHING GENETIC SEGMENTS

The most important pieces of genetic information needed to connect genealogical and genetic data are its location on a specific chromosome and the length of the shared genetic segments (including exact beginning and end points). Segments of chromosomes are measured in centimorgans (cm), which represents approximately one million base pairs of DNA sequence. GEDmatch and ftDNA provide this information for all genetic matches that they report, while 23andMe provides it only for those users whose privacy options are set to "Open Sharing" or who agree to share genetic information with particular individuals following the acceptance of a sharing invitation. Just as 23andMe truncates the list of genetic matches, it also sets a limit on the size of genetic segment about which it will provide information.

Genetic genealogists disagree regarding the segment size at which triangulation is possible and accurate. Whether having the names of the thousands of distant genetic matches with whom what is shared is a single tiny IBS segment is useful at all is arguable; some users have had success with small segments, against the odds, and want every match they can get. Others are looking for a glimpse of their most distant ancestry and see these IBS segments as clues to geographic origin rather than genealogical ancestry. Uploading genomes to multiple genetic genealogy services is a common practice among the most dedicated users of these services, since it serves to increase the total list of genetic cousins identified and also the chance that some of these people will have an extensive enough family tree to make a genealogical connection as well.

Three of the four services, 23andMe, ftDNA, and GEDmatch, allow users to download (or cut and paste) data into a spreadsheet, providing a wealth of information about matches, including the location and size of all matching segments. 23andMe cuts off those who share segments smaller than 5 cm, while ftDNA provides downloadable spreadsheets of matching segments as small as 1 cm. GEDmatch will provide information on such tiny segments through some of its tools but not others. Of the four services, only Ancestry fails to provide any genetic segment information at all.

## NAMES OF GENETIC MATCHES IN COMMON

All four services provide names of people who are related to both the user and their genetic matches. The three commercial sites use their own internal algorithms to determine how many cousins-in-common matches will be provided, a truncation calculated separately from the list of a user's own matches and based on a segment size cut-off. On 23andMe this produces an odd side effect: genetic matches that have been truncated in users' own lists may still show up as common matches on their relatives' lists because that cousin happened to inherit a slightly longer segment that is shared with that match than the user did. Ironically, the segment that their algorithm has identified as too small to warrant inclusion may well be IBD since it triangulates with a larger segment inherited by a known cousin. All services truncate their matches, but GEDmatch analytic tools allow users to set cut-off points themselves. Conservatism in this regard is justified by the services as a feature that improves the reliability of information provided. This argument does not persuade those genetic genealogical researchers who wish to rely on their own judgment regarding the point at which a given genetic segment is too short to be genealogically meaningful. Size-based truncation for the sake of reliability is not a desirable feature for these users.

## LOCATION/LENGTH OF GENETIC SEGMENTS SHARED AMONG MATCHES IN COMMON

Knowing the names of cousins in common is not yet enough to achieve triangulation. Even pinpointing the location and size of segments shared between the user and two common matches is not enough. A user may match two different individuals on the same genetic segment, *but on the opposite chromosome*; in other words, one match may be a maternal cousin and the other a paternal cousin. In other words, they are not related to each other the way they are related to the user. In order to distinguish genetic matches on any particular chromosome as either maternal or paternal in descent, a process known as *phasing*, it is necessary to know whether those who share a genetic segment with a given user also match each other. 23andMe and GEDmatch provide tools to accomplish this with relative ease. ftDNA does not allow users to view the location of segments shared between users' matches, but it does offer a matrix tool that can report whether or not two genetic cousins match each other, though not which segment, if there is more than one. In order to accomplish triangulation of a segment, on ftDNA a user must contact their genetic matches and ask them to do the analytic test between themselves and the cousin match they have in common. This can be a frustrating operation, given that many users don't answer email queries, and only a subset of users know how to use the data analytic tools. No tools are provided by AncestryDNA to assess overlapping cousin matches, since they don't share segment information with users.

## NAMES OF GENETICALLY UNRELATED MATCHES

The reason why genetic genealogists want to know the identity of their cousins' cousins (who they may not themselves match genetically but with whom they suspect they share ancestry) has to do with the inheritance of autosomal

DNA, the genetic information that comes from our twenty-two pairs of autosomal chromosomes rather than our single pair of sex chromosomes (XX or XY). Siblings who are not identical twins randomly inherit half of each parent's autosomal DNA; as a result of this process, siblings may be almost identical or almost completely different from one another genetically. Differences in genetic inheritance are amplified in each generation, so that a pair of distant cousins with a confirmed genealogical connection may share no detectable genetic segments at all. In other words, though shared genetic segments can confirm a proposed genealogical connection, lack of genetic evidence of connection is not enough to rule out the existence of a genealogical connection because we do not share genetic material with everyone to whom we are genealogically related. Genealogists who become genetic genealogists typically are interested in ancestry as a separate issue from genetic inheritance; in other words, they want to know everyone they are descended from regardless of whether they carry those ancestors' detectable gene segments. The information needed to break through a dead end in genealogical research, therefore, does not necessarily exist in the genetic information a user shares *with* their distant cousins but could well be found in the genetics shared *between* their distant cousins, which the user did not themselves inherit.

The original build of 23andMe allowed users to download the spreadsheets of the genetic matches of anyone they were sharing with through a tool called Countries of Ancestry. This tool was removed due to privacy concerns. Now comparisons between two genetic matches can only be done one segment at a time, only with permission of the other user, and this information must be added manually to an off-site spreadsheet. The solution that many genetic genealogists have come up with is to ask their family members for their logins and passwords so they can go and do the necessary tests themselves after determining that their family members have no interest or willingness in figuring out how to do so. It is not uncommon to meet people on 23andMe who administer a dozen or more different accounts, including their own family members', their in-laws', and, for professional genealogists, their clients' as well.

Of the four services, only GEDmatch will allow users to evaluate the genetic relationships between people genetically unrelated to the account holder. Astonishingly, users can not only employ the available data analytic tools on their own genetic information but can analyze the genetic segments of anyone in the database in relationship to anyone else, regardless of whether either match the user. That is why GEDmatch is useful for law enforcement purposes. It should be noted that GEDmatch only provides genetic triangulations; to be genealogically meaningful, they would need to be connected with identified common ancestors as well. In the collecting of genealogical information through family trees, Ancestry leads the pack.

## FAMILY TREES

All four services allow users to input family tree data to their websites. AncestryDNA benefits tremendously by its ability to "link" genetic information to the enormous collection of user-created family trees in Ancestry. com. These can be private or public; public trees are fully searchable, while private trees provide user names and an invitation to contact them for access to their tree. Ancestry's trees are a powerful resource because of the sheer size of their database. AncestryDNA urges its users to consent to linking their Ancestry.com tree to their DNA results or to create a tree on Ancestry.com expressly for this purpose. The reason they do this is so that they can conduct genetic genealogical analysis and triangulate users' genetic matches. They then provide users with hints regarding their common ancestry with other users. They will provide the names of the common ancestors in question in cases where they discover triangulation and both users have linked trees.

Users of ftDNA can create family trees. Though functional, this aspect of the service is underutilized. The first build of 23andMe incorporated a less than fully effective family tree, which ceased to be editable when they rolled out their first big upgrade in 2015, called the "New Experience." Eventually it was removed altogether. Instead of replacing it, for a period they encouraged users to link to trees created on other services, including Ancestry.com and MyHeritage.com, a commercial service based in Israel that also owns another popular site, Geni.com. After a few years without its own tree feature, 23andMe recently rolled out an automatically generated tree based on their algorithmic predictions of genetic genealogical relationships. It triangulates behind the scenes, as Ancestry does. The point of having a tree, in the other services, is so that genetic matches can search for familiar surnames. The new tree on 23andMe is not currently searchable by other users (though there are indications that it will be in the future). The main point of the tree at the moment appears to be to encourage users to collaborate with the company on triangulation, much as Ancestry does through their trees (though Ancestry doesn't use that word). Users can confirm or reject proposed relationships and can manually add known relatives as well. What is different about this process compared to how Ancestry links genomes to trees is that 23andMe users are given access to the genetic segment information that 23andMe is using to make its predictions as well as tutorials about what it all means.

Until recently on GEDmatch, only a minority of users uploaded their genealogical information (via gedcom files, the standard format for sharing genealogical information). Since becoming a for-profit company, improved and advanced tools for the linking of genetic information to trees appear to be increasing the sharing of genealogical data. Some of its user-organized research groups require that members upload a gedcom file, since without it a few analytic tests won't work. In every case, and for all four services, success in triangulation still requires communication between users, and the person-to-person sharing of private information beyond the consent that users grant to other users to view and analyze their genetic information. The degree to which the corporations facilitate and encourage such communication differs among services.

## COMMUNICATION AND COLLABORATION

Both ftDNA and GEDmatch encourage the use of private email as the main method of direct communication between their users; email addresses are provided without the step of soliciting them, as is required by Ancestry and 23andMe, which have internal messaging systems. Since the New Experience, 23andMe has made it difficult to send messages to people with whom users share no genetic segments or who "scrolled off" when closer cousins were added to the lists. This is not a problem in AncestryDNA, which makes use of the messaging system of Ancestry.com; it allows messages to be sent to any unblocked user account. But in both cases the usefulness of messaging for collaboration is limited because they disallow file attachments. As a result, users of all four services typically employ regular email for conducting ongoing collaboration or participating in private, third-party, or social media discussions. These may be organized around a single surname, a cluster of surnames associated with a particular region, or a geographic area by itself.

GEDmatch-connected research groups are proliferating outside of GEDmatch, with many appearing on Facebook, where the quick creation of private groups allows for easy sharing of information among group members. Some of the wide range of internet-based genealogical groups are public, but the Facebook groups tied to GEDmatch are explicitly private and limited to people with the appropriate genealogical or genetic connection. Membership in these closely moderated groups differs somewhat in terms of the degree of pertinent evidence required for entry; all require an acceptance of a code of conduct and privacy-related restrictions. Users of any and all genetic genealogy services gather and comingle on Facebook. Popular Facebook pages like DNA Detectives, founded by CeCe Moore, a genetic genealogist who has become a television celebrity, can have many thousands of members. These discussions inadvertently act as marketing for commercial services since discussions of which service is best for a particular purpose is a common topic across them.

Finally, websites hosted privately by extended families can still be found across the internet, though their significance in the genealogy world has diminished since their heyday in the 1990s when information sharing happened largely as a relational act between individuals or was facilitated by public institutions such as local history organizations and libraries and by energetic genealogists who took up the task of serving the communication and genealogical research needs of their extended families or communities. Such websites, which may still feature traditional family trees, often now include the results of collaborative genetic projects—an assumed ancestral connection proved or disproved, for example, or the discovery that not all carriers of a particular surname descend from the same patrilineal founder.

## PRACTICES OF PRIVACY

During the first few years after the release of 23andMe in 2007, users frustrated by the truncation of genetic matches at about a thousand discovered that the number could be increased by sending messages to all their matches—including the anonymous users—asking them whether they would like to share information. The majority of these invitations would never receive a response. No matter, the software wouldn't remove matches when there was an invitation pending. In this way, determined users were able to increase their lists to 1,400 matches or more. In actor network theory, *drift* is said to occur within a network when actors use technologies in ways other than the way they were intended. In this drift, users of 23andMe successfully resisted the tool's intended constraint on the flow of information, a removal of unreliable data that 23andMe may have viewed as appropriate but that users judged to be parsimonious. When the New Experience arrived, the company responded to the drift by announcing they were voiding invitations to anonymous users. This prompted an outcry from genetic genealogists who had spent many hours sending those invitations; 23andMe accommodated them by doubling the upper limit on matches provided.

A second conflict occurred during the transition from the old to the new user experience of 23andMe over the loss of the Countries of Ancestry tool. Although users had to consent to share private information in order to view a chromosome chart showing the geographic origins of the grandparents of their matches, they were unaware that the tool also allowed people other than themselves to download a spreadsheet showing the names of *their* genetic matches, including segment location and length. Having access to other people's data in spreadsheet form is extremely useful to genetic genealogists because it allows for accomplishment of the genetic half of the triangulation process. Users could then contact genetic matches to request specific genealogical information, already knowing quite a lot about the nature of the genetic connection. People who had consented to participate in the Countries of Ancestry tool because they wanted to know their ethnic origins but had chosen to be anonymous in the rest of the 23andMe website were unpleasantly surprised when they were contacted by genetic relatives who knew their name and the names of their genetic matches. As a result, the tool and the ability to access other users' matches through it were done away with in the New Experience. The resistance to that privacy accommodation from the genetic genealogical users was swift. On social media and in public forums, these users declared 23andMe to be no longer a viable platform for doing genetic genealogy. As incompatible privacy norms collided, the "context collapse" caused distress all around.

During the period between Countries of Ancestry being shut down and the New Experience being unveiled, the company tweaked the website, its tools, and its consent policies, and a new privacy practice was established. The informational preferences of each side of this privacy conflict were both constrained and appeased. The ability to download a spreadsheet of other users' matches was gone forever; however, anonymous users were no longer allowed to operate as privacy "free riders," with access to other people's personal information without sharing any of their own. In its current privacy configuration, if 23andMe users want to see their list of genetic matches, they must now provide a pseudonym, at least, and their personal page will contain a list of cousins in common without any sharing invitation process required. Segment information, however, is not shared unless the user explicitly allows it. Users may also withhold a host of other personal information, including their real name and their ancestral surnames and locations. Through their privacy settings, they can also block particular people from seeing their information or sending them messages.

Because 23andMe's offerings include health-related genetic tests and services with their own consent processes, some subset of their users will never have an interest in communicating with genetic cousins for genealogical purposes. From an STS perspective, such users are not *enrolled* in the genetic genealogical kinship network, and so they practice their privacy differently. This can be frustrating for both their close and distant genetic relatives who cannot get them to respond to a message, much less to share useful genetic or genealogical information. Balancing the desire of some users to be anonymous with the desire of other users to have access to information about their genetic matches without having to beg for it, 23andMe resisted and accommodated its users as its corporate decision makers, staff genetic genealogists, web programmers, and lawyers collaboratively fine-tuned the flow of private information on their site. Even with access to the names of cousins in common, and the exact segments shared, other types of personal information are needed for triangulation to be achieved. 23andMe does not have the database of family trees that Ancestry boasts. So, like extended family genealogists of old, genetic genealogy researchers on 23andMe must still communicate with and persuade distant cousins to view themselves as part of a network of genetic kin.

Unlike 23andMe, ftDNA does not allow users to withhold the names of cousins in common, nor their segment information, nor email addresses. Only GEDmatch makes emailing matches as easy as ftDNA does. The one thing they limit is users' ability to see the location of segments shared between cousin matches. If users want to know how their genetic matches match each other, they must connect with these distant cousins via email and ask them to use the appropriate tool to check who they match on a given segment. By constraining one type of information flow while enabling another, they are, in effect, requiring users to communicate outside the ftDNA website. This policy makes sense in the context of their business plan, which encourages collaboration between users in order to attract customers to their more expensive DNA tests, which are meaningless unless multiple people take the test and join together to analyze the results. Inside private discussion groups, such users can organize and communicate with one another, but they still will need to recruit outside of ftDNA if their projects are to be successful. The fact that ftDNA provides smaller segments than 23andMe on their downloadable spreadsheets also reflects their financial interest in encouraging users to explore more distant, "deep" ancestral, and particularly patrilineal, connections comparing mutations on the Y chromosome among men who have the same surname. This comparison necessitates significantly more expensive testing than the autosomal comparisons used in segment triangulation.

AncestryDNA's practice of privacy in relationship to the other two commercial sites is unique in that it fails entirely to accommodate the central informational need of genetic genealogists while putting extensive pressure on its users to disclose private genealogical data. After clicking on the name of a genetic match from the list provided, users have in the past been greeted with the following pop-up message: "Your DNA results show that you may be related and comparing family trees is the best way to find out exactly how. We've got a few tricks up our sleeves to make it easy—automatically showing the surnames, places and people that both family trees share in common." The "trick" they have up their sleeve is the very genetic genealogical analysis they do not allow their users to conduct for themselves. With the combination of users' decoded genomes and uploaded family tree information, AncestryDNA searches for correspondences between users' family trees and their common genetic segments. In short, they triangulate. As a result, they are able to provide the names of common ancestors to their users with some confidence. The fact that they refer to the information as "hints" without reference to triangulated segments is both ironic and self-revealing, evocative of magicians whose livelihood depends on their audience not knowing how their magic tricks work. While both ftDNA and 23andMe offer tutorials regarding triangulation and how to achieve it, AncestryDNA spends its communicative energy on encouraging users to fill in their family trees and link them to their DNA.

The early years of internet-based genealogy were marked by collaboration and the free sharing of genealogical information within online networks that drew heavily from real-life hobbyist genealogical networks. Ancestry.com successfully monetized the information that was being crowdsourced through these networks and shared online, selling easy access to uploaded family trees, along with the added value of archival materials they were collecting themselves and putting behind their paywall (even as much of it was and continues to be available through familysearch.org for free). This seems to be the general business model underlying their genetic genealogy service as well. While the other three services sell data and genetic genealogical analytic tools, AncestryDNA sells (or rather, intends to sell in the future) easy results. This strategy is not lost on genetic genealogists, whose complaints regarding AncestryDNA's refusal to share segment data have gone unheard for more than a decade.

Resistance to AncestryDNA's withholding of segment data has created a definite drift. Genetic genealogists desiring to make better progress in their research download their decoded genomes from AncestryDNA (or from ftDNA or 23andMe or other services) and upload them to GEDmatch. It is not uncommon for people to set up accounts with multiple services, combining technologies, tools, and data provided by all of them. It is clear that the sociotechnical networks of genetic genealogical kinship do not live within self-contained online services and their user communities but rather sprawl between and across them in a messy network of crisscrossing networks, with private information flowing online and offline between users and their close family, extended family, and distant genetic kin, some who test on one service or another, or on as many as they can afford. This development was not likely anticipated, or even perhaps desired, by the various services, but it is increasingly accommodated.[22] GEDmatch, in particular, works with the other services to streamline the uploading of genomes, functioning as an extension of their own tools and services and effectively attracting the most interested and active genetic genealogists from all three of the other sites.

GEDmatch gained public notice beyond the genetic genealogy community when its database was used to catch Joseph James DeAngelo, the Golden State Killer. Law enforcement agents working with skilled genetic genealogists employing their knowledge of how genetic segments are inherited, and their ordinary genealogical know-how of document searches and family trees, were able to identify potential suspects and eventually the killer. A few other cases followed before GEDmatch users became fully aware that their data could be used in such a way. A privacy paradox followed, and the result of the outcry was that the company may only provide law enforcement with genetic data that comes from users who have explicitly opted in.

GEDmatch, which began as a not-for-profit genetic genealogy cooperative, was purchased in 2019 by Verogen, a California-based forensic genomics company. Anecdotally, many users left GEDmatch when it was purchased, despite the "opt-in" system, the retention of the well-liked founder of GED-match as an administrator of the site's day-to-day functions, and the company's assurance that the essential tools would remain free.[23] Users may choose from four privacy settings that affect what private information other people can access: "private," "research," "public + opt-in," and "public + opt-out." Opt-in and opt-out refer specifically to law enforcement's use of the data. A year after the sale of GEDmatch, only about a tenth of GEDmatch's users had given their consent, reducing the efficacy of the investigative technique.[24] Low levels of buy-in for the forensic use of their information, as well as user departures, suggest that users' willingness to share private data in the old GEDmatch may have been based on a professional kinship among genetic genealogists; they were willing to take the risk on behalf of collaborative knowledge creation but were unwilling to extend that affective sense of kinship to include the new corporate owner and its connection to lawyers and law enforcement agencies.

True to promise, the site design hasn't changed very much. Its web interface remains old-fashioned and spare. There is still no cost to use many of its powerful analytic and more server-intensive tools, and beta versions of new tests continue to require a fee—paid month by month or as a yearly subscription, but they did not become dramatically more expensive after the website was purchased, and there is no hard sell to users to consent to have their genetic information used by law enforcement. Still, it doesn't quite feel like the same grassroots cooperative it was in the beginning. The naïve sharing of genetic information for genetic genealogical purposes that went on in the nonprofit GEDmatch rested on a trust that fellow users wouldn't abuse the openness of the system. Before the sale, this notice was printed at the top of every generated list of genetic matches: "Please DO NOT send emails to anyone on this list without first using the one-to-one utility to verify that it is a legitimate match. DO NOT create mass mailing lists from these results." This notice was whistling in the wind, of course; they were unable to prevent either of these things from happening. The potential risks associated with sharing data with the for-profit GEDmatch are more clearly expressed in the current terms of service that greet users now: "DNA and Genealogical research, by its very nature, requires the sharing of information. Because of that, users participating in this Site agree that their information will be shared with other users. . . . We take steps to prevent your Genealogy Data from being available to the casual web surfer or to the search engines (e.g. Google). However, we cannot guarantee that your information will never be accessed by individuals other than GEDmatch users. If you require absolute security, you agree that you will not upload your Genealogy Data to GEDmatch. If you have already uploaded it, you agree to delete it immediately."[25]

Even though GEDmatch is no longer a nonprofit site, it remains a collaborative cooperative of researchers; it is in that context that GEDmatch users will share both information and risk in equal measure. One of its newest features allows users to link their family trees with their genetic information, as occurs on Ancestry and 23andMe, but their rhetoric is distinctive. You are told that you are doing this not only for yourself but for the benefit of other users: "You will be given the opportunity to link your Genealogy Data with your DNA data. This is a powerful tool and we encourage people to use it. It also provides a means of access to your Genealogy Data to people who may have no Genealogy Data of their own at GEDmatch. It will also enable identification of individuals within the provided Genealogy Data, even if the individuals are not identified in the Genealogy Data." The gift to other users described here is genetic genealogical knowledge. GEDmatch is asserting that this knowledge belongs to individuals who complete the full (genetic and genealogical) triangulation of their genetic segments and that sharing it is a social good. Arguably, such knowledge truly is a gift to people who are adopted, without access to their medical, ethnic, or genealogical ancestry. Equally grateful are genealogists who are able to resolve a decades-old dead end on their family tree. This generosity in genetic genealogy strikes the familiar chord of the free-sharing genealogy of an earlier era; it appeals not to the ties of family but of kinship.

That the company also wants to use this knowledge to solve crimes is no secret; it is key to Verogen's mission and the reason for their acquisition of GEDmatch. The company has kept its main features free for a reason other than sentimental generosity; they need users' information and their genetic genealogical expertise in order to conduct the business of forensic genealogy successfully. Some people are bothered by this use of their data; others just aren't. The practices of privacy on GEDmatch may well seem inexplicable to people not fully enrolled, in an actor network sense, in a genetic genealogical kinship network, among whom the open sharing of private information is an established good. To be fair, the risks associated with extreme sports may appear similarly unreasonable to those outside those networks of pleasure and play. But it would be a mistake to judge membership in GEDmatch as inherently riskier than membership in the other commercial websites. The risks are just easier to see when the web interface is less slick.

The differences between services, from the point of view of a consumer who must choose between them, are not immediately obvious. Because of the size of its user database and its encyclopedic family trees, AncestryDNA provides the best genealogical resources for adopted people in search of birth families. 23andMe is commonly judged to offer the most accurate estimations of "ethnic" ancestral origins, and it also tests for a wide variety of health-related genetic markers for a cost that is significantly less than what must be paid to get the tests done through regular medical channels. ftDNA is the only service of the four that provides tests that investigate "deep" ancestry, including advanced genetic testing of the Y chromosome for those interested in the ancient origins of their patrilines. Serious genetic genealogists congregate on GEDmatch, collaborating in their own investigations while facilitating the investigations of others. With its suite of powerful data analytic tools and its wild west approach to privacy and information sharing, GEDmatch is where the collaborative work of genetic genealogy gets done.

## CONCLUSION: SOCIOTECHNICAL NETWORKS OF PRIVACY

I began by arguing that in genealogical networks privacy decisions are more a matter of belonging than of choice. As privacy is practiced, it reveals itself as a relational act that doesn't necessarily follow from a rational assessment of risk. If a user of these services feels that they are part of a genealogical network, and that using genetics to establish and prove genealogical connections is a positive good, then they will share their private information with their genetic cousins and with the available services that facilitate the necessary tasks to do so. They share private information as a matter of course, whether the rest of the world considers that an unreasonable risk or not, just as in bygone days people would tell the stranger on the phone their daughter-in-law's maiden name and the birthdates of their new grandchildren. They trust that this information will only be used for the good of their extended kin, where *kinship* includes ancestors, the living, and generations not yet born.

Being able to "read" someone's ancestors in their genes is the holy grail for all four genetic genealogy services. AncestryDNA has staked its claim by setting up a system that encourages both genetic and genealogical information coming in from its users, but it only releases *genealogical* information back to them. The company protects its ownership of the collaboratively produced knowledge (the triangulated segments connecting specific genetic information with specific ancestors) by withholding the data that would allow its users to comprehend where this knowledge came from. In contrast, users on the other three sites are encouraged to understand, and are free to share with others, the significance of the triangulations they discover and the knowledge that is produced as a result.

AncestryDNA is looking toward the not-so-distant future in which their customers will submit their DNA and, for a price, receive a list of their ancestors. Anecdotally, that's what some disappointed users of genetic genealogical services think they are buying today. However, the knowledge that AncestryDNA wants to sell to its users does not yet exist. The names of our ancestors are not yet written in our genes, at least not in our individual genes. But the dogged work of triangulation, segment by segment, proceeds surely enough to beg the question: If this bio-digital dream comes true, to whom will the genome maps of our ancestors belong?

Anthropologist and STS theorist Marilyn Strathern has argued that traditional genealogical kinship networks, though they may seem endless, in practice are not: "Social relations depend on multitudinous factors that truncate the potential of forever-ramifying biological relations. Biological relatedness—'blood ties'—can thus be cut by failure to accord social recognition (someone is forgotten), just as social relationships can be cut by appeal to biological principles (dividing 'real' kin from others)." Strathern analyzes the patenting of genetic information as a truncation of a network, another kind of cutting, where ownership replaces belonging as the salient relation. The parts of a network that are left out in the patenting of a genetic process include researchers whose work provides the technical basis for the future work of others: "Any one invention is only made possible by the field of knowledge which defines a scientific community. The social networks here are long; patenting truncates them. So, it matters very much over which segment or fragment of a network rights of ownership can be exercised. In another case, forty names to a scientific article became six names to a patent application; the rest did not join in. The long network of scientists that was formerly such an aid to knowledge becomes hastily cut. Ownership thereby curtails relations between persons; owners exclude those who do not belong."[26]

Strathern's insight, that ownership truncates belonging, clarifies what is going on when scientific processes—or genes—are patented.[27] Through a similar process, the practice of privacy in genetic genealogical kinship networks initially reflects an expansive view of belonging that connects all human beings to each other. We should be attentive to truncations of belonging and the stripping of provenance and context, not only in the practices of online genealogy and genetic genealogy but in other collaborative and crowdsourced processes as well. As reassembled maps of our ancestors' genomes emerge through the collaborative production of genetic genealogical knowledge, they will, invariably, be commodified and the crowdsourced labor that was necessary to accomplish the monumental work erased—just as, decades ago, credit for the diligent research of traditional genealogists was lost in the furious proliferation of unreferenced family trees that scraped the data from others' work and uploaded it all over the internet. Enabling a free flow of information leads to the production of genetic genealogical knowledge; truncating it reestablishes the knowledge as property. Within sociotechnical networks, belonging enables a flow of private information that can be knowledge-generating, but we must be wary. Constraints on the flow of information may well be establishing norms, values, practices, and legal barriers relating to the protection of ownership and not "privacy" at all.

## NOTES

1. See Sangita Chari and Jaime M. N. Lavalle, eds., *Accomplishing NAGPRA: Perspectives on the Intent, Impact, and Future of the Native American Graves Protection and Repatriation Act* (Corvallis: Oregon State University Press, 2013).

2. See Helen Nissenbaum, *Privacy in Context: Technology, Policy, and the Integrity of Social Life* (Redwood City, CA: Stanford University Press, 2010), and Helen Nissenbaum, "A Contextual Approach to Privacy Online," *Daedalus* 140, no. 4 (2011): 32–48. Her work was shaped by foundational scholarship from law: Samuel Warren and Louis D. Brandeis, "The Right to Privacy," *Harvard Law Review* (1890): 193–220; Alan Westin, "Privacy and Freedom, 1967," *Washington and Lee Law Review*, no. 25 (1970): 166; from psychology: Irwin Altman, *The Environment and Social Behavior: Privacy, Personal Space, Territory, and Crowding* (Pacific Grove, CA: Brooks/Cole, 1975); and from sociology: Georg Simmel, "The Sociology of Secrecy and of Secret Societies," *American Journal of Sociology* 11, no. 4 (1906): 441–498; Erving Goffman, *The Presentation of Self in Everyday Life* (London: Harmondsworth, 1973).

3. Nissenbaum, *Privacy in Context*, 231.

4. Alice E. Marwick and danah boyd, "Networked Privacy: How Teenagers Negotiate Context in Social Media," *New Media and Society* 16, no. 7 (2014): 1051–1067.

5. See, for example: Daniel Solove, *Understanding Privacy* (Cambridge, MA: Harvard University Press, 2008); Rath Kanha Sar and Yeslam Al-Saggaf, "Contextual Integrity's Decision Heuristic and the Tracking by Social Network Sites," *Ethics and Information Technology* 16, no. 1 (2014): 15–26.

6. Important works on the psychology of privacy and the privacy paradox include: Krystelle Shaughnessy, Jessica N. Rocheleau, Somayyeh Kamalou, and David A. Moscovitch, "The Effects of Social Anxiety and Online Privacy Concern on Individual Differences in Internet-Based Interaction Anxiety and Communication Preferences," *Cyberpsychology, Behavior, and Social Networking* 20, no. 4 (2017): 212–217; Sören Preibusch, "Guide to Measuring Privacy Concern: Review of Survey and Observational Instruments," *International Journal of Human-Computer Studies*

71, no. 12 (2013): 1133–1143; Patricia A. Norberg, Daniel R. Horne, and David A. Horne, "The Privacy Paradox: Personal Information Disclosure Intentions versus Behaviors," *Journal of Consumer Affairs* 41, no. 1 (2007): 100–126; and Andrew Gambino, Jinyoung Kim, S. Shyam Sundar, Jun Ge, and Mary Beth Rosson, "User Disbelief in Privacy Paradox: Heuristics that Determine Disclosure," Proceedings of the 2016 CHI Conference Extended Abstracts on Human Factors in Computing Systems (May 2015): 2837–2843.

7. Marwick and boyd, "Networked," 1053.

8. Marwick and boyd, "Networked," 1064.

9. Carsten Ochs and Petra Ilyes, "Sociotechnical Privacy: Mapping the Research Landscape," *Technoscienza: Italian Journal of Science and Technology Studies* 4, no. 2 (2014): 73–92. Their work draws on these foundational works: Michel Callon, "Society in the Making: The Study of Technology as a Tool for Sociological Analysis," in *The Social Construction of Technological Systems: New Directions in the Sociology and History of Technology,* ed. T. Huges and T. Pinch (London: MIT Press, 1987), 83–103; Bruno Latour, "Technology Is Society Made Durable," *The Sociological Review* 38, no. 1 supplemental (1990): 103–131; and Wiebe E. Bijker and John Law, eds., *Shaping Technology/Building Society: Studies in Sociotechnical Change* (Cambridge, MA: MIT Press, 1994).

10. Ochs and Illyes, "Sociotechnical," 2.

11. Michel Callon, "Economic Markets and the Rise of Interactive Agencements: From Prosthetic Agencies to Habilitated Agencies," in *Living in a Material World: Economic Sociology Meets Science and Technology Studies,* ed. T. Pinch and R. Swedberg (Cambridge, MA: MIT Press, 2008): 29–56; Adele E. Clarke and Susan Leigh Star, "The Social Worlds Framework: A Theory/Methods Package," *The Handbook of Science and Technology Studies,* no. 3 (2008): 113–137.

12. Michel Callon, "Some Elements of a Sociology of Translation: Domestication of the Scallops and the Fishermen of St Brieuc Bay," *Sociological Review* 32, no. 1 supplemental (1984): 196–233; John Law, "Notes on the Theory of the Actor-Network: Ordering, Strategy, and Heterogeneity," *Systemic Practice and Action Research* 5, no. 4 (1992): 379–393.

13. Bryn Williams-Jones and Janice E. Graham, "Actor-Network Theory: A Tool to Support Ethical Analysis of Commercial Genetic Testing," *New Genetics and Society* 22, no. 3 (2003): 271–296; Catherine Bliss, "Translating Racial Genomics: Passages in and Beyond the Lab," *Qualitative Sociology* 36, no. 4 (2013): 423–443; Indrit Troshani and Nilmini Wickramasinghe, "Tackling Complexity in E-health with Actor-Network Theory," in System Sciences (HICSS), 2014 47th Hawaii International Conference on Systems Sciences, IEEE (January 2014): 2994–3003; Catherine Heeney, "An Ethical Moment in Data Sharing," *Science, Technology, and Human Values* 42, no. 1 (2017): 3–28.

14. Andrew Pickering, *The Mangle of Practice: Time, Agency, and Science* (Chicago: University of Chicago Press, 1995).

15. Pickering, *Mangle,* 22.

16. See, for example, Sören Preibusch, "Guide to Measuring Privacy Concern: Review of Survey and Observational Instruments," *International Journal of*

*Human-Computer Studies* 71, no. 12 (2013): 1133–1143; Emily Christofides and Kieran O'Doherty, "Company Disclosure and Consumer Perceptions of the Privacy Implications of Direct-to-Consumer Genetic Testing," *New Genetics and Society* 35, no. 2 (2016): 101–123; Hsiao–Ying Huang and Masooda Bashir, "Direct-to-Consumer Genetic Testing: Contextual Privacy Predicament," *Proceedings of the Association for Information Science and Technology* 52, no. 1 (2015): 1–10; Peter Chow-White, Stephan Struve, Alberto Lusoli, Frederik Lesage, Nilesh Saraf, and Amanda Oldring, "'Warren Buffet Is My Cousin': Shaping Public Understanding of Big Data Biotechnology, Direct-to-Consumer Genomics, and 23andMe on Twitter," *Information, Communication and Society* 21, no. 3 (2018): 448–464; and Tobias Haeusermann, Bastian Greshake, Alessandro Blasimme, Darja Irdam, Martin Richards, and Effy Vayena, "Open Sharing of Genomic Data: Who Does It and Why?" *PLoS One* 12, no. 5 (2017): e0177158.

17. See, for example, Catherine Nash, "Genealogical Relatedness: Geographies of Shared Descent and Difference," *Genealogy* 1, no. 2 (2017): 7.

18. See Susan Leigh Star and James R. Griesemer. "Institutional Ecology, Translations and Boundary Objects: Amateurs and Professionals in Berkeley's Museum of Vertebrate Zoology, 1907–39," *Social Studies of Science* 19, no. 3 (1989): 387–420; and Susan Leigh Star, "This Is Not a Boundary Object: Reflections on the Origin of a Concept," *Science, Technology, and Human Values* 35, no. 5 (2010): 604.

19. See Marwick and boyd, "Networked."

20. David Koh, "Their Isolation Creates Gene Lab," *Baltimore Sun*, October 6, 2003, https://www.baltimoresun.com/news/bs-xpm-2003-10-06-0310060146-story .html.

21. The term was coined by genetic genealogist William Hurst in 2004. See William Hurst, "New Words for This New Field of Genetic Genealogy," Genealogy-DNA mailing list, December 16, 2004, https://isogg.org/wiki/Triangulation#cite_note-1.

22. Another genealogical and genetic genealogical website, MyHeritage.com, links seamlessly to the free family trees collected on Familysearch.org, the portal to the massive collection of genealogical resources curated by the Mormon Church, the digital content of which is both public and free.

23. Verogen's press release on the acquisition of GEDmatch appeared on December 9, 2019: "GEDmatch Partners with Genomics Firm," Verogen December 9, 2019, https://verogen.com/gedmatch-partners-with-genomics-firm/. For context, see Nila Bala, "We're Entering a New Phase in Law Enforcement's Use of Consumer Genetic Data," *Slate*, December 19, 2019, https://slate.com/technology/2019/12/gedmatch-verogen-genetic-genealogy-law-enforcement.html.

24. Nanci Carr, "Cold Cases Freeze: Law Enforcement Locked Out of DNA Database Used for Investigative Genealogy after Consumers Object to Being Genetic Informants," *Washington University Law Review* 98 (2020): 1–15.

25. GEDmatch.com Terms of Service and Privacy Policy, December 9, 2019, https://www.gedmatch.com/tos.php.

26. Marilyn Strathern, "Cutting the Network," *Journal of the Royal Anthropological Institute* 2, no. 3 (1996): 524.

27. Marilyn Strathern, "What Is Intellectual Property After?," *The Sociological Review*, 47, no. S1 (1999): 156–180.

## Chapter Ten

# The "One Hundred Percent Corner"

## *Information Architecture for Intergenerational Communities*

### David Hopping

For to him that is joined to all the living, there is hope.

Ecclesiastes 9:4

In 1994 an entirely new type of retirement community was imagined and realized, almost inadvertently, as a side effect of meeting a different challenge. Hope Meadows was formed as a hybrid foster-adoption agency and retirement community in a rural town in central Illinois, and it quickly gained national recognition as a promising innovation on multiple levels: seniors could find a safe and affordable place to live, families could receive adequate support for the often-overwhelming task of providing foster care to "special needs" kids, and the children themselves could find an end to (or even avoid) a long series of temporary placements and painful disruptions.

Since it was developed, this multifaceted program design has been adapted dozens of times around the country to a range of other social challenges, always entailing the common feature of enlisting older adults—mostly retired or semiretired—into "everyday" roles that support and even potentiate professional interventions.

This chapter foregrounds the informational aspects of the many layers, structures, and affordances of the core "program" at Hope Meadows, most of which are information systems in their own right, composing an overall integrated system that lends itself to modeling and critique as "information architecture" (IA). But it also ventures beyond the conventional scope of IA, which addresses the findability of information and the means of making information systems navigable and understandable, and suggests ways of bringing the complexities of everyday information into scope as well.

The goal is to track not only the professional and structural components of such programs as information systems but to also explore how natural networks and everyday systems of interaction can be integrated into, and even cultivated, as strategic resources within a more comprehensive IA design.

Especially important in the case of Hope Meadows is the design of systemic/cybernetic processes, where information flows in continuous circuits, much like the circuits by which personal and social identity develop within webs of human relationship and circuits of informational feedback. As a practice, this kind of IA also implements design patterns that cultivate emergent structures within the next-larger system (such as a mission-focused neighborhood community) in order to channel everyday signals of commitment and evidence of the tangible value of continued social engagement—such that it makes sense to take on audacious later-life ventures demanding personal risk and transformative effort.

Among these design patterns is the "100 percent corner" concept borrowed by architect Victor Regnier to describe hubs of concentrated social interaction and flows of both formal and everyday information.[1] This pattern can serve as a unifying metaphor for a range of other innovative patterns, which continuously stabilize and orient individual engagement, promote collective efficacy, and support successful aging in community.

## COMMUNITY AS INTERVENTION

The Hope Meadows neighborhood was created from housing on a decommissioned Air Force base, which was renovated and converted into sixty-four units of various sizes, with fifteen allocated to foster and adoptive families, forty-four to senior citizens, and five for administrative and community activities. There are no fences, and the neighborhood is indistinguishable from other base housing, with which it is contiguous on three sides. The structures consist of split-level duplex and fourplex clusters with external carports, arrayed along tree-lined streets that meander in typical suburban fashion between larger thoroughfares.

Hope Meadows was designed from the outset as an opportunity to serve—to support and engage with fledgling adoptive families as they worked through the challenges of including "hard-to-place" children from the foster care system into their existing family systems. The children who were referred to Hope by child welfare services had generally suffered multiple traumas and insults to their physical and emotional well-being as well as the disintegration of kinship and other social network ties.

They arrived at Hope, sometimes as sibling groups of three or four, having spent an average of 58 percent of their young lives in foster and/or institutional care. The challenges facing foster-adoptive families can be daunting and typically entail considerable "emotion work" on everyone's part and adjustment of expectations and reworking of personal and family identities.[2]

A small staff of professionals (social caseworkers, therapists, consultants) was available to provide critical information and guidance to families and to intervene in crises when necessary. But from the beginning, one supervening goal was also integral—to cultivate a different kind of socioemotional resource in the form of older adult neighbors. These ready-to-go prospective grandparents would eventually extend the reach and impact of formal interventions and enfold families into a natural social web, tapping into natural processes for restoring the capacity for trust and resilience and age-appropriate development to children who had spent too much time in the "care" of the state.

The founders knew that programs that are successful in improving the lives of children have certain identifiable attributes. As characterized by Lisbeth Schorr, they are flexible and persevering, they see children in the context of families and families as part of neighborhoods, they are guided by long-term visions and continue to evolve over time, they are competently staffed and provide responsive services, and they encourage mutual trust and respect between practitioners and families.[3] But the founders also recognized, with Schorr, that to improve the lives of children, one must go beyond program practices to include emotionally salient interpersonal relationships. Citing Urie Bronfenbrenner, the "dean of child development scholars," Schorr observes that to grow up whole, be able to learn and develop a conscience, children need to experience—especially in the early years—the irrational love, attention, and commitment of at least one adult. "Bronfenbrenner," she suggests, "summarizes volumes of studies: 'Somebody has to be crazy about the kid.'"[4]

## THE 100 PERCENT CORNER

For over a decade, retired Hope Meadows resident Al Peña would make his way every morning to the Intergenerational Center (IGC) at the heart of the neighborhood and make coffee for the neighbors who would soon drift in. Many of them had also been part of realizing the original vision, filling it out with innovative detail, creating it tangibly in carpentry and landscaping and organizing.

Al continued to find his way, day after day, from his front door, across the street, and down the sidewalk to the IGC even after early signs of dementia started to appear, because every detail of his routine had become fixed and established, and every person around him was watchful, knowledgeable, and alert to his situation and status.

Sipping coffee with his companions, Al sat at the center of a system of everyday information flows. Neighbors could watch through their low and wide picture windows, separated from the sidewalk by a narrow strip of lawn, as he progressed in his everyday journey there and back again. The early-morning cohort would settle at one of several long tables in the large area that had been created by opening up and connecting the living rooms of two units of a duplex apartment—and thus had the same picture window layout and perspective on the street but situated at the geographic heart of the neighborhood.

I visited frequently, at first doing dissertation research during the earliest years of the program and later doing administrative and research work in the office down the street (another converted duplex). I would drop in to the IGC at various times of day to observe, participate, and chip in with minor projects, such as helping Doug Riley (a retired engineer) troubleshoot networking problems in the downstairs computer lab or helping Al shorten a closet door so that it would swing freely over the new carpet. The seniors had built out the IGC space themselves, as one of their first volunteer activities, in anticipation of the arrival of new families and a steady stream of new children, which would eventually bring the neighborhood to full capacity by 1998.

During its most bustling hours, the IGC conjured a multiplicity of transformative spaces into transient existence—providing a potentially powerful vehicle of psychosocial intervention constructed without the formal direction of licensed professional experts. Each of its specialized rooms (for tutoring, play, gathering, computers, library, etc.) had its own distinct ambience, and each would be hosted by one or more volunteers according to a regular but flexible schedule.

I recall noticing that by early evening one chair would typically end up in a particular spot near the large front window, oriented sideways to it. I might not have thought much about this, or even noticed, had I not been recently sensitized to this pattern in a seminar on architecture and aging. The instructor, architect Victor Regnier, recounted a similar experience when researching designs for assisted living. While visiting one facility, he noticed that a certain chair in a common dining area seemed to keep finding its way to a particular spot away from its assigned table, despite being diligently returned by staff from time to time. He went over and sat in the chair, casually looked around, and realized that this vantage provided clear lines of sight into every path and corner and activity and conversation going on around him.

**Figure 10.1. View from the wayward, window-seeking chair in the IGC at Hope Meadows.**
David Hopping

The wayward, window-seeking chair at Hope Meadows was no different—sitting in it, one could monitor the main entry door to the IGC, the doorway and half-flight of stairs to the basement, the stairway to the upper level of the building and all the traffic that coursed along this route, at least half of the double living room area, activity in the kitchen through the open pass-through window, all the vehicle and foot traffic at this end of the neighborhood, and the front door and driveway of the main office, half a block down the street (see figure 10.1). It was an information superhub.

This reliable, welcoming center of gravity of community life in the neighborhood is a design pattern that could in principle be built into the program architectures for supportive, assisted, even independent living housing anywhere. Regnier would famously tag this pattern as the "100 percent corner," a term borrowed from urban planning, where it is typically applied to the busiest intersection in a downtown metropolitan district as measured by pedestrian flow or car counts:

> In this context, the phrase refers to the most socially active place in the building. A successful 100% corner usually requires a nexus of features to make it attractive and engaging . . . [beginning with] a table that seats six to eight, positioned so residents can easily converse and interact. The table should overlook stimulating activities in adjacent rooms and outside areas. Having a proximal connection to major circulation pathways generates visits. . . . A successful 100% corner is often busy throughout the day. It is a place that is equally comfortable for spontaneous interaction or for planned activities.[5]

By using his wandering-chair story to introduce the 100 percent corner concept in the seminar, Regnier was also drawing attention to the *informational* significance of the pattern and to the basic human imperative to track the environment and sustain general situational awareness. The story also introduces another easily overlooked element, relating to the "everydayness" of this process—the "100 percent information" effect was achieved not by design and foresight but by a creative, messy, mildly transgressive reappropriation of affordances that *were* designed, but for other proximal purposes, such as sitting correctly at a dining table.

From the outset, Hope Meadows' senior residents were afforded wide latitude for inventing the rest of an ultimately complex and defining portfolio of structures and programs for interaction and engagement—children's library, computer lab, play space and regular activities for toddlers and preschoolers, after-school tutoring and endless games and creative activities both indoor and outdoor, monthly potlucks and special celebrations for birthdays, adoptions, and holidays, including national Grandparents' Day (September 12), and a very full Black History Month.

The evolving program of events and volunteer opportunities also established serendipitous venues for connection, both within and between natural affinity groups, thus weaving a complex network of networks. The specific connections often entailed multistranded relationships (a senior might connect with a child, for example, as friend, neighbor, confidant, tutor, mentor, or "grandparent") depending on the specific context of the moment, and all such program-scaffolded networks (volunteer system, event attendance, proximal neighbors, book club, quilting group, etc.) were also interlinked—resulting in an extremely high "density of acquaintanceship" overall (effectively 100% within the neighborhood) and a rich web of further relationship opportunities.[6]

## SYSTEMS, CYBERNETICS, AND IDENTITY WORK

Social network analysis conceptualizes and traces the things that flow through networks, such as support, resources, recognition, status, authority, prestige, influence—leading to sometimes surprising insights into how human beings are connected.[7] For designers of large heterogeneous ventures such as Hope Meadows, one of the most important of these considerations is the flow of information through the whole system, including especially the circuits of feedback and coordination that weave it all together.

In this hybrid organization/community system, the "everyday," routine, often transient information loops play an outsize role, because this is how this particular peculiar system was designed to work. Underneath the innovative program of volunteer work and scheduled activities and meetings, Hope Meadows also sustained both a significant property management operation and a licensed foster and adoption agency—implemented as a more conventional layer of policies and practices. Information in this more formal system flowed largely from the organizational periphery to the center via reports and records and was largely structured in ways mandated by regulations and common standards.

Information about events, activities, volunteer duties, and so on also flowed back out to the community via mostly conventional patterns, including the *Seedlings* weekly newsletter, formal parent and senior training sessions, informational "coffees" with guest speakers, occasional community-wide meetings, and a rich schedule of celebrations. The work of keeping track of the combined total system, with a fairly complex conventional structure and even more complex informal network of networks, was accomplished mostly intuitively, supplemented by regular ethnographic research.[8]

Not surprisingly, there remained a productive but sometimes frustrating tension between professional practice and community autonomy, requiring a continuous negotiation of boundaries and responsibilities. It might be said that the literal and figurative "architecture" of the overall system was being continuously cocreated by multiple parties in multiple interconnected roles and relations.

The term *information architect* acquired its modern meaning when architect Richard Saul Wurman applied it to himself quite casually in the mid-1970s and more definitively in 1997 in his seminal book *Information Architecture*: "I don't mean a bricks and mortar architect. I mean architect as used in the words architect of foreign policy. I mean architect as in the creating of systemic, structural, and orderly principles to make something work—the thoughtful making of either artifact, or idea, or policy that informs because it is clear."[9]

The term was adopted by Peter Morville and Lou Rosenfeld in the mid-1990s to describe a new field of practice, addressing the design and management of information resources on the World Wide Web, and this meaning has since become dominant. Information on a website should be findable and understandable, and the site itself should be easily navigable. Information itself implies something that can be collected, stored, and retrieved, and the architect makes this work for "users" who are seeking access in order to accomplish something. More recently IA has come to include a closer attention to the context and timeline of interaction, even framing the user's experience in terms of conversation and relationship and extending its gaze to encompass the user's journey of engagement with an organization across multiple "touchpoints" over an extended period of time.[10]

This perspective can be logically extended to the broader task of service design, and in a program like Hope Meadows, it could help smooth out some of the inevitable frictions in the conventional side of the program (social services, property management, etc.). But to be relevant to the intentional community side, a deeper dive into the "everydayness" of information processes and flows is required, along with an exploration of relational networks and interactions. A starting place is the restorative identity work accomplished through such networked interactions, which is key to mitigating and reversing the effects of deep damage to children's socioemotional resilience and their consequently faltering identities.

Modern identity theory understands identity as something developed and sustained in relation to others, a process that is intrinsically embedded within networks of social relations and vulnerable to disruption by trauma or neglect. In cases of damage to a child's identity development, therapy can launch the process of restoring socioemotional resilience and (re)construction of a secure identity, and well-supported and informed family systems can take the baton from there. But in cases of prolonged and severe damage to a child's development, the challenge can outpace a family's best efforts and overwhelm the task of realizing a new family identity at the next level of social organization.

All the children arriving at Hope Meadows for adoption had sustained severe traumas and losses and sometimes persistent disconfirmation of their identities; one would cringe at physical contact and would collapse emotionally under praise, another apparently had developed no self-concept and was unable to use personal pronouns or express preferences or desires.

Identity theory proposes a systems/cybernetic model of social and personal identity, highlighting the role of information and feedback in a continuous looping-and-comparison process. The basic idea, as described by Jan Stets and Peter Burke, is that "people did not just act in ways that were consistent with their identities. Rather they used feedback from others (reflected appraisals) as well as their own direct appraisals to understand the meanings of the behaviors they were enacting. On the basis of this, they altered their behavior in order to make their perceptions of the meaning match the meanings in their identity standard."[11]

When this cybernetic formulation first appeared in 1991,[12] it was actually rather subversive, running counter to the entrenched notion that people controlled their behavior: "The idea that people controlled their perceptions by engaging in whatever behavior worked to match perceptions of meaning to identity standard meanings was not commonly understood. Again, the perceptual control perspective emphasizes the idea that it is the meaning that is important not the behavior itself, and meaning is subject to social confirmation. By looking at others' responses, one can confirm that one is adjusting the meaning of the situation in the desired manner."

An individual's identity entails an internalized identity standard and a complex of expectations, plus an accumulated repertoire of responses to situations. In any given encounter, one's performance of this identity can either be confirmed in reflected appraisals from others or disconfirmed, and disconfirmation will trigger a response and behavior to bring things back into alignment. The theory predicts that unwarranted praise is equally disconfirming of identity, and while in psychologically healthy persons it may elicit a positive or (at worst) embarrassed response, it will still trigger action to "close the discrepancy" (discounting, negotiating, explaining) in terms of the cybernetic flow of information within the space and circuit of encounter.[13]

In the normal course of development, children will play at multiple identities and tune their skills and repertoires through interaction with adults and other children in a (hopefully) wide variety of contexts and in response to a range of confirmations and disconfirmations, successes and failures, and outcomes that are neither, just purely exploratory.

## THE MAGIC OF THE ORDINARY

Most of us weather the daily barrage of influences that affect our identities, positively and negatively, with a capacity referred to in other literature as socioemotional resilience. Confirming and disconfirming information received from the world is continuously and immediately compared to a stable internalized reference source, and significant disparities ("differences that make a difference") trigger subsequent thought and action to reduce them.[14]

For most of the children referred to Hope Meadows for fostering and adoption, such resilience had either been reduced by years of neglect and trauma to threshold levels or never fully developed in the first place. The Hope Meadows program/community system was designed (if tacitly) to redress this resilience gap and help restore and strengthen broken identities.

A key design pattern for achieving this involved cultivating what might be thought of as the "obverse" of information—a distended state of playful uncertainty—held open in interpersonal spaces of risk and trust. This was managed in the first instance within the proven context of play therapy—a well-bounded, confidential, comforting, and permissive environment set up to elicit tentative explorations of feelings and interaction patterns.

The reach of this "crucible" pattern was extended through the various formal engagements of the cadre of seniors (whose households outnumbered

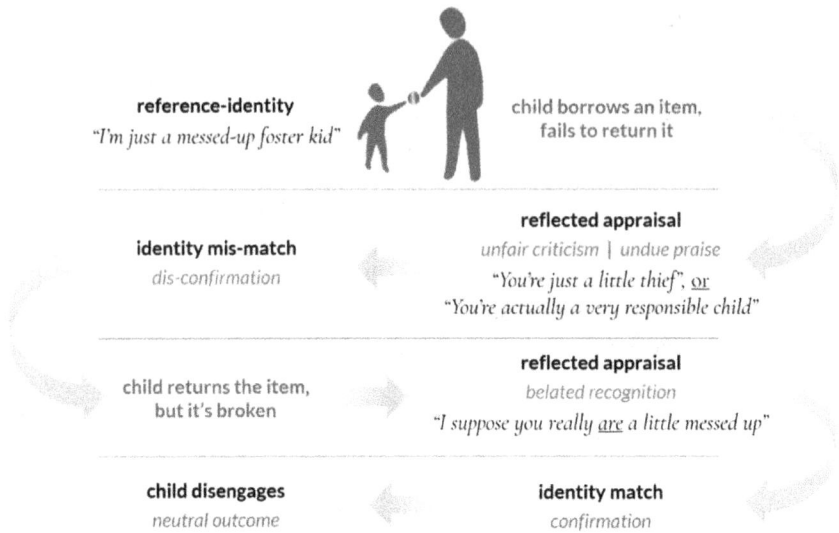

| | |
|---|---|
| **reference-identity** | child borrows an item, |
| *"I'm just a messed-up foster kid"* | fails to return it |

| | |
|---|---|
| | **reflected appraisal** |
| **identity mis-match** | *unfair criticism | undue praise* |
| *dis-confirmation* | *"You're just a little thief", or* |
| | *"You're actually a very responsible child"* |

| | |
|---|---|
| | **reflected appraisal** |
| child returns the item, | *belated recognition* |
| but it's broken | *"I suppose you really are a little messed up"* |

| | |
|---|---|
| **child disengages** | **identity match** |
| *neutral outcome* | *confirmation* |

Figure 10.2.   An overture may collapse for failure to recognize how identity works, especially in the counterintuitive case of a "spoiled identity"a child will work to get confirmation of even a liminal status and identity, because this is how humans actually function. Overly-harsh or overly-generous "reflected appraisals" will precipitate round after round of interaction, but no basis for a longer-term relationship.
David Hopping

families by a factor of four to one) into more serendipitous encounters and activities throughout the child's social ecosystem: a new family, new extended fictive kin, and an entire neighborhood, all signed on to the same mission—distributing a myriad of micro-instances of potentially resilience-building interactions across the widest range of contexts and roles.

The contours of such little crucibles of interaction are thus similar to the fifty-minute-hour framework of professional interventions—but differ both in sheer multitude (see figure 10.3) and, perhaps more importantly, in the fact that they unfold within a relational horizon with no expiration date—seniors are an everyday copresence and fact of common life and represent an open-ended commitment to the intertwining of personal futures.

That children can intuitively recognize and work naturally within these crucibles is illustrated in the vignette with which author Wes Smith closes his book on Hope Meadows:

Five years after Debbie and Kenny Calhoun began parenting the toddler who had been "failing to thrive," widowed Hope senior Irene Bohn answered the doorbell in her apartment down the street from the Calhouns' home. She found Marty standing on her doorstep.

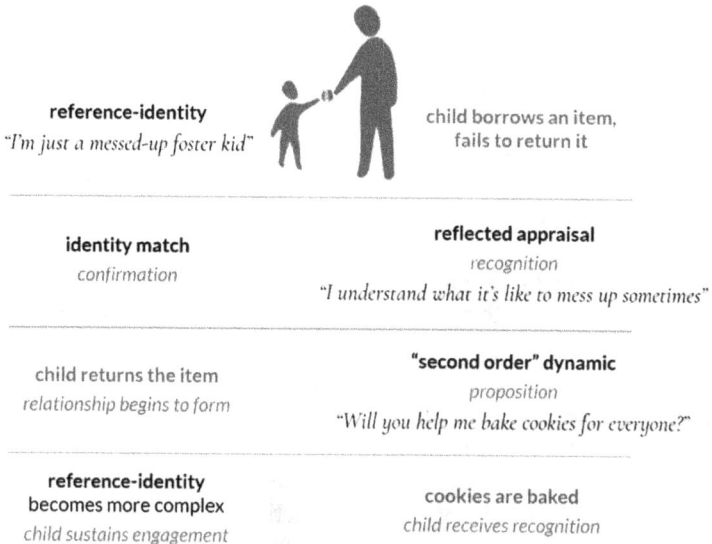

**reference-identity**
*"I'm just a messed-up foster kid"*

child borrows an item,
fails to return it

**identity match**
*confirmation*

**reflected appraisal**
*recognition*
*"I understand what it's like to mess up sometimes"*

child returns the item
*relationship begins to form*

**"second order" dynamic**
*proposition*
*"Will you help me bake cookies for everyone?"*

**reference-identity**
becomes more complex
*child sustains engagement*

cookies are baked
*child receives recognition*

**Figure 10.3.** Longer-term relationships are based on recognition, which can open up space for venturing into a "second order" cybernetic process in which a subsystem's "reference signal" (the child's identity in this case) can be modified or even reset. Both parties must adopt an information strategy that embraces uncertainty (the "opposite" of information) about what exactly will emerge.
David Hopping

"Do you live alone, Grandma?" he asked.

"Yes, I do," Bohn replied.

"Your husband's dead?"

"Yes, he is."

"Did you kill him?"

"No."

"Did he get real sick?"

"Yes, he did."

"Do you miss him?"

"Yes."

"Do you cry?"

"Yes."

"Well, I'm going to come and live with you."

"You are?"

"Yes, you need a man in the house."

That night, Debbie Calhoun reports, she found her six-year-old adopted boy intently packing his suitcase, fully intending, it seemed, to carry on the Calhoun family's caring tradition and a new pattern of behavior born of a caring community.[15]

Some seniors had grown up in foster care themselves and were indispens-able companions for some of the most troubled children, bringing an intimate understanding of their fragility and of the debilitating effects of what sociolo-gist Erving Goffman called "spoiled identities."[16]

Al Peña's wife, Loralee, was able to recognize the anger and frustration that shadows many of the children, having grown up in long-term foster care and having spent years trying to discover and understand why.[17] "In my mind," she said, "I was always waiting for my real family to show up. Anger wells up unexpectedly to me. For a child, it's probably like that, and it prob-ably goes further than they expect, so it's scary." When this does happen to kids at Hope Meadows, says Peña, "I want to be there."[18]

The crucible effect also sometimes induced profound transformations of identity in the seniors themselves, even precipitating dramatic resilience ef-fects. When George and Effie King first moved to Hope Meadows, he had begun to experience a serious physical and emotional decline and needed a home health aide for help with routine activities. "I was in a state of with-drawal from the world," he said, "but when I came here, I got involved immediately with the kids and the community and my life began to mean something. I had a goal—to help the kids—and that turned my life around."

Effie would often remark that "I've watched this man come alive again be-cause of this place." Within a few weeks, George would send the home health aide away permanently, as he was now "just too busy" to make time for her.[19]

Psychologist Ann Masten has studied the human factors and environmental conditions promoting socioemotional resilience and offers the following defini-tion: "Resilience refers to a class of phenomena characterized by good outcomes in spite of serious threats to adaptation or development. Research on resilience aims to understand the processes that account for these good outcomes."

The surprising result of resilience research, she writes, is the ordinariness of the phenomena: "What began as a quest to understand the extraordinary has revealed the power of the ordinary. Resilience does not come from rare and special qualities, but from the everyday magic of ordinary, normative hu-man resources in the minds, brains, and bodies of children, in their families and relationships, and in their communities."[20]

Such everyday informational circuits, cultivated formally and informally and (in a sense) stochastically, make up the final layer of the broader IA de-sign for purpose-driven intergenerational communities.


## CLOSING THE LOOP

The 100 percent corner venues within the IGC (morning coffee, weekly potlucks, informational workshops, game nights, etc.), as well as various vol-

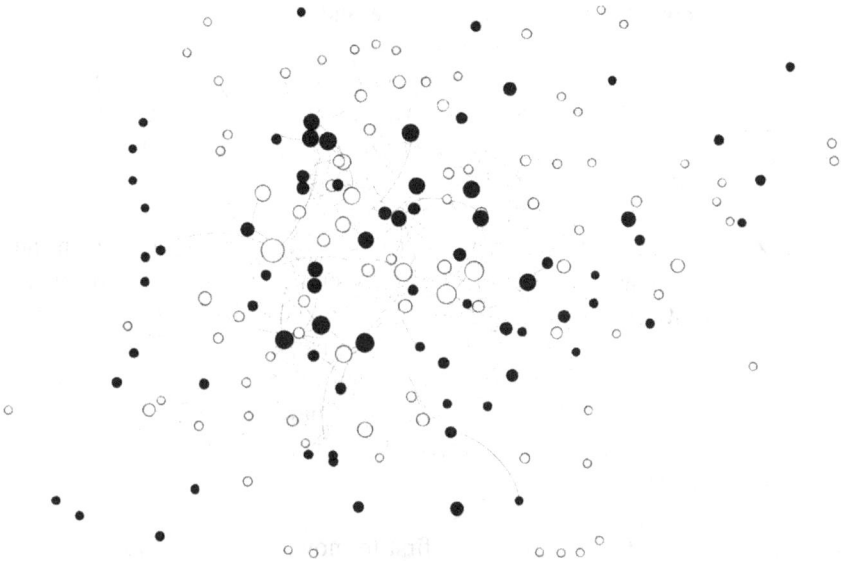

Figure 10.4. Network of especially close senior-child relationships (mentor, "grand-parent") as they accumulated over the first fifteen years of the neighborhood's history. Each line connects a child (solid dot) with one senior (open circle), and represents a relationship capable of functioning in a "crucible" fashion, supporting identity-work and recovery. Multiple seniors connect with multiple children in multiple ways. Larger dots indicate more connections, and recently arrived residents tend to be located on the graph's periphery.
David Hopping

unteer capacities that brought them randomly together with others, afforded opportunities to compare notes and relate experiences or to coordinate ad hoc support to families as needs arose. Mutual reassurance, reframing of problematic behaviors in light of small victories, and little breakthroughs with children as they responded to hundreds of minor acts of care—too numerous and mostly too small to warrant recording and reporting—were celebrated nonetheless in these informal informational circuits.

The emergence of these circuits, through networks that had been scaffolded by more formal programmatic structures, represents a different register of information architecture—that of a myriad of small and transient spaces for unconditional engagement. The crucible pattern, whenever realized in the moment, meant that these would be potentially playful and undetermined and would always imply a tangible and predictable underpinning of security, of tacit commitment and care.

This extended level of (tacit) information architecture was integrated into, and supported through, the more formal programmatic architecture, which prepared the conditions for its emergence and captured and constantly reflected back stories and accounts of small acts of care and recognition into the community. These would then recirculate—through casual conversations at morning coffee or via small posts in the weekly *Seedlings* newsletter, or even via a steady succession of national news media productions and publications (*New York Times*, *Chicago Tribune*, *ABC Nightline*, *60 Minutes II*, *Oprah Winfrey*, and dozens of others).

These sources of "reflected appraisal" further leveraged the small gains and minor moments of achievement and development, valorizing the ethos of care and responsibility, and fed back into the evolving collective neighborhood consciousness as propositions about the identity of Hope Meadows itself.

They also shaped the standard role-identity of "Hope Senior" per se and contributed in this way to the socialization of new arrivals to the neighborhood and program, affording prospective residents a sense of what was expectable and possible.

Al and Loralee had been among the first to move into Hope Meadows, and Marty had been among the first foster-adopted children to arrive. By age six he could be seen carrying Al's gasoline can as the two of them roamed the fifteen-acre neighborhood whacking weeds.

Many years later, Loralee recounted an episode when Al needed to be taken to the hospital and had become distressed at the presence of the ambulance crew. His dementia was advanced by now, and he was fractious, confused, and resisting. Marty, who lived just a few houses away, had noticed the ambulance and come over and quietly talked Al down, reassuring him that he was safe and that things were as they should be and there was no reason to be afraid.

Al had entered a period of life when his own capacity to acquire and use information about his immediate circumstances and status had become severely diminished. What he needed in that moment was access to something else: that same crucible of trust and release that he had helped to proliferate and establish as a canonical resource within the community—a resource that could be invoked spontaneously as the moment might demand, and a basic element of everyday information architecture at Hope Meadows.

*In memory of Debbie Calhoun, 1957–2021*

## NOTES

1. Victor Regnier, *Housing Design for an Increasingly Older Population: Redefining Assisted Living for the Mentally and Physically Frail* (London: Wiley, 2018).

2. Martha Bowman Power and Brenda Krause Eheart, "Adoption, Myth, and Emotion Work: Paths to Disillusionment," *Social Perspectives on Emotion* 3 (1995): 97–120.

3. Lisbeth B. Schorr, *Common Purpose: Strengthening Families and Neighborhoods to Rebuild America* (New York: Doubleday, 1997), 225.

4. Schorr, *Common Purpose*, 225.

5. Regnier, *Housing Design*, 77–78.

6. For more on the application of social network analysis to the dynamics at Hope Meadows, see David Hopping, "Thinking Further Outside the Box: Can Program Evaluation Keep Up with Program Innovation?," in *Changing Welfare*, ed. Rachel A. Gordon and Herbert J. Walberg (Boston: Springer, 2003), 179–199; and David Hopping, "Modeling Hope: Boundary Objects and Design Patterns in a Heartland Heterotopia," in *Where to Live: Informational Aspects in the Internet Era*, ed. William Asprey and Melissa Ocepek (Washington, DC: Rowman and Littlefield, 2021).

7. See for example, Nicholas A. Christakis and James H. Fowler, *Connected: The Surprising Power of Our Social Networks and How They Shape Our Lives* (New York: Little, Brown Spark, 2009).

8. See for example, Martha Bowman Power and Brenda Krause Eheart, "From Despair to Care: A Journey of the Old and the Young at Hope Meadows," *Children and Youth Services Review* 23 (2001): 691–718.

9. Richard Saul Wurman, *Information Architecture* (Lakewood, NJ: Watson-Guptill, 1997).

10. James Kalbach, *Mapping Experiences* (Sebastopol, CA: O'Reilly Media, 2020).

11. Jan E. Stets and Richard T. Serpe, eds., *New Directions in Identity Theory and Research* (Oxford: Oxford University Press, 2016). See also Jan E. Stets, Peter J. Burke, Richard T. Serpe, and Robin Stryker, "Getting Identity Theory (IT) Right," in *Advances in Group Processes*, ed. Shayne R. Thye and Edward J. Lawler (Bingley, UK: Emerald, 2020).

12. Peter J. Burke and Donald C. Reitzes, "An Identity Theory Approach to Commitment," *Social Psychology Quarterly* 54, no. 3 (September 1991): 239–251.

13. See Jan E. Stets, Scott V. Savage, Peter J. Burke, and Phoenicia Fares, "Cognitive and Behavioral Responses to the Identity Verification Process," in *Identity and Symbolic Interaction*, ed. Richard T. Serpe, Robin Stryker, and Brian Powell (Cham, Switzerland: Springer, 2020), 65–88.

14. Ann S. Masten, "Ordinary Magic: Resilience Processes in Development," *American Psychologist* 56, no. 3 (March 2001): 227–238.

15. Wes Smith, *Hope Meadows: Real Life Stories of Healing and Caring from an Inspiring Community* (New York: Berkeley Books, 2001), 209.

16. Erving Goffman, *Stigma: Notes on the Management of Spoiled Identity* (London: Touchstone, 2009).

17. Rob Gurwitt, *Raising a Neighborhood: Hope Meadows* (San Francisco, CA: Civic Ventures, 2001), 10.

18. Rob Gurwitt, "Fostering Hope," *Mother Jones*, March–April 2002.

19. Smith, *Hope Meadows*, 111.

20. Masten, "Ordinary Magic," 235.

## Chapter Eleven

# Mapping the Research on Digital Information Issues for Older Adults

Unmil Karadkar

Earlier chapters in this book have described how information is increasingly a key factor in enhancing the quality of daily life of older Americans—and indeed, the wider populace. The sources of information—government agencies, nongovernmental organizations, and businesses, several of which are included in chapter 1—are responsible for ensuring the accuracy of the disseminated contents. In addition to information from these sources, older adults rely on other, often changing information, such as weather, traffic, or construction updates. They are interested in information for which no official channels exist—for example, updates on friends and family—and consume information that is designed for use by the general public, without accounting for the particular infirmities of old age. They use devices such as tablets, mobile phones, and computers, which are typically designed to appeal to the younger generations, although accessibility features such as increasing text size or adjusting brightness are helpful for reading. In addition to facilitating information access, mobile devices also shape social and communication patterns. Understanding how older adults access, understand, and share information is important for ensuring its relevance and utility. Researchers from a variety of disciplines, including information studies, gerontology, psychology, sociology, computer science, design, and medicine, study the information needs of and the use of software and hardware by older adults.

The authors and editors of this book have benefited from and conducted such research. We have summarized, analyzed, and contextualized scholarly research for telling stories of the lives of older Americans. For example, chapter 3 describes an ethnographic case study of Jane's information ecosystem. This chapter also includes results of a large-scale survey that situates Jane as a typical older American—"two-thirds of Jane's cohort have home broadband, and 92 percent of those who do, access the internet." While other chapters have cited research that is necessary to tell their story, this chapter tells a story of the research being conducted at the intersection of information and aging, as viewed through the lens of published articles. It includes details about my survey of the published research conducted by other scholars, how this research relates to significant milestones such as the release of the iPhone—the first broadly adopted smartphone—the topics covered by researchers, and the demographics they have studied. Description of these aspects helps us understand which populations have received attention and, conversely, which have not and where additional insights are required. Tracing arcs of research studies as well as technological advances helps identify emerging areas and future research trajectories.

## METHODOLOGY

Research findings are published as scholarly books, journal articles, and as conference proceedings by several publishers and made available through their web portals. These portals offer different features for fine-tuning searches by title, topic, or author, and while a few support bulk download of citations, the download formats vary significantly. Thus, locating and downloading articles of interest from tens of publisher portals is a challenging task. A partial remedy is to use citation indexes,[1] which aggregate materials from multiple publishers—for example, Google Scholar[2] (all disciplines) and PubMed[3] (biomedical research). Of these aggregators, Google Scholar likely indexes the highest number of articles, but it does not support fine-tuning the search terms. Viewing ten results at a time, a user must manually sift through thousands to millions of results, which likely include a high percentage of irrelevant articles (false positives). Most major publishers as well as citation indexes do not support bulk download of search results, which hinders tasks such as large-scale filtering, relevance judgment, analysis, and pattern-finding tasks, which are essential for reviewing articles published in research areas such as aging studies, gerontology, or supervised learning algorithms.

In order to overcome these challenges, this review is based on data from two citation index portals: Web of Science[4] (WoS) and Scopus,[5] which allow both fine-tuning and bulk download of search results. WoS result sets can be downloaded in batches of five hundred, a vast improvement over browsing individual results but still a significant task when thousands of matching articles are found. Scopus, in contrast, supports a single download of search results regardless of the number of matching citations. Both are subscription-based services and index articles from a variety of disciplines, including social sciences, physical sciences, life sciences, arts, and humanities. While both sources include articles from major journals and publishers, Scopus also indexes articles from conference proceedings, which are key publication venues in the physical and computational sciences.

I searched for articles of interest using a two-step process, beginning with a trial-and-error phase to identify the best search terms and then using a selected set of terms to download relevant citations. In the first phase, I coupled with the phrase *older adults* a variety of terms, such as *internet*, *web*, *worldwide web*, *information*, *digital information*, *Internet of Things*, *IoT*, *digital devices*, and *mobile devices*, counting and skimming the results to assess their volume, relevance, and uniqueness. This quick task helped identify coarse patterns: for example, terms such as *information* and *web* predominantly returned articles that were outside the scope of this study (a negative, indicating that the search term was too broad), while results for terms such as *Internet of Things* and *IoT* overlapped significantly (a positive, since one is an acronym for the other). Building on this initial assessment, I retrieved matching articles from both WoS and Scopus for the following four keyword searches:

- "older adults" and digital information
- "older adults" and internet
- "older adults" and "Internet of Things"
- "older adults" and mobile devices

The quotation marks indicate that the entire phrase must occur together, exactly as specified, for an article to match, while unquoted words may appear separately in the article. Table 11.1 summarizes the citation counts returned for each search. A quick glance at the table indicates that the number of articles that matched the search term *internet* is significantly higher than those for the terms *mobile devices* and *Internet of Things*, which aligns with the expectation that technologies that have existed longer have also likely been studied and reported on more extensively.

The citations returned for each of these queries were saved and analyzed via ScientoPy[6]—an open-source software for scientometric analysis.[7] ScientoPy ingests and merges saved downloads from both WoS and Scopus data formats to create a single corpus for analysis. In this process, it removes duplicate articles and omits those that are not research articles. Table 11.2 summarizes the results of this operation. The seemingly higher number of duplicates found in the Scopus results is an artifact of the order of processing— ScientoPy read the WoS results before those from Scopus. One hundred and ninety-three duplicate articles were found in the WoS records, likely a result of articles matching multiple searches that I conducted. After this cleaning up

**Table 11.1.   Relevant Articles Retrieved from Web of Science and Scopus**

| Search Terms | Web of Science | Scopus |
|---|---|---|
| "Older adults" and digital information | 376 | 464 |
| "Older adults" and internet | 1,496 | 1,667 |
| "Older adults" and mobile devices | 107 | 521 |
| "Older adults" and "Internet of Things" | 57 | 138 |
| Total | 2,036 | 2,790 |

of the downloaded citations, ScientoPy created a "clean" dataset consisting of 3,065 articles for further analysis.

ScientoPy includes features for analyzing articles using a variety of criteria, including subject areas, author-provided keywords, publisher-provided keywords, author names, institutional affiliations, and countries. The software interface supports filtering results by count and by year—for example, to analyze only the top ten topics between the years 1995 and 2010. A user conducts each analysis separately, and ScientoPy displays a graphical overview and makes available the resulting data for further customization and analysis.

## FINDINGS

An exploratory analysis on the dataset of 3,065 articles illustrates a growing interest in and an expanding scientific community that studies information issues related to older adults. Figure 11.1 displays the articles published by year. The first article reporting on the impact and inclusion of older adults was published in 1993,[8] in the context of broadening the computing community at the College of St. Catherine, a small liberal arts college in Minnesota. This article explicitly mentions training women on technologies such as Gopher, BBS, email, vax notes conferencing, and accommodating the "issues related to the physical limitations of older adult learners." Whether

**Table 11.2.   Article Preprocessing Summary from ScientoPy**

| Articles | Web of Science | Scopus | Total |
|---|---|---|---|
| Search results (table 11.1) | 2,036 | 2,790 | 4,826 |
| Omitted (not research papers) | 59 | 217 | 276 |
| Retained | 1,977 | 2,573 | 4,550 |
| Duplicates | 193 | 1,292 | 1,485 |
| Analyzed | 1,784 | 1,281 | 3,065 |

coincidentally or not, this article was published soon after the debut of the Worldwide Web (in 1991), at the onset of the web-based information access revolution. While there were sporadic articles about "senior citizens" and the use of computers that were published prior to this time frame, a large-scale digital information ecology did not exist and computers were not central to individuals' daily life. The number of articles relating to older adults and information technology has exploded since the year 2000, increasing to five hundred in the year 2020. More than a fifth of the articles in this dataset have been published since January 1, 2020, showcasing the growing publication volume. In the first four months of 2021 alone, 139 articles were indexed by WoS and Scopus, indicating that the trend is continuing.

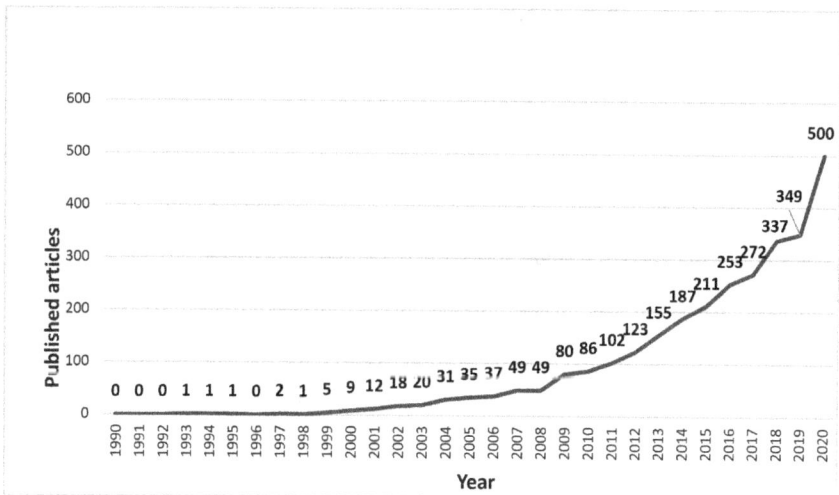

**Figure 11.1. Number of Articles Published Annually.**
Unmil Karadkar

Figure 11.2 groups the articles by the subject area of their publication. Of the 3,065, over 370 articles (more than 10%) have appeared in books, journals, and conferences that self-identify as being related to geriatrics and gerontology. Articles in these publications have consistently led the subject-based tallies since 1998. Other significant topics relate to health publications of various flavors—physical, mental, public, environmental, and occupational (neurosciences, nursing), followed by technology—computer science, engineering, informatics, and information science. Finally, fewer than twenty articles, all since 2012, have appeared in publications related to business, economics, and law, indicating a nascent interest from these disciplines. The data

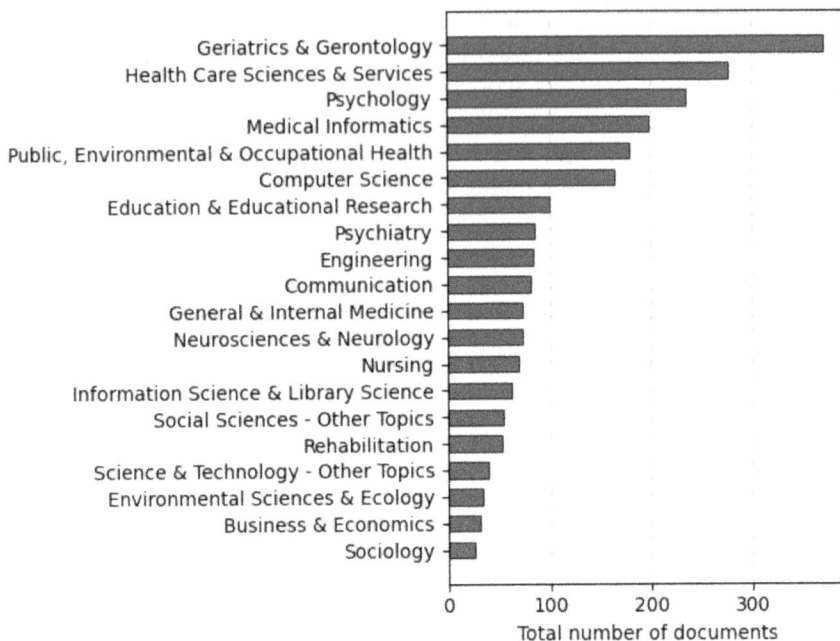

**Figure 11.2.  Top 20 Publication Subject Areas.**
Unmil Karadkar

shows a noticeable spurt in articles published in the top ten subjects in 2009, following the release of Apple's iPhone (2007) and the resulting large-scale adoption of mobile devices.

Many scientific publications enable authors to include keywords and phrases that best convey the topics covered by their article. Such keywords fall into two broad categories: those selected from a publisher-provided list—usually, a controlled vocabulary[9,10]—and those freely chosen by the authors. The ACM computing classification system[11] (CCS) is a hierarchical disciplinary organization system developed by the Association for Computing Machinery (ACM) and used to categorize ACM journal and conference articles in addition to free-form, author-provided keywords. Medical Subject Headings[12] (MeSH), developed and maintained by the National Library of Medicine (NLM), is another such controlled, hierarchical vocabulary. In addition to the terms themselves, the NLM has developed tools,[13] such as the MeSH Browser[14] and MeSH on demand,[15] that help authors find matching terms for their articles. ScientoPy's keyword analysis feature supports the exploration of such publisher-approved as well as author-specified keywords. Table 11.3 shows the one hundred most frequently occurring author-provided

**Table 11.3. Most Frequent Author-Specified Keywords**

| Aging | Health | Technology | Health Technology |
|---|---|---|---|
| Older adults (691) | Dementia (90) | Internet (317) | eHealth (70) |
| Aging (187) | Physical activity (74) | Technology (151) | mHealth (45) |
| Elderly (128) | Depression (65) | Internet use (62) | Telemedicine (43) |
| Aged (53) | Loneliness (52) | Social media (62) | e-Health (29) |
| Seniors (46) | Cognition (48) | Mobile devices (53) | Telehealth (29) |
| Older people (45) | Exercise (41) | Usability (52) | Mobile health (26) |
| Age (42) | Mental health (33) | Internet of Things (47) | Digital health (24) |
| Ageing (39) | Health (32) | ICT (39) | eHealth literacy (20) |
| Older adult (35) | Social isolation (32) | Smartphone (36) | |
| Geriatrics (21) | Well-being (31) | Mobile phone (36) | *Aging Technology* |
| Gerontology (16) | Chronic disease (30) | Assistive technology (32) | Gerontechnology (32) |
| Adults (15) | COVID-19 (29) | Computers (31) | Technology adoption (24) |
| | Caregivers (26) | Information technology (25) | Digital literacy (23) |
| *Research* | Cognitive impairment (24) | IoT (21) | Technology acceptance (23) |
| Systematic review (27) | Anxiety (24) | Information and communication technology (19) | |
| | | | *Other* |
| Survey (21) | Mild cognitive impairment (22) | Information and communication technologies (18) | Digital divide (104) |
| | | | Health literacy (46) |
| Randomized controlled trial (20) | Ambient assisted living (19) | Artificial intelligence (17) | Quality of life (39) |
| Review (17) | Hearing loss (19) | Mobile phones (17) | Social support (35) |
| Qualitative research (16) | Alzheimer disease (18) | Participatory design (17) | Self-management (34) |
| | Memory (18) | Health information technology (17) | Communication (31) |
| | Falls (17) | Mobile technology (16) | Accessibility (26) |
| | Prevention (17) | Sensors (16) | Health promotion (24) |
| | Frailty (17) | Online (16) | Education (22) |
| | Health care (17) | Social networks (16) | Health information (20) |
| | Primary care (16) | Computer use (15) | Digital inclusion (20) |
| | Insomnia (16) | Internet of things (IoT) (14) | Gender (19) |
| | Intervention (15) | | Self-efficacy (18) |
| | Disability (14) | | Activities of daily living (15) |
| | Rehabilitation (14) | | Attitudes (15) |
| | | | Design (15) |

keywords along with the number of articles in which they appear. I have presented the keywords as retrieved, without modifying for grammar, spelling, or capitalization, nor merged similar terms. For the purposes of this discussion, I have separated these as relating to aging, health, technology, intersecting categories among these three, the research process, and those that do not belong to any of these categories. These categories are illustrative and certainly not definitive. A discerning reader will find plenty to disagree with. These keywords highlight the areas of emphasis within the older adult–information domain and facilitate the discussion of similarities and differences in the descriptive terminology. The keyword *aging* first appears in the literature in 1995, and the most popular current term, *older adults*, has been used consistently since 2001. Health issues and experiences typically associated with older age have been identified most frequently, indicating their dominance in the number of studies conducted: dementia, physical activities, depression, loneliness, and cognition top this list. One heartening feature among these topics is that research has included the study of mental health, cognitive, and social issues in addition to physical infirmities, indicating that scholars are interested in tackling different aspects of aging. The COVID-19 pandemic appears in the top one hundred terms with twenty-nine mentions in articles published in just over a year. Technology topics include recent developments (social media, Internet of Things, mobile devices, artificial intelligence) as well as the study of inclusive design and assessments of technology use by older adults.

The keywords also include the adoption of digital technology in health care (Health-Technology) and the adoption and adaptation of digital devices by and for older adults (Aging-Technology). Other topics that have received scholarly attention are health literacy, gender issues, digital divides, and attitudes of older adults toward technology. Finally, topics in the "Research" category describe the research methods used to conduct these studies. Relatively few articles list methods as keywords, and reviews of existing studies, much like this chapter, top this category.

A quick glance within the categories points out a glaring problem with these keywords—several are repeated in some form. For example, spelling variations American (aging) and British (ageing), singular-plural variants (older adult/s, information and communication technology/ies), abbreviations (ICT—information and communication technology, IoT—Internet of Things, mHealth—mobile health), and variants (mobile phones versus smartphones versus mobile devices or eHealth versus e-Health). Such variations can be attributed to a variety of causes. Some are regional variations. Use of abbreviations may indicate familiarity that emerges with the adoption of technology (e.g., IoT). Yet others indicate an evolution of terminology—while *mobile phones* and *mobile devices* have both been used since 2006, the earliest use of the term *smartphone* in this dataset dates to 2013. These variations in author-provided keywords highlight the challenges in locating relevant articles through query-based search techniques.

In order to enhance the reliability of indexes, research publishers have developed and adopted controlled vocabularies such as CCS and MeSH described previously. However, while the individual vocabularies contain unique terms, the different vocabularies were developed without coordination, a problem that comes up when searching for articles from multiple publishers, as illustrated in table 11.4. Like table 11.3, this table also displays the terms as retrieved from the citation index, which, in turn, retrieved them from the publisher's website. A glaring feature of this table is the use of all-caps terms, which researchers do not use to describe their work but are commonly used in classification and database systems. Other than the difference in case use, the variation in terms used is similar to that used by researchers. In order to allow comparison between the two lists, table 11.4 groups the terms using the same categories as table 11.3 where possible. Within the categories, the publisher keywords have not kept up with the quickly advancing intersection of technology with aging or with health. While authors have used terms like *gerontechnology*—a term used to describe studies conducted at the intersection of gerontology and technology—initially in 2004 and consistently since 2011, and mobile health or mHealth since 2012, these terms have not yet been included in the controlled vocabularies. Thus, the stability of usage provided by controlled vocabularies complements the avant-garde terms chosen by authors to describe their novel contributions, demonstrating the utility of each type of descriptor. It is important to mention that table 11.4 only shows terms from the controlled vocabularies that were applied by article authors and not the vocabularies in their entirety.

Within the aging category, the controlled vocabularies distinguish between old and very old adults (one number used is over eighty years), while researchers' keywords do not distinguish between these groups. The descriptors in the health categories are more restricted as well and do not adequately cover cognitive issues or physical impairments such as frailty and falls. The vocabularies are more extensively developed to label gender-specific research findings and research methods, while researchers' keywords do not typically use these terms. The only geographic area identified is the United States, in 121 articles, but the dataset includes articles that report on studies conducted in several other locations, such as Singapore, the Netherlands, China, Taiwan, and South Korea, indicating that those studies were published in journals that do not label geographic areas. Corresponding to the mention of the United States in the keywords, authors are predominantly affiliated with universi-

**Table 11.4. Most Frequent Publisher-Specified Keywords**

| Aging | Health | Technology | Health-Technology |
|---|---|---|---|
| Aged (810) | HEALTH (270) | INTERNET (928) | Telemedicine (137) |
| OLDER-ADULTS (695) | Depression (148) | TECHNOLOGY (260) | |
| Middle aged (381) | CARE (129) | INFORMATION (210) | *Human Descriptors* |
| Adult (321) | Exercise (109) | INTERNET USE (150) | Female (647) |
| Older adults (304) | DEMENTIA (106) | Human computer interaction (148) | Male (642) |
| Age (185) | LONELINESS (100) | Mobile devices (81) | Human (549) |
| "Aged, 80 and over" (175) | Cognition (95) | COMPUTER USE (68) | Humans (445) |
| Aging (153) | PHYSICAL-ACTIVITY (73) | Devices (67) | PEOPLE (173) |
| Very elderly (132) | RISK (73) | Internet of Things (66) | GENDER (56) |
| Young adult (83) | INTERVENTIONS (63) | Computer (66) | POPULATION (46) |
| Adolescent (69) | Health care (59) | Mobile application (62) | |
| Age factors (57) | Physiology (54) | Information processing (61) | *Other* |
| ADULTS (53) | INTERVENTION (53) | INFORMATION-TECHNOLOGY (60) | Article (333) |
| | Geriatric assessment (52) | Mobile applications (60) | EDUCATION (130) |
| *Research* | ANXIETY (51) | ONLINE (59) | United States (121) |
| Controlled study (119) | Physical activity (50) | Smartphone (59) | COMMUNICATION (106) |
| Questionnaire (114) | OUTCOMES (47) | Usability (48) | IMPACT (105) |
| Priority journal (101) | Chronic disease (46) | User interfaces (48) | SOCIAL SUPPORT (98) |
| Procedures (94) | | | DIGITAL DIVIDE (94) |
| PREVALENCE (87) | | | Quality of life (91) |
| Major clinical study (82) | | | LIFE (88) |

Review (71)
RANDOMIZED CONTROLLED-
  TRIAL (69)
Methodology (60)
Randomized controlled trial (59)
METAANALYSIS (51)
Qualitative research (51)
Human experiment (50)

SUPPORT (86)
QUALITY-OF-LIFE (77)
Psychology (75)
ADOPTION (74)
PERFORMANCE (73)
ACCEPTANCE (71)
ATTITUDES (68)
Design (66)
Independent living (65)
BEHAVIOR (64)
Health promotion (64)
MANAGEMENT (57)
Clinical article (57)
Health literacy (55)
LITERACY (51)
ACCESS (50)
HEALTH INFORMATION (49)
PROGRAM (49)
Knowledge (49)
Health education (47)
PERCEPTIONS (46)

ties in the United States and Canada, with those with European affiliations being the second-largest geographic group. While this dominance of articles reporting on the experiences and needs of those from the developed countries bodes well for older Americans, these studies leave out the experiences of older populations in the rest of the world or, worse, could be generalized inappropriately, assuming that the reported experiences are representative of those encountered everywhere.

Another important highlight from the tables is that both author and publisher keywords emphasize the intersection between health, age, and technology but leave out other key aspects of our increasingly technology-enabled aging process. Only fifteen articles relate to "activities of daily living" and nineteen mention "ambient assisted living," all since 2014. As older adults adopt technology for other activities, future research should investigate the nature, quality, and value added by this adoption. The trajectory of the research trailing technology introduction by about two years for the Worldwide Web, social networks (Facebook, for example), and mobile phones indicates that researchers will soon turn their attention to the broader information needs of older Americans.

Research articles are also recognizing that impairments exist on a spectrum, as demonstrated by the use of terms such as *mild cognitive impairment* (in addition to *cognitive impairment*) and *hearing loss* (as opposed to *deafness*) and that changes in communication or activity patterns (indicated by the studies on "loneliness" and "physical exercise") can improve the quality of life. Younger and older Americans alike have adopted video-conferencing apps such as Zoom, WhatsApp, and Skype to stay in touch with their friends and family during the COVID-19 pandemic. Perhaps the breadth of communication options afforded by such apps will result in their long-term adoption, providing intermediate relief for issues such as loneliness.

## LIMITATIONS

While this review of 3,065 articles provides a significant insight into the threads of research that have been followed over the last three decades, it is neither exhaustive nor definitive. First, the reliance on the two major citation indexes leaves out scholarship that these indexes do not cover. WoS and Scopus predominantly index articles in English, to the exclusion of scholarship conducted elsewhere around the world in other languages. Within the indexes, the retrieval of relevant articles is likely not complete due to the limitations of search algorithms and the variation in terminology adopted by authors and publishers to describe their research. Finally, I have analyzed the metadata of the articles but have not read each article, which makes it harder to capture the nuances within and between the research studies.

## EMERGING TRENDS

Older adults' increasing acceptance and adoption of digital technology is well recognized. However, we are only beginning to study systematically the impact of this change on areas beyond health. As devices and sensors are increasingly embedded in the lives of older Americans, what does this mean for the data generated about their lives? Who will control this data, and how will this data be used to improve their quality of life? How do older Americans think about privacy and data collection issues?

While the studies regarding the breadth of activities being conducted by older Americans are encouraging, the differences in adoption by adults of different socioeconomic strata and, conversely, the impact of technology adoption on their socioeconomic status are still unclear. Technology adoption as well as the ongoing COVID-19 pandemic have affected several aspects of the aging life, including national and local economies, communication, living situations, and work practices, the effect of which on older Americans will need to be investigated, especially as the pandemic subsides and the health situation normalizes.

Increasing life spans around the globe have captured the attention of policy makers as well as researchers. Since 2014, the Social Sciences and Humanities Research Council of Canada has funded the Aging+Communication+Technology project,[16] which brings together an international coalition of aging-technology researchers. Explicitly recognizing that the studies of older adults often revolve around the topics of technology and health, the Volkswagen Foundation[17] has announced research funding to support humanistic inquiry of aging populations in Europe.[18] Titled "Challenges and Potentials for Europe: The Greying Continent," this program challenges researchers to study the transformative impact of the aging population on individuals, governments, business, and civil society. This funding opportunity specifies that the research projects will be led by researchers in the humanities and social or cultural sciences and that those in life or natural sciences and data or technological sciences act in supporting roles.

At the transnational level, the United Nations has declared 2021–2030 as the "decade of healthy aging,"[19] an initiative that aims to foster global collaborations of "governments, civil society, international agencies, professionals, academia, the media, and the private sector to improve the lives of older people, their families, and the communities in which they live." This initiative explicitly recognizes the role of technology in enhancing the quality of life for older adults. A key acknowledgment within this initiative is the need to conduct more research and gather empirical data about the lifestyles of aging adults. Older people are living longer and more diverse lives. Over a billion people around the world are over sixty years old. Developing information resources and gathering reliable data is necessary to support older Americans in accomplishing their goals in their golden years.

## NOTES

1. Wikipedia, "Citation Indexes," accessed July 27, 2021, https://en.wikipedia.org/wiki/Citation_index.

2. Google Scholar indexes research articles across disciplines. While Google does not publish the number of indexed articles, estimates run into hundreds of millions of articles. Google Scholar, accessed July 27, 2021, http://scholar.google.com/.

3. PubMed is developed and maintained by the National Library of Medicine, National Institutes of Health (https://pubmed.ncbi.nlm.nih.gov). It indexes over thirty-two million biomedical research articles as of May 2021.

4. Web of Science (WoS; https://clarivate.com/webofsciencegroup/solutions/web-of-science/) is a subscription-based service offered by Clarivate Analytics, which many large universities subscribe to. I accessed this service through the University of Graz. WoS provides access to over 171 million articles as of May 2021.

5. Scopus (http://www.scopus.com/) is a subscription-based service provided by Elsevier. I accessed this service through the University of Graz. As of January 2021, Scopus indexed over seventy-eight million articles.

6. ScientoPy (http://scientopy.com/en/) is an open source, freely available tool for scientometric analysis described in the research article J. Ruiz-Rosero, G. Ramirez-Gonzalez, and J. Viveros-Delgado, "Software Survey: ScientoPy, a Scientometric Tool for Topics Trend Analysis in Scientific Publications," *Scientometrics* 121 (2019): 1165–1188.

7. Overreliance on scientometric analysis for incentivizing and rewarding research has faced significant criticism. This study uses a software designed for scientometric analysis because it facilitates convenient data processing. It does not subscribe to or adopt the critiqued scholarly productivity and reward metrics.

8. C. Krey, "Expanding the Campus Computing Community: User Support of Non-traditional and Distance Learners at a Small, Liberal Arts College for Women," *Proceedings of the 21st Annual ACM SIGUCCS Conference on User Services* (November 1993): 288–291, https://doi.org/10.1145/263814.263902.

9. "Controlled Vocabulary," Wikipedia, accessed May 2021, https://en.wikipedia.org/wiki/Controlled_vocabulary.

10. P. Harpring, "What Are Controlled Vocabularies?," in *Introduction to Controlled Vocabularies: Terminology for Art, Architecture, and Other Cultural Works,*

ed. M. Baca (Los Angeles, CA: Getty Research Institute, 2010), http://www.getty
.edu/research/publications/electronic_publications/intro_controlled_vocab/what.pdf.

11. "ACM Computing Classification System," Association for Computing Machinery, accessed May 2021, https://dl.acm.org/ccs.

12. "MeSH Home," National Library of Medicine, accessed May 2021, https://www.nlm.nih.gov/mesh/meshhome.html.

13. "Suggestions for Finding Author Keywords Using MeSH Tools," National Library of Medicine, accessed May 2021, https://www.nlm.nih.gov/mesh/authors.html.

14. "MeSH Browser," National Library of Medicine, accessed May 2021, https://meshb.nlm.nih.gov/search.

15. "MeSH on Demand," National Library of Medicine, accessed May 2021, https://meshb.nlm.nih.gov/MeSHonDemand.

16. ACT Project, accessed July 27, 2021, https://www.actproject.ca/.

17. Volkswagen Foundation, accessed May 2021, https://www.volkswagenstiftung.de.

18. "Challenges and Potentials for Europe: The Greying Continent," Volkswagen Stiftung, accessed May 2021, https://www.volkswagenstiftung.de/en/funding/our-funding-portfolio-at-a-glance/challenges-for-europe.

19. "UN Decade of Healthy Aging," World Health Organization, accessed May 2021, https://www.who.int/initiatives/decade-of-healthy-ageing.

# Index

Page references for tables, textboxes, and figures are italicized.

60 Plus Association, *11*, 102–4, 105, 107. *See also* organizations

AARP (formerly American Association of Retired Persons), 2, *9*, *69*, *75*, 91–102, *103*; competitor organizations, 102–11, 112; criticism of, 95–96, *103*, 105–6, 110, 114n12; diversity of membership, as concern of, *94*, 99, 101; health/health care, as concern of, 96, 97, 99–100; history of, 94–96; information delivery means, 99–101, 116n45; as information organization, 91, 94, 97, 98–102, 111–12, 152, *211*; issues addressed by, *93–94*, 114n8; Medicare, as concern of, *93*, 96, 99, 149, 152–53; as political organization, 92, 94, 96–98; Social Security, as concern of, *93*, 97, 99. *See also* organizations
ACM. *See* Association for Computing Machinery
Affordable Care Act (ACA). *See* Patient Protection and Affordable Care Act
ageism, 126–27, 134, 184

aging: active aging, 164; activities of daily living (ADLs), 165, 166–67; aging in community, 248; and cognitive processing, 20–23, 28–30; falling, as consequence of, 170; falling, monitoring/prevention of, 170–71, *172*; "fourth age," 65, 81; infirmities associated with, 18, 20, 40, 274; in an information society, 127; "old," defined, 123; "old old," defined, 123; research on, considerations related to, 31–32, 35–37, 38, 48, 49–50, 53, 57n39; stereotypes about, 81; "third age"/"younger old," 49, 65, 81, 82; wandering, as a consequence of, 171. *See also* successful aging
aging in place, 163–64; early independence systems, 165–67; independence and, 164–65, 184; modern independence systems, 167–69
American Association of Retired Persons. *See* AARP
American Seniors Association (ASA), 110–11

279

Andrus, Ethel Percy, 94, 95
Association for Computing Machinery (ACM), 49, 268
Association of Mature American Citizens (AMAC), 107–10, 112, 121n100

Biden, Joseph R., 102
Bohorquez, Claudia Grisales, 129, 130–32, 137
boyd, danah, 225
Burke, Peter, 254
Bush, George W., 97, 104

Christ Above Politics (CAP), 105–6, 112
Clinton, William J., 96–97, 110
cognitive ability: aging and cognitive processing, 20–23, 28–30; bottom-up processing, 26, 27; brain training, 34, 35–36, 37–38; crystallized intelligence, 22–23, 24–25, 28, 44, 51–52; fluid intelligence, 22–23, 24–25, 28, 31, 44, 55n19; information "out there" vs. knowledge, 24–26; information retrieval, 44–47; interactions of life and, 28, 30, 33, 38, 45, 47, 48, 53; personal space of information (PSI), 51; skill acquisition, 33, 34, 36, 39; skill transfer, 34, 37, 39; top-down processing, 26–27, 48, 56n29; "training to function" hypothesis, 33–38; "use it to keep it (longer)" hypothesis, 31–33. *See also* memory
cognitive decline:
as concern of older Americans, 20; inevitability of, 33, 38, 41; interventions to compensate for, 41, 42–47; interventions to prevent, 28–31, 33–38, 39; research on, considerations related to, 31–32, 35–37, 38, 55n15, 57n39. *See also* memory

computer (laptop/desktop), use of by older people, 2, 7–8, 65, 78, 80, 177, 200, 201, 212
COVID-19 pandemic, *75*, 79, 83, 99, 274, 275; tele-communities and, 204–5, 209, 213–14, 215–16

Davis, Leonard, 94, 95, 114n11
Deming, W. Edwards, 85

Ellis, Katrina, 209, 212, 216

Fisher, Karen E., 78–79
foster-adoptive families, 247, 248–49

Geertz, Clifford, 65, 84
genealogy: access to information and, 223–24; belonging and, 224, 226; communication/collaboration and, 221, 222–23, 239; genetic genealogy and, 228; information management and, 226; information technology and, 226–27, 235–36; kinship and, 223–24, 226, 241, 243; online services, 234, 235
genetic genealogy, 221–22; belonging and, 227, 243–44; challenges in, 228–29; communication/collaboration and, 235–36, 238; family tree data, 234–35; forensic genealogy, 239–40, 241; genetically unrelated matches, 232–33; information types used in, 229–30; kinship and, 237, 238, 239, 240, 241, 242; online services, 227–28, 229, 230–43; privacy considerations, 229, 231, 233, 235–42; tasks of, 227–30
Gilleard, Chris, 82
Goffman, Erving, 258
Granovetter, Mark, 14n9

Health Care and Education Reconciliation Act of 2010, 145. *See also* Patient Protection and Affordable Care Act health insurance, in the US: affordability, and older people, 150, 157; decision-making about, by older people, 156–58; health insurance literacy, 143–44, 150–51, 154–56, 157; information sources, 151–53; intersectionality and knowledge of, 151, 153; "Medigap" policies/ Medicare supplement insurance, 147, 159n15; overview of, 144. *See also* Health Care and Education Reconciliation Act of 2010; Medicare; Patient Protection and Affordable Care Act

Higgs, Paul, 82

Hope Meadows, 247–52; background, 248–49; children living in, 254, 255; information flow in, 252–54; Intergenerational Center (IGC), 249–51, 258; senior residents, as caregivers for adopted children, 247, 249, 255–56, 258; senior residents' design/build-out of, 249–50, 252; socialization of new residents, 260

identity theory, 254–55, *256, 257*

Ilyes, Petra, 225

infirmities, of older people, 18, 20, 40, 65; tools/procedures addressing, 40–41

information architecture, 247, 253; the "100 percent corner" as design pattern of, 248; circuits of information as feature of, 248, 252, 255, 258; planned-community design and, 254, 258, 259–60

information behavior: accessing of information, 56n21; collecting of information, 72, *73,* 80, 81; digital literacy, 127, 137; drift, 236, 239; within family networks, 222–23; informatics life course, 127–28, 133, 134; information ownership, 243–44; information retrieval, 44–48; information-seeking behavior, 3,

13, 79; of older people, 1, 13, 63, 80–81, 83–84, 263; personal space of information (PSI), 51; social engagement and, 83; types of, 72. *See also* information technology, help with

information ecosystem, 63, 66, 68–73, *75,* 84

information flow, 236, 238, 244; the "100 percent corner," 249–52, 258; in circuits, 248, 259; in family/ kinship networks, 221, 222, 223, 226; social network analysis and, 252–53; technology and, 225

information infrastructure, 67, 73–80, 84; community-based information infrastructure, 133, 134–36, 137, 139; content of, 74;

internet as component of, 79–80; management of, 75–77; physical component of, 73–75, 77; spatial component of, 76–78

information issues: ageism and, 126–27, 134; digital divide, 124–25, 127, 208, 216–17; disability divide, 200; of older people with disabilities, 3–4, 199, 201–202; of older people, in general, 5–6, 8, 65, 80, 127

information sources, for older people, 7, 68, *69,* 72, 73, *75,* 263; on health insurance, 151–53; libraries as, 8; organizations as, 7, 102–3, 106, 108–11, 112

information studies, 1; information-seeking behavior, as topic of, 3–6, 44–47, 67, 79; information sources, as topic of, 6, 68; methodological considerations, 48, 49–50, 53, 63, 66–67; of older people, 52–53, 63, 137, 182, 263

information studies, of older people: challenges to, 2–3; document processing, as topic of, 42–44; emerging trends in, 275–76; gaps in, 274, 275; increasing number of,

266–67; informatics life course, as topic of, 127; information-retrieval interfaces, as topic of, 44–47; information-seeking behavior, as topic of, 4–6, 67; information technology help, as topic of, 128–37; information technology use, as topic of, 7; publication venues for, 264, 267; and technological improvement, 48–50; tele-communities, as topic of, 204–7, 212–14; topics of, 267, *268–69*, 270–71, *272–73*
information technology: cognitive decline mitigation and, 41–47, 50; full-screen text editors, 42–44; genealogy and, 226–27, 235–36; genetic genealogy and, 226, 227, 229, 230–43; improvement of and older people, 48–49, 127, 177–78, 183–84; information retrieval and, 44–48; privacy concerns and, 165, 171, 181, 182–83, 229, 231, 233, 235–46; quality of life and, 6, 83; social connections of older people and, 177–79; use of, by older people, 7–8, 46–47, 52–53, 65, 79–80, 123, 138, 263. *See also* information architecture; Internet of Things
information technology, older people and help with, 123, 125–26, 128, 129–30; agents, not users, 131–32, 138; building digital mazeways, 133–34, 138–39; each one teach one/collective intelligence, 128, 137; experts-together, 136, 139; informatics moment, 125–26, 131, 133, 134, 136, 138; nonjudgmental awareness, 136, 139; shaping community-based information infrastructure, 134–36, 139; strategic patience, 132–33, 138
internet, 8, 65, 67, 73; as component of information infrastructure, 79–80; information sharing and, 128; limited access to and older people, 199, 208, 210, 212, 214; search services, 45–46, 47, 48, 79, 106
Internet of Things (IoT), 163; chronic health conditions of older people and, 175–76; concerns of older people about, 163–64, 171, 173, 180, 181–82; design considerations of devices for older people, 169, 183; exercise by older people and, 174–75; falls by older people and, 170–71; family networks of older people and, 178–79; health management of older people and, in general, 176–77; independence of older people outside the home and, 168–69, 171–72; nutrition of older people and, 173–74; peer networks of older people, 179; security of older people and, 180–83; sleep of older people and, 174; voice assistants, 167–68; wandering by older people and, 171–72;

James, William, 36

Kahn, R. L., 18, 19–20
Kay, Marilyn, 129, 130–32, 135, 136, 137

Lenstra, Noah, 130, 132, 133, 136
Lévy, Pierre, 128, 137
libraries, use of by older people, 8, 65, 74, *75*, 129–30; health insurance literacy and, 153; technology help and, 126

Marwick, Alice E., 225
Masten, Ann, 258
media: online news, 79; print, *7*, *75*; radio, *7*, 63, 70, 74; television (TV), *7*, 8, 63, 65, 70, 73, 74
Medicaid, 146, 147, 150
Medicare, 3, *7*, 92, *93*, *103*, 108, 110, 111, 150, 151; history of, 145–46; overview of, 143; Part A, 143, *148*;

Part B, 143, *148*; Part C, *148*; Part D, 143, 144, *148*, 154; sources of information about, 147, 149, 151–52; structure of, 147; Veterans Administration health insurance and, 145

Medicare Catastrophic Coverage Act, 104, 118n64

memory, 24, 25–26, 34; aids to, 42–43, 53; long-term memory, 37; short-term memory, 39, 41, 55n19, 56n26; working memory, 37, 41, 43, 44, 55n19. See also cognitive ability; cognitive decline

Morville, Peter, 253

National Association of Conservative Seniors (NAOCS), 111

National Library Service for the Blind and Print Disabled (US Library of Congress), 3, 14n6

Nissenbaum, Helen, 224, 225

Obama, Barack H., 97, 103, 145

Obamacare. *See* Patient Protection and Affordable Care Act

Ochs, Carsten, 225

older people: agency of and technology, 131–32, 134, 136, 138, 139, 169, 178–79, 181, 183; aging-in-place technology and, 164–69; baby boomers in the US as, 49–50, 82; blogging by, 201, 202; as caregivers for adopted children, 247, 249, 255–56, 258; chronic health conditions of and technology, 175–76; cognitive decline/impairment, as concern of, 20; concerns of, in general, 92; concerns about monitoring technology, 163–64, 171, 173, 180, 181–82; demographic characteristics of in the US, 1–2, 19, 64–65; digital security of and technology, 182; with disabilities, 4–5, 199, 200–202, 214–15; diversity of, in the US, 3, 4,

99, 216; exercise by and technology, 174–75; falls by and technology, 170–71; family networks and technology and, 178–79; financial scams and, 181, 182; health/health care, as concern of, 1, 2, *5*, 6, 68, *70*, 92, 96, 143–44; health insurance decision-making of, 156–58; health insurance literacy and, 143, 150–51, 154–56, 157; health management of, 173, 184; health management of and technology, in general, 176–77; independence of, in general, 164–65, 184; independence of, outside the home, 168–69; information consumption by, in general, 63, 80–81; information-seeking behavior of, 3, 13, 65, 70–72, 79; information technology help and, 80, 123, 126, 128, 129–33, 135–36, 137; information technology use by, 7–8, 65, 123, 127; information transmission, modes of, 79; internet access and, 199, 208, 210, 212, 214; isolation/loneliness and, 164, 177, 204–5, 212, 213; nutrition of and technology, 173–74; "old," defined, 2; peer networks of and technology, 179; physical security of and technology, 180–81; quality of life of, 2, 6, 85; retirement, 2, *6*, 31, 49, 57n39, 64, 66, 81, 83; safety of and technology, in general, 169–70, 178; security of and technology, in general, 180, 182–83; self-perceptions of, 82, 85n1; sleep of and technology, 174; social connections of and technology, in general, 177, 179–80; social media use by, 65, *69*, *75*, 200; wandering by and technology, 171–72. *See also* ageism; aging; cognitive ability; Medicare; Patient Protection and Affordable Care Act; successful aging; tele-communities organizations (public/private), serving older Americans, 8–13, 15n16, 112; as information sources, 102–3, 106, 108–11, 112; Medicare, as concern of, 92; membership-benefit plus advocacy organizations, 107–11; with a political focus, 102–5; with a religious focus, 105–6; Social Security, as concern of, 92. *See also* AARP

Patient Protection and Affordable Care Act (Affordable Care Act/ACA; Obamacare), 97, 102, *108*, 110, 145. *See also* Health Care and Education Reconciliation Act of 2010
Peña, Al, 249–50, 258, 260
Peña, Loralee, 258, 260
Pettigrew, Karen E. *See* Fisher, Karen E.
Pickering, Andrew, 226
privacy: genetic genealogy and, 229, 231, 233, 235–42; Internet of Things and concerns regarding, 165, 171, 181, 182–83; practice of, 226, 236–42; theories of, 224–26

Regnier, Victor, 248, 250, 251–52
retirement communities, 129, 247. *See also* Hope Meadows
Rosenfeld, Lou, 253
Rowe, J. W., 18, 19–20

Salthouse, T. A., 31–32, 49
Schorr, Lisbeth, 249
seniors centers, 123, 126, 208–9, 214, 215–16. *See also* Silver Center
Seniors Coalition, 104, 105, 107. *See also* organizations
seniors communities. *See* retirement communities
Silver Center, 207, 209–14, 216–17. *See also* seniors centers

smartphones, use of by older people, 7–8, 65, 78, 79–80, 210; disadvantages of, 208; vs. landline phones, 199, 202; monitoring of wandering by, 172
Smith, Wes, 256
social media, 112; genetic genealogy and, 235; use of, by older people, 65, *69*, *75*, 200
social networks: of older people, 157, 164, 177, 179, 213, 248; social network analysis, 252
Social Security program. *See under* US Social Security Administration
socioemotional resilience, 255–56, 258
Stets, Jan, 254
Strathern, Marilyn, 243
successful aging: behaviors/interventions fostering, 20, 28, 39–40, 83; crystallized and fluid intelligences and, 23–25; definition of (MacArthur model), 17; factors for, 17–19; information tools ("cognitive spectacles") fostering, 28, 40–47, 50; interactions of life and, 28, 30, 45, 53; mental exercise and, 31, 32–33, 39, 72; personal space of information (PSI) and, 51; physical exercise and, 31, 72, 90n60; societal benefits of, 19–20. *See also* aging

tele-community: asynchronous/synchronous combination, 203; asynchronous tele-community, 199, 201–207, 214–15; defined, 199; synchronous tele-community, 199–200, 207, 209–14, 215–17
telephones (landline), 199, 201–202. *See also* smartphones
ties (weak/strong), *7*, 14n9
Thompson, Mindy, 131, 133
Thorndike, Edward, 36
Trump, Donald J., 102, *103*, 121n100

United Seniors Association, 104–5, 107
US Social Security Administration, 2, *7*, *11*; Social Security program, 92, *93*, 97, *103*, 104, 108, 110, 146, *148*

Veterans Health Administration (VHA), 145
video-conferencing apps, 274

Williams, Kate, 129, 130
Wilson, Norvena, 209, 212, 216, 217

xPress, 201–202, 204–7, 213, 214, 215

Zola, David, 135
Zuboff, Shoshana, 132

# About the Editor
# and the Contributors

## ABOUT THE EDITOR

**William Aspray** is Senior Research Fellow at the Charles Babbage Institute at the University of Minnesota, Twin Cities. He has previously held leadership positions at the Babbage Institute, IEEE History Center, and Computing Research Association and senior faculty positions in the information schools at Indiana (Bloomington), Texas (Austin), and Colorado (Boulder). He has also taught at Harvard, Penn, Virginia Tech, and Williams. His research interests include information history, computing history, information behavior, information policy, underrepresentation in computing, food studies, and history and philosophy of mathematics. His most relevant publications to this book are *Everyday Information* (ed. with Barbara Hayes, MIT Press, 2011) and *Deciding Where to Live* (ed. with Melissa Ocepek, Rowman & Littlefield, 2021). He received his PhD in history of science from the University of Wisconsin, Madison.

## ABOUT THE CONTRIBUTORS

**Pallabi Bhowmick** is a PhD student in informatics at Indiana University and is being advised by Professor Katie A. Siek. Her research interest is broadly focused on developing Internet of Things devices to support older adults in living more independently using technology. She is particularly interested in investigating how older adults connect with each other and empowering them to build better social connectivity with the help of technology, thereby reducing social isolation. She earned her B.Tech degree in computer science and engineering in India and pursued an MS degree in informatics from the

Technical University of Munich, Germany. She worked as a developer in Wipro and Intel before joining Indiana University, Bloomington.

**Claudia Grisales Bohorquez** is a doctoral student in informatics at the University of Illinois at Urbana-Champaign. She is interested in participatory design of information systems and technologies that can support communal work in a damaged world. Her research looks at the possibilities of design to contribute to futures of collaboration, care, and reconciliation in areas of entangled environmental and armed conflict in Colombia. She is also a researcher for the Center of Alternatives to Development.

**Robin Brewer** is an assistant professor in the School of Information at the University of Michigan. She holds a courtesy appointment in computer science and engineering and affiliation with the Digital Studies Institute. Her research lies at the intersection of human-computer interaction, accessibility, and computer science. Robin's recent work focuses on how voice-based interfaces can improve information access for older adults and people with disabilities as well as the design and study of technology for social well-being. Robin received her PhD in technology and social behavior; a joint doctoral degree in computer science and communication studies from Northwestern University; an MS in human-centered computing from University of Maryland, Baltimore County; and a BS in computer science from University of Maryland, College Park.

**Clara Caldeira** is a Computing Innovation Fellow in the Department of Informatics at Indiana University, Bloomington. Her research in human-computer interaction involves topics such as aging-in-place technology, chronic condition management, cultural and psychosocial aspects of users' experiences, and human-data interaction. She earned her PhD and master's degrees in informatics from the University of California, Irvine, and her bachelor's degree in computer science from University of Brasilia, Brazil.

**Kay Connelly** is a professor in the Department of Informatics and the associate dean for research in the Luddy School of Informatics, Computing, and Engineering at Indiana University, Bloomington. Dr. Connelly's research interests are in the intersection of mobile and pervasive computing and health care. In particular, she is interested in issues that influence user acceptance of health technologies, such as privacy, integration into one's lifestyle, convenience, and utility. Dr. Connelly works with a variety of patient groups, including very sick populations who need help in managing their disease, healthy populations interested in preventative care, and senior citizens looking to remain in their homes for as long as possible. Her research is supported by the National Institutes of Health, National Science Foundation, and private foundations such as the Lilly Foundation. She received a BS in computer science and mathematics from Indiana University (1995) and an MS (1999) and PhD (2003) in computer science from the University of Illinois.

**James W. Cortada** is Senior Research Fellow at the Charles Babbage Institute at the University of Minnesota, Twin Cities. He worked at IBM for nearly four decades, holding leadership positions in sales, management consulting, and research. He has published extensively on the history and management of information and information technology. He currently studies the role of information ecosystems and infrastructures. His most recent publications include *IBM: The Rise and Fall and Reinvention of a Global Icon* (MIT Press, 2019) and *Building Blocks of Modern Society: History, Information Ecosystems, and Infrastructures* (Rowman & Littlefield, 2021).

**David Hopping** is a teaching assistant professor at the University of Illinois, Urbana-Champaign, in the School of Information Science. His research interests include intergenerational community informatics, digital inclusion and digital literacy, relational sociology, and sociological theory. Hopping helped to build the not-for-profit community development organization Generations of Hope and served as the organization's executive managing director from 2006 to 2015 and as executive director in 2016. His current research involves the use of biofeedback and gaming technologies to enhance human capabilities and to mitigate vulnerabilities through the fostering of socioemotional resilience and the augmentation of carefully designed spaces of interaction in ways that promote bonding, learning, and playful engagement across generations. He received his PhD from the University of Illinois, Urbana-Champaign in the Department of Sociology.

**Mary Janevic** is an associate research scientist in health behavior/health education at the University of Michigan School of Public Health and is a faculty member of the University of Michigan's Center for Managing Chronic Disease. Her work focuses on interventions to promote self-care among individuals with chronic pain and other chronic illness, particularly older adults and women; family support for chronic illness management; physical activity among individuals with chronic illness; and the effects of having multiple chronic conditions on self-care and health outcomes. Previously Dr. Janevic was a postdoctoral fellow at the Department of Epidemiology and Public Health at University College London, UK, where she assisted with the English Longitudinal Study on Aging. She has also worked at Kaiser Permanente, Northern California Region, where she coordinated health education programs focusing on chronic disease management.

**Ben Jelen** is a PhD student in informatics at Indiana University, Blooming-ton. His research has focused on how to engage older adults in technology through craft-based electronic toolkits, breaking down technophobic stereo-types and bringing them into the design of older-adult-focused technology. He is advised by Dr. Katie Siek in the ProHealth lab, where his work is funded through the National Science Foundation, including a fellowship through the NSF Graduate Research Fellowship Program. He earned an MS in informatics at Indiana University, Bloomington, and a BS in biomedical engineering from The Ohio State University.

**William Jones** is a research associate professor emeritus in the Information School at the University of Washington. He continues to work on the chal-lenges of "keeping found things found," both as a research topic and in his own life. He is recently interested in the relationships between information, knowledge, and successful aging. William has published in the areas of per-sonal information management, human-computer interaction, information retrieval (search), and human cognition/memory. He wrote the book *Keep-ing Found Things Found: The Study and Practice of Personal Information Management* and more recently the three-part series *The Future of Personal Information: Part 1: Our Information, Always and Forever*; *Part 2: Trans-forming Technologies to Manage Our Information*; and *Part 3: Building a Better World with Our Information*. William holds six patents relating to search and personal information management.

**Unmil Karadkar** holds a dual appointment: as a senior scientist in the Center for Interdisciplinary Research in Aging and Care at the University of Graz, Austria, and as a research associate in the School of Information at the Uni-versity of Texas at Austin. Blending techniques from social, information, and computer sciences, his research focuses on the intersection of research data and the communities that create, use, and manage such data. The increasing significance of research data has enabled him to collaborate and publish with scholars in diverse areas, including archival studies, biology, geosciences, educational technology, mental health, history, nursing, astrodynamics, and power systems engineering. His research has been funded by the National Science Foundation, Andrew W. Mellon Foundation, and Texas General Land Office. Unmil earned a PhD in computer science from Texas A&M University and worked as a tenure-track assistant professor in the School of Information at the University of Texas at Austin.

**Marilyn Kay** is a retired educator living in Urbana, Illinois. She is the founder and former director of The Reading Group, a not-for-profit reading organization. She was a classroom teacher for eleven years, prior to receiving a master's degree in education at the University of Illinois in 1968. She has given lectures, workshops, and in-service training in schools throughout central Illinois as well as presentations at the International Reading Association and other state, national, and international organizations. Since 2006, she has coordinated programs for LEAP—Linking Educators and Parents—a dyslexia study group providing information for teachers and parents dealing with dyslexia and other learning differences.

**Noah Lenstra** is an assistant professor in the School of Education's Department of Library and Information Science at the University of North Carolina at Greensboro. He holds a courtesy appointment in the UNCG Gerontology Program, where he serves on the Gerontology Research, Outreach, Workforce and Teaching Hub executive committee. His research focuses on how public libraries start and sustain community partnerships to contribute to collective impact in the domain of public health. Recent work focuses on how public libraries support healthy, age-friendly communities through programs, spaces, and services. He received his PhD in library and information science from the University of Illinois.

**Novia Nurain** is a PhD student in health informatics at Indiana University and is currently working with Professor Kay Connelly. Her research primarily focuses on understanding older adults' experience of socialization and technology usage. She has received both MSc (Engg.) and BSc (Engg.) degrees in computer science and engineering from Bangladesh University of Engineering and Technology, Dhaka, Bangladesh.

**Judith Pintar** is an associate teaching professor and the acting director of the undergraduate program in the School of Information Science at the University of Illinois at Urbana-Champaign. Her recent work centers around collaborative knowledge practices and game studies. She is a game designer and director of an Illinois campus-wide game studies initiative, Games@ Illinois: Playful Design for Transformative Education. Her broader interests include narrative artificial intelligence, digital storytelling, suggestibility and media manipulation, collaborative game design, collective memory-making, and social narrative approaches to trauma and memory studies. She received her PhD at the University of Illinois at Urbana-Champaign in the Department of Sociology.

**Katie Siek** is a professor in informatics at Indiana University, Bloomington. Her primary research interests are in human-computer interaction, health informatics, and ubiquitous computing. More specifically, she is interested in how sociotechnical interventions affect personal health and well-being.

Her research is supported by the National Institutes of Health, the Robert Wood Johnson Foundation, and the National Science Foundation, including a five-year NSF CAREER award. She has been awarded an National Center for Women and Information Technology Undergraduate Research Mentoring Award (2019), a Computing Research Committee on Widening Participation in Computing Research Borg Early Career Award (2012), and Scottish Informatics and Computer Science Alliance Distinguished Visiting Fellowships (2010 and 2015). Prior to returning to her alma mater, she was a professor for seven years at the University of Colorado, Boulder. She earned her PhD and MS at Indiana University, Bloomington, in computer science and her BS in computer science at Eckerd College. She was a National Physical Science Consortium Fellow at Indiana University and a Ford Apprentice Scholar at Eckerd College.

**Emily Vardell** is an assistant professor at the School of Library and Information Management at Emporia State University. Her research interests are in the area of health information behavior with a focus on health insurance literacy and how people make health insurance decisions. She teaches graduate courses on the foundations of library and information science, research methods, reference, consumer health, health sciences librarianship, and disaster preparedness. Her first book, *The Medical Library Association Guide to Answering Questions about the Affordable Care Act*, was published by Rowman & Littlefield in 2015. She earned her PhD from the School of Information and Library Science at the University of North Carolina at Chapel Hill in 2017.

**Kate Williams** (PhD Michigan) is an associate professor at the School of Information Sciences at the University of Illinois at Urbana-Champaign. She also teaches on occasion in China. Her research asks if community is possible in the digital age by looking at how people use technology in communities. Part of this question is: What is the role of the public library in this process? And how do ordinary people get and give tech help? Overall, she has found that people are more ingenious and resourceful than they get (or give themselves) credit for. Professional librarians who understand this make for better and freer libraries.